Keir Starmer

ALSO BY TOM BALDWIN

*Ctrl Alt Delete: How Politics and the Media
Crashed Our Democracy*

*England: Seven Myths That Changed a Country and How
to Set Them Straight* (with Marc Stears)

Keir Starmer

The Biography

Tom Baldwin

WILLIAM
COLLINS

William Collins
An imprint of HarperCollins*Publishers*
1 London Bridge Street
London SE1 9GF

WilliamCollinsBooks.com

HarperCollins*Publishers*
Macken House, 39/40 Mayor Street Upper
Dublin 1, D01 C9W8, Ireland

First published in Great Britain in 2024 by William Collins

1

Copyright © Tom Baldwin 2024

Tom Baldwin asserts the moral right to be identified
as the author of this work in accordance with the
Copyright, Designs and Patents Act 1988

A catalogue record for this book is
available from the British Library

HB ISBN 978-0-00-866102-1

Set in Adobe Garamond Pro
Printed and bound in the UK using 100%
renewable electricity at CPI Group (UK) Ltd

For Rebecca

Contents

Part III: Making

Three decades of 'fighting for justice and the rule of law'

Part IV: Standing

From becoming an MP to becoming leader

Part V: Running

Back from the brink and on to the gates of government

Introduction

The origins of this book can be found in another one that Keir Starmer started writing himself not so long ago.

In those days much of Westminster was covered by a great fatty slab of conventional wisdom under which almost everyone agreed he would never beat the 'charismatic' Boris Johnson. In an effort to break out from this narrative, the Labour leader decided to produce an autobiography to explain where he came from, what he stood for, and how he would change Britain.

The reason, however, that leaders of political parties rarely do such books is that it takes up a vast amount of time they generally do not have. After a few months, I was asked to help him stitch together various notes and interviews. And it slowly became clear that Starmer had some reservations about the project.

For a start, he kept asking why he would publish his memoirs before having even had the chance to take some decisions in government. He felt uneasy about writing so much about himself or turning his life into some shining arc of narrative in which he was the hero of every page. He worried – a lot – about whether it would cause his family to get unwarranted attention from the media or, worse, put them in danger.

And then the political terrain began to be upheaved. Johnson was forced to resign, and his replacement Liz Truss lasted just seven weeks before Rishi Sunak took over. That slab of conventional wisdom flipped itself over. Suddenly, it seemed Starmer didn't need thousands upon thousands of words to explain himself, when just four would do: 'I am not them.'

In the spring of 2023, we met for a drink in one of the dimly lit pubs he knows in London's Kentish Town. Starmer swiftly put his autobiography out of its misery. He then bought another round and I made the case for another book. My argument was that, even though every opinion poll showed he was heading to Downing Street, most voters still knew little or nothing about him. I said that politics abhors such vacuums and he risked letting this one be filled by his opponents, just like they had for so many of his predecessors. And I suggested he would never, even with a fair wind from the media, be able to tell his story properly in just a single speech, video or podcast profile.

By the end of the evening, we had struck a deal. I would write a book using some of the material already prepared and interview him for some more, while he would encourage others to talk to me too. In return, I promised not to abuse that access nor approach members of his family without permission.

The result is not the first book about the Labour leader. At the last count, three were available, although none have been written before now with any degree of cooperation. But this biography is not 'authorised' in the usual sense of the word because Starmer has neither handed over boxes of correspondence for me to look through, nor had control over what I write.

Although I'm fully aware that even the tiniest detail can take on inflated significance ahead of what promises to be a nasty and deeply personal election campaign, I felt it was important that neither he nor his office should have approval over this text. There will probably be elements of this book that he doesn't like or thinks I have got wrong. Writing about someone else's life is inevitably intrusive and so it's worth saying here that any mistakes in the chapters that follow belong to me alone.

At this point, there are plenty of people out there who will say, some politely and others less so, that I'm not exactly an impartial observer. In my own past I was a pro-Labour journalist who went on to work, with limited success, as the party's communications director. And, though I don't agree with him on everything – and might still wish he took a different stance on Europe, for instance – it's only fair to warn those hoping to find these pages spattered with blood that they will be disappointed.

Nonetheless I have tried to give as full and fair an account of Labour's leader as I can. It is impossible to tell Starmer's story without acknowledging he has many critics or recognising that, sometimes, they have a point. But it's equally true to say he has so far frustrated their efforts to define him.

Is he a radical with a Marxist past who will tax private schools and force the super-rich to flee this land forever, or part of an immovable 'Establishment' that resists all kinds of change? Is he a 'well-heeled lefty lawyer from north London', or the nasal non-entity snobbishly nicknamed 'Keith' Starmer? He cannot, logically, be all of them.

Certainly, he is a moving target. But he is not necessarily one being deliberately evasive. Instead, this biography will argue that Starmer is peculiarly hard to pin down, especially for people who work in politics, because he resists being fitted into the clean lines within which politicians usually project themselves.

For instance, he is the most working-class leader of the Labour Party for a generation and also the first in its history to have the prefix 'Sir' attached to his name before he got the job. Starmer is a private man who has chosen to place himself in the white light of public scrutiny, while showing a determination that is itself exceptional to maintain a semblance of normality. In spite of being instinctively cautious, he has taken a series of gigantic risks to transform his party and, though often appearing uncomfortable at being a politician at all, he has hurdled barriers at speed while many more polished or 'charismatic' rivals have fallen.

In exploring all these contradictions, I have found myself writing a different, and hopefully more revealing book from the one he would have written. I have interviewed more than a hundred people, ranging from members of his family, his closest friends and colleagues, to political opponents and even a protester who attacked him on stage. I have sat on trains with him between campaign stops and in his kitchen as he makes toast; trudged across the field behind his old home where his parents once kept donkeys and stood upon the Astroturf where he plays football; seen his eyes well up in private and wondered why, when in public, that same person can seem so cramped.

The resulting picture is a messier or more paradoxical one than politicians are supposed to have and, therefore, just as complicated as real people usually are; it is the biography of someone who is both extraordinary and very ordinary.

This book is divided into five parts, each of which begins by sketching a moment since he became a politician when this tension is most apparent. All of them also include descriptions of some-times traumatic episodes that have wrenched him back to real life and away from the febrile – often fake – world of Westminster politics.

The rest of the structure is more straightforward and chronolog-ical. The first part covers the young Keir Starmer's childhood and schooldays in Surrey. The second chronicles his time as a student in Leeds and Oxford, then as a trainee barrister in London. The third spans almost three decades of a legal career that saw him tran-sition from a human rights lawyer into the country's chief prosecutor. The fourth describes how he became an MP, a member of the shadow cabinet and leader of the Labour Party. The fifth examines that leadership, before assessing what kind of prime minister he would be if he makes it to Downing Street.

And yet, as I write these words in the final weeks of 2023, it's still by no means certain that Keir Starmer will be prime minister. The speed with which he has transformed Labour's electoral pros-pects means that work can just as swiftly be undone. The electorate is so volatile that only a fool would take his victory for granted.

And Starmer is, most definitely, no fool. He has grown a tougher skin over the past few years because he will need it. Whatever must be done, he will do his best to do.

He knows the months ahead will test him in ways he has not been tested before. Perhaps a terrible scandal I have missed will be revealed. Maybe one will be invented or puffed up out of all proportion. Certainly, I do not claim to have discovered all there is to know about a man whom I both like and trust, but still sometimes find hard to fathom.

More importantly, a lot of his story is yet to come, especially if he wins the next election and becomes Britain's prime minister.

One day, Starmer may tell us everything. That is, if he ever finds time to write his autobiography.

Part I

Beginning

A ramshackle childhood and
Surrey education

1

Strangers on a train

An ordinary-looking man in a hurry to get somewhere. There is nothing much to mark him out as he strides through Victoria railway station. Average height, middle-aged and solid in his suit; maybe only the hair suggests it once had something to say.

He has left it a bit late, craning his neck until he reaches the front of the queue for the ticket machine. Destination … Standard … Day return … But even when it's printed, he still resists the impulse to run full tilt for his train.

That's 'never the best look' for a politician, he tells himself. Only a quarter of an hour ago he was still in Parliament, where there had been carnage all day. It is late November in 2018 and the government might fall.

He makes it to Platform 16 just in time to board the 15.08 service heading south out of the capital. The train slides through the suburbs and past stops – Clapham Junction, East Croydon – hardwired into him from countless childhood journeys back home. But he's not going home, or not exactly. Right now, he needs to reset his thoughts and focus.

The carriage is only a third full and he finds an empty bay of four seats, answering a message from his office from someone worrying about what will happen tomorrow, then switching his phone off because he is more worried about today. A man looms into view, sits down opposite and utters words that invariably mean the start of a much longer conversation.

'Hi, Keir Starmer? Can I talk to you about your position on Brexit?'

'No, you can't,' replies the Shadow Secretary of State for Exiting the European Union, folding his arms and turning to stare out the window until his fellow passenger goes away.

*   *   *

Politicians hoping to be prime minister don't usually start a story about themselves by describing how they slipped off from work early in the middle of a crisis or were rude to a voter who asked them about a policy. But Starmer is telling one that involves him doing both.

A few hours later that night, when he looked at his phone again, he saw a tweet about him written by the man on the train. Although he can't recall the exact words, he knows they were fairly critical. You can still find them if you do a Twitter search of posts for that day.

Saw @Keir_Starmer on train today. Didn't want to talk. Disappointing. He looked scared. I was offering support. Solution starts with talking.

Even now, when he hears this, there is a flicker of irritation in his eyes. Not because of anything to do with Brexit; nor is it a sign he feels particular regret about being so abrupt. It's because this short trip on a train is carved on his memory for another reason: he was going to see his father who was close to death.

The doctors at East Surrey Hospital had telephoned and suggested, as gently as they could, that he should try to get there soon. 'I was trying to think about what was happening at the hospital and what I would say,' he explains. 'Frankly, that mattered more to me than hearing this man's opinions about Brexit – it mattered more than anything.'

But the way Starmer describes the journey matters too. He often talks about 'a gap between politics and people', or how what happens in Westminster is seen as remote and disconnected from everyday lives. In recent years, that gulf has often seemed wider than the two swords' lengths separating rival parties shouting at each other across the House of Commons. And the few inches between Starmer and this stranger on a train that November evening also symbolise the divergence he so often feels between the politician he has become and the person he has always been.

Much of this book is devoted to explaining the way Starmer's experiences outside politics have shaped him but, until recently, he really had not spent much time thinking about a 'backstory'. In his long career as a lawyer, he never sought to persuade judges and juries by making reference to his parents' jobs or describing the kind of house in which he grew up. According to his oldest friends, he wasn't the type to talk about himself all the time and generally disapproved of those who did.

That has changed, of course: since becoming leader of the Labour Party, he has come under constant pressure to make his grey, even opaque, public image more interesting by adding a few splashes of human colour. Inevitably, he has faced endless questions, some fairer than others, about his background. Several times, when he speaks about this in conversations for this book, and once or twice in front of cameras, he has appeared anguished as he tries to work out the answers.

Yet no one forced him to enter Parliament or set his sights on Downing Street and, whether he likes it or not, talking about these things is now part of his job.

In the past three or four years, he has got used to describing a stylised version of his background, telling audiences so often about the 'pebble-dashed semi' of his childhood – 'my dad was a toolmaker and my mum was a nurse' – that the lines have become the object of eye-rolling ridicule for the sneerier parts of the media.

However, the reality of this upbringing, which was sometimes very far from normal, has too many jagged edges to slip inside the simplicities of a few paragraphs. And, although going to see a parent about to die is something that will 'happen to almost everybody at some point', he says that when such things happen to anyone, 'they don't feel ordinary, they matter very much.'

On that November afternoon, Starmer made it to the hospital just in time for a meeting with his sisters and the doctors. 'They asked us a few questions about whether they should try to keep Dad going or begin ramping up the morphine,' he says. 'Either way, they told us it would not be long before he was dead.

'I went down to see him again a few days later. I had been in a lot of hospitals before when my mum was sick and they are not my favourite places. But now it was Dad lying there. I could tell there was something different about him: he was giving up.

'I understood too how any chance Dad and I might have had to speak properly – to sort everything out – had gone. We hadn't hugged each other for years. Not since I was a kid. I thought about trying to put my arms around him in that hospital room but – no – it wasn't what we did.'

Starmer has described how, instead, he walked away. 'I knew he was dying and I didn't turn around, to go back and tell him what I thought. And I should have done.'

His story about being rude to a stranger on the train could, of course, be presented as the entitled demand of a powerful man for some privacy. Alternatively, the cynical might dismiss it as merely the conceit of a politician trying to show he's really down to earth. But, listening to him tell it, he seemed to be revealing a bit more than he intended.

Starmer gave a glimpse of how he – just as much as anyone else – is filled with ambiguity, doubt and guilt. He was admitting something that politicians don't say often enough about anything, least of all themselves: life is complicated.

2
Out of the ordinary

'A pebble-dashed semi'

In recent years, political leaders have often had something remarkable in their background. John Major's father was a music hall performer and trapeze artist; David Cameron is a distant relative of the royal family; while Ed Miliband's parents had been refugees from the Nazis.

Keir Starmer's immediate ancestors, by contrast, generally worked with their hands for other people. They were farm labourers, millers, servants and laundresses in a slightly ramshackle and chaotic extended family, most of whom seemed to live close to where he grew up on the Surrey–Kent border. And, far from obsessing about his genealogy or trying to trace his pedigree back through the generations, he squints with the mental effort of remembering the names of people who left few written records behind.

His maternal grandmother was called Marge and worked nights as a nurse, while his grandfather Ron was a bus driver during the day. Their jobs kept them apart most of the time because they were always arguing. 'I was fond of them in their cranky way,' says Starmer. 'We used to see them for tea every other Sunday and they were very generous with things like Christmas presents even though neither had much money.' The marriage broke up after they retired and Ron later ended up in a psychiatric hospital.

In contrast, his other set of grandparents adored each other and used to say there had 'never been a cross word' between them. Bert earned a living as a wheelwright and later a mechanic, while Doris stayed at home to raise four children. Starmer vaguely recalls meeting his great-grandfather, Gus, a retired gamekeeper who lived in a cottage near Godstone and always had that 'respectable sort of working-class attire like wearing a shirt even on weekends'. There were uncles and aunts too. His dad had a couple of brothers, one who became a schoolteacher and another who went off to tarmac roads in the Middle East, as well as a sister, Bib, to whom he has remained close, even after she moved to Norfolk. On his mum's side there was David, 'a bit of a recluse whose home was somewhere in Worthing', as well as Roger, who joined the Navy and lived in Plymouth.

As for Starmer's parents, they grew up not far from each other in the same Surrey village of Woldingham. Rodney Starmer was a little older than Josephine Baker. He had gone to Purley Grammar School for Boys, she to Whyteleafe Grammar School for Girls. Both were bright, but neither went to university. He became an indentured apprentice at a toolmaking firm and then did two years National Service with the Royal Electrical and Mechanical Engineers; she went off to be a trainee nurse. They were married in the summer of 1960 at Woldingham Church. Always known as Rod and Jo, they had four children: Keir was born on September 2, 1962, in between Anna the previous year and the twins – Katy and Nick – in March 1964.

Starmer still has his NHS medical card from when he was a baby, showing an address in Woodchurch, Kent. But soon after, the family moved into 23 Tanhouse Road in Hurst Green, a village near Oxted in Surrey, just a couple of stops down the railway line from Woldingham.

Hurst Green is as indistinctive as Starmer himself. It is neither urban nor suburban, but not quite the countryside. Very few would ever know where this village is unless they lived there or looked it up on a map. It's a place as untraceable as his not-exactly-London accent. For a boy like Starmer who fell in love with football, there was no big club nearby around which to form an identity. So he picked Arsenal, as lots of children growing up far from north London still do.

For all that, few politicians have made as much as he has of where they grew up. His family home on Tanhouse Road has featured in countless interviews, speeches, newspaper profiles and a party political broadcast. He was sufficiently self-aware to preface another such anecdote in his speech to the Labour Party conference in 2023 by saying he had tried 'really hard not to mention the house I grew up in again'. But then he added: 'Seriously, that pebble-dashed semi was everything to my family. It gave us stability through the cost of living crises of the seventies. Served as the springboard for the journey I've been on in my life. And I believe every family deserves the same.'

This home, Keir Starmer's 'ground zero', is on a quiet road flanked by sycamores and conifers or hedges of privet and beech, part of what is sometimes described as the 'Stockbroker Belt' and a place where these days a working-class family would probably be unable to afford a mortgage. But it was never that grand a house. When it was sold for £455,000 in February 2021, the estate agent's pictures showed not much had changed since Starmer's boyhood half a century ago. Brown curtains hung above a stained old Aga; there were three bedrooms; a living room with a brick fireplace decorated with a vase and some knick-knacks; the wallpaper had wide vertical stripes.

'My first memory, from when I was four or five, I'm pretty sure, is Dad buying a blue Ford Cortina,' he says. 'It was a big moment when he came home with it because we'd never had a car before.' He also remembers the house's black front door, which they eventually replaced with a more cheerful yellow one. 'At the back was a field and not far away is a bridleway that went through Tandridge, where you can still walk up into the Oxted Downs.

We also had a decent-sized garden, where I had a hard, brown football made of half-inch-thick plastic that really hurt if you got it kicked at you.'

Life inside was cramped. 'There were six of us and only one bathroom, which would always cause a bit of shouting or banging in the morning,' says Starmer. 'I shared a bunk bed with my brother in a room with an airing cupboard and just enough space for a couple of small desks where we'd do our homework.' They taped posters to the wall, often pulled from the pages of the football magazine *Shoot!*. Later, like countless other teenagers, they put up one of Debbie Harry from Blondie.

The chaos of these early years was not eased by each child being given a dog for their tenth birthday. Anna had Pip, a spaniel, while Nick and Katy had a pair of Jack Russell terriers – called Greg and Ben – 'because by then I don't think we could have coped with anything bigger'. Starmer says: 'My dog, Percy, was a red setter and anyone who has ever owned one knows about the little bump on top of their head which, we say, is their brain. Percy was a beautiful dog but hard to contain in a field, let alone our house.'

All this sounds normal enough for an English childhood in the 1970s: a semi-detached in Surrey, dogs in the kitchen and a plastic football in the garden, a Cortina parked on the drive. There was an orange space hopper, bikes with dropped handlebars and flared jeans too.

But every family has its own story which is out of the ordinary. Starmer's revolves around his mother's illness and his father's all-consuming devotion to her.

'My mum was a nurse'

When she was ten, Jo Baker wasn't given a dog but the first in a long series of medical appointments about her painful and swollen joints. Eventually, doctors at Guy's Hospital diagnosed Still's disease, a relatively rare condition in which the immune system attacks itself. While for some people it can be quite mild, she got it about as badly as anyone can.

Jo was left with the kind of severe rheumatoid arthritis more normally only seen in someone very old. At the age of eleven, she was told two things about the rest of her life: that she would be in a wheelchair by her twenties and she should forget about ever having children.

That her eldest son is telling this story proves not only that the doctors were wrong but also, in his words, 'how she was a very determined person and – in a way – a lucky one'. Jo was given what was then an experimental treatment with cortisone, which reduced the inflammation and meant her body didn't deteriorate as quickly as had been expected.

Even so, you can get a sense of her disability from an account Rod wrote for her funeral about their first meeting, when Jo was sixteen and gatecrashed a party organised by his local cycling club. Noticing she wasn't joining in, he asked her for a dance. She declined, saying she was having a 'flare up' in her joints and couldn't. Despite having taken a different girl to the do, Rod was intrigued, so they sat and chatted. As he put it, in his stilted fashion, 'close friendship followed and we met regularly'.

Within a few years they were getting married and inviting a Guy's Hospital doctor called Ken MacLean who lived in Woldingham and had taken a personal interest in Jo's condition. At the reception, MacLean told them: 'If you want children, do not wait. There may be unseen side effects from the cortisone and I will arrange for them to be born at Guy's.'

They didn't wait. 'Rather than being in a wheelchair in her twenties, she gave birth to four children in three years, including me,' says Starmer. 'But by the time I began my life, she had already been living with Still's disease for most of hers.' Jo would have to have her hips and knees replaced twice, big operations that took months to recover from each time. Though always disabled and in pain, she really wasn't one to make a fuss.

'Mum was very ill many times as I got older,' he says. 'She was often told she would never walk again. But then she did walk again, again and again. She would never dwell on her problems – "How are you, Mum?" – "I'm all right, how are you?"'

A lot has been written about the link between childhood adversity and the drive that many successful people appear to have, with one 1970 study finding that around half of British prime ministers had suffered the early death of a parent, far more than the average for the population. It has become commonplace for US presidents to discuss in lengthy and sometimes mawkish detail their struggles with angry, alcoholic, deadbeat or just plain dead parents. More recently, the journalists Rachel Sylvester and Alice Thomson have created an entire podcast series and a book from seeking the seed of unhappiness in the backgrounds of famous people that germinated into ambition.

For most of his life, however, Starmer has been reluctant to indulge in any such self-analysis. He admits to having an instinct to 'hold back' that goes beyond the standard emotional diffidence of his generation. For him, it seems to stem from a childhood desire not to stand out or be different from other families that appeared more 'normal' than his own.

Starmer once admitted he had been a bit embarrassed at being named Keir, saying: 'When I was at school, at about thirteen, I thought, why couldn't they have called me Dave or Pete?' He is still unnecessarily sensitive about his middle name, Rodney, possibly because he shared it both with his father and the member of the fictional Trotter family so often called a 'plonker' in the 1980s BBC comedy *Only Fools and Horses*. Even now, when describing his family's often tight finances, it's noticeable how Starmer invariably adds that he's not trying to 'plead poverty or greater hardship than anyone else'. And, when he talks about Jo's illness, he usually emphasises how keen his mother was for everything to seem as normal as possible.

'Some of my friends later told me they could see how Mum's hands were twisted by the arthritis,' he says, 'but I don't think I ever really noticed much more than how she walked with a limp. There was always this question being asked around the house about whether she'd remembered her pills – she had to take handfuls of them, three times a day – but that was how it was and, as far as I was concerned, how it always had been.'

He acknowledges his teenaged self probably didn't properly appreciate the importance to Jo of the family's holidays, always spent in the Lake District, having driven up to Cumbria overnight from Surrey. 'Two parents in the front, four kids and four dogs in the back,' he says. 'There were no seatbelts in those days so there would be Anna and me on either side of Katy and Nick in the middle. They had to sit forward with two of the dogs behind them, while the other two were by our feet.

'This was my mum's choice because she loved the place and I don't think it ever crossed her mind to go anywhere else,' he says. She never owned a passport and only got on a plane once in her life, flying to Manchester for a honeymoon that had, inevitably, also been in the Lake District.

On that trip, at the top of Loughrigg Fell, the newly wed Rod and Jo had come across a man with a sketchpad sitting on a rock who told them the best route down. He turned out to be Alfred Wainwright, an iconic figure for walkers largely thanks to his idiosyncratic series of bestselling books, *A Pictorial Guide to the Lakeland Fells*. The writer was known to be reclusive, and, according to legend, if you tried to talk to him when he was out walking he would turn away and pretend to urinate. But the Starmers – unusually – were given a pass so, for the next thirty years, would pop over to see Wainwright at his home every summer. Whenever Jo was sick, he'd send a card telling her 'the hills are waiting for you'.

Along with his sisters and brother, Starmer didn't even get to meet this Lake District celebrity because his parents thought the children might make a nuisance of themselves. 'We always stayed in the same row of miners' cottages – dark, damp, small – next to a quarry in the Langdale Valley, which wasn't exactly the definition of fun for me in the 1970s,' he says.

But he now thinks Jo's resolve to visit the same place each summer was 'one of her ways of showing she was still the same person she had been the year before and the year before that'. He says: 'These trips might have been boring for me, but they were remarkable for her. Here was a woman who had fought a battle to walk all her adult life, insisting on a holiday where pretty much the only thing to do was not just walk, but walk to the top of high, windswept hills.'

Sometimes she had to rest completely the next day, but she refused to accept she was disabled, even making four attempts to get to the top of Scafell Pike, England's highest mountain. When she eventually managed it, with four children and four dogs in tow, Rod quoted what he described as 'the immortal words' of Edmund Hillary to Tenzing Norgay after they climbed Everest: 'We knocked the bastard off!'

Every now and then, however, came a reminder Jo was different from other people's mothers. Starmer describes such a moment when he was seven or eight, walking home the couple of miles from primary school with his older sister. 'At the top of our road was a busy junction, and the rule was that we had to wait there for Mum,' he says. 'One day we saw her coming up to meet us on the other side of the road. Then she just toppled over and fell face down in the gutter. She couldn't get herself up. We couldn't get to her because cars were speeding past. The dog was barking, with its lead all twisted, and Mum seemed so helpless. She was shouting at us, "Stay there! Don't cross!" Anna and I were both crying. It must have been only a couple of minutes or so, but it felt a lot longer. I think a motorist stopped and got her up because we weren't strong enough to do that then.'

Once again, Jo just tried to make everything seem as normal as possible. 'Mum was never one to make a fuss,' says Starmer. 'When she was back on her feet, she joked about what had happened, paid lots of attention to the dog, and took us home.' Many years later, he would pick his mum's favourite song, Jim Reeves' 'Welcome to My World', as one of his tracks on Radio 4's *Desert Island Discs*. 'She would listen to that when we came home from school,' he told the programme. 'We'd arrive home and she would make us jam sandwiches and have it on in the background. And that's an image of Mum that sticks with me forever.'

While the life Jo made for herself was testament to her resilience and determination, it would not have been possible without Rod. 'He managed all her medication, knew exactly the symptoms of everything that might possibly go wrong, and then what drugs or combination of drugs or injection would be needed,' says Starmer. People who met them often recall the couple's devotion to each other. 'Whenever I think of Rod and Jo,' says one, 'I have this image of them always holding hands.'

Helena Kennedy, who later became a friend and mentor to Starmer when he was a barrister, has said that listening to him talking about his childhood in broadcast interviews over recent years helped her to understand him better. 'When you're in a family with someone who has got something really seriously wrong with them, you don't feel you can complain, you don't emote,' she says. 'You learn to close off your needs and emotions … it makes you less expressive.'

As he got older, Starmer kept his home life largely separate from his school friends, many of whom have only become aware Jo was disabled since he started talking about it in interviews. 'Keir kept all of that quite private,' says one, 'he's always been a very compartmentalised person.'

His sister, Katy, remembers how he shouldered a lot of responsibility from a young age: 'When Mum was ill and Dad was at work or at the hospital, it was Keir who took charge. It was quite tough for him because he's had to be grown-up all his life. I've always been quite open about my feelings – Keir is good at most things but not that. He will always say he's all right even when I know damn well that he isn't.'

On one occasion, while the two of them were mucking about on their walk home from school, Katy jumped down from a metal fence, tearing the new dress her mother had made. 'As soon as we got home,' she recalls, 'Keir said, "Just give it to me", then went off and sewed the dress back up before Mum and Dad would notice. Now, when I think about it, he must have been only little himself – and learned how to sew by watching Mum – but he didn't make a big deal of it or want to be thanked, he just went off and solved the problem. That's what he's like.'

She says he was always very protective of her twin brother, Nick, who had suffered complications during his birth and subsequently had some fairly severe difficulties with learning. Jo had helped teach him to read, once again defying all the doctors who had told her he would never manage that. But Starmer remembers how the school labelled his brother as 'remedial' and put him in a special group that went to be taught in a village hall. 'They had no expectation of him or anything and I'm not sure he even sat exams, so he had nothing to show for coming out of education,' says Starmer.

'We were a family of six, so it didn't feel lonely and I shared a room with him, but Nick didn't have many friends and got called "thick" or "stupid" by other kids.' This bullying clearly still bothers Starmer, who says that 'even now I try to avoid using words like that to describe anyone'. Katy admits both she and Keir got into fights because of Nick. 'I certainly punched a few people,' she says with a little flash of a smile.

During one of their mother's overnight hospital stays the family's defiant façade of 'getting on with it' began to crumble. 'I think I was about thirteen,' says Starmer, 'and the phone in the kitchen rang. It was Dad saying he didn't think Mum was going to make it. He wanted me to warn the others.

'That evening, I had this idea I should stay up all night to keep watch in case he rang again, but I must have fallen asleep eventually because I woke up to hear the sound of Dad's car outside our house at seven-thirty in the morning. We didn't know what the news was until he came in. She'd pulled through, he told us, as matter-of-fact as ever, then he drove back to the hospital while we went to school. I had never really thought about Mum dying before then, but I did quite often after that night.'

Jo 'pulled through' other times too. After having to give up her job as a nurse, she refused to let her mind go the same way as her legs, achieving a first-class degree in sociology from the Open University while studying at home and bringing up four children. But the huge doses of steroids she'd taken since childhood couldn't hold the disease back and exacted a heavy price for the life she had managed to lead. By her late thirties, the medication 'had made her skin tissue-paper thin and her bones crumbly like Weetabix – they stopped her body from healing itself,' says Starmer. Something as innocuous as an insect bite on her ankle would become 'a hole the size of a fifty-pence piece and then get bigger and bigger until she had to go to hospital', a place where her suppressed immune system faced the constant danger of another infection.

He remembers hating trips to the hospital, seeing his mum with 'all kinds of tubes in her', and his parents always trying to get everything back to normal as swiftly as possible. 'We'll get you walking again, you're not giving up,' Rod would tell her, to which Jo would reply, 'I'll be fine, we'll get on with it, don't worry about me,' then turn to her children, asking: 'Now tell me about what happened at school. Have you eaten? How are the dogs?'

No one, not least Starmer himself, would pretend he is unique among politicians in having experienced some childhood trauma. For instance, he has more in common with Sir Ed Davey than having a knighthood prefixed to his name. The Liberal Democrat leader has described the death of his own father when he was very young and having to administer morphine to his terminally ill mother while a schoolboy.

But there is no hierarchy in pain and everyone is uniquely affected by their childhood. Starmer tries to explain the way his affected him. 'I suppose they have made me slightly intolerant of people who complain about being ill all the time even if there really isn't much wrong with them,' he says. 'It's not my best trait, but you don't need to be the world's greatest psychiatrist to see why it's there.'

More than anything, Starmer says his mother's 'sheer determination' and her belief in 'just getting on with it' have stayed with him. He still draws strength from a woman who, after being warned she could never have children, had four, and despite being told she would not walk again, did walk – again and again – until she could do so no more. 'Whenever I'm faced with a problem or a challenge,' he says, 'I think of her and walk towards it because, compared to what she went through, some of the tougher things I have to do just pale into insignificance.'

'My dad was a toolmaker'

Early on in Keir Starmer's childhood, people often used to come over to the house on Tanhouse Road to see his mother, who made friends easily. She had a network through St John's Church, a five-minute walk past the village's wooden war memorial, where she was part of the congregation most Sundays. But as she became more infirm and housebound, the family gradually withdrew into itself behind their yellow front door.

'Everything revolved around keeping her well and I didn't bring many friends back,' he says. 'I didn't know how Mum would be when I got home. And in any case, Dad controlled what happened there.'

His father avoided chatting with the neighbours and had a presence about him that ensured not many tried. He was a similar height to the five foot nine to which his son Keir grew, but had a stronger build from having worked for so long lugging around lumps of metal. Rod wore the same clothes in all seasons: a buttoned-up shirt sometimes cut off at the sleeves, baggy shorts, socks and sandals. This was topped off with a huge straggly beard without moustache, 'Amish-style', so it framed and enlarged his face. In photographs, he looks like a cross between a Victorian patriarch and an American frontiersman emerging from a few years of living alone in the woods.

What Keir Starmer says about his father has evolved over the past few years so it's worth spending a little time unpicking two different strands. Usually, Rod has appeared in speeches or interviews as proof of a working-class background – 'my dad worked on the shopfloor of a factory'. But Starmer has also talked about how he feels about a father who could be overbearing and sometimes block out the light for his eldest son.

The facts are easier to establish than the feelings. Rod was clearly intelligent; he was someone who loved classical music and read serious books on history. Having been denied the chance to go to university by the circumstances and time of his birth, he went to technical college and completed a long apprenticeship to be a tool-maker. This was a job with a special status among other workers who aspired to own their own tools and regarded those who made them as a kind of aristocracy. The Marxist historian Eric Hobsbawm, chronicling the decline of Britain's factory workers in the 1980s, wrote about how 'the tool-room was to remain the last stronghold of the craftsman in the semi-skilled mass production engineering works of the twentieth century'.

Starmer recalls his father's 'immense pride in his craftsmanship – the jigs, dies and moulds, the stocks and castings – the kind of precision machine engineering that had once helped make Britain prosperous'. In his speech to the Labour Party conference in 2021, he quoted W. H. Auden's lines about how 'you need not see what someone is doing to know if it is his vocation, you have only to watch his eyes', before describing the 'eye-on-the-object look in my dad' and the dignity – 'the beauty' – of his work.

Rod had done such work for a long time in the Twinlock factory at Elmers End on the southern outskirts of London, then moved to a smaller workshop in Caterham, becoming friendly with a boss who his family thought 'was a bit flash because he drove a Saab and had a big sheepskin leather coat'. For a while, he also worked in a factory at Thornton Heath, which Starmer mainly remembers now as a place where he was sometimes given some spare change to get a doughnut or a Mars bar from the shop nearby.

It has occasionally been alleged he has exaggerated these proletarian roots for political purposes. A biography written under the name of Michael Ashcroft, a billionaire donor to the Conservative Party and sometime Tory member of the House of Lords, devoted several pages to a theory that the Labour leader's father was really '*petit bourgeois*'. According to Ashcroft, 'It is hard to accept that Rodney Starmer was a straight-up-and-down member of the working class, as his son has so often suggested.' Later he went further in an article for the *Mail on Sunday* accusing Keir Starmer of having 'overplayed his supposed working-class credentials'.

Such claims rely heavily on the fact that for a time Rod owned his own business, the Oxted Tool Company, as well as him having written that his eldest son once spent a few months 'in my factory operating a production machine'. The inference appeared to be that this man ran a factory, rather than just worked in one.

However, the most obvious aspect of Rod's working life was not so much its socio-economic classification as its loneliness. Even Ashcroft's book concedes that the absence of any Companies House records for the business 'indicates he may have remained a sole trader' and appeared to have 'almost always worked alone'. Starmer's own account bears this out: 'As Mum's health became more precarious, Dad wanted to be close to her at all times, so he quit his job and moved his machines into an old canteen, more or less derelict, near our house where he persuaded the owners to give him a lease of half of it. This became the Oxted Tool Company.'

As for working for his father, Starmer says he was 'paid sixty quid a week' to help out during his gap year after leaving school, doing not particularly skilled work: 'Some engine blocks had been sent down from Croydon – hundreds of them – and my job there was to put eight bolt holes in them, then do the next one.' But for most of its existence, the Oxted Tool Company 'was usually only Dad in there with just the noise of the machines to keep him company', doing 'hard and dirty' work: 'He would be standing there all day long in steel toe-caps and overalls, scrubbing himself clean with Swarfega afterwards.'

Nor did it confer the kind of prosperity on the family that might have been expected had Rod really been a thrusting 1980s entrepreneur running his own business in the Home Counties. The household bills were not always paid, the telephone was cut off and the family home became increasingly shabby. Paul Vickers, a childhood friend, once compared the Starmers' home to 'a building site', where there were 'holes in the wall, bits of masonry missing – it was always like they were trying to finish the house but never got quite around to completing the job'.

Katy remembers when the River Eden flooded during their childhood and the water reached the top of the stairs: 'We couldn't afford to get the house redecorated so there was just bare plaster for years.' On another occasion, after a football was kicked through the back window – 'That would have been Keir's fault,' she says, laughing – 'we never fixed the glass because that cost money. Dad just boarded it up.'

The emotions inside the house, however, could be more tightly bound than the décor – or even as nailed shut as that window. Starmer's recollections of the warmth and love he felt over jam sandwiches with his mother are in sharp contrast to those he has of his father coming back from work. 'If Dad was there, meals were usually eaten in silence so that he could read his newspaper,' he says.

As Jo's disability became more severe, 'Dad retreated further and further into himself. He would go to work at 8 a.m., come home at 5 p.m. for what he would always call his tea, then go back to his machines from 6 until 10 at night. It was work, come home, work, go to bed, repeat. That was his routine.'

3
Class politics

Turning in

When people remember Keir Starmer's father now, most of them eventually revert to describing him as 'a bit of a character' as a way of hinting at something else.

According to Paul Vickers, Rod was 'very powerful' and a 'slightly intimidating figure', who would 'always ask questions about politics'. Mark Adams, who used to go back to Tanhouse Road after school, says: 'If Keir's dad was there, he would sort of confront us, try to take us on in an argument and want to know what we had to say for ourselves. That was unusual for parents in those days. I found it quite scary at the age of thirteen or fourteen.'

Starmer remembers such exchanges being generally one-sided. 'We didn't have debates in which everyone had a chance to express their views – Dad's view was the only view – what he thought was not up for discussion. Other opinions would swiftly be shut down. Mum would have liked to have people round a bit more, but as he isolated himself, she had to too. She couldn't exist without him – and he drove people away.'

Someone who refused to be put off, however, was one of those who knew Jo from the church. Mary Seller had moved to Hurst Green in 1975, become a lay minister at St John's, and had coincidentally been working as a laboratory scientist at Guy's Hospital when Jo was having lengthy spells of treatment there. 'Whenever she was in one of the wards at Guy's, I would pop over to see her during my lunchbreak,' says Seller. 'Jo was a warm and lovely lady who would always make light of her troubles.'

Seller became a friend of the family and often went to see them at home. 'If Keir was there, he would be cheery enough and then disappear up to his room, like any ordinary lad,' she recalls. 'But Rod was really quite rude. He would answer the door and say something like, "Not you again – what are you doing here?"

'Jo would just smile this sort of secret smile to herself when he behaved like that. I really don't know how she put up with him. At one point I decided I couldn't go round there anymore because he was so aggressive. But someone told me that was his way of show-ing he liked you and, over time, I think I came to understand Rod a bit better.' In Seller's words, he was 'a talented and complex man with, for whatever reason, chips on his shoulders' who kept his 'underlying decency' well hidden. She remembers his skill at 'making medical and other fine instruments', and once telling her he had invented something and bitterly regretted someone else taking out the patent.

But she also describes how Rod could be 'extremely thoughtful and generous', for instance letting her use his photocopier when the one in the church was broken, even though he was a declared athe-ist. Rod eventually became friends with David Butlin, the vicar at St John's for twenty years, possibly because he had no religion. 'It's sometimes quite difficult to be close to people because you have a pastoral duty to them,' says Butlin, as he walks around his old parish on a sunny spring day. 'With Rod, it was different because he wanted nothing from me. I'd see him around the village and he would say something like, "Still doing all that religious mumbo-jumbo then?" I would try to be equally rude back and we got along just fine. There were certainly no frills with Rod.'

Although this former vicar says 'it's hard to know what makes us tick', he suggests: 'Perhaps the way he presented himself and his directness were symptoms of the strength of his political beliefs.

But there was a very gentle side to him. My wife had a brush with cancer and he would always ask after her, as well as make sure that on her birthday she had a posy of sweet peas that he had grown in his garden.'

Butlin also tells the story of Rod's unexpected arrival at the vicarage during his last year at Hurst Green, in 2012. 'He had heard my daughter was getting married and brought three teapots with him. "I want to give you a present," he said to her. "You can't have all of them, but you can have the one you like the best."'

Another unlikely bond was with the Lake District's Alfred Wainwright, who, though known to be a hang-'em-and-flog-'em right-winger, maybe saw in the left-wing Rod Starmer someone who matched his own gruffness. Rod later contributed to a book of tributes to his friend. 'I'm not renowned for being chatty, nor was Mr Wainwright himself of course, but we got on very well,' he wrote. 'We never talked politics or religion, we just knew to avoid such subjects.'

To the young Keir Starmer it sometimes seemed his father was trying to avoid much of the outside world altogether. Although an active member of the cycling club and volunteer marshal for road races, Rod 'preferred to do time trials so that he could be on his own'. For many years, he wouldn't let the family have a television set, relenting only after Jo began her Open University degree and needed to watch the BBC programmes on during the daytime.

Even then, access to this small black and white TV was strictly rationed. Starmer negotiated 'a weekly dose' of *Match of the Day* on Saturday nights, 'but we weren't allowed to watch the shows – *Starsky & Hutch*, *Tiswas* and the like – that other people were watching back then … We couldn't play pop music on the radio if Dad was there. He would come in and switch it off without saying a word or put his Shostakovich or Beethoven on.' Indeed, Starmer says that one of the reasons he played football during 'every break, every lunchtime' at school was to avoid the conversations that everyone else was having about what they had watched the night before.

At weekends the family sometimes went shopping at the Whitgift Centre in Croydon, which has since been redeveloped because the council decided it was an eyesore but was an exciting place to go if you came from Hurst Green in the 1970s. 'We might pick up a lunch like Cornish pasties for when we got home,' says Starmer, 'or something made with pasta which I can hear Dad even now complaining about. He'd call it "foreign food".' Starmer's sister, Katy, remembers one of their Saturday treats being 'a big pot of strawberry-flavoured yoghurt which we'd divide up between us into four bowls' and her mum making wholesome soups, baking cakes and 'meringues with cream in the middle'.

On special occasions, they might go for a meal at a pub just up the road from their house called the Haycutter. Starmer says his mum liked to order scampi and chips with a white wine and lemonade, 'but Dad wouldn't drink or say very much – he just sat there behind his beard'.

'Just, sort of, piecing it together'

When Starmer talks of time he spent with his father, he always conveys a sense of a rigidity and distance between them. Remembering the long night-time journeys to the Lake District the family made every summer in a packed car, he describes how Rod would drive and everyone else would fall asleep. 'For some reason I always felt I needed to stay awake for him, but we would sit there in complete silence.' Asked if they bonded more when working together, he says, 'I can't remember any kind of long conversation. He was doing his job and I was doing my job. It was functional. I was putting holes in metal, he'd get on with doing what he needed.'

This bottled-up tension never turned violent or anything like that. 'There might have been some swearing at times – words like "bloody this" or "bugger that" – but nothing worse,' says Starmer now. 'I didn't really have arguments or confrontations with Dad;

we just didn't have that point of connection. There was space in him for Mum and not much else.'

And yet the language he uses about Rod has subtly changed as the two distinct stories he tells about him – the factory worker, the remote father – have become tangled around each other.

In 2020, he described 'a difficult man, a complicated man', someone who 'kept himself to himself'. The following year, in another interview, he said his dad 'had real difficulty expressing his emotions'. Asked if he understood his relationship with his father now, Starmer replied that he was only 'beginning to unravel bits of it', adding: 'I've never really talked about it. I've never had this conversation that we've just had, and I need to probably.' In an interview at the end of 2021, Starmer talked about the way his dad 'had carried quite heavily' a sense that other people 'looked down on him' because he worked with his hands. A few months later, he said this sense of not being valued had affected his father's outlook and made him withdraw into himself. 'I'm not sure I saw this clearly at the time, but I can see it very, very clearly now.'

Around this time, Starmer had a couple of lengthy Zoom chats with Barack Obama, organised by David Lammy, a member of the shadow cabinet who has been friends with Obama since their days at Harvard University together. 'When Keir started talking about his dad, he got quite emotional,' says Lammy, 'and Barack just came alive.' The former American president's political rise had been accelerated by the popularity of *Dreams from My Father*, his autobiographical book about race and his relationship with a largely absentee Kenyan dad. 'He started interrogating Keir further and drawing on his own challenging background,' says Lammy. 'Barack is one of the best storytellers of his generation and he could see something in what Keir was telling him that could become the architecture for a genuine campaign; one where we could talk more about how too many people have been looked down upon by the Establishment, and how too often working-class people have struggled to find their voice in recent decades.'

Sure enough, the Labour leader began 2022 with a speech outlining a new contract with the British people based on 'security, prosperity and respect'. He said: 'My dad always felt undervalued because he worked in a factory. He felt people looked down on him. And he wasn't wrong about that. People have their dignity and it needs to be respected. I want to live in a country in which crucial skills are valued, in which everyone is respected for what they contribute.' None of this is to suggest that the way Starmer or, for that matter, Obama have spoken about their fathers is just some political tactic. In both cases, it is more interesting than that.

Starmer was by then continually being asked for details of his backstory and facing criticism for failing to make more of an early impression on voters. As someone who had come late into politics, he once told the writer Donald Macintyre, 'It's a bit odd for a man in his fifties to be talking about his mum and dad quite as much, frankly. In most walks of life, people are judged by who they are. Politics is different.' He accepted that voters were entitled to ask 'who you are and what you come from', but added, 'I don't like it'.

As such, he appears to be a man who feels obliged to talk about his childhood more than a politician trying to exploit it. At one point in his interviews for this book, Starmer is almost apologetic when he is briefly overcome with emotion while talking about his parents. 'I'm just – sort of – piecing this together,' he says, between deep breaths.

In doing so, however, he also tells a story about what was happening to Britain in the years he came of age, when the titanic battles between trade unions, business and government – strikes, privatisation and factory closures – resonated even in a commuter village in Surrey. If many manufacturing industries were already in trouble before Margaret Thatcher entered Downing Street in 1979, Rod Starmer felt her government relished shutting them down, treating jobs like his as if they were relics of a bygone age from which whole swathes of Scotland, Wales, the North and the Midlands needed to be scrubbed clean. This was also the time when the docks of east London were being razed to the ground to be replaced by the steel and glass towers of global investment banks at Canary Wharf, and when Rod's old workplace the Twinlock factory made way for a Tesco Superstore. 'Dad detested Thatcher,' says Starmer. 'He couldn't understand why she wanted to destroy so much and so few people seemed to care. "We've got to make things, Keir," he'd say. "If we don't make things, what kind of future do we have as a country?"'

Still a fairly mixed community in the 1970s, Hurst Green encompassed some well-to-do houses around the church, but also some poorer homes in a housing estate near the shops. A working-class family in this village back then would not have had the collective experience of an industrial town or city where neighbours would have known what a toolmaker did and respected him for it.

Starmer describes the kind of occasion, infested with petty snobbery, that his father feared most. 'There would be a bunch of grown-ups standing around chatting and someone might ask, "What do you do for a living?" One would be a solicitor, another an accountant, or maybe there would be a teacher and someone who worked for the council. Dad didn't want to tell them that he worked in a factory because he knew it would be followed by a little moment of silence, when everyone was judging him, when no one would have anything to say.'

Starmer says that, growing up, he failed to notice the way this lack of respect hurt his father: 'I didn't think about how much all this mattered, what it did to him, how it changed him.' Nor did he appreciate enough that 'eye-on-the-object look' of a real craftsman. 'Dad was always worried his worth was less than that of other people,' he says. 'He was a talented man, part of what a good economy should be, but no one saw his worth.'

Using the c-word

In a country as obsessed and often riven by class as Britain, the background of any political leader is always going to matter. But none more so than the leaders of a party created for the purpose of governing in the interests of working people and one now desperate to do so again.

Starmer cites as his role models the three predecessors who are the only people to have led Labour to a general election victory in the last ninety years. All of them came from wealthier and more educated families than his own. None had any real roots in the party.

Clement Attlee grew up in a large house with servants, a tennis court and a Liberal-supporting father. Harold Wilson's mother was a teacher, his father an industrial chemist and manager of a dyestuff factory who also had links to the Liberals. Tony Blair's barrister father was also a university lecturer who wanted to be a Conservative MP until a stroke put paid to his ambitions. Each was able, in their own way, to offer reassurance to voters wary of Labour. Attlee had the demeanour of a high street bank manager or country solicitor with the social conservatism to match. Wilson alchemised his past into the story of a meritocratic society driven by a thirst for science, knowledge and technology, while Blair fashioned a wand from his Tory background and private education that he waved over Middle England to make the doubts of voters disappear.

By contrast, the Starmers were both relatively poor and so Labour they named their eldest son after Keir Hardie, the party's first leader who as a child had worked down the Lanarkshire coal mines. At election times, the house in Tanhouse Road would be covered with Labour's red and gold posters and placards supporting striking miners and firemen, which must have been an unusual sight in Tory-voting Surrey during those years.

Starmer has described his father as a socialist who devoured the *Guardian* every day, while his mother's own politics included an immovable commitment to the NHS. 'She would never allow anyone to be even mildly critical of it,' he says, let alone countenance the idea she might go private – 'she would not have been able to bear that'.

His advisers grind their teeth over why these roots are not more widely recognised. Instead, reports from focus groups conducted with working-class voters whose support he needs to win often show that some voters see him as 'posh', as 'a member of the Establishment', or even that his knighthood is a hereditary title. Remarkably for a man who likes a pint as much as he does, one focus group quoted participants saying he would never drink beer but 'probably something like gin and tonic'.

Early in his political career, Starmer shrugged his shoulders at this and said he found it a bit frustrating that people think 'your dad was probably a judge or your mum was this, that or the other'. More recently, however, he had begun to talk about class in a way very few political leaders have done for a long time.

Whereas Blair felt bold enough in 1999 to declare 'the class war is over', Starmer has said: 'My political project is to return Labour to the service of working people and working-class communities. There may have been times in the recent past where Labour was afraid to speak the language of class at all – but not my Labour Party.' He has said the last Labour government didn't do enough to 'eradicate the snobbery that looks down on vocational education, didn't drain the well of disrespect that this creates, and that cost us'.

Asked about this new emphasis on class now, he says: 'It isn't something remote that I've read in a textbook when I was at Oxford about this group of people who really ought to be helped along the way. It's part of my lived experience.' That's also the case for much of his shadow cabinet team, who come from even more precarious working-class backgrounds: Angela Rayner grew up on a council estate and left school while pregnant without any qualifications; Wes Streeting's grandmother was released from Holloway prison to give birth to his mother; Bridget Phillipson lived off benefits for much of her childhood and has never met her father.

None of this should be taken to mean, however, that he is reverting to some sort of Marxist ideology that sets the working class up in conflict against everyone else, because in large part Starmer's talking about opportunity and social mobility.

One person in a good position to judge this is Nick Thomas-Symonds who, as well as being a member of Starmer's frontbench team and one of his closer friends in politics, has also written well-regarded biographies of both Attlee and Wilson. 'Keir is far more working class than either of them, not only in terms of the background alone but because it's combined with a defining story of aspiration,' he says. As such, this is a story about where Starmer was headed, as much as where he was from.

The state boy

The starting point of this journey is probably the day he sat the 11-plus exam in September 1973, even though he doesn't remember it being that big a deal at the time. 'It seemed routine, just another one of the tests we had to do every now and again,' says Starmer. Nor, when he passed, did that seem so important. He remembers his dad coming into his room saying, 'Well done. I'm proud of you', then turning away and shutting the door behind him. It's the only time he can remember his father saying such a thing.

The eleven-year-old Starmer was one of around half a dozen children in his year at Holland Middle School to pass the exam and, for a boy like him from Hurst Green, that meant going to Reigate Grammar School about a dozen miles away. This gave him, he says, 'a sense of heading in a different direction to Anna, Nick and Katy', who went to Oxted County School, closer to home, 'growing up with different people, doing different things'.

Starmer became increasingly aware of expectations around him changing and his parents discussing the kind of career he might end up having, even though they tried to avoid singling him out for attention and his siblings teased him if he got big-headed. Katy says: 'We used to call him "Superboy" because he was so good at everything he tried – music, football, whatever he did, he did it well.' Was she jealous of his success? 'No, no,' she says, smiling, going on to describe watching him play football for the village team. 'He was incredibly competitive even then. He always wanted to be the best at everything and to win. If his team lost, Keir would just stomp off the pitch afterwards.' She starts bouncing her fingers across the table to explain what she means. 'Stomp, stomp, stomp, it was so funny – we'd just laugh at him.'

But Starmer recognises he 'got a better chance in life than my sisters and brother', and goes out of his way to praise his siblings. Anna went on to horticultural college, which was what she had always wanted to do, before raising a family and later working at a garden centre. Katy was a nurse and now works with adults who have Down's syndrome. Both, he says, 'have touched people's lives in a very different way to how a lawyer or a politician can'.

He describes his brother's technical qualification as 'an achievement against the odds' because 'Nick was dealt a very different set of cards to me and he's had problems all his life – problems I've never had to face.' Starmer says: 'I admire him, not in spite of the way his life has taken another course to mine, but because of it.' Then he talks about how Rod and Jo instilled in them the idea you respect people for what they overcome, adding: 'I remember Dad saying to me, many, many times, "Nick has achieved as much as you, Keir."'

When he was awarded a place at Reigate in the mid-1970s, debate was raging about abolishing grammar and secondary modern schools. Starmer doesn't claim to have had profound insights about this at the time, saying, 'I was, after all, only eleven.' And that is one of the reasons why he believes the old system was profoundly unfair: 'It tests kids at too young an age; it has a bias towards those from educated backgrounds and, worst of all, it separates off a few children from everyone else.'

Emphasising his support for the kind of mixed-ability streamed comprehensives that his own children attend, he says they should be able to develop 'at their own pace at different subjects – crucially – in the same space and the same place as everyone else'. In the decades since, a lot of the argument about different education systems has focused more on the unequal life chances given to children at private schools. And Starmer didn't go to one of these – or at least, not at first.

In September 1974, when he started at Reigate Grammar School, it was still entirely state-funded. But its headmaster, Howard Ballance, was determined to resist the tide of comprehensive education. He tried to enlist the support of the Conservative government's education secretary, Margaret Thatcher, in keeping Reigate as a direct grant grammar school, which she had praised 'as a half-way house between the independent and state systems'. In reality, however, Thatcher would approve the opening of more comprehensive schools across both county and country than any education minister has before or since.

This led Ballance to decide his only option was to transform his school slowly, year by year, into a private one. In 1976, he did a deal with Surrey County Council under which Reigate could charge fees for new pupils while the local authority would continue to pay for the 'state boys' already there. At the same time, the headmaster began marketing the school to middle-class parents as offering the trappings of a private education, putting fresh emphasis on the success of the rugby team, the strength of its combined cadet force and the teaching of Latin, as well as having a strictly enforced uniform code – dark blue blazer and cap with silver strips – that marked its pupils out from their comprehensive counterparts.

All of which was disliked, even resisted, by one of the school's self-consciously 'state boy' pupils. Starmer wore his school tie fat, short and low, often with the top buttons of his shirt undone. He grew his hair long in a style described by friends at the time as a throwback to the Bay City Rollers. When the Jam – a band from nearby Woking – topped the charts, friends remember how Starmer's tie became skinnier and his hair shorter. A trace of his teenage self can still be heard when he talks about those days. 'I took that blazer and cap off whenever I could because I thought it made us look ridiculous. I didn't want to be taught Latin, pretend I was a soldier by marching around the playground in uniform, or play rugby – because football was my sport.'

Mark Adams, a longstanding friend from schooldays, says: 'I suppose Keir was what would have been called a bit of a tearaway – trouble seemed to follow him around. We were being told by the headmaster that football was for "oiks", but Keir refused to conform. He wouldn't accept what he thought were stupid or pretentious rules. He kicked against it and played football just about all the time.'

Starmer idolised the 'Dutch master' Johan Cruyff who, like him, was left-footed. 'I'd always take free kicks and would practise my corners endlessly until I got good enough to curl an inswinger from the right into the top corner of the net.'

There is some schoolboy satisfaction in him still when he points out that Adams, who went on to have a career as a journalist and now works for the International Olympic Committee, 'injured himself while attempting a "Cruyff turn"'.

But Starmer is more serious when he insists that the transition of Reigate to a private school 'didn't change the way I was educated because my parents certainly couldn't have afforded to pay fees'. He says: 'As far as I was concerned, I started school as a "state boy" and I finished as one too.'

And that is true in spirit, if not entirely in substance. The wrinkle in this account is that Ballance's deal with Surrey Council lasted only until the state boys like Starmer had finished their O-levels.

In the autumn of 1976, Shirley Williams, the Labour government's education secretary, received a letter from some parents at Reigate complaining it was unfair of the council to end funding at the age of sixteen because it would prevent their children staying on to do A-levels. Parliament was told that she saw 'no need to intervene' because the local authority was able 'to offer comparable A-level courses in their sixth form college'. Starmer accurately says that his parents did not pay a penny for his education, but only because the school allowed those state boys with good grades to stay on, free of charge, by cross-subsidising them with bursaries and the income from fees paid by other parents.

And yet Starmer isn't the only pupil from this time to be vague about how he was financed through sixth form. One of his class-mates, Andrew Cooper, recalls: 'I always felt like I was a state kid, doing my A-levels in the same school where the taxpayer had always funded my education. We didn't really think about how it was paid for.' Another, Andrew Sullivan, says: 'My parents never paid for anything so – no – I don't think of myself as having been privately educated.'

Both are among a remarkable number from Starmer's year to have had prominent careers. Neither have any reason to exaggerate their 'state school' credentials or to downplay the notion of going to a private school, though it's worth noting that both say they would happily vote for Starmer now. Cooper, who was a strong Labour supporter at school, later became strategy director for two Tory leaders and a Conservative peer. The precociously right-wing Sullivan went on, via Oxford and Harvard universities, to become a hugely influential libertarian writer and political commentator in America.

These 'state boys' – Sullivan, Cooper and Starmer – would be among those who would meet each morning on the top deck of the 410 bus to Reigate at the start of a day at school punctuated by passionate political arguments.

4

The top deck

'Loud and gobby'

'Margaret Thatcher had just taken over as leader of the Tory party; it was a very exciting time to be a swotty right-wing boy like me,' says Andrew Sullivan. 'I had the 1979 general election written into my calendar weeks in advance. But Keir was more rough and ready, quite macho. He was always very Labour, that was the whole point of his name.'

The writer describes the young Starmer variously as both 'my main sparring partner' and a 'bit of a wild man, without any of that lawyerly restraint you see today'. He says: 'There were a few times when the boys on the 410 got called out in morning assembly because all kind of stuff was going on with us on the top deck. It wasn't just Keir and I shouting at each other – but a lot of our arguments probably became a bit of a performance with other people gathering round to watch.

'We used to wind each other up. I'd bring something up in class just to piss him off. A lot of it would be about union power or strikes. Keir even showed up at a Christian Union meeting to get at me,' says Sullivan, who comes from a strongly Catholic background. 'At times it would get heated, but Keir was pretty sophisticated. He would bring in books or newspaper cuttings to prove me wrong.'

But he always liked Starmer. 'And I still like him when I see him now,' he says. 'Actually, I'm really fucking proud of him. Though

I'm sure Keir has to do political things, like politicians do, he's not a cynical person. Unlike a lot of people in his position, he doesn't have this disrespect for ordinary people. I think there's a core of integrity in there.'

For his part, Starmer also says that, for all the sound and fury generated between them, he never fell out with Sullivan: 'We argued about everything – politics, religion, you name it – all the time. I was on the left, he was on the right, but Andrew was a friend.' He acknowledges there were a few incidents on the bus. 'Some of the other passengers would have thought I was a bit loud and gobby. I think the driver had to stop a few times and come upstairs to tell us to shut it.' Just as the teenaged Starmer would probably be among those now denouncing his older self for being insufficiently left wing, the adult version admits, 'If I saw someone behaving like we did then, I would have told us to shut it too.'

According to Mark Adams, 'Keir certainly knew how to look after himself and would defend his space. He took the view that if someone hit him, he'd hit them back harder, but I don't think he would be the one to start it.' Cooper remembers them being hauled out of school assembly with other regulars from the 410's top deck after one complaint from a member of the public. 'Keir had a bit of a reputation as one of the hard lads,' he says. 'He'd be the first to take the piss out of the teachers. He was popular, always at the centre of a gaggle, telling the jokes. If he saw someone walking round in the school caps – he really hated those caps – he might grab it off their head and toss it around a bit. But he wasn't nasty or a bully – I don't think that's in him.'

Starmer has talked publicly about his detentions for fighting 'around the back of the bike sheds', admitting there were 'always bits and bobs going on'. He hints at clashes with the rugby types at Reigate 'who thought they were comic geniuses for finding a word that rhymed with the name Keir', telling the story of how he became friends with Colin Peacock after seeing this new arrival at the school picked on by some of these boys in a nearby cemetery. 'Colin's quite a big fella now but was very skinny and small back then. I could see them sellotaping him to a gravestone. I ran out – there was probably a bit of pushing or shoving, but nothing serious. They weren't being really malicious. I sat down next to Colin in the graveyard and, together, we unwound all those yards of tape to set him free.'

Peacock, who has been friends with Keir ever since, says: 'He looked out for me and for other people too. He didn't like any sort of bullying. At one point we started calling each other John, not sure why, but it really confuses our kids now.'

'Good, when roused'

It's possible that these flashes of colour about Starmer's teenaged rebelliousness have distorted the picture of him because they stand out, when he is usually portrayed as monochrome and dull. The truth appears to be that this 'hard lad' was also a bright pupil who made the most of his opportunities and was generally seen as some-one who 'joined in' with school activities.

Starmer's end-of-term school reports show him a bit wilder and less focused than he is now but still recognisable. As he prepared for his O-levels, his teachers describe a capable and positive member of classes, who did not always do himself justice in exams. Most say he tried hard enough but his handicraft teacher didn't seem to like him much, issuing a 'D' for making 'very little effort' and occasionally being 'silly'. In Latin, he was described as 'a borderline candidate'.

When he entered the sixth form, Starmer decided on A-levels in maths, music and physics, choices he would later regret because he had always been more interested in history and geography. His physics teacher wrote that, having 'thrown himself wholeheartedly into a multitude of activities this year', Starmer 'has not managed to perform to the best of his abilities'. In maths, the verdict was he would do better without 'too many other distractions'. But he shone in cross-country races, captained the football team (the school having finally allowed this sport to be played in the sixth form), played flute in the orchestra, acted in plays, helped younger children learn the recorder, and became a prefect. He did the Duke of Edinburgh Award scheme, volunteering at Netherne Psychiatric Hospital where his grandfather Ron later ended up as a patient. Starmer was one of the few pupils to get a Gold Award, which he received at a ceremony in Buckingham Palace from Prince Philip himself in December 1981.

His sixth-form reports mix praise for his 'lively' contribution to debates and 'marvellous' achievements in music with a certain amount of disapproval for his politics. 'His rather extreme views found expression in discussion' was all the teacher of someone whose future political career would be overshadowed by Brexit had to say about his performance in 'European studies' during the summer term of 1980.

In English, he was described as 'good, when roused, but unable to distinguish between proper pride and the old-fashioned sort'. Starmer's form teacher M. G. Bullen wrote: 'He is an able boy who promises well. He is clearly enjoying life in the sixth form. He is well-liked by his form-mates even if they remain suspicious of his political views!' At the end of the following term, when Starmer was beginning to think about studying law, Bullen was writing: 'It is good to see him arguing his beliefs with cheerful vigour ... I venture to observe to an aspiring lawyer that the law is the law, even if it is bad, and that dealing with the views of others with anything other than scrupulous courtesy merely demonstrates the weakness of your own arguments. Belief and commitment he has in full – maturity will come, I'm sure.' In his final year at Reigate, however, the same teacher seemed to have come round to the eighteen-year-old Starmer, recording the 'respect and affection in which he is held' by pupils and teachers.

By this time a dozen or so girls had been allowed into the previously all-male school to attend the sixth form, a move Starmer calls a 'much-needed culture change'. They included Sarah Hargreaves, who arrived from a girls' private school and recalls being taken aback at the sight of Sullivan and Starmer locking horns.

'I was a fairly standard Surrey Tory, I suppose, and Keir was very political in a way I had never really encountered before,' she says. 'There were different groups of people – rugby types, nerds – and then there were these politicos like him in the year above me.' Over time, however, 'Keir grew on me,' she says, 'or maybe he just grew up a bit.'

Big dreams in a small town

At sixteen, Starmer joined the youth wing of the Labour Party, at that time called the Young Socialists. 'Our branch in East Surrey consisted of about four members and we would meet, have some sort of earnest discussion and then see if we could get served in a pub,' he says. The local Conservative MP was Geoffrey Howe, the then chancellor, and there were some half-hearted efforts to disrupt his events. Sometimes they would set up street stalls or knock on doors at the end of long gravel drives in the vain hope of persuading those who lived behind them of the case for mass nationalisation.

Andrew Cooper, still in his left-of-centre phase, usually chaired the Young Socialist meetings, which were often held in a room above his parents' garage. 'We were in a minority of people who were Labour in what was a very Conservative area,' he says. While 'Keir was always more left wing than me', he is proud that their youth branch was beyond the reach of the Trotskyite Militant Tendency that was becoming such a force in this period and says it was praised as a 'beacon of light' by a visiting party official during Denis Healey's titanic 1981 battle against Tony Benn for the party's deputy leadership.

Many of Starmer's friends believe there has always been something of the 'small town patriot' about him. This includes an affinity for the countryside, real ale and national sports teams that makes him distinct from sections of the 'north London metropolitan elite' of which he is sometimes portrayed as being a card-carrying member. But this part of his character expressed itself in other ways too.

When the Argentine military junta invaded the Falkland Islands in the spring of 1982, Starmer remembers instinctively supporting Britain taking military action. He had a family interest in the success and safety of the Royal Navy's task force as it set sail for the South Atlantic. His mother's brother – Uncle Roger – was serving on HMS *Antelope*, a navy frigate that was later sunk by Argentinian bombers at the entrance to San Carlos Water on May 23. 'Mum was desperately upset,' says Starmer, 'and we didn't know until about a week later that Roger had survived.'

But, as he got older, Starmer had also begun to shake himself free of a life both at home and school that he found a bit stifling. 'I wanted to expand my horizons, hear other ideas and opinions, do other things,' he says, 'I wanted to explore.' He sought to get out of his house as often as possible. On weekday mornings, he would wake at 5.45 to practise the flute, take his dog for a long walk across the fields, and two hours later be waiting at the bus stop to take him to school. In the evenings he did football training with his local team, Bolt Hurst Athletic, or, later, Edenbridge FC in the Kent Boys League. On Sundays, he played matches, travelling to away fixtures in a van with two parallel benches in the back.

On Saturdays, he would head up to London and the Guildhall School of Music. Starmer was a serious and accomplished flautist for whom all that pre-dawn practice had earned him a youth scholarship at this prestigious institution. Going there every weekend for more than six years was, he says, 'a big deal for a boy from Hurst Green'.

But he quickly recognised that any talent he had in music would never be enough to make it as a professional. Although he loved playing quartets – particularly Mozart who had a 'special place for the flute' – he felt himself stumbling into a world of brilliant musicians who could improvise and do things he couldn't. Some people are 'properly gifted', he says, 'whereas I was just someone who had got to a certain level through practice, repetition and hard work.'

It's hard to tell if such a reaction is an early example of what he calls the 'class ceiling' that made people from his background feel they didn't belong or merely a hard-headed pragmatism. In any case, he also got to a good level on the piano and the recorder, as well as for a time learning the violin alongside someone who would later be very famous under a variety of different names but was still called Quentin Cook when he left the grammar school after his O-levels. He became Norman Cook at Reigate Sixth Form College, where he met Paul Heaton with whom he would go on to play bass guitar in the Housemartins. Much later, he would earn a Guinness World Record for the most Top 40 hits under different names, including Beats International, Freak Power, Pizzaman, and, of course, the DJ Fatboy Slim.

Cook says he didn't really hang out much with Starmer outside school but remembers a 'decent person' and says he's been 'pleasantly surprised' by his rise over the years since, adding: 'Thankfully, Keir is a way better politician than he was a violinist.' For his part, Starmer has hazy memories of going to see the first band formed by Cook and Heaton, a punk forerunner of the Housemartins called the Stomping Pond Frogs, at gigs in local village halls.

But he says his social life was usually confined to a bit of under-age drinking in pubs with landlords who were willing to turn a blind eye or going to parties at friends' houses while their parents were away. Coming back from one, he was in a car that overturned on the A25 and Starmer says he was very lucky to escape serious injury. The accident also helps explain why even now he prefers to drive himself, although he concedes that may also be because of 'my slight control-freakery'.

As the seventies became the eighties, old certainties were being challenged by punk rock and strikes, social and economic upheaval.

A teenaged Starmer was all too aware that everything 'happened elsewhere' and this leafy corner of England remained a very conservative sort of place. This was underlined by the experience of a friend from Hurst Green called Graham who went to school at Reigate and had come out as gay. 'It was a brave thing to do in 1980, even though it wasn't much of a surprise to any of us,' says Starmer. 'Graham's dad, who ran the Diamond Inn down the road, did that "You're no son of mine" thing and threw him out.'

Starmer refers to him only by his first name because Graham later disappeared off to London and neither he, nor other friends, heard from him again. But Starmer does tell a story about how, in the summer after their A-levels, Graham joined him and Mark Adams working at a holiday centre for the Spastics Society – now called Scope – in Cornwall. One night, instead of the usual quizzes and musicals they organised, the three went to a nightclub. 'Graham didn't do much to conceal that he was gay,' recalls Starmer, 'and some of the local kids decided the way to prove they weren't gay too was by punching and kicking him. Mark and I got involved, so all three of us ended up getting beaten up.'

He says: 'When I'm told how "things were better in the old days", people forget about the ways Britain has become less cruel and less full of hate. We can all take some pride in that.'

5

'Reunited'

The pilgrim

For all that the young Keir Starmer felt at odds with that early eighties era and the system in which he was educated, he still has some fond recollections from those days.

Many involve a teacher called Aubrey Scrase – or 'Aubs' as he was universally known – who taught Latin. Though it wasn't this pupil's favourite subject, Starmer says Scrase was his favourite teacher, someone who took him and his friends on trips to London to see plays and had 'a calm way of allowing you to be an adult'.

After Scrase died in 2016, Starmer went back to Reigate for a reunion of sorts as a newly elected Labour MP to deliver a tribute in front of a two-hundred-strong audience in the school's dining hall. 'We trusted him and he would never judge us,' he said. Pointing to the image on the screen behind him, he added: 'Look at that face, blue shirt, messy hair, big glasses. Then look at the smile and ask yourself, "What was he thinking?"' Starmer raised a glass and toasted 'Aubs' with what was apparently the teacher's catchphrase: 'Silly sod!'

He has returned to his old school on other occasions, giving a talk to sixth formers about his work as director of public prosecutions, as well as appearing at fundraising dinners for charities that subsidise pupils whose parents cannot afford the £23,000-a-year fees. When Starmer became leader of the opposition in 2020, the school's headmaster Shaun Fenton proclaimed this to be 'the highest political office that any Reigatian has achieved to date', and a former staff member lauded Starmer's 'staunch' support of the school and its foundation.

That relationship has soured since, however, because Labour is committed to removing the exemption that private schools get as charities from paying VAT on their fees, a policy that has been denounced by the *Daily Mail* as 'Marxist' and 'a blatant attempt to incite class envy'.

Starmer's occasional attendance at fundraising events for the school's charitable foundation has been seized upon as proof of double standards by sections of the Conservative press. And, almost half a century after Reigate Grammar began charging fees to those who weren't 'state boys', the *Daily Telegraph* decided to make it front-page news with a headline saying, '"Hypocrite" Keir Starmer benefited from private school charity', along with a picture of his face concealed in shadow.

The Labour leader himself wearily emphasises that he has no ideological objection to private education and explains that his party's policy is a pragmatic one, ending a tax break for such schools in order to raise more than £1 billion in additional funding for the state sector.

Fenton, however, has become one of the more prominent critics of the proposal, saying Labour's plan will prevent less wealthy families who already 'scrimp and save and sacrifice' to afford it from sending their children to private school. He provocatively compares Labour's expectation of tax revenue for state schools to the promise that Boris Johnson once made that Brexit would mean £350 million extra for the NHS every week. 'Keir was better educated here than to believe all that,' he says.

In his headmaster's office, where on the wall behind him is a photograph of the 'Old Reigatian' David Walliams wearing a dress but none of the Labour leader in any form of outfit, Fenton insists: 'We really are very proud of Keir and would welcome him back at any time.' For all their disagreements, he says the school would not dream of disclosing embarrassing details of Starmer's time there, adding: 'I expect he got up to a few things the teachers didn't know about – I would be disappointed if he didn't – but he was seen as an interested, bright and successful member of the school community.'

The headmaster's father was a 1970s glam rock singer, Alvin Stardust, known for his huge jewellery and trademark single black leather glove. So Fenton may be talking with a degree of expertise when he laughs off suggestions that the young Starmer had been a 'tearaway' by pointing out that 'Keir playing Mozart on his flute in our school orchestra' was 'not particularly rebellious' at a time when the Sex Pistols were scandalising society and being banned by the BBC.

Then he shakes off this brief interlude into rock culture and reverts to being all headmasterly, saying: 'Keir will remember having to sing our school song at assemblies, "To Be a Pilgrim", which is all about going on a special journey with a purpose. My advice to him is to go on and be a pilgrim and do good in the world.'

The sanctuary

Starmer probably does not need such advice right now, having spent the four decades since he left school going on and, at the very least in his view, trying his level best to do some good in the world.

Those years are detailed in the chapters to follow but in closing this one, it's worth describing what happened in the home he left behind. Although his relationship with Rod softened a bit over the years, the emotional gap between them remained. 'We just couldn't find a point of contact,' he says, 'we never found a way of dealing with it.' He describes a typical phone conversation from those days. '"Hi Dad. It's Keir." There would be a pause and then he would just say, "I'll get your mum."' And she would ask her son everything – 'what I was doing, who I had seen, where I had been' – as if she knew she had to make up for his dad.

Although Jo's failing health gave her more to complain about than most, a combination of her positivity and Rod's increasing eccentricity lightens this somewhat grim family history.

There was, for instance, a small herd of rescued donkeys. Rod and Jo had always loved animals, but seemed to develop a particular empathy for these. The first two donkeys were given to the Starmers to look after by a family moving away from Oxted and they roamed about the garden, keeping Jo company when Rod was at work. But then more began arriving. 'Whenever Mum and Dad heard one was being treated badly or waiting to be shipped to an abattoir, they'd turn up with a trailer and a bit of cash to buy its freedom,' says Starmer. 'There was a Horrace, a Daisy – and others too whose names I can't remember.'

Within a few years, their eldest son had bought them the field behind their house so they could have what he calls 'a sort of donkey sanctuary'. He tells a story of how his dad had once 'flagged down a bloke with a JCB and asked him to dig a grave'. The explanation was that one of the donkeys had died. 'This poor guy then had to stay for the funeral, probably thinking he had a really implausible excuse for being late to work, while my dad conducted a ceremony in loving memory of Horrace or whoever.' Did his father perhaps see a bit of himself in a hard-working but notoriously grouchy animal that lacks the privileges of a horse or a pony? 'There might be something in that,' replies Starmer doubtfully. 'But I think it was more that he just wanted to keep Mum happy.'

The donkeys became part of the fabric of Hurst Green community life. David Butlin, the vicar at St John's, remembers how for a number of years his atheist friend would bring one of them into church at Easter, livening up the Palm Sunday story of Jesus Christ riding such an animal into Jerusalem. 'Rod would still be wearing his shorts, of course, and there was no question of him staying for the service afterwards.'

Back in London, Starmer's legal colleagues were bemused by the way this ambitious lawyer would reschedule meetings or race down to Hurst Green after court had finished because he was on 'donkey duty'. One of them who witnessed such a visit later remembered Jo as an 'extraordinary woman … ruddy-cheeked and packed with energy', as well as how the animals 'nuzzled up to this frail lady as she went about her business tending to them, feeding them and caring for them'.

As Starmer's career took off, however, the worsening condition of his mother's health could swiftly bring him back to earth. Once, after he had won a human rights award and, he says, 'I was feeling pretty good about myself, a phone call came from the hospital to tell me she was very ill.' She had developed MRSA and, by the time he got there, Jo had 'no fewer than four nurses around her bed trying to keep her alive'. He describes how 'this frenzy of activity went on for hours without any of them taking a break', adding: 'When Mum's condition finally stabilised, all I wanted to do was get on my knees and thank them.'

His parents still kept going up to the Lake District, eventually clocking up seventy-seven holidays there over the course of fifty-four years. By 2000 they had climbed all but two of the 214 fells described in Alfred Wainwright's books. Rod used his engineering skills to adapt Jo's wheelchair so he could push her up mountains, but it was on one such holiday in 2008 that she fell and broke her leg badly. Her weak bones couldn't be pinned and the doctors decided they had to amputate. When Starmer went to see her before the operation, she was, as usual, doing her best to make light of it: 'I've got one good leg, one bad leg,' she told him. 'I just hope they don't cut the wrong one off.'

'After her leg was amputated,' says Starmer, 'something in her broke.' Jo became totally immobile and no longer able to speak. Rod built an outhouse with a big window at the back of the garden so she could look at their donkeys, then installed a kitchen and moved her bed in there too. One of Starmer's regrets is that his children never got to know her or feel the love she had given him. 'She couldn't feed herself, go to the toilet, or move. She was in a bad way. It wasn't just that she stopped speaking, she couldn't communicate in any way. She just stared out at the field,' he says.

Each Sunday Rod would wheel Jo into church, before sitting outside until the 'religious mumbo-jumbo' was over, then complain to some of the other congregants about how they'd parked their cars on the pavement and made his job of getting the wheelchair in more difficult. For similar reasons, he had what was said to have been a 'spectacular falling out' with the landlord of the Haycutter in the village over a refurbishment that made it harder to get her wheelchair through the door.

More enlightened policies were in place at Oxted's Barn Theatre, where in 2005 Rod was persuaded to swap his shorts for a suit during a visit from a member of the royal family. Pictured in the theatre's newsletter, the Starmers were described as 'patrons', proudly showing off to the Duke of Kent a new lift designed for disabled access.

Rod would use this same newsletter in 2014 to tell Oxted's theatregoers about his son's knighthood at a ceremony in Buckingham Palace. 'Keir was treated like a Lord and we were looked after like a Lord's Mum and Dad!!' wrote the old socialist. 'The Citation at the ceremony was: "Sir Keir Starmer, for services to Law and to Criminal Justice." I can think of nothing better. Prince Charles did the Honours.'

Making his father proud was almost certainly one of the reasons Starmer accepted the honour, even though he has more usually called it a mark of respect for the thousands of people who worked for him at the Crown Prosecution Service. And Rod's account of the ceremony was accurate, up to a point. Starmer likes to fill in some of the extra details with a story that grows slightly more elaborate with each telling. But there is a sense of genuine affection in his voice as he describes the scene: 'Dad rocked up at the gates in his beaten-up old Volvo estate with my mum in the front seat, her wheelchair in the boot and their Great Dane, Tiffy, in the back seat because they thought it would have been unfair to leave the dog at home.

'Apparently, he just rolled the window down and told the police guarding the entrance to the palace: "We're here for Keir's knighthood." None of this – the massive dog, the car, the strange beard hanging off his chin – had been cleared with the authorities. By the time I got on the scene, the car was rocking with this really loud barking from the dog and it was surrounded by security people.

'I managed to negotiate Dad, Mum, Tiffy and the Volvo through the gates. Then we started worrying about what to do with Tiffy. We couldn't just let him out of the car – what if he met the Queen's corgis in the gardens? So Dad asked these royal attendants if they would mind looking after this ginormous drooling dog for the next hour or so. And they did.'

The grave

Jo died in April 2015, a few days before Starmer was elected as an MP. While he says her death was 'a release' from suffering, it left Rod without his focal point in life. He had been planning to take her to Parliament to watch their son be sworn in, having made all kinds of special designs to get her there. But once she died, he decided there was no point in going on his own.

For her funeral at St John's, Rod had written a eulogy for Jo but was unable to read it out and asked David Butlin to deliver it instead. So it was the vicar who described in great detail their holidays in the Lake District, their friendship with Alfred Wainwright and the different mountains they had climbed over the years. There was brief mention of the four children they had raised together but, as ever, Rod did not want to single out one of them by saying Keir had just become an MP. His eulogy merely stated that they were 'now all grown up and leading useful lives'.

In the months that followed, Starmer says, 'Dad more or less abandoned the house and moved into the outhouse he had built for Mum, turning it into "a bit of a shrine", arranging all their photo albums there and placing her wedding ring beside the bed.'

Even in his eighties, this still physically strong man refused all offers of help. Mary Seller remembers him insisting on having his Christmas lunch sitting on his own by Jo's graveside which he visited most days, eating a pack of sandwiches. By the summer of 2018, however, after a cut on his leg turned septic, he started drinking heavily to ease the pain. He was forced into hospital, and his family assumed he would be out again in a few days – but he developed blood poisoning, becoming delirious. When Starmer took his son to see Rod a few times, he had to listen to 'grandpa telling him about money hidden behind the bed or how they let goats eat his feet at night'.

In his more lucid moments, Rod asked about Lettie, his latest dog, or if things were okay back at the house. In truth, they were not – his children had decided not to tell him about a fire in the outhouse that had burned everything to a cinder, including the dog. 'Mum and Dad's photo albums were destroyed, together with every relic of the life they had made,' says Starmer. 'We found Mum's wedding ring eventually in the ashes, all bent and broken. Everything Dad had was in there. And we hadn't told him it was gone. "The dog's fine," we'd say. "It's all fine, just waiting for you to come home."'

And so, on that November night described at the beginning of this section, when Starmer raced down on the train to see him, the Labour leader's whirlpool of emotions also included a measure of relief because it meant his father need never be told about the fire.

'Dad died when I was back in London,' he says. 'I had gone out with football friends for our Christmas do. But about forty-five minutes in I went home, I just knew something. I didn't want to be out. So I was sat on the sofa when the call from the hospital came.'

Rod was buried at Oxted cemetery alongside Jo. 'It wasn't the biggest funeral,' says Starmer, 'because Dad had fallen out with most people he met and so those that turned up were either family or there under some form of duress. I did a eulogy that morning which began: "Since we're in a church I had better be truthful. He was a difficult sod." The other mourners nodded and laughed at that. They knew what he was like too.' By the grave he shares with his wife, there is now a simple wooden cross with a brass plate saying simply: 'Jo & Rod Starmer. Reunited.'

After they had finished at the church, there were sandwiches and tea but Starmer couldn't stay long because he had to get back to his job and away from what he had already left behind.

In the way that many people do as they get older, Starmer has realised there is sometimes more than just a bit of his dad in him. When having difficulty explaining a point, he will often reach for a pen and paper to draw a map or design, just as his engineer father would have done. There is also an attention to detail, a stubbornness and refusal to emote in public that seems familiar too. His old childhood friend Mark Adams likes to tease him that he is getting more like Rod, then adds: 'Keir hates it when I do that.'

The house at 23 Tanhouse Road was sold in 2021 to Andrew and Sarah O'Neill. He is an architect who has moved walls around, excavated the garden and made it his own. Andrew says, 'It's just bricks and mortar to me.' But Sarah sometimes worries when 'people speak badly' of the politician who once lived there, because 'I sort of think there might be ghosts and memories in these walls.'

The land at the back of the house used as the donkey sanctuary was sold the following year, albeit for a small fraction of the ludicrous eight-figure sum one newspaper alleged it to be worth. Some traces of the Starmers were still there in the summer of 2023, including some of Rod's old yellow cycling club vests and – you notice this with a start – Jo's old wheelchair. Upturned and abandoned, it's still recognisably the same one that had been adapted at the front by her clever toolmaking husband.

But the story of his parents does not quite end there, because real life is untidy too.

While helping clear out the house before it was sold, Starmer found a scrapbook hidden right at the back of a cupboard, filled with newspaper cuttings from when he was younger, then about his career as a lawyer and an MP. 'I knew it was Dad's because he had done it so neatly with his craftsman's hand and he had written in dates beneath the pictures,' he says. 'But I didn't really know what to think about it, why he had taken all that trouble, then hidden it.'

At the time he had just begun to talk publicly about the strained relationship he'd had with his father – and perhaps with the scrapbook still on his mind, he said: 'I only once remember him saying he was proud of me.'

It was all too much for Mary Seller, who wrote to the Labour leader at the House of Commons. 'She wanted me to know I had got him a bit wrong,' Starmer recalls.

The family's old friend from Hurst Green can't remember the exact contents of the letter, but says: 'After watching Keir on television talking about him, I felt it was important for him to know his dad loved him.' Seller describes how she had carried on dropping by the house after Jo died: 'Rod would always be watching the BBC Parliament Channel in the hope of catching sight of Keir. He may not have been able to tell him how proud he was of what he had achieved but he was, he really was. Rod would always tell me about him.'

None of which is to say Starmer has painted a false picture of his father. Seller confirms Rod remained a peculiarly difficult person to the very end. When she went to see him in hospital, for instance, he told her: 'I don't want to talk to you. Go away.' She remembers leaving so quickly she didn't even have to pay for parking. Later, when Rod was close to death, she tried again and, as priests do, offered a few comforting words about Jo being in heaven. 'He opened one eye and replied: "What makes you think there is a heaven?"' Yet Seller is adamant that behind the rudeness and irascibility, there was a sincere and principled man who was proud of all his children.

Starmer remarks on the strangeness of how an interview on national television resulted in him getting a fresh insight into his dead father. 'Mary had told me something I didn't know: Dad was proud of me and loved me, even if he couldn't tell me to my face,' he says.

'And it's now too late for me to tell him – to his face – that I was proud of him, that I loved him too.'

Part II

Underpinning

Foundations laid and lessons
learned from Leeds to London

6
Feet on the ground

A late penalty!

There's a half-hearted effort to contest the decision that doesn't last long because Keir Starmer is both captain of one team and the unofficial match referee.

He takes the ball, places it on the spot, steps back and steadies himself as he stares into the eyes of the keeper. 'No pressure, Keir,' says an opponent, just within hearing range. Starmer strides forward, plants his right foot, then smashes the ball with his left into the corner of the net. 'Getiiiin!'

It is March 4, 2023, a Sunday, one resembling countless others in his life in that he's on a patch of worn Astroturf running around in pursuit of a football. He's wearing shorts and a blue-green Gaelic football top that is now a tighter fit than when he bought it in Donegal fifteen years ago, while an elastic sports bandage on his right knee provides another hint the march of time has not left him entirely unscathed. Even at the age of sixty, however, Starmer is still organising and playing football in these eight-a-sides with some of his oldest friends on a pitch near his home in London's Kentish Town.

At other times on a weekend, he's watching the game as a season ticket holder at Arsenal in the upper tier of the West Stand, where he sits next to more of these friends who have nothing to do with Westminster. Before or after a game, he goes to pubs like the Pineapple near his home to drink beer with people he knew long before he ever contemplated becoming prime minister. Later, he will go home to his family where, he says, 'as soon as I walk through the door, I am just Dad.'

Football, friends and family are, he says, the everyday experiences that keep his 'feet on the ground' even though the world he inhabits now seems so slippery.

Yet, as he wheels away in celebration after scoring that Sunday, the familiar clicking noise of a camera can be heard from pitchside. The press photographer who has been standing for the whole game seems friendly enough and even goes to fetch the ball after it is kicked over. And, if the Labour leader says the best thing about his football games is that the other players 'don't give a stuff' what his job is for the rest of the week, it's clear that Jeremy Selwyn is there precisely because of what Starmer does when he's not playing football.

This is the same photographer who took a picture of a previous Labour leader making a bit of a mess of eating a bacon sandwich in 2014. This was regarded as so damaging to Ed Miliband it was front page of the *Sun* on the day of the general election a year later along with the headline: 'Save Our Bacon'.

Selwyn says that 'taking pictures of politicians in off-guard moments and in situations they might not want to be shown' is justified because press officers usually control their image so tightly. He describes Starmer as 'one of the nicer politicians I've come across' and goes out of his way to say the Labour leader seemed 'quite athletic that day', before emphasising it's not his fault if newspapers decide to use – out of hundreds of different shots he takes – just one picture showing someone in a bad light.

And the photograph published by the *Sun* on the Monday morning after this eight-a-side game in Kentish Town did not, of course, show Starmer scoring a goal or looking 'quite athletic'. It showed the Labour leader bent over, elbows splayed and knees turned in, apparently flinching as the ball came towards him. The headline helpfully pointed out he had ended up on the 'losing side' in this 'London kickabout'. And he hates losing.

*   *   *

Starmer is all too aware this local football pitch is not the only habitat for his real life that is now endangered. He worries about being photographed when he goes to the beach on family holidays. He also has to be a 'bit careful' at Arsenal games nowadays because 'everyone's got a camera on their phone – I'm conscious of a few eyes glancing over at me' – and he can't get into an argument with 'someone who's shooting their mouth off'. Does he still sing at matches? 'Sometimes,' he replies, cautiously. 'But I'm not one of those with his shirt off and arms out doing "Fooor-tee-nine, for-ty-nine, un-de-feat-ed" on their own when no one else is joining in.'

At the same time, researchers from the Conservative Party's attack unit have been heard to claim they've placed spies in the Pineapple pub to get a video of him drinking too much or talking indiscreetly. This might just be the kind of idle boast that is some-times heard around Westminster in the hope it will spoil the taste of his beer, but Starmer doesn't seem too fussed. He says there have been a few occasions journalists have sniffed around local shops and been into the pub asking questions. The bar staff usually let him know and say 'we told them nothing'.

Part of the problem is that, having been well into his fifties before becoming an MP, he had carved out a life outside the narrow grooves demanded by politics. He worries now how his job constricts what his family can do. He talks about how his son and daughter are teenagers and should be getting up to 'all sorts' with-out any risk of media intrusion while his wife, Vic, wants to carry on walking to work and meeting her friends for coffee. He admits that when they first met, the prospect of him becoming a politician was 'not on the cards', and at the time, she would 'much rather I had become a judge or something'.

At home, even with the blinds down and the curtains closed, Starmer finds the presence of reporters and camera crews outside deeply uncomfortable. He shows an ordinary father's resentment as he remembers how the media, gathered on his doorstep at dawn, once woke his daughter up before an important school test. He tries to protect his children as best he can by asking the media not to use their names or take photographs of them.

If he mentions his children at all it is usually through a pair of self-deprecating anecdotes: returning home one evening with an award, he was greeted by his son asking, 'Where did you blag that then?' Leaving home for a fundraising event, his daughter asked: 'Why would anybody pay to hear you speak?' He has probably used these same stories a dozen times because they are tried and tested and he doesn't want to feed journalists' interest by giving away any more. As he says of his children, 'I talk about them less, because they matter most.'

Such a pressure point is not only about how he adapts to the scrutiny and intrusion that is an inevitable aspect of his job, it is also about the extent to which he uses his refuges from politics to authenticate himself within it. Every time he does so, he risks making them a bit less authentic and loosening the connection to a real life outside Westminster which is both a release valve for him and a genuine source of his values.

He does podcasts about his passion for football, usually begins big speeches with a joke about Arsenal's latest result, and has recorded an interview walking around the Emirates Stadium with Robbie Lyle of the unofficial fan channel AFTV. For all his unease about photographers taking pictures of his eight-a-side games, his own press officers – who Selwyn complains want to control politicians' image – have posted an edited video, entitled 'What football means to me', of him playing there.

Starmer is certainly not the first person running to be prime minister to highlight an everyman passion for the national sport. That's the kind of thing politicians do. And there will always be some observers determined to prove it's synthetic.

New Labour appeared almost symbiotically linked to the football fashions of the 1990s but Tony Blair also found himself accused, unfairly as it later turned out, of exaggerating his connections to Newcastle United. David Cameron was justifiably ridiculed when, having spent several years professing his love for Aston Villa, he got confused at a campaign rally and announced he supported West Ham. More recently Rishi Sunak has spoken about being a 'massive fan' of Southampton FC since he was a child and his father was the club doctor, yet has made the mistake of letting himself be photographed grinning among otherwise miserable-looking supporters when the club's relegation from the Premier League was being confirmed.

The columnist Stephen Bush has suggested Starmer sounds 'highly unconvincing' when talking about football because he's too cheery and doesn't complain enough. That's a little unfair to his fellow Arsenal fan who can moan away with the best of them about some things. He has slated the 'so-called fans' who 'don't know what they're talking about' or leave before the final whistle when the result is still in the balance – 'I'll never really understand that' – as well as the new-fangled managers who try to improve perfor-mance with gimmicks like banning tomato ketchup from players' diets. At the same time, Starmer can also verge on the lyrical when he wants as he describes the feeling when a late winner is scored and thousands of fans simultaneously forget themselves. 'Everyone stands up, hands in the air,' he once said, 'like there's a magnet in the sky above the stadium.'

All of which means Starmer generally passes the sniff test of being a 'proper fan', even to the point where journalists have asked him, perhaps half-seriously, if he would prefer to see Arsenal win the league than become prime minister.

Yet, as such questions imply, his passion for football has an intensity that makes him simultaneously more 'ordinary' than other politicians and less so. His friend from school, Mark Adams, puts it this way: 'If most politicians try to invent a love of football to make themselves appear more normal, Keir probably needs to downplay the football side of things because he really is pretty obsessive about it all.'

Starmer has always used football to normalise his life, even the parts that are not normal. The schoolkid, kicking a ball around as a way of avoiding the conversation others were having about TV he hadn't been allowed to watch, became someone who has since continued to use the sport as both ice breaker and anchor. More than half a century after his competitive debut, he plays football not just to stay fit or because he likes it, but to reassert a sense of himself.

Before an eight-a-side game, he can be seen pacing outside the changing rooms impatiently waiting for late arrivals. He'll usually have picked himself on the left side of midfield, but these days probably talks a better game than he plays. Actually, he hardly stops talking for ninety minutes of cajoling team-mates and winding up opponents.

'They include some of my oldest friends,' he says, 'along with friends of friends, sons, cousins, friends of a cousin's friend, or, maybe, someone we roped in because we were short of a player and they just carried on from there. There's one guy I play regularly with who we always call "Blocker" for obvious reasons. It was only when we got invited to his wedding that we found out his real name and, even then, I fear I may have referred to his bride as "Mrs Blocker".'

One of those to whom he is closest, in every sense, is Colin Peacock. Apart from the years he was away at university, he has never lived more than fifteen minutes from this friend he met at school. Their careers have taken different paths, with Peacock working with Gillette – Starmer's father would always call him 'Razorblade – and then Procter & Gamble. 'Given the choice,' the Labour leader says, 'I would much rather go to the pub with Colin than another of the receptions I get invited to these days. When I'm with him, there's no need to hold back or pretend.'

Peacock is among the old friends on whom Starmer leans precisely because they don't want to discuss politics every evening and there's 'complete trust' with them. 'The life I've got is quite weird and I have to find a space to just get away from it,' he says.

Although he spends less time in the pub than he once did, Peacock describes how they still 'eat pizza, have a pint and talk nonsense to each other' before matches and, afterwards, 'we might stop off for another cheeky half'. That, too, is not entirely normal in politics, where party leaders often only venture into a pub for the photo opportunity of them 'pulling a pint'.

Peacock says: 'I think he really values friendship in a way a lot of people don't. He works out who are the fake and the frauds. I'm not a good footballer, never have been really, but Keir always puts me in his team for our games. He must be a nightmare to play against – so lippy – but I don't get too much grief off him provided I work my socks off.

'He has this big thing on the pitch about "working hard and playing hard". It's sort of his approach to life in general.'

As philosophies go, it is a simple one, but it also probably explains more about his beliefs than any textbook on political theory.

7

Playing hard

Snakebite and curry chips

In the year after leaving school when he did some work for his dad 'putting holes in metal', Keir Starmer earned enough money to buy his first car. It wasn't much to look at: a battered Morris Minor Estate with wooden panels that had moss growing out of them. But it was in this vehicle that he had what he describes as 'one of the best days of my life' when, in September 1982, he drove away from his past towards the future.

'With every mile that went by,' he says with unusual force, 'I told myself I was never going back.'

He did go back – of course he did – and, as he drove away from Hurst Green, he was also carrying a certain weight of expectation from his family because he was the first of them ever to go to university.

There had been lengthy discussions about what he should study. He had lost interest a bit in the subjects he did at A-level but still ended up with two 'B's and a 'C' which, he says, 'was then considered reasonably good'. He had toyed with the idea of studying politics or maybe something to do with theatre and music production, but Rod and Jo – like so many working-class parents before them – wanted their son to study for a 'proper profession'. In the end, they settled on law and he won a place at Leeds University, one of the better ones for this subject at the time.

When Starmer arrived in the city, however, he says it dawned on him that he had 'neither met a lawyer nor really knew what they did' and remembers feeling that almost everybody else had 'a better idea of what they were doing'. He says: 'I was surrounded by a lot of people who had wanted to be lawyers all their lives, some of whose parents and grandparents had been lawyers too. They talked knowledgeably about specialising in this or that field or arranging their summer internship at some or other barrister's chambers.'

Although he has faced similar moments in his life since, he says this was his biggest leap. When he makes speeches now about 'breaking the class ceiling' and that 'nagging voice inside saying, no this isn't for you, you don't belong here, you can't do that' – he is thinking about this time in his life.

The disorientation he felt was made worse by being so far from home. He had never lived anywhere bigger than a Surrey village and now found himself in a great northern city, two hundred miles distant, full of a million strangers. While a friend from school, Geoff Scopes, had driven up with him, they were in different halls of residence. Starmer's was a big 1960s building called Charles Morris, nicknamed the 'Charlie Mo', where he knew no one.

As so often happens in student life, the immediate solution involved alcohol. On that first night, he says, 'a couple of lads knocked on my door and asked if I wanted to go to the pub'. He did. One of them was from Liverpool, the other from the Midlands, a fact he remembers only because he had never really met anybody from either. Nor were they much interested in hearing about where he was from. 'I didn't ask for your life story, mate,' said one. 'Are you going to buy me a pint?'

In those days, Starmer's idea of a pint was Snakebite, a mixture of lager and cider seen as dangerously anarchic in the 1980s for reasons no one really understood. Almost two decades later, such was the reputation of this drink a pub landlord in Harrogate reportedly refused to serve it to the visiting former US president Bill Clinton on the implausible grounds that it was 'illegal in the UK'.

Within a week of being in the north, Starmer discovered curry chips – basically normal chips covered in a spicy brown-green sauce – but they were so alien to this Surrey boy in 1982 he made the mistake of soaking the first batch he bought with vinegar. And, of course, there was football. He played for Charlie Mo on Saturdays and the law school team on Wednesdays, frequently hanging around the sports centre in between until he could pick up a five-a-side game. A few times, he went to watch Leeds United play at Elland Road.

There was little sign at this stage that Starmer would become much of a lawyer. He found his first term studying 'the nuts and bolts of contract law' pretty dry and hadn't much warmed to some of the more entitled students on the course. One day in the canteen that October, someone sat down opposite him who started talking and, he says, 'really hasn't stopped talking since'. John Murray has a clear memory of their first conversation. He'd been staring at a letter on the table which bore Starmer's name.

'Are you related to Lady Starmer?' he asked.

'Who?'

'She's a dignitary where I come from,' he said. 'Lives in a big house near me and is famous – well – in Darlington …'

'Never heard of her.'

'Still, there can't be a lot of Starmers around.'

It transpired Murray was doing the same course and had been similarly spooked by the self-confidence of the other students. But, before they could work out how to crack their class ceilings, there were more urgent matters to be sorted out. After inspecting Starmer's thin collection of Status Quo and Boomtown Rats albums, Murray decided this Surrey boy needed 'an emergency re-education programme'. He had started a music fanzine called *Nag Nag Nag!* to sell to 'skinny indie kids' back in Darlington, which in its first edition had declared a mission to drag people just like Starmer 'kicking and screaming into the 1980s'.

And Starmer acknowledges his debt to a friend who 'seemed to know about every underrated album or unknown band doing an underground gig'. He says: 'We must have looked like an incongruous pair at first. John looked like Ian McCulloch from Echo and the Bunnymen, had trendy half-mast trousers and a copy of his fanzine under each arm. I was fresh from the village of Hurst Green in Surrey with heavy jeans, woolly jumper and a haircut apparently modelled on Ray Clemence [the then England goalkeeper].'

Together, they went to see bands like Orange Juice, Aztec Camera and the Smiths. Murray even hung out with Keith Gregory and David Gedge, who were in a local indie band called the Lost Pandas, which a few years later became famous as the Wedding Present. They knew him as 'Talkin' John', to distinguish him from another John who could tolerate a conversational vacuum. 'Talkin' John' even gets a 'without whom' credit on the 1985 single 'Go Out and Get 'Em Boy', after lending Gregory a bass guitar which he never got back.

A book published in 2023 has hundreds of stories from fans of the Wedding Present and in the middle of it – incongruously – is a picture of a man described as 'Sir Keir Starmer, KCB KC MP, Leader of the Labour Party', saying he had met Gregory and Gedge a few times in the early eighties. He then names his top song by the band as 'My Favourite Dress', adding: 'David has managed to perfectly distil the tortuous agonising feelings of jealousy into three minutes of angst. The guitar hook is pretty great too …'

Murray noticed his friend got a new 'shorter, sharper haircut' and started wearing 'dead man's raincoats from Oxfam'. Starmer learned the shuffles, spins and flips of northern soul dancing. Before long he was going out with Angela O'Brien, a psychology student and one of seven children from an Irish Catholic family in Manchester, the first in a series of strong women in his life who have all known how to keep him in check. They would be together, on and off, for the next decade. Given his difficulties with his own dad, it's noteworthy how close he became to Angela's father who, as a welder by trade, also worked with his hands. Even now Starmer remembers Ged O'Brien fondly as 'an extraordinary, generous and interesting man', someone with whom, on trips back to Angela's, he would slip off to the pub, down pints of mild and – though Ged was a Manchester United fan – go to watch the then perennially unsuccessful Manchester City at Maine Road. because 'we could never get tickets to Old Trafford'.

In his second year, Starmer shared a house with friends from school like Geoff Scopes and Debbie Bacon, as well some new ones, including Murray, Alison Jenkins and Simon Head, living in the Hyde Park area of Leeds at Chestnut Avenue. It is an address that became notorious a decade later as the 'most burgled street in Britain' after being described by the *News of the World*, with the dose of exaggeration for which that publication was famed, as a place where 'trembling residents cower behind their front doors' while 'gangs of drug-crazed thugs roam menacingly' outside. When one householder reportedly dared to approach an intruder in his garden, 'he was told down the barrel of a gun: "Get back in or die."'

Murray doesn't remember anything like that at all but concedes, 'We didn't have much worth stealing.' He says, 'All we had was an ancient black and white TV, which was no doubt left by the deceased person the landlord bought the house from. In those days there was no wi-fi or fridge freezers; it was whatever floral wallpaper and sticky swirly carpets the previous owner had left behind.' He has, however, described the moment he and Starmer 'waded in' to protect another friend and fellow law student, Andy Symms, who was being beaten up because 'a group of lads had taken exception to his haircut'. 'I got knocked out,' says Murray, 'actually saw stars and was carted to hospital by ambulance, but Keir got off scot-free – so typical – with not even a mark on him.'

High times

Many of the stories from this time in Starmer's life combine descriptions of a general scuzziness familiar to generations of students and his more unusual desire to establish some order.

The Morris Minor in which he had driven to Leeds – by then known as the 'mobile hedge' thanks to the vegetation growing from its bodywork – required the use of a starting handle before becoming mobile and was sparingly deployed once a week for a trip to the supermarket. But Starmer also took it upon himself to organise everything, with each housemate making an equal contribution to a shopping bill that included a flat-rate tax of twenty-five pence each for petrol money.

He remembers mastering his 'signature dish' of chilli con carne, then advancing to 'bits of chicken in a creamy pink sauce made with powder from a packet', before encountering less success with a curry that was discovered a few weeks later, 'rock-solid', round the back of the cooker. And yet he would also patrol the house at night trying to cut down on the use of electricity. 'What bothered him most was people turning lights on and off all the time,' says Murray. 'He had this thing about that being more expensive than anything.'

A sense of what Starmer was like back then can be found in a black and white picture of him posing, as if for an album cover, with his housemates in an art studio. At the back is Murray, apparently lost in thought. Bacon is wearing sunglasses even though it is dark outside, while Jenkins reclines in heels, white jeans and a hat. Starmer, lying on the floor beside a human skull which Murray insists was real, sports a check shirt with its sleeves ripped off like Stuart Adamson from the Scottish band Big Country. Slightly exotically, he is also wearing eyeliner as he gazes intently into the distance.

According to the *Guardian*'s art critic, who reviewed the photograph in 2021, 'Starmer is clearly the star of this putative indie band' and has 'a fervent light in his eyes'. Jonathan Jones continued: 'He may be all too aware of his look, and his looks, but he also projects a romantic dream of some kind – nay, a vision. Young Keir appears to believe in some big idea or better future. He can see it.'

By then, Starmer and Murray were hitchhiking down to London, Manchester and Leicester for gigs. 'We weren't interested in going to summer balls or any of that hooray stuff,' says Murray. Instead, the two were going to cheap nightclubs on Friday nights and even turning the basement of the university's law society into their own 'DIY disco', so they could experiment with being DJs.

Unsurprisingly, such tales have prompted the question of whether Starmer also experimented with drugs. In one interview he was asked no fewer than fourteen times without giving a categorical answer either way. The subject of what substances were inhaled or otherwise ingested by political leaders when they were younger has become a wearisome media ritual, even though these days there is little evidence the public care too much about it either way. Starmer's stock response is to say, usually accompanied with a knowing grin and a little incline of his head, that 'I had a very good time at university.'

Although many have taken this to be a tacit admission that he did take drugs at some point, it has so far been impossible to find anyone – on or off the record – who will say they ever saw him do it. Maybe this is just another instance of his friends' loyalty. For what it's worth, they point out Starmer never got into smoking cigarettes, let alone anything stronger, because he was worried that polluting his lungs might damage his performance on the football pitch. There is said to be a photograph of him posing with a cigar at a Christmas party but those present say they're not sure if he even smoked that.

Some suggest his abstinence comes from a dislike of being out of control, with one friend describing how 'he will just take himself off to bed and go to sleep – Keir never totally loses it'. Others believe he may have been demonstrating a respect for, and obedi-ence to, the law that perhaps goes with the territory of someone preparing to be a lawyer. Certainly, there is no sign in any Labour law and order policy under his leadership that a Starmer govern-ment would adopt a more liberal approach to drugs.

Murray does, however, describe an occasion when this student of the law found himself on the wrong side of it. In the summer of 1984 he and Starmer headed to the south of France after seeing an advert suggesting they could make money selling ice creams and doughnuts on the beach. It wasn't until they got off the coach in Toulon that anyone told them hawking to tourists was technically illegal. Murray remembers them both being 'carted off' by sweating gendarmes on various occasions but says the worst that happened was the police would cheerfully consume all the illegal merchandise before letting them go.

'They even gave us a receipt for the food,' says Starmer, 'because they knew it was a bit of a game and we needed to show our employer we hadn't eaten them all. It was sort of "see you tomor-row" with a wink and a nod. I don't think anyone was actually arrested. They didn't really want to do over these hapless nineteen-year-olds.'

Murray has a photograph of the pair of them leaning back on benches at Toulon railway station as they wait for a train at the end of the trip. Pointing to his friend's footwear, he laughs and says: 'Keir should have been arrested just for wearing those espadrilles.'

Low times

When they returned to university, however, much of Yorkshire was locked in a struggle for the survival of jobs and communities that involved a very different relationship with the police.

The miners' strike that had begun in April that year had turned ugly while Starmer and Murray were heading for France to share their ice creams with the *Gendarmerie*. Thousands of police from across the country had been drafted into the coalfields and the notorious Battle of Orgreave an hour or so away from Leeds has since become a byword on the left for some of the worst excesses of state power.

The impact of all this was even spilling over into students' lives and Starmer remembers 'a really tough winter for the city'. He went on demonstrations and gave money to support miners' families – 'someone was always rattling a tin for them back then'. He says: 'It was impossible to be there at that time and not be moved by the miners' defiance.' For all the compliments he has offered since to the then Tory prime minister's capacity to bring about change, he hasn't forgotten the impact she had on real people's lives forty years ago. 'These were the British citizens who Margaret Thatcher branded as "the enemy within". They didn't deserve that,' says Starmer.

For his third year, he had moved into a new house at Brudenell Avenue in the city. Murray and Head went with him, joining up with another group of women, Katie Munson, Anne Cummings and Sarah Hargreaves, the last of whom he had first known at school where she had been slightly shocked by his left-wing politics. Hargreaves remembers how 'Keir liked to cook curries that would cover the entire kitchen in a sort of yellow sediment. We made it clear they couldn't carry on like that. We sat the boys down and told them there would be a cleaning rota. And, to my amazement and their credit, they stuck to it.'

Hargreaves still had fairly mainstream Tory views in those days and recalls some late-night arguments about the miners' strike with Starmer in the house. But she emphasises they 'never fell out' and now – to her former housemate's genuine delight – plans to vote Labour for the first time. 'A lot of people have asked me these days what he was like back then,' she says. 'What's always stuck in my mind is how he was with a friend of ours whose dad died in the third year. Students can be a bit selfish or immature. But Keir could not have been kinder or more sensitive to her. I've seen the same quality in him over the years with other people. It matters.'

Although a member of the university's Labour Club, Starmer had little appetite for the factional in-fighting that characterised the party in this period. John Erskine, the club's chair, was one of those engaged in a struggle against the Militant Tendency, but says Starmer was 'non-aligned' and largely absent from such conflict. He wasn't one of 'those selling papers on the streets and trying to get themselves arrested on picket lines', says Erskine. 'I remember him as part of a fairly trendy crew with sharp haircuts who hung out at Charles Morris Hall and the law school.'

This wasn't a good time to be a Labour Party member. In 1983, Thatcher had won a landslide, increasing her majority from 44 seats to 144. It became fashionable in political circles to predict that a shrinking working class meant Labour would never win another general election. Over the same period, organised labour through the trade unions fared no better with the defeat of the miners being followed by legislation making it harder to take legal strike action or form picket lines outside a workplace.

According to Murray, however, Starmer was always much more interested in politics than he was. On a trip back to Darlington he remembers introducing him to his Tory-leaning mother as a 'future Labour prime minister', though once again he says this was really just a way of 'winding both of them up'.

Concealed behind all the dancing, drinking, wind-ups and piss-takes of being a student was Starmer's capacity to study with a ferocious intensity. Indeed, one of the characteristics pointed out by almost everyone who knows him is his power of recovery. 'No matter what had gone on the night before which had left the rest of us lying in a heap somewhere,' says one, 'Keir would always be up at six the next morning, getting on with his studies.'

8

Working hard

'The essence of being human'

Starmer says that he soon realised that some of the other law students at Leeds who had seemed so confident when he first arrived were 'bullshitters'. It's a phrase he uses often to describe people in politics and elsewhere who, he says, 'go round talking loudly about things but don't know what they are talking about'.

In contrast to those school reports expressing concern that he wouldn't do as well as he should or was too prone to distraction, Starmer seems to have found his focus at Leeds. He spent a lot of time in the university's old law library on Lyddon Terrace, while also attending lectures and tutorials from professors like Clive Walker – with whom Starmer would later write a couple of books about miscarriages of justice – and Michael Passey, whose office was so cluttered with books and newspaper cuttings he often had to find another room in which to teach.

Passey specialised in civil liberties and human rights, and took a particular interest in Starmer, even expressing concern the loud music at gigs might damage his future as a lawyer if couldn't hear what was being said in a courtroom. At the end of one term, after Starmer and Murray both got firsts for his course – the only ones in their year – the professor took them out for a celebratory meal, where he made an arch comment about the similarity of their exam papers.

'Keir was his golden boy and his immediate instinct was that I must have copied him,' says Murray. 'I didn't really mind and I've only mentioned it twenty or thirty times since. We both worked hard and drove each other on. But Keir was always so disciplined. He never stopped – he's always been the same – sometimes, it makes me feel weary just thinking about the life he leads and his forward propulsion.'

From the outset of their friendship, Murray and Starmer had been splitting the cost of textbooks, both learning some of what they needed to know, then taking it in turns to explain to the other. There were also endless disputes about how to look after the books they bought. 'Keir liked to underline bits and make notes in the margins while I wanted them kept looking pristine and unread,' says Murray. Before exams, they walked miles along the Leeds and Liverpool Canal with their revision cards testing each other, 'because it was the only way to stay awake when the student hall kept the heating on all through the summer months'.

Sarah Hargreaves also witnessed his capacity for work. 'I've never seen anyone be able to study like him,' she says. 'I would always get distracted too easily. But Keir would go up to his room and be at his desk for hour, after hour, after hour.'

By then Starmer knew not only how to study but also what he wanted to learn, describing international law and human rights as 'a revelation' compared to the dry stuff of the first year. In these subjects, he found something fundamental to his belief system even now. He puts it like this: 'The essence of being human, irrespective of who you are, where you come from and what your circum-stances, is dignity. It means all people have rights which cannot be taken away. This idea of irreducible human dignity became a sort of lode star which has guided me ever since; it gave me a method, a structure and framework, by which I could test propositions. And it brought politics into the law for me.'

This triggers a reaction among Brexity Conservatives like Dominic Raab and Daniel Hannan, the last of whom wrote a book entitled *How We Invented Freedom & Why It Matters*, who see it as confirmation of Starmer's affinity for a foreign, 'continental', conception of human rights. They have sought to draw a distinction between Europe – with its 'Roman' tradition of law being derived from first principles and then enforced in 'Napoleonic' systems – and the gently evolving and older English concept of common law freedom they trace back through the Civil War, Magna Carta or even to pre-Norman 'Englalond' whose warriors, they like to imagine, gathered around oak trees debating ancient liberties.

This isn't a sterile debate from a law library in the 1980s because these *folkmoot* theories of freedom have taken root on the Conservative right and feed the desire of politicians like Suella Braverman to leave the European Convention on Human Rights or, indeed, Downing Street's description of the Labour leader now as a 'lefty human rights lawyer' because he opposes its plan for sending asylum seekers to Rwanda.

Starmer has dismissed such views as based 'on a fundamentally flawed analysis of their origin and relevance to our society'. 'England did not "invent" freedom, as some of today's more far-out politicians like to say, nor are the rights we have in the UK part of an exclusive racial birthright,' he says. Instead, he sees human rights as being part of an inclusive patriotic tradition which has helped our country always be 'at the heart' of a debate, from the Chartists in the nineteenth century to the suffragists in the twentieth, about what freedom means.

A particular inspiration for him was the 1948 Universal Declaration of Human Rights that emerged from the ashes of the Second World War when, he says, the world came together to find a way of preventing any repetition of the 'horror of Nazis being able to pass legislation in Germany which allowed them to torture, murder and massacre their own citizens'. Starmer is proud that Britain – and British values – played a big part in codifying these rights for other nations, saying: 'This was a way in which any government could be held to account for their actions, not because they had broken their own laws, but because they had committed crimes against humanity itself. Britain helped ensure that all people all around the world – the weakest as well as the most powerful, those who are different from us as well as those who are the same – have a right to demand freedom.'

He points out that it was a Conservative prime minister in Winston Churchill and the British diplomat David Maxwell Fyfe, a future Conservative home secretary, who helped enshrine human rights into the European-wide convention from which so many in that same party now wish to resile. Later on, as former colonies won their independence, Britain helped them craft constitutions built around this same crucial concept of human dignity, 'because they saw how human rights made them stronger as nations, not weaker'.

Although, as a left-wing student in the early eighties, Starmer probably wouldn't have put it quite that way at the time, he maintains that 'the Universal Declaration struck a deep chord with me – and it still does'. What's more, it raised the summit of his ambition.

In 1985, he became one of only a few in his year to be awarded a first-class degree in law from Leeds. And he hasn't forgotten his debt to the university, opening the law faculty's new Liberty Building in 2011 and delivering a lecture to its Centre for Criminal Justice Studies. For much of his time there he envisaged a career as a trade union solicitor and had started out looking for jobs with local firms in a city so badly bruised by the miners' strike that there was no shortage of this kind of work.

As he drilled deeper into the law, however, and felt what he calls 'a genuine sense of achievement for the first time' from his academic success, he began to think about becoming a barrister and fighting for those human rights in the highest courts of law. That ambition took him south again, to Oxford and a university he had never seriously countenanced going to before.

Off to the 'ivory tower'

Much has been written about Oxford in the 1980s. Boris Johnson, David Cameron, Michael Gove and Jeremy Hunt were all there at the same time. So too was the Liberal Democrat leader Ed Davey, as well as future Labour politicians like Yvette Cooper, Ed Balls and the Miliband brothers – first David, then Ed. A few years later came Liz Truss and Rishi Sunak.

If he succeeds Sunak after the next election, Starmer will be the fifteenth out of nineteen British prime ministers since the Second World War to have studied at Oxford. But the caricature of this university as an 'ivory tower' makes it too easy to lump all these people together as part of some homogenous elite. Not every experience of Oxford fits the stereotype and you won't find any photographs of a young Keir Starmer wearing the royal blue tailcoat with cream lapels of the Bullingdon Club like there are of David Cameron, Boris Johnson and George Osborne.

Starmer was a postgraduate doing a Bachelor of Civil Law (BCL) the university says is only offered to students with 'outstanding first law degrees'. This grindingly difficult course was crammed into a single year of three eight-week terms. And, unlike generalist subjects like politics, philosophy and economics (PPE) – that so many future MPs studied – the BCL was almost training in preparation for a real job.

All of which meant that, even had he been so inclined, there wasn't room in his schedule for punting down the Cherwell, sipping champagne at summer balls, or pretending to be a grown-up politician by dressing in white bow ties to debate at the Oxford Union.

Starmer remains suspicious of the kind of networking conversations that mention this or that university – quite often Oxford or Cambridge – 'and how someone must know so-and-so because they went there too'. Nor did he have much tolerance at the time for some of the obviously ambitious and extremely privileged people there who, he says, 'boasted about doing as little work as they could'. He says: 'None of that made much sense to me and I didn't waste any time with them. I just worked and then worked some more.'

He lived in graduate accommodation, playing football during his occasional free time or taking the train to Reading, where Angela O'Brien was doing her postgraduate course. For him, Oxford was 'not about who I could get to know so much as what I could learn'. The university's Bodleian Library holds a copy of just about every book that has ever been published in English and he describes the wonder at how he could submit a list the night before and arrive at his desk the next morning to find everything he possibly needed waiting for him rather than having to 'scramble around' for texts like at Leeds. Some of the books' authors were teaching his course: 'I had read a lot by Ronald Dworkin, the American philosopher, and here he was, lecturing law students like me in Oxford.'

The university is divided into around three dozen colleges and his was St Edmund Hall, sometimes known as 'Teddy Hall'. It was regarded as one of the more conservative colleges at the time with much of its identity linked to sports like rugby and rowing. On the college website, where he's now listed along with other famous former students, Starmer has provided a quote that doesn't say much more than that 'my intense year there confirmed me in my choice of pursuing a career as a human rights advocate'. It also shows that, when director of public prosecutions, Starmer went back – as he had to both Reigate and Leeds – to give a lecture to a later generation of students.

But he had an uneasy relationship with the college back in 1986. Its undergraduates that year had debated whether or not to ban newspapers owned by Rupert Murdoch, after it sacked thousands of printworkers and moved production to a heavily fortified new plant at Wapping in east London. The students not only voted against a boycott but decided to order an additional copy of the

Sun every day. By contrast, Starmer went to Wapping to act as a left-wing 'legal observer' of what he later described as the 'paramilitary policing' methods used to crush the protests. He watched what became an almost medieval scene as mounted police charged the crowd and trucks were set on fire. John Bowden, one of his fellow legal observers, was hit by a police baton and later made a speech from the platform with blood pouring down his face.

Starmer joined the Oxford University Labour Club at a time when the extreme left was in the ascendant. Ed Balls has described attending one of its meetings that year and 'finding the main item on the agenda was whether or not to include the hammer-and-sickle on the club's new banner'. Starmer does not recall seeing Balls but confirms he did come across David Miliband, then leading a more moderate faction, though neither he – nor Miliband when contacted about it – can remember what they talked about.

There is a solitary reference to Starmer in the Labour Club newspaper that hints at his demeanour in the period. A gossip column published on June 17, 1986: 'I am not one to deny the existence of macho politics. Now just look at Keir – "I am not macho and this is not a Talking Heads jacket so just shut your bloody mouth – Starmer."'

Even so, he managed to make some friends among Oxford's Labour students and remains close to Alex Harvey, who gives a familiar account of Starmer's diligence and drive mixed in with a bit of politics and a lot of football. 'The way he plays the game is the essence of him,' says Harvey before comparing his style to 'Captain Marvel' – Bryan Robson, the England skipper for much of this time, 'who was always the leader although he wasn't necessarily the most skilful or talented'.

Harvey's description of a holiday they took in France sums up Starmer's work-hard, play-hard mentality: 'As soon as he arrived, Keir went off for a five-mile run in the searing heat, then staggered back when everyone else was sitting around. It was like he had to almost destroy himself before he could chill out.'

Nor was Harvey the only person Starmer got to know at the Oxford Labour Club that year and, for a little while at least, another of them would have a big influence on his political views.

Exploring alternatives

The editorial collective

Many of those involved in Oxford's student politics during the mid-eighties remember someone usually referred to as 'the Frenchman' and not merely because he had briefly been the chair of the university's Labour Club.

Ben Schoendorff exuded a certain sort of leftist chic in an era when foreign students were comparatively rare and perhaps seemed even more sophisticated because he had got married to the equally glamorous Florence Berteletti while still at university. Harvey describes Schoendorff as 'this very tall, charismatic creature' and rumours swirled about his origins. Some said he was really Belgian, others that he was related to a famous European artist, while the proto-Tory politicians convinced themselves he was aristocratic, if only so they could go round calling him 'the French Count'.

In the summer of 1986, as Starmer's year at Oxford came to an end, Schoendorff persuaded him and Harvey to join the 'editorial collective' of a new magazine, *Socialist Alternatives*, that would propagate an obscure left-wing ideology called Pabloism. For the next two years, Starmer would combine training to become a barrister in London with being an editor, production manager and writer.

By any measure, *Socialist Alternatives* was a failure. Only a handful of copies were ever sold, and it appears to have disappeared by the end of the decade and was then forgotten until, thirty-four years later, one of its more regular contributors became leader of the Labour Party.

A few editions have since been disinterred and posted on the internet, to be occasionally drawn upon by journalists seeking to illustrate claims that Starmer has a 'Marxist revolutionary past'. One well-known newspaper columnist even used the material to compare him to a Soviet double agent in a John le Carré novel.

They would have got even more excited if they had known Starmer had taken two trips as a young man to Communist Eastern Europe. The first with Mark Adams came in between school and university, when they were curious about what lay behind the Iron Curtain so diverted off an Interrail holiday to cross into Hungary and then Romania. A few years later, Starmer and Murray went to Czechoslovakia, and helped restore a memorial to civilians murdered by the Nazis in the village of Lidice. But there is zero evidence Starmer was ever attracted to Soviet Communism and he describes his repulsion for much of what he saw, particularly in Nicolae Ceauşescu's Romania. 'We were robbed at one campsite and spied on the whole time we were there,' he says. 'I got a glimpse of a totalitarian regime – I wouldn't want to live like that.'

More interesting is the question of whether he flirted with some of the myriad revolutionary Marxist groups around during the 1980s. Even some writers sympathetic to Starmer say *Socialist Alternatives* was 'a Trotskyist front'.

His articles are, in truth, quite hard to decipher, with many of them written in what feels almost like a lost language from the 1980s, when left-wing acronyms and splinter groups proliferated as rapidly as the ranks of those who understood what they were going on about have since dwindled.

Pabloism was so called after Michel Pablo, one of more than a dozen aliases for Michalis Raptis, a Greek Trotskyist whose life story included running guns to Algerian nationalists in the 1950s and spells in jail. By the time Starmer came to it in the 1980s, Pablo had split with orthodox Trotskyism and begun advocating a form of local 'self-management', whereby socialism would be built, not top-down by the state but bottom-up. Such ideas were seen as a form of 'revisionism' or, even worse in the eyes of the hardcore Trotskyists, 'centrism'.

John Foot, the son of the investigative journalist Paul Foot, was another member of the Oxford Labour Club recruited by Schoendorff to help run the magazine, and says: 'To understand the whole Pabloism thing you have to understand the Frenchman – Ben – because none of us would have ever heard about it without him. He was like a whirlwind.

'There were probably about thirty Pabloists in the entire country back then, but Ben would go over to Paris and have these mysterious meetings in smoke-filled rooms. He was such a presence it made us feel we were part of something. But none of us ever used the term "Pabloite" or "Trotskyist". In fact, most of us hated the actual Trots.'

This was a decade when the left seemed further from power than ever. Ken Livingstone's Greater London Council was abolished in 1986 and the following year Thatcher would win her third consecutive election with another hundred-plus majority. Parliament was not proving much of a bulwark against a government that many people, not just those who were working class, regarded as unjust and oppressive.

Starmer's articles supported a 'red-green' alliance in which the Labour Party and the trade unions might be reinvigorated by the energy of new social movements like feminism and environmentalism, as well as groups campaigning for lesbian and gay rights or racial equality. Much of what he wrote, however, really wasn't as terrifyingly left wing as some selective quoting might suggest. In an article written after the Wapping dispute, he asked what role, 'if any', police should play in society, concluding in terms that would be utterly uncontroversial today – and Starmer himself would later have some experience of implementing in Northern Ireland – that the police should be more accountable to 'the community they are meant to serve'.

He joined the Socialist Society, an organisation set up by Ralph Miliband, the Marxist academic father of Ed and David, and the left-wing MP Tony Benn, to bring together groups from inside Labour with those outside it who were actively resisting the Thatcher government. He also attended socialist summer festivals in Benn's Chesterfield constituency in 1987 and 1988. Hilary Wainwright, who later founded *Red Pepper*, a significantly more successful 'red-green' magazine still published today, remembers Starmer and Schoendorff being in a 'little group of Pabloites who were idealistic young people trying to widen their appeal', adding: 'They probably thought we were more influential than we were.' Both got on to the steering committee of the Socialist Society, she says – 'it wasn't that difficult, all you had to do was turn up' – but Schoendorff 'tended to dominate discussions'.

Foot, now a professor of Italian history at Bristol University, says: 'I think, after a while, we all began to ask why we were dedicating so much time to the magazine. We were going into shops and trying to persuade them to take a single copy. It was all a bit bonkers really and just faded away.'

Starmer himself shrugs when the magazine is mentioned, saying it covered a short period of his life 'at the tail end at Oxford, then the early days of when I was in London – it never really went anywhere'. He has long since lost touch with Schoendorff, now a psychologist in Montreal, described on his social media profile as an 'anti-imperialist ecosocialist'.

Like the question about whether politicians took drugs when they were younger, the media's mild obsession with Starmer's youthful political outpourings is all a bit pointless unless it can be shown they have any relevance to what he believes in now.

Somewhat surprisingly, however, the Labour leader answers that they do – a bit. What he wrote was part of his evolution and, as such, traces of it can still be found in his DNA. For instance, there is an interview he conducted with Tony Benn for *Socialist Alternatives* in 1987 in which you can get a sense of his earnestness as he asked: 'Is it possible to create this emancipatory alliance as it could be called without, on the one hand, subordinating the demands of the new social movements to the class struggle and without, on the other hand, undermining the importance of the class struggle?' The language can easily be parodied these days, but it's arguable the question he asked remains relevant to his own efforts to ally Labour's traditional working-class base with the progressive politics opponents might now call 'woke'.

Starmer has sometimes gone out of his way in the years since to say he still believes in this red-green agenda. For instance, in a 2020 interview, he asserted: 'The big issue we were grappling with then was how the Labour Party, or the left generally, bound together the wider movement and its strands of equality – feminist politics, green politics, LGBT – which I thought was incredibly exciting, incredibly important.'

Asked about it now, he says: 'I'm not going to disown all of that … There's no point in putting the idea of dignity and respect at the centre of our politics if we only stand up for some people who are being denied it.' But, before anyone gets too carried away, he senses the danger and emphasises that doesn't mean he stands by every word he wrote in a magazine published before the end of the Cold War. 'As a student in my twenties, I may have thought I had all the answers, but – guess what? – it turns out I didn't.'

The words he is keenest to withdraw from that time are those he used to criticise the Labour Party's leader, not least because he's someone Starmer has since come to like and admire. 'I was wrong about Neil Kinnock,' he says. 'The challenge of knitting together an election-winning coalition from all the different strands of progressive politics looked so easy from a flat on Archway Road. Now that challenge sits on my desk and I still don't have all the answers. I do know, however, that listening to other arguments – reflecting on what's been said and being willing to change my mind – is the best way to find them.' They don't live far from each other these days and when Kinnock's wife, Glenys, died in December 2023, the former Labour leader says Starmer was 'one of the first people through the door' of the family's home in Tufnell Park to comfort him.

Putting aside the content of his youthful articles, the unrelenting focus with which he tackled the task of magazine publishing may say more about him now than anything he wrote back then. According to Alex Harvey, Starmer was less interested in a long ideological discussion than getting an outcome, saying: 'It's like that question the left is always meant to ask itself: "What is to be done?"'

Even those who strongly dislike his politics now, such as Richard Barbrook, an activist who later worked for Jeremy Corbyn, concede that getting the magazine out was probably the most noticeable feature of Starmer's contribution. 'There were only about half a dozen of them,' says Barbrook of the *Socialist Alternatives* group, 'a bunch of friends who'd met at Oxford producing this tiny magazine. Keir was the backroom guy, the one who did the hard work. He got all the articles in, laid them out on the page, got it to the printers, distributed it at the bookshops, got the money from the bookshops. That's what he was like. The rest sat around and talked. The magazine wouldn't have existed without him.'

In any case, publishing a few articles calling for a participatory bottom-up form of socialism was a relatively small part of what Starmer was doing at the time. In September that year, having turned twenty-four and secured what was later said to be 'a goodish BCL from Oxford', he headed to the capital to train as a barrister at the Inns of Court's Middle Temple.

'Property is theft'

For someone such as Starmer, who appears to have been self-consciously edgy and anti-elitist at Oxford, it must have seemed he had arrived at another deeply conservative institution.

To help pay his fees, he applied for and was awarded the prestigious – if stodgy sounding – Queen Mother Scholarship, a bursary
that even today the Middle Temple's website points out is granted
only on the basis of academic excellence, so as not to discourage
those who 'come from more traditional or privileged backgrounds'.
Studying for the Bar also required Starmer attend twenty-four
formal dinners in the Middle Temple's Elizabethan dining hall
which begin with a procession of gown-clad barristers followed by
lots of toasts and bowing.

None of the pomp appealed to him. 'Like some of the stuff to do
with Oxford,' he says, 'it didn't seem to have much to do with
being the kind of lawyer I wanted to be.' Nor was it the most obvious setting in which to convert to vegetarianism, though he did just
that at one of the dinners, after a woman sitting opposite challenged this apparent radical about the animal flesh on his plate. 'If
I can't justify what I'm doing,' says Starmer, 'it's usually a good
sign that I should knock it on the head.' Aside from a few lapses far
from home, he has generally eschewed any meat except fish ever
since.

Having sailed through his last set of exams, he applied to be a
'pupil' – an apprenticeship with an established barrister – at a relatively liberal set of chambers at 1, Dr Johnson's Buildings. One of
its more celebrated figures was Geoffrey Robertson, who had
already earned fame for defending *Gay News*, *OZ* and the National
Theatre's production of *The Romans in Britain* against the ever-cen-
sorious Mary Whitehouse. Robertson took an immediate shine to
Starmer because he had been to 'a state school [and] a redbrick
university', but needed all his powers of persuasion to get Starmer
a place after some of his stuffier colleagues complained they
couldn't take 'someone who wears a cardigan', who seemed so
'nervous and awkward'.

Within a year, however, Starmer appeared to have lost some of
his nervousness and upped his awkwardness. His interview for a
permanent place, or 'tenancy', at the chambers has entered folklore

in legal circles, especially since his rise to become director of public prosecutions. Asked how he would defend a first-time shoplifting offender, he replied: 'Isn't all property theft?'

'Yes, he did say that,' declares Gavin Millar, one of the barristers on the interview panel. 'And I think one of my colleagues raised his eyes to the ceiling in response.' But, he adds: 'Keir put a good case. It wasn't just lefty political waffle, he had an argument grounded in rigorous academic thinking. He explained why locking everybody up wasn't the answer to criminality and said we needed to do more to address the causes of offending. Afterwards, we all agreed we had to give him a job. It was a no-brainer.'

Starmer's own account of this interview is that a previous question, about whether he understood how much work was involved in becoming a barrister, had annoyed him because he was already doing sixteen-hour days, 'working my arse off for them'. But he admits his line about defending theft was 'disrespectful' and didn't even properly reflect what he thought at the time. He says: 'One of the senior barristers interviewing me, Stephen Irwin, later took me round the corner where he more or less put me up against a wall and told me in the clearest possible terms I had been a fool.'

Another story indicating the tension within Starmer as he took his first steps at the Bar is told by someone who later became one of his greatest friends, the barrister Ed Fitzgerald. 'Keir was always very serious and passionately left-wing, someone who found it a bit awkward when he first joined this bastion of privilege. I think he was probably slightly suspicious of me as some sort of awfully posh debauchee. But when the bailiffs turned up to repossess my desk because I hadn't paid my VAT, suddenly I was no longer just a toff but a "victim of oppression". Keir really warmed up to me after that.'

Starmer joined the Haldane Society of Socialist Lawyers, leading an unsuccessful effort to abandon the first part of its name so it sounded less like a 'barristers' club' and later becoming its secretary and a regular contributor to its journal, *Socialist Lawyer*.

These articles are as good a way as any to track his evolving attitude to the legal profession. The earliest of them focused on the exploitation of tenants, the treatment of immigrants and Thatcher's trade union laws. In the spring of 1988, he used a piece about the dominance of Oxbridge-educated white men in the judiciary, to highlight a deeper problem preventing even the most enlightened judge from doing much to change a system of laws 'which pay much more attention to individual property rights than they do to the collective rights of ordinary people … How can any judge deal with an unemployed person who comes before them pleading guilty to burglary, when he or she does not have the power to alter the system which denies that person the human right to a decent livelihood?'

But, as Britain entered the final decade of the twentieth century, political change was opening up new paths in this conservative profession. Labour was heading in a different direction to the Conservatives over Europe, with the former warming to the idea of Brussels guaranteeing some basic social rights as a protection against Thatcherism while the latter cooled on closer integration for precisely the same reason. At the same time the collapse of Soviet Communism was triggering a debate about freedom and the reshaping of national constitutions. Liberal opinion began to clamour for a new Bill of Rights through the 'Charter 88' campaign for democratic reform.

Although Starmer was still to the left of this, he was writing more about miscarriages of justice, the heavy-handed policing of peaceful protests and raves that he rather naively insisted had nothing to do with illegal drug use. In the summer of 1989, he attended a socialist summer festival with a couple of hundred others in the Haute Loire region of France. He met the human rights campaigner Peter Tatchell, who was seen as a martyr figure on the left following the vicious treatment dished out to him six years earlier when he had been the Labour candidate in the Bermondsey by-election. That had been when sections of the press decided being gay made him unelectable and even the Liberal Party issued a leaflet asking, 'Which Queen Would You Vote For?' Tatchell remembers Starmer as being 'analytical and thoughtful', and someone who combined 'radicalism with pragmatism'. But he says: 'I would never have seen Keir as a politician. He was a non-dogmatic grassroots activist back then who was very much against the old top-down establishment structures of politics.'

That year, *Socialist Lawyer* published an interview Starmer had conducted with John Platts-Mills, an elderly barrister and former Labour MP with known Communist sympathies. After asking, perhaps a little sarcastically, whether 'with the benefit of hindsight' it had been a mistake to attend Joseph Stalin's funeral, Starmer wanted to know what role – if any – radical lawyers could play in the cause of progress. Platts-Mills told him they shouldn't be 'too eager to thrust forward too fast'.

Such advice reflected the suspicion on the left towards a legalistic conception of rights that Marxist theory regarded as 'bourgeois individualism' by failing to recognise the fundamental economic causes of injustice. Even some of the more mainstream voices were suspicious of relying too heavily on an Establishment judiciary because they didn't want to do anything that might limit the power of a Labour government. Neil Kinnock, the Labour leader, is alleged to have dismissed Charter 88 as a bunch of 'whingers, whiners and wankers'. His deputy, Roy Hattersley – who may have been the real source of that quote – said, 'True liberty requires action from the government', and the adoption of a written constitution 'actually prevents or inhibits that action from being taken'.

As late as 1991, Starmer remained sceptical of relying on legal institutions to bring change because, he wrote, that would be 'putting the cart before the horse'. He warned instead the left would never be able to participate properly in debates about civil rights and constitutions until it had developed 'a concept of socialist law'.

Only after a fourth consecutive general election defeat in 1992 was the Labour Party persuaded to embrace a statutory guarantee of fundamental rights. And, as a Conservative government that had been in power for Starmer's entire adult life began to ebb away over the next few years, there came a noticeable shift in his position too.

Writing in 1995 for *Socialist Lawyer* about the prospect of an incoming government led by Tony Blair passing a Human Rights Act, Starmer began by saying that 'Karl Marx was right' about any declaration of fundamental rights being a product of the era in which it was made. But then he added: 'It does not necessarily follow from this that the entrenchment of fundamental rights, drawn up in this time and place – on the eve of the twenty-first century in Britain – is incapable of contributing to the realization of progressive change.' The real test of such a law, he emphasised, would not just be whether it defended liberal rights like freedom of speech or protest – 'that part is easy' – but the extent to which it allowed social and economic rights 'for all those burdened with poverty, oppression and exploitation in Britain today'.

Anthony Barnett, the director of Charter 88 at the time, remains irritated at the way the campaign's liberal demands had been initially opposed by much of the left. When shown a copy of that Starmer article in *Socialist Lawyer*, Barnett suggests that Starmer was one of those belatedly adopting an 'opportunist' position – 'the bus had left and they had better get on' – while still making the mistake of not being able to 'recognise as leftists that Marx had been wrong'.

Nonetheless, by 1996, Starmer had produced a detailed audit of Britain's democratic failings, finding no fewer than forty-two human rights violations of international standards in the previous years. His co-authors were the human rights academic Francesca Klug and Stuart Weir, the founder of Charter 88. Although the book sidestepped some of that campaign's constitutional agenda, it did say the first-past-the-post voting system appeared to breach the human rights principle of political equality because it 'does not give electors votes of equal value'.

Starmer's early writing will probably continue to be used occasionally as evidence by the left to show he has 'sold out' his deepest-held beliefs and by the right to claim he is only pretending to be a moderate, while the centre can wistfully wonder what happened to his support for voting reform. And yet, even during this most radical phase of his life, his approach to politics appeared to have been characterised more by the practical details of getting things done, like distributing a magazine, than highfalutin ideology.

Bill Bowring, who was chair of the Haldane Society when Starmer was its secretary and describes his own politics as 'Marxian', saw a lot of him in those years, but never heard him utter the words 'Trotsky', 'Pablo' or 'Marx'. 'He kept company with a lot of radicals,' says Bowring, 'but I always saw him as a technocrat, a very good organiser but not very political at all and not a natural politician. He was certainly not a Marxist.' Helena Kennedy, one of the senior barristers at his chambers, largely agrees. 'I don't think Keir was ever a Marxist,' she declares. 'He wanted to change people's lives in sensible ways from a position of principle, not from a perspective of ideology.'

Indeed, for all his prolific left-wing writing from the mid-1980s to the mid-1990s, Starmer was never cut out for a career as a polemicist. Instead, he had more success later as the author of a series of legal textbooks, shorn of any grandiloquent language or vision, about how lawyers could use human rights legislation. As he put it in one interview: 'I've always been very focused on outcomes – what am I trying to achieve, what is the goal, how do you get to that goal – rather than having a conversation with myself about what does all that mean … You can achieve the same thing in different ways.'

Living above the (knocking) shop

When Starmer moved to London, the accommodation he found could not have been further from the grandeur of the Middle Temple or the honeyed stone of Oxford's colleges. It was a large flat at 285 Archway Road, spread over three floors, at the start of the old A1 heading north out of the capital and close to the cemetery where Karl Marx is buried.

Conditions resembled those of the TV comedy series *The Young Ones* that was popular at the time. There were blocked drains, rotting floorboards and occasional sightings of rats. The exact list of tenants was fairly haphazard. Paul Vickers, a friend of Starmer's from school, was already there and notionally in charge of paying the bills. At various times, Starmer's girlfriend Angela O'Brien, as well as friends from school and university – including Colin Peacock, Alex Harvey, Mark Adams and John Murray – moved in too.

Murray likes to tell the story of someone being sick into a bath at one of their parties and how, instead of cleaning it up, they just stopped using that bathroom. On another occasion, a dead pigeon was discovered in the water tank and no one knew how long it had been decomposing in there. Vickers sometimes paid for his drinks at the Shepherds Tavern or the Woodman with a pile of ten-pence pieces taken from the flat's payphone. On another occasion, he broke up some chairs for the wood burner to keep warm. Starmer himself describes how the washing machine leaked so badly the floorboards rotted away and eventually it fell into the room below. 'The flat was really grotty,' he says. 'but it was cheap, you know I was with mates, we were young and having a good time.'

And all that was just what was happening upstairs. A year before Starmer moved in, the landlord, Victor Mehra, had been jailed for nine months after being found guilty of living off the earnings of prostitution. The sauna and massage parlour that he had once operated, however, remained, sharing its entrance with the flat above.

Peacock's father, who had a very respectable job at the Lawn Tennis Association, was worried he might be photographed going through the entrance to a brothel when he came to visit. Vickers, who was later to work as a journalist for the BBC and *Private Eye* before his death a few years ago, liked to tell elaborate stories of erotic costumes he claims to have seen when exploring the facilities below. 'I think you have to take that with a pinch of salt because Paul always had a pretty vivid imagination,' says Starmer firmly.

The occupants of the Archway flat undoubtedly played hard, thanks in part perhaps to its location opposite Highgate tube, which meant their parties often included guests they had never met before who had just wandered in off the street after hearing the music playing. There were also trips to the nearby Jackson Lane community centre to watch comedy acts like Patrick Marber and Jo Brand, who were breaking through, or cabaret night. Friends say that Starmer was always at the centre of everything but are far too loyal to provide copies of the photographs still circulating between them of him wearing fancy dress costumes.

Starmer says the massage parlour at least meant 'we didn't have the kind of neighbours who would complain too much about the floors shaking or people arriving and leaving late at night'. But he also describes how he got to know the names of the women working downstairs. 'They would always shout hello and share a joke with us,' he recalls. 'They had tough lives and deserved to be treated with respect.' Eventually the women did a 'moonlight flit', leaving the flatmates with no one to pay rent for two years, as well as a circular bed and a baby grand piano in the room downstairs.

A regular set of visitors in those days was the *Socialist Alternatives* group. Schoendorff is said to have stepped lightly past 'Carlton', the homeless man who often slept in the doorway, entering the flat with a 'mystical air about him', then sitting as far as possible from some of its permanent inhabitants so he could 'think big thoughts'. Colin Peacock complains: 'I spent more time lugging piles of that magazine around different rooms or up and down stairs than I ever spent reading it.'

In the midst of all the squalor and parties, however, it's notable that Starmer kept his room spotless. There is a picture of the young human rights lawyer from those days sat at a desk surrounded by neat stacks of files and an array of early computer technology. Fingers poised over the keyboard, he is looking over his shoulder and grinning at the camera as if disturbed from the guilty pleasure of hard work.

Indeed, everyone who lived with him back then pays testament to his powers of concentration, usually by reference to a particular incident. One night, Vickers and Adams came home late to find a couple of intruders carrying away their television and video recorder. 'I ran upstairs thinking I was going to find an empty, ransacked house,' said Vickers, 'and there was Keir sitting at his desk working. He was so obsessed with his books, so buried in his texts, he didn't notice two burglars walking round the house, helping themselves to our stuff.' Starmer doesn't deny the story, but suggests it became 'more of a legend' among his friends 'as the years went on and I was put in charge of the criminal prosecutions'.

And, grating though this will sound to all those now suspicious of Starmer's motives, there does appear to have been a bit more of a social conscience among this group of friends than among some other upwardly mobile young professionals arriving in London at the tail-end of the Thatcher years. Theresa Hendrickx might have been one of these 'yuppies' until she moved into the flat. 'I was working in the City for Prudential until Keir inspired me to do something better with my life and train as a criminal solicitor,' she says. 'I still blame him for that.'

Many of the early cases he took on as a lawyer were on behalf of tenants living in terrible housing that might have been thought of as similar to his own. 'There were parents with young children getting chucked out of their homes by landlords or living in flats so damp their kitchens were covered in mould,' he says, before recognising 'there is a big difference between roughing it as young people with some prospects' and feeling 'trapped in such conditions'.

Starmer acted for the National Council for Civil Liberties, which renamed itself Liberty in 1989, when he remembers feeling bemused by marketing and branding conversations about whether the dot of the 'i' in the organisation's name could float around the page 'to represent freedom'. More meaningful was the work he did for the

National Union of Mineworkers as part of the team that challenged the provision for workers made redundant by the final pit closure programme of the early nineties. Even a decade later, when being profiled by *The Times*, Starmer proudly cited the case on behalf of the NUM as the 'most memorable moment' in his career.

Alex Harvey recalls him giving legal advice during this period to the women from the massage parlour downstairs. 'It was typical of Keir that he did some work for them, he's more interested in practical things like that than some ideological posture,' says Harvey. 'But he's not completely explainable by all his component parts because the whole is greater than the sum. I've been friends with him for nearly forty years and he really isn't like other politicians I've known, there is something both enigmatic and genuinely different about him.'

This was the first time in his life Starmer started watching football regularly because they lived close enough to Arsenal's old Highbury stadium to race down the Holloway Road at short notice on a Saturday afternoon. He remembers paying 'a fiver' at the turnstiles and pushing through to a preferred spot on the terraces at the top on the left-hand side of the North Bank: 'The crowd would sway and surge, moving you around as you handed over physical control of your body to the energy and emotion of thousands of others around you,' he says. 'I thought it was brilliant, though it wasn't everyone's idea of fun back then.'

Quite often he would see punches thrown. Violence simmered after almost every match as he walked home past the away fans, at a time when hooliganism and racist abuse of players were regarded as part of the game. English clubs had been banned from Europe in May 1985, after a group of Liverpool fans were blamed for causing a wall to collapse at the Heysel stadium in Belgium, resulting in the deaths of thirty-nine – mostly Italian – supporters. A few days earlier, a fire in a dilapidated wooden stand at Bradford City had killed fifty-six fans. For several months there had been no football on television at all because neither the BBC nor ITV were willing to pay what now seems minuscule amounts for the privilege. 'It became fashionable for newspapers and politicians to talk about football as dangerous, backward-looking and a source of national shame,' says Starmer. 'But most people who watched football were neither violent nor racist. The clubs they supported mattered hugely to the identity and pride of communities. All that couldn't just be written off.'

The sport hit rock bottom in April 1989 at an FA Cup semi-final in Sheffield. The Hillsborough Disaster would eventually lead to ninety-seven Liverpool fans losing their lives. Senior police officers – with the help of a right-wing MP, the *Sun* newspaper and Downing Street – went for what must have seemed to them the easy option of trying to cover up their mistakes by blaming supporters.

Yet Hillsborough also instigated the start of football's renewal with Lord Justice Taylor's report into the safety of football grounds. And, though nothing can ever compensate for the awful loss of life that day, for many Arsenal fans the sport's redemption began barely a month later, with the club's penultimate-minute goal at Anfield to bring the league title to Highbury for the first time in nearly twenty years. Although the losing team was Liverpool, whose fans had already suffered so much, this match also provided a reminder to others of how magical the sport could be. More than three decades on, when Starmer saw the scorer of that winning goal across a crowded room at a reception in the House of Commons, he could barely contain his excitement. 'I suspect it became a bit too obvious that I was more interested in talking to Michael Thomas than Michael Thomas was interested in talking to me,' he says.

In the summer of 1990, after England reached the World Cup semi-final in Italy, the nation took Bobby Robson's team into their hearts, before a defeat to Germany on penalties. Starmer watched it all in northern France, with friends who had organised the first of many 'international tournaments' of their own, and whose chief concession to continental French culture back then was apparently mixing Pernod with their beer.

After four years in Archway the flat was condemned as unfit for human habitation. Starmer moved out to other rented houses in Brondesbury Park and Islington, until he had earned enough money to buy a flat at 60 Ellington Street, close to Arsenal's ground. Nonetheless the Archway days were important in forming his values because it was when and where he put down roots. 'This bit of London became the centre of my world,' he says, 'and I kind of knew I wasn't going to leave it.' He still sees his old friends from those days whenever he can and is generally credited for making sure he is around if something goes badly wrong in their lives. 'We're a slightly unusual group in that we have stuck together,' says Hendrickx. 'It's not all about Keir but he has been, sort of, the glue.'

10

The value of roots

'Footballism'

These days, Archway Road has been smartened up quite a bit. Some of the kebab and pizza shops Starmer remembers have been turned into delicatessens, while the massage parlour is now an upmarket gym. The Shepherd's Tavern has become a music venue called the Boogaloo. 'Wishee-Washee Splishee-Sploshee Cleanee-Knickee Vellee-Quickee' (that really was the name of the launderette where he sometimes 'washed his smalls') no longer exists, which may be just as well.

Arsenal have moved to their expensive all-seater stadium, where tickets no longer cost a fiver and Starmer acknowledges the worry of fans who feel the game has lost a bit of its soul, with clubs traded as commodities to owners who live far away and know next to nothing of their history.

But lots of people who know him say Starmer finds his best expression of himself with his friends in the West Stand. The Labour leader talks about getting to know other people who sit nearby, including the man who sits in front of him and brings homemade and freshly fried pakoras to hand around as an end-of-season tradition. He says it feels as if 'we've been through a lot together'.

Sometimes, Starmer even talks about his children in this context because he seems so pleased they come with him to games. Before his son's first match, he asked those nearby to alter the words of 'We've got a Big Fucking German' with which Arsenal fans sere-naded their six-foot-six defender Per Mertesacker. Remarkably, they all sang 'big fuzzy German' instead. Starmer's son is now a committed Arsenal fan, while his daughter 'takes the piss' out of him for muttering instructions to players or pointing to where the ball should go. 'They can't hear you, Dad,' she says. 'I know,' he replies, making a diagonal hand-slice gesture. 'Dad,' she sighs, 'they can't see you either.'

There are occasions when all this talk of football can go too far and risks confusing a national audience in which not everyone likes the game as much as he does. In the summer of 2023, referring to a minister who had criticised her own government's record, he said it was like the Arsenal coach doing a speech 'on this-is-what-Arse-nal-ought-to-do – if you're in the job, it's your job to do it'. Only slightly more comprehensible to non-football fans was when he compared the prime minister boasting about some marginally improved quarterly economic indicators to 'a football manager, bottom of the league at Christmas, celebrating an away draw three months ago'.

He may also be in danger of sounding a bit 'laddish' sometimes, although he did take his family to watch England's Lionesses in the summer of 2022 and was struck by the look on the face of his daughter who had been accustomed to watching only men play.

Occasionally, you see glimpses of a cultural hinterland in Starmer that extends beyond football and the pub. He has often talked of the value of art and music in the education system and in a Fabian pamphlet written in 2021, he said he wanted every ten-year-old to 'have had the chance to play an instrument, join a competitive sports team, visit the seaside, the countryside, or the city, go to cultural institutions, ride a bike and learn how to debate their ideas'.

Although he gave up playing the flute as soon as he left home, music has left its mark on him. He has talked of his abiding love of composers such as Mozart, Brahms, Fauré and especially Beethoven, saying the latter's 'Emperor' Piano Concerto's second movement can still take him 'to a different place … away from all the other strains of the day'. Starmer says he prefers to listen to music intensely rather than just have it on in the background because it is one of the 'release valves' he needs.

In an interview with a community newspaper when he was first elected as an MP, he picked Daniel Barenboim as his favourite musician, even though the Israeli pianist-conductor might be known as a 'difficult person'. But then Starmer retreated into more familiar territory to explain what he meant, as he added that, 'Like talented footballers, you accept this.'

Football, however, is more than just a private obsession and metaphor of choice to him. It is both a symbol of that 'work hard, play hard' maxim examined in this section and a source of values that almost certainly go deeper than any of those left-wing ideological 'isms' he explored in the mid-1980s.

In the spring of 2023, the Labour leader injured his knee in a match shortly before he was due to embark on a gruelling round of campaign visits. He asked Jill Cuthbertson, his admirably no-non-sense office gatekeeper, what that meant for his schedule. 'What it means,' she sighed, 'is that you should stop running around playing football with your friends.'

In the months that followed, however, even when he remained on the injury list, Starmer continued booking the pitch, selecting the teams and sending a weekly text message to the players with the details of when to turn up, just as he has done for the past thirty years. For some, this might seem to be an exercise in control such as that of Jimmy Carter who infamously felt he had to manage the White House tennis court rota during his presidency. But those who work with Starmer say it's more like an electrical earthing system. Even the long-suffering Cuthbertson concedes football is an activity that 'grounds him' and keeps the Labour leader in touch with normality or, at least, his version of it.

Starmer acknowledges that 'I don't do that it's-not-the-winning-it's-the-taking-part-that-counts thing very well' and almost anyone who has played with him has a story about his competitiveness. A constituent who has occasionally been roped into a game in Camden says: 'The way someone plays sports tells you a lot about them. Keir is fair – always fair. But, my god, he's also hard.' Anas Sarwar, the Scottish Labour leader, likes to recount how the referee in a 'friendly' game was forced to allow thirty-five minutes of injury time and only blew his whistle when 'Team England' captained by Starmer had taken the lead for the first time.

The Labour leader also plays in the occasional midweek five-a-side with staff from his office, whose stand-out player is his relatively youthful press officer, George Mason, someone who a few years ago turned down the chance of a professional league career at Morecambe. If Starmer finds himself lining up against Mason, he will jab a finger in the winger's direction and tell teammates: 'Just sit on him!'

He has met England's head coach Gareth Southgate to whom he has sometimes been compared for getting results without the flamboyance associated with some of their predecessors. He believes political leaders can learn from different management styles in sport. 'What I noticed about Southgate,' he says, 'is that he listens – he's not trying to dominate the whole room.'

Even those old football clichés about 'playing for the team' or 'getting our best players out there' and 'doing your talking on the pitch' are suffused with fresh meaning by Starmer as he wheels them out to discuss shadow cabinet reshuffles or Labour's plans for government. But he can make subtler points, such as during a discussion of the barriers holding people back, referring to the way a player like Paul Gascoigne was labelled 'thick' or 'daft as a brush'. Starmer says you could see Gascoigne's intelligence by the way the former England star could read the game or anticipate the spin of a ball.

More than anything, 'footballism' has probably helped him understand people's sense of place. He has often spoken about the demise of smaller clubs like Bury and, after visiting Accrington Stanley, he said it is really important for people to come together in this former mill town in Lancashire, where government can seem more distant than ever, and say: 'This is my team, my community.'

Other clubs he has been to since becoming Labour leader include Carlisle United, Port Vale, Stevenage, Walsall and Wycombe Wanderers, as well as non-league Ilkeston Town and Glasgow Perthshire. The sheer number suggests it's more than just to be photographed by the local paper as a suited politician kicking a ball into an empty net. There is real interest in his policy team, for instance, over how the owner of Grimsby Town is trying to revive a sense of civic pride in a fishing port that became a symbol for northern decline.

And yet he also faces the persistent charge he is too 'north London' to understand the rest of Britain.

One of Rishi Sunak's better lines is that the current Labour leader, along with his two predecessors, all live in the 'same square mile' of a corner of the capital that many see as dominated by a remote and wealthy liberal metropolitan elite. Another Tory prime minister, Theresa May, once called such people 'citizens of nowhere'.

'Take me home'

Starmer will have none of that. 'Try telling the people I play football with on Sundays that they come from nowhere. Ask the people who sit next to me at Arsenal if they have no roots or identity,' he says. 'And don't dare suggest to my wife who works in a local hospital, or my kids who go to a local school, that they're not part of a community.'

Wherever he goes, he carries a wallet with the words 'Take Me Home to Kentish Town' written on the back. His constituency of Holborn and St Pancras is 'not one but a series of neighbourhoods all of which are a bit different', he says, adding: 'There are people who've been left out of the globalised economy in north London as well as north Tyneside. There are thousands of people in my constituency who are struggling to pay their heating bills, find a decent home, or get their kids through education. There is a ten-year gap in life expectancy between the richest and poorest parts of my constituency. Inequality exists everywhere in our country, not just one part of it. And most of us, wherever we live, care about that very much.'

Many MPs feel equally passionately about the seats they represent but it is nonetheless a big feature of Starmer's make-up. Georgia Gould, leader of Camden Council, has described him leaving talks in Downing Street in the middle of a Brexit crisis in the spring of 2019 so he could see the bereaved family of a knife crime victim. According to Gould, he spoke to them in exactly the right way, with compassion and no cameras –'because that's exactly who he is, someone who turns up in the difficult moments'.

Drive through these streets with him and he'll tell you where to get the best curry, explain why some of his favourite Bangladeshi restaurants around Euston are closing down because of HS2, then wave an arm in the direction of the hospital where his wife and two children were born.

He is a regular with Chris at the Blue Steel Barbers on Dartmouth Park Hill, buys his milk and newspapers from Mehmet at the corner shop near his home, leans out of the window of his car to ask Danny – the caretaker at his children's old primary school – to ask where he's watching the football and then jogs down the road to join him in front of the big screen at the Boston Arms in time for kick-off. So well does he pride himself on knowing these neighbourhoods he once asked a minicab driver to stop outside a newsagent's so he could get a copy of an *A–Z* and show him a better route.

When he gets home, he is likely to be asked immediately to clear up something the cat has brought in. 'The most exciting part of my life is seeing the kids, I know it sounds naff, but they make me laugh, they are annoying, it's great, it's hopeful.' Not many people in politics get to see inside his home but it's clear this doesn't just belong to him. The walls are covered with pictures of the children and Vic. Her sport is not football, but horse-racing. And on the wall of their kitchen facing the cooker, the largest photograph is of a close finish at Doncaster Races – known for its rambunctious meetings at the end of the summer – where Vic's mother took her as a child. On Saturday nights, if he's not too busy, Starmer moves into this territory and still tries to cook. 'I put on the radio and pick the most complicated recipe I can find,' he says. 'The more chopping up and preparation there is, the better the music sounds. After an hour or so, everyone is moaning at me.' Vic wonders why he has to use ten different saucepans. His children will declare they don't want what he's cooking and ask if they could have some pasta. 'The beauty of my system is that by the time I'm ready they're all so hungry they'll eat anything,' says Starmer.

He maintains a vast network of friends and is assiduous in remembering anniversaries or meeting up for the big birthdays – forty, fifty and now sixty – as well as funerals. 'Sometimes I'll call Keir and he'll send me a text back saying, "I can't talk now, I'm at work",' says Colin Peacock. 'Then I'll see on the TV he was doing a big speech in front of hundreds of people or meeting some foreign leader. I don't think many politicians would just say "I'm at work", but it's an important part of how he approaches it.'

Although he can sometimes come across as distant in media appearances, there is often a genuine warmth in the way Starmer talks about places and people. 'Every town and village seem unremarkable,' he says, 'but they're not.'

In the summer of 2023, while on holiday in the Lake District he visited so often with his parents, there was a flurry of newspaper stories about Starmer handing out leaflets in a café – not about the Labour Party, but to help a family find their lost dog. When asked about it, he smiles and launches into a different anecdote about taking his children back to the row of Langdale Valley cottages he stayed in so often when he was their age.

'We knocked on the door and a woman was kind enough to let us in and show us around. She noticed our car moving and thought someone was stealing it, so I explained that was just my police protection team. Her husband started laughing and saying she hadn't clocked I was a politician. She said if I told her that earlier she would have taken the chance to push me down the stairs.'

This might be neither the funniest nor the most inspirational story you'll ever hear from a political leader, but it's one worth recording because it shows the pleasure Starmer takes at still being anonymous within all that muddle of Britain.

All of this is why a precise definition of Starmer's values is almost impossible. His 'sense of place' might be labelled 'communitarian'; the way he talks about losing himself in a big crowd or the team ethic of football is more 'collectivist'; while the individual human rights he discovered in Leeds are undoubtedly 'liberal'. Asked about it, he grudgingly recognises all of this in himself but insists it isn't really about different 'isms' as much as friends, family and football mixed up with a bit of the law as the different legs of a slightly wonky stool.

Opponents will inevitably want to dismiss much of this as fake or even cover for some harder, more elaborate ideological apparatus lurking beneath the surface of a carefully constructed public image. The evidence, however, suggests they're digging in the wrong places.

Part III

Making

Three decades of 'fighting for
justice and the rule of law'

11
All the same?

By mid-morning, Keir Starmer has drunk five cups of tea and done as many media interviews. He's pulled on boxing gloves with the word 'vote' embroidered on one and 'Labour' on the other, and been asked to hit a punch bag in slow motion for the cameras. Later he waves at people he's never met, pats someone's tiny dog outside a hair salon, and knocks on doors to be told 'all you politicians are the same'.

And yet, climbing aboard a train at Hull station in the afternoon, he reflects how it felt good to talk with people in the places where they live and take a local election campaign out to the country. It's what politicians are supposed to do.

This is late spring in 2021 and, although Starmer is more than a year into his leadership of the Labour Party, he could be forgiven for feeling it's barely begun. He's spent several months largely at home in Covid lockdowns, during which his main contact with the outside world has been through video meetings on a laptop. The rules have eased a bit by the time of this local election campaign, with people allowed to meet indoors for work where they can eat or drink together or sit outside pubs in groups of six.

However, the pandemic is far from over and Starmer's prospects are looking a bit sickly themselves. Boris Johnson is riding a post-lockdown wave of popularity that will see him win the Hartlepool by-election in a few days. The Labour leader, by contrast, is getting what's becoming familiar criticism about lacking charisma or just being insufficiently 'political'.

When a story about him does cut through, it's often a bad one. During his visit to Bath a few days ago, news bulletins led with footage of a pub landlord shouting at him about how Labour's support for the lockdown 'had fucked the economy'. A slightly dazed-looking Starmer was shown being bundled out before he could pose for the perennial photo opportunity of a politician pulling a pint.

For all that, the severe restrictions on people's freedom have generally been supported by a public that recognises why they're needed. And, if it seems particularly important for the MPs who voted for them to obey the laws, few politicians can have felt this more keenly than Starmer. Having spent almost thirty years as a lawyer before entering Parliament, his whole professional identity has been built around the rules that determine relations between citizens and the state.

You can get a sense of this from an itinerary prepared for Starmer's visit to Hull. During the door-to-door canvassing for local elections, it insists staff be split into two separate Covid-compliant teams so there can be no question of them breaking the 'rule of six'. In bold type, the memo says: 'Team B to stand on the opposite side of the road to Team A unless swapping places with someone from Team A.'

Later, when Starmer and his masked-up staff arrive at their overnight destination, they go to a hotel and get a room key from the receptionist behind a plastic screen, who tells them not to wander around and that breakfast won't be in the dining room but will be left outside their doors in the morning. He goes to the old Miners Hall where the Labour MP has her constituency office, complete with socially distanced desks. There, he's taken off to do campaign videos and an interview with a nearby radio station, as well as speak to an online 'Get Out the Vote' rally. At about 9.35 p.m. some takeaway food arrives.

The reason for all the detail is because the events of that evening have since been speculated on by the media, pored over by his officials and examined by a team comprising no fewer than nine police detectives, who spent a total 3,200 hours investigating them.

The date is April 30, 2021 and Starmer is in Durham for a night that will become briefly infamous, under various names ranging from the predictable 'Beergate' and 'Currygate' to the snappier 'Keir's Beers'.

And it's why this, the third part of Starmer's biography, focuses on a career in the legal profession that not only was the making of him but also sets him apart from some of those in his most recent profession in politics.

In Durham that evening, he ate his dinner standing next to the window, drinking from a bottle of lager, while discussing the campaign with Mary Foy, the MP, and Angela Rayner, Labour's deputy leader. According to the evidence Starmer later provided to the police, he finished his food in less than twenty minutes and went back into the office because there was more work to be done. One of Foy's staff members asked him to pose for a photo posted to social media with a Consett AFC football strip ahead of their FA Vase trip to Wembley. He read and signed off a press release. He got briefed on the plan for the next day. By the time Starmer and Rayner got into the car to head back to the hotel, it was about 10.30 p.m., and he remembers looking out the window and thinking lockdown Britain 'was still pretty quiet'.

The next morning was sunny. He and Rayner went to a building site at Durham Cathedral, donning hard hats and yellow hi-vis jackets for photographs of them pointing at things and gazing with visionary purpose into the distance, as so many politicians have done before.

Only in the car afterwards was he told to look at a video of him standing by the window the night before that had been filmed by Ivo Delingpole, a Durham University student. Perhaps coincidentally Delingpole is the son of a journalist who at the time was working for Breitbart News, an organisation associated with the American far right. The footage had been passed to the anti-lockdown activist and former actor Laurence Fox, who had posted it on social media.

Starmer quickly issued a statement, explaining briefly why the meal had been necessary for work purposes. The *Sun* ran the story on an inside page, but it was largely ignored by the rest of the media. That was because Durham police had swiftly issued a statement saying they'd seen no evidence of a crime being committed or any need to investigate.

*　　　*　　　*

Fast forward a year to April 2022. Boris Johnson was clinging to office after revelations of a dozen or more parties held in Downing Street while the rest of the country was in lockdown. Starmer had overtaken him in the popularity polls. There was a by-election in Wakefield, a Red Wall seat captured by the Tories in 2019, that Labour was favourite to win.

This was when the thirty-second video of him drinking a bottle of beer stirred back into life with a string of 'exclusive' stories making the front pages of Conservative-supporting newspapers for twelve days running. Eventually, under severe pressure from a local Tory MP, Durham police agreed to open an official investigation into whether he and Rayner had broken lockdown laws.

The decision by the police wasn't merely embarrassing, it was potentially fatal for Starmer's leadership. A few months earlier, after the police had announced they were investigating Johnson for breaking Covid rules, Starmer had – uncharacteristically – joined the clamour demanding the prime minister's resignation.

Even sympathetic commentators asked why he wasn't applying the same standards to himself. 'Having climbed onto a very high moral horse,' wrote one, 'Sir Keir is now at risk of falling off.' A more hostile columnist reached for some overripe alliteration to describe the Labour leader's 'tortuously woven web of dissembling, double standards and alleged dishonesty'.

Named after Labour's first leader, the one-year-old Keir already looks pretty serious.

On a walking trip as a boy, probably one of many he went on in the Lake District with his family.

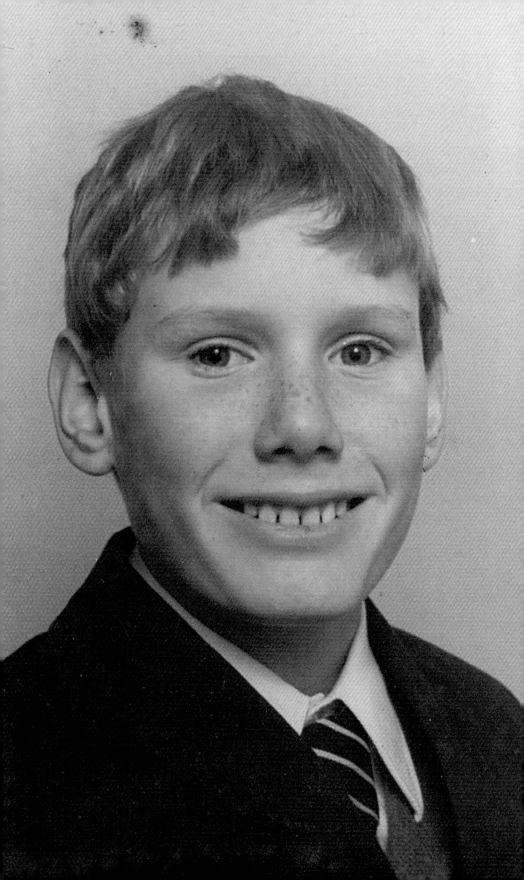

In his first year at Reigate Grammar School in 1974,
where he got a mixed bag of reports from teachers.

He is an able boy who promises well. He is clearly enjoying life in the Sixth Form. He is well liked by his form-mates even if they remain suspicious of his political views!

N G Buller _____ **Form Master**

House Master's Report He has never failed to use his all round ability in support of the house. A valued member of the house.

J M malign. _____ House Master

Handicraft **M.** | **c** | His work has not been halted by silly behaviour. He can do better!

I have a feeling that next year he will set about demonstrating his real academic ability but he must beware being over-confident or complacent. It is good to see him arguing his beliefs with cheerful vigour. It is with diffidence that I venture to observe to an aspiring lawyer that the law is the law, even if it is bad, and that dealing with the views of others with anything other than scrupulous courtesy merely demonstrates the weakness of your own argument! Belief and commitment he has in full — maturity will come, I'm sure.

N G Buller _____ **Form Master**

A very promising boy.

H Pallant _____ Headmaster

European Studies | His rather extreme views found expression in discussion. | *JWy*

English | Good when roused but unable to distinguish between proper pride and the old fashioned sort. | *C Jn.*

A favourite photo of Starmer's mother, Jo, whose 'smile could light up a room'.

Teenage time trials as part of the Surrey cycling club his father helped run.

Starmer (*front centre*) wearing eyeliner and 'projecting a romantic vision of some kind' with student flatmates in Leeds (*left to right*): Alison Jenkins, John Murray and Debbie Bacon. The skull, apparently, was real.

At Toulon railway station in the summer of 1984 after a brush with the law. John Murray (*left*) says, 'Keir should have been arrested just for wearing those espadrilles'.

'Caught in the guilty pleasure of hard work' at his desk, surrounded by neat stacks of files, in the otherwise filthy Archway flat above a sauna and massage parlour he shared in the late 1980s.

Celebrating his first-class degree in Law from the University of Leeds with his parents Rod and Jo in 1985.

'Captain Marvel': Starmer leads Homerton Academicals to a cup triumph in 1997.

Enjoying a pint after victory with Jo (*foreground*) and assorted nieces and nephews.

Three generations: Starmer's mother, sister Katy and paternal grandmother Doris at a family wedding in 1986.

Decorating a Christmas tree with his maternal grandmother, Marge Baker.

Reporters stationed outside his house shouted questions at him like 'Are you a hypocrite?' as he hurried into a car. A Conservative 'attack unit', which had pushed 'Currygate' into the media, was handed gold stars from party bosses for taking the shine off Labour's local election campaign. The political editor of *The Times* tweeted it was the most successful such operation the Tories had mounted 'in living memory'. Labour's sense of unease grew after suggestions that fresh disclosures had been leaked from party officials still loyal to the previous leader, Jeremy Corbyn.

It was an episode redolent with what Starmer has called the 'darker side of Westminster' politics and he immediately told aides that he would have to resign if police fined him for breaking the rules. Yet some of them urged him to 'tough it out', arguing there was no equivalence between a single bottle of beer in a constituency office and the suitcases of wine going into Downing Street for lockdown parties.

The stakes were high, with speculation about his position growing, his authority beginning to drain away, and the most ambitious members of the shadow cabinet reportedly preparing for an imminent leadership election. Eventually, it was agreed he should think about it over the weekend, during which he consulted family and friends from outside politics.

He told Vic if he was forced to quit there would be 'no comebacks, no hanging around in Parliament like a bad smell – I'll do something else with my life'. Then, three days after the story broke, Starmer delivered a statement, reiterating that he had done nothing wrong and then said he would quit as Labour leader if issued with a fixed-penalty notice. 'This is my decision about what is the right thing to do in these circumstances,' he said. 'This is about me. It's about what I believe in … It's about integrity.'

Such weighing of advice and attention to detail is more typical in the law than in politics, where taking time over a decision can be mistaken for indecision. And those who know Starmer best say they were not surprised by how he reacted. Parvais Jabbar, a close friend from his legal career, says: 'I spoke to him during that weekend and I've rarely known him so upset about anything. A lot of people thought this whole thing was just about politics but look at those words where he said it went to the heart of who he is as a person. You can disagree with Keir about all kinds of stuff – he knows that's part and parcel of his job – but it's an entirely different matter if you question his integrity.'

Vic was particularly incensed on her husband's behalf because she knew to what lengths he had gone in order to remain on the right side of all the guidelines, rules and laws during that period. For instance, the family had been dropping off food or clean clothes for her recently widowed father who'd been forced to isolate during the pandemic. When the 'rule of six' came in, she and Starmer would go with their children and her sister to spend time with him chatting on the doorstep. On one occasion, a neighbour started walking over to join them and there was a danger of six people becoming seven. 'You just disappeared,' Vic told him, 'you must have taken yourself off for a walk or something – even though nobody would have batted an eyelid probably – because you didn't want there to be any risk of breaking the rules.'

That is not explainable merely as the behaviour of a politician who doesn't want to be caught out. Long before becoming a recognisable public figure, Starmer would cycle home from work with a friend of his, Jonny Cooper, who delighted in telling people how he'd always 'sail through' red lights, leaving the punctilious Starmer waiting behind. Rayner makes a similar point, saying the Labour leader would 'probably beat himself up for a day for parking on the double yellow ... the idea that he would break lockdown rules was just ridiculous.'

Looking back at the Durham episode, Starmer says: 'Some people were surprised by how much this got to me, but it did, and in ways I've never properly acknowledged. I felt angry and humiliated.' His son was asking him about the police investigation, what it was about, whether it was true what people were saying and when it would be over. For the next two months, while the probe continued, Starmer couldn't even bear to hear it mentioned and would just switch the radio off. He recalls: 'The investigation into Durham meant the Tories were doing this false balancing act – "Boris Johnson did this while I'm accused of doing that".' He believes they wanted people to think there's no real difference, that political leaders all say one thing and do another: 'They wanted to make out I'm just like Johnson or worse, a "posturing hypocrite" as one newspaper called me. I'm never going to get used to that sort of coverage. It stings, because it should.'

On July 7, 2022, Johnson was finally forced to announce his resignation. His reputation had never recovered from being found to have broken the law during lockdown. The next day, Durham police cleared both the leader and deputy leader of the Labour Party of any wrongdoing. Starmer came out and said what he'd been wanting to say for eight weeks: 'Political leaders are not all the same.'

Speaking about it now, he says: 'Obeying the Covid rules didn't make us paragons of virtue or better than the hundreds of MPs or tens of millions of British citizens who quietly followed the rules without making a fuss. It shouldn't have been controversial to say that those who make the law can't break the law, or anything except the barest minimum the people have a right to expect of us. It shouldn't ever have been a point of difference between any prime minister and any leader of the opposition. Sometimes in politics all you can do is tell people who you are. The lockdown was a moment when we had to show it.'

An episode that started more than a year earlier with him out on the campaign trail trying to prove he could be like other politicians, had ended with Starmer drawing a clear line between how he saw himself and the most prominent politician in the country; someone he had truly come to detest.

Politicians aren't all the same, but Johnson and Starmer are particularly different because they both had formed much of their identities in long and successful careers prior to entering Parliament. Johnson had been a louche and irreverent celebrity-cum-journalist who never appeared to take anything, including rules, very seriously. Starmer, by contrast, had spent the best part of three decades as a barrister and public prosecutor where the law was just about everything.

In the death throes of his premiership, Johnson complained about the Labour leader's 'sanctimonious obsession' with rules and 'the great gaseous Zeppelin of his pomposity'. Those attack lines are not without appeal and they could well be dusted down in the next general election, when there will be many people – and not just in the Conservative Party – who will hope Starmer chokes on his elevated moral tone about enforcing the rule of law.

Such is the state of British politics some of its most successful practitioners believe having high standards of integrity is a weakness to exploit. The obvious hurt caused to Starmer by accusations he behaved with anything other than complete propriety means his opponents will want to keep punching that bruise. 'He does seem – how can I put it – rather over-sensitive to this sort of criticism,' says one senior Conservative who probably wisely insisted on being quoted anonymously.

The Tories have long since believed Starmer's record in the legal profession is a rich seam for them to mine for evidence of double standards or proof he is really 'Sir Softee' – one of those 'lefty lawyers' they say represents an existential threat to Britain's way of life. At the same time, his critics on the left believe that same career shows him as the vengeful dark angel of an authoritarian state.

In reality, neither comes close to the truth. They are political caricatures of a story that encompasses thousands of legal cases. In some areas, Starmer has changed his mind, in others he has adapted to new circumstances, and in still more you can see a clear line of consistency.

But this long career lies at the core of his identity and he remains properly proud of it. In his first party political broadcast, Starmer summed it up as 'fighting for justice and the rule of law'.

12
On the outside

Doughty Street

'There is no version of my life that does not largely revolve around me being a human rights lawyer,' says Starmer. And at the start of this career, he deliberately positioned himself on what was then its most radical cutting edge.

He was one of the youngest in a group of thirty progressive barristers who sought to change their profession in 1990. They moved out of the Temple, that stodgy old slice of London sandwiched between Fleet Street and the Thames, where most barristers' chambers were located. Their leader, Geoffrey Robertson, talked of escaping 'the smug, self-satisfied' atmosphere of a 'sclerotic caste-based institution'.

They found an office building in what was then a shabby Georgian terrace over a mile away in Bloomsbury. This was Doughty Street where coincidentally the *Spectator* – edited for much of this period by Boris Johnson – also had its offices. And the new set of barristers' chambers would become the base for the kind of 'lefty lawyer' that magazine has since spent much of its time fulminating against.

A brightly lit end-of-the-millennium idealism ran through the Doughty Street Chambers, which promised not only fresh ground coffee to visitors and a crèche for the children of those working there, but also a seminar room for lectures and the donation of profits to good causes. Robertson said the only cases that would be turned away would be those upholding the death penalty because justice should be afforded to all, 'regardless of the popularity or the cause or the client'. The Bar Council hauled them in for being so vulgar as to publish a brochure advertising their services. This boasted about having 'modern communications systems', and included a photograph of a flat-topped twenty-eight-year-old Starmer staring with furious intensity at a computer screen.

In those days he was still venting against the formality and ostentation that accompanied so much of the legal system. In his first appearance on national television he called for courts to become more like a health centre where the 'ordinary person feels they can go' without feeling intimidated by judges and barristers in old-fashioned wigs and gowns. He would have been one of those cheering away at the launch party of Doughty Street Chambers as Robertson stood on a packing crate and declared they had 'moved out of a museum and into the real world'.

That real world was still elite, in its own way. Doughty Street was to be found at the nexus of progressive thinking at a moment when, for the first time in a generation, such ideas appeared to be capturing the future. But their chic was the shabby kind. These offices consisted, as they still do, of pokey rooms found at the top of narrow, rough-carpeted stairs with exposed pipes on the walls and mousetraps on the landings. Some stardust has more recently been sprinkled by lawyers like Amal Clooney, married to the Hollywood actor, George, but a big night out for most of this set in the 1990s usually revolved around the Duke of York pub, or 'the Duke' as they call it, followed by a curry at the Salaam Namaste restaurant.

More important than form, however, was the substance. According to the chambers' founding principles, half the cases would be paid for by legal aid – normally earning less than a third of the commercial rate – or free of charge altogether. Helena Kennedy, one of the campaigning barristers who set up these chambers, recalls a great feeling of camaraderie between them all back then because they thought they were doing something important. She had a sharp eye for up-and-coming talent and often this alighted on Starmer. 'Oh, we loved him!' she says. 'We'd all fight to have Keir as our junior counsel. He was brilliant, crystal clear, very meticulous.'

Although for the time being Starmer himself was content to play a supporting role, he still felt at odds with a system in which justice could be sought only for 'one individual at a time'. He remembers repeatedly suing a paper factory near Ipswich on behalf of workers who kept getting terrible injuries. 'Every time we took the factory to court, the owners would pay out a bit of compensation because it was cheaper for them to do that rather than improve the safety of their dangerous machinery to stop people being hurt in the first place,' he says.

But an opportunity to work on a big case, one that would reverberate around the world, turned up at his office door just a few months after he'd moved to Doughty Street. The fast food giant McDonald's had launched libel actions against a group of British environmental activists over leaflets they had produced alleging it mistreated animals, exploited children, underpaid workers and much else besides. This huge corporation, busy back then promoting its hamburgers as harbingers of freedom in Eastern Europe, could be ruthless in deploying legions of lawyers to protect both its reputation and an annual revenue bigger than the entire economy of some of these countries.

Understandably, most of those being sued quickly rolled over and apologised, but a pair of vegan anarchists – Helen Steel, a part-time bar worker, and Dave Morris, an unemployed postman – decided to fight. Only after they had boldly declared they would represent themselves in court, did they begin to realise what they were taking on. 'We didn't know the first thing about libel,' admitted Steel. 'We didn't know what to do.' Morris remembers one solicitor they consulted told them they were on a 'hiding to nothing', even if they were right. Nearing the end of their tether, they met someone at an anti-poll tax protest who mentioned the name of a young lawyer at Doughty Street who apparently would work for free.

'Helen and Dave came to see me, explained they were in an unequal fight and asked if I could help,' says Starmer, picking up the story. Though by no means a specialist in this area of the law, he recognised there wasn't exactly a long line of barristers queuing up to help them and agreed to do what he could. At the time, the case was expected to last about three or four weeks. It turned out to be the longest in the history of libel law.

Starmer has always emphasised his role was strictly behind the scenes, but Steel has said he helped them navigate the legal system, teaching them everything from the details of an argument to the correct way to 'tie a ribbon' on a court file. 'If Keir hadn't offered to write the defence for us and draft the document, we'd never have been able to fight the case,' she said.

'We thought he was a saint,' said Heather Williams, one of his colleagues at Doughty Street who observed this epic battle. 'He literally spent day after day, unpaid, sitting with Helen Steel and Dave Morris ... going through the documents with them, explaining the documents to them, explaining the issues to them, explaining what they were going to do.' She added that, because he was working in the background, this young lawyer wasn't even going to be the star turn in court, and so did it all 'without any sense of consolidating his personal reputation'.

Maybe it was the kind of case he gravitated towards because it was about helping a pair of outsiders and he still felt like that a bit himself. In interviews at the time, he described them as challenging the system: 'Even with limited resources, even unable to bring all the evidence to court, you can still win significant victories, through a belief in what you're saying, a belief in free speech, and the courage to continually put your case forward.' He added: 'After this, things are going to have to change ... This case will change the future of libel law.'

Talking to Starmer about McLibel now, it's still possible to get a sense of that side of him. 'Seeing two ordinary people go head-to-head with this very expensive legal team was inspiring. And, because this was just about the first time anybody had stood up to McDonald's, it didn't know what to do. Instead of silencing criticism, the trial only drew more attention to the original claims.'

His eyes flash as he describes the time the corporation flew its executives over from America in 1995 to seek peace with Steel in her tiny Tottenham flat. They offered her a settlement, on the condition that neither she nor Morris talk about McDonald's to anyone, except in private. Starmer helped them write a letter back saying Helen and Dave would consider the terms, provided they could add a condition of their own: if they weren't allowed to say what they thought, it was only fair that McDonald's should cease telling other people what it thought too and stop all advertising. And, of course, this agreement wouldn't prevent the corporation from recommending its burgers to its friends and neighbours – in private.

'There was no way Helen and Dave were ever going to settle,' he explains. 'Whether or not most people agreed with their view of McDonald's, I don't think there are many who believe big corporations should be able to use the law to shut everybody up.'

At the end of a trial lasting two and a half years and costing McDonald's an estimated £10 million in legal fees, the judge delivered a 762-page mixed verdict, ruling that Steel and Morris had not brought sufficient evidence to prove McDonald's contributed to the destruction of the rainforests and starvation among the world's poorest, but also that some of the leaflet's claims, about the nutritional quality of its food and the exploitation of children in its advertising, were justifiable. McDonald's was awarded limited damages but wisely didn't pursue Steel and Morris for money they didn't have. The McLibel Two were back leafleting outside its restaurants within days, while corporations around the world filed the lessons under the category of 'What Not to Do' if you want to avoid a public relations disaster.

Even after the judge's verdict, the case rolled on for another seven years as Steel and Morris appealed all the way to the European Court of Human Rights in Strasbourg, where Starmer represented them. In 2005, they won a ruling that the lack of a level playing field in libel trials, including the absence of legal aid for underdogs like them, infringed their democratic right to freedom of expression. Starmer issued a portentous statement declaring the case 'a milestone for free speech'.

Since then, there has been some reform of the defamation legislation to make it less likely that people will be sued by a gigantic corporation. But Starmer recognises the victory was only partial, saying: 'We have this fantastic legal system but there hasn't always been justice for ordinary people. It's like a Rolls-Royce – a great car – but one only a few can afford.' What one former colleague called 'Keir's first rodeo' was perhaps already showing him the limits of what could be achieved working on the outside.

McLibel has had other lasting impacts on him. He still can't bring himself to eat in a McDonald's, though he says it's out of habit as much as anything else, and is teased for it by family members suggesting he try a 'McPlant' burger. 'Maybe I will one day,' he replies sceptically.

The episode also continues to generate controversy over the use of so-called 'spy cops'. Starmer says: 'London Greenpeace only ever had about twenty members, but McDonald's had sent in spies to infiltrate the group from two different agencies who were spying on each other some of the time. The police sent in their undercover officers too.' Ridiculous as it sounds, he says, this was a time when vegan anarchists were deemed to be a danger to our way of life. At some meetings of the group there were probably more infiltrators than genuine members. But more sinisterly, Helen Steel was in a relationship with a man she knew as John Barker, who she had met at these meetings. He vanished during the trial but she later tracked him down and discovered he was an undercover policeman called John Dines. 'This was devastating for her and clearly something that should never have been authorised,' says Starmer.

Even so, his later work with the police and intelligence agencies has convinced him that sometimes undercover operations are necessary, particularly in fighting terrorism. In one of his first clashes with the left after he became Labour leader, he insisted the party's MPs abstain and not vote against legislation giving such agents immunity against prosecution over crimes they commit to maintain their cover. 'If our enemies know these officers have red lines about what they can do written in law which they cannot cross, we might as well draw a target on their backs for them to be shot,' says Starmer now. 'But it's also really important that there are proper safeguards and democratic oversight of these operations, otherwise we're undermining the very freedom they are supposed to protect.'

Another legacy from that case might affect him now in more ways than one. *McLibel*, an award-winning documentary made by Franny Armstrong, has an interview with an awkwardly blinking Starmer recorded in 1996 in which he explains the legal concepts involved. When he appears again, eight years on, hailing a taxi on his way to the European Court and examining legal papers over breakfast in Strasbourg, he is a big-shot barrister and looks much more in charge.

But there was also some footage not used at the time from a party where he is wearing a sports shirt and leaning back in his chair over the remains of his dinner. Starmer is asked about how his career has gone since, and he mentions being made a Queen's Counsel – a title bestowed on Britain's top lawyers – before seeming to check himself for sounding too cocky and adding that it 'was odd since I often used to propose the abolition of the monarchy'.

This clip has since been aired multiple times by opponents as proof that, for all his subsequent avowals of support for the royal

family, he may not be quite what he seems. The right-wing blog
that claimed to have unearthed the clip said 'a smirking Starmer'
had been caught 'smugly boasting about his long-held republican
views'.

The Labour leader, aware that this is unlikely to be the last time
such footage gets aired, swiftly points out how his use of the past
tense should show anyone interested in what he thinks now that he
had changed his 'teenage views' about the monarchy. More inter-
estingly, perhaps, he also suggests that 'shooting my mouth off' in
such a way during this early encounter with the media had underlined to him the danger of relaxing too much in front of a camera.

It's possible that he learned the lesson of needing to be risk averse
and shrouding his personality when in public rather too well.
Indeed, some of the friends he made as a lawyer find it difficult to
reconcile the person they know with the sometimes bland politician
they see on television.

Death Row

Edward Fitzgerald, to whom the word 'bland' has never been
applied, is one such friend. This devoutly Catholic, slightly rumpled
and eccentrically brilliant barrister acted as the leading counsel in
many of Starmer's early cases and therefore in these pages stands as
what his profession might describe as an expert character witness.

'We laugh when we see Keir being described as boring,' says the
joint head of Doughty Street Chambers, 'because we know him.'

By way of illustration, Fitzgerald recalls the night they found
themselves in the bar of the Radisson Hotel in Belize on a work trip
together. 'There was some obnoxious American, surrounded by
cronies, being rather loud about his views on human rights. We
had to, well, sort of restrain Keir. Otherwise, I think he might have
punched him.' On another occasion, while consoling themselves
over a verdict that had gone against them, Starmer was reluctantly
persuaded it would not be a good idea to turn up at the judge's

front door and remonstrate further. 'Keir can certainly take things a little bit to heart when he feels an injustice has happened,' says Fitzgerald, eyes twinkling.

Both cases were about the death penalty. While nobody has been executed in the UK since the Labour leader was still a toddler in 1964 – and capital punishment was formally removed from the statute books in 1998 – it remains in place for many countries in the Caribbean and Africa as a grim legacy of the British Empire's legal system. For three decades, Starmer was among a group of human rights lawyers who mounted increasingly successful challenges to the death sentence imposed on prisoners in Commonwealth countries around the world.

Anyone who suggests his policy shifts since becoming Labour leader show he doesn't believe in anything have clearly never had a conversation with him on the subject. The people whose lives he was trying to save were often guilty of terrible murders but he wasn't trying to get them acquitted or escape justice, as implied by the *Sun* in January 2024, in a story about how he fought to 'save baby killers and axe murderers'. Instead, he says it was because 'the death penalty horrifies me – it's a process involving dozens of people methodically planning to exterminate another human being in the name of the law'. He adds: 'No matter how good your courts are and how terrifying or awful the crimes committed, there will always be miscarriages of justice. And, in far too many countries where they still have capital punishment, there isn't even much chance of a fair trial.'

Usually, Starmer was acting for convicts who faced being hanged by the neck until dead, a very difficult form of execution to carry out cleanly because human bodies weigh different amounts. 'They practise with a sack of sand the day before,' he says. 'If the drop is too far, people's heads can be pulled right off; if the drop is not far enough, they are slowly throttled.'

His efforts to prevent fellow human beings being killed in this way were no more glamorous than they were paid. Almost always, they began with a phone call from Parvais Jabbar or Saul Lehrfreund, a pair of lawyers who run the Death Penalty Project from the offices of a legal firm in London and have dedicated much of their own lives to saving those of others.

They had a rule which meant they never said no, however tough the case, says Starmer: 'And that meant I could never say no to them either when they would call, whatever the time.'

Jabbar, who joined the tight circle of Starmer's friends in those years, still exudes passion for his cause. 'It might sound good heading off to exotic places, but we weren't drinking rum punch at the beach,' he says. 'We would be spending two or three days in a prison seeing the client, taking instructions and meeting with local lawyers. These jails are old and dirty. We would stand in the baking sun to talk to the prisoner through the bars of their cells.'

On one such trip with Starmer, they arrived late in Malawi after a delayed ten-hour flight, only to find the court hearing at 9 a.m. the next day was taking place 250 miles away in a different part of the country. They took another flight at five that morning on a plane they doubted would have passed its MOT, got changed hurriedly in the toilets and were present in court on time, to discover the entire journey had been pointless because the hearing was adjourned until the following week.

Yet Starmer continued to be willing to drop everything and fly out at short notice for death penalty work, a huge commitment because it meant taking four days out of his diary, says Jabbar. 'And he'd do it maybe eight or nine times a year, for individual cases and wider work too.' During one uncomfortable flight back to London from the Caribbean on which everyone else was trying to sleep, 'Keir spent the entire night drafting a five-page strategy note.'

Jabbar credits Starmer with helping bring international human rights law into the domestic sphere of those countries, asserting: 'Courts could easily just turn around and say, "Well that's very interesting but it doesn't apply here", but Keir was always very skilled at showing why it did.'

The very unradical-sounding Judicial Committee of the Privy Council offered another legal route they could pursue, as it's still the final court of appeal for many Commonwealth countries. These nations also used the English common law system, which meant their courts could be persuaded by rulings made in other countries, and many incorporated the European Convention on Human Rights into their constitutions.

They won a key victory in Jamaica, where two convicted murderers, Earl Pratt and Ivan Morgan, had been facing the gallows for more than fourteen years. The two men had repeatedly been prepared for execution, measured for their coffins and 'weighed for the drop', before receiving last-minute reprieves. In 1993 the Privy Council declared the mental anguish they suffered to be 'an unintended extra element of punishment' and that no one should spend more than five years on Death Row. As a result, hundreds of convicts had their sentences commuted to life imprisonment and, as the judgment began to be applied over the following years across the Commonwealth, hundreds more escaped the death penalty too.

While he began as a very junior member of that legal team, more than a decade later, as one of Britain's leading human rights barristers, Starmer travelled with Lehrfreund and Jabbar to a heavily fortified prison atop a hill west of Kampala. The trip was meant to be merely for meetings with the campaigning Ugandan lawyer John Katende, but the London lawyers encountered a scene, as they described in a later newspaper article, that would stay with them for the rest of their lives.

'As we stepped through an archway, we stopped in our tracks. Before us were all the male prisoners on death row – hundreds of men standing, sitting or squatting in a space no more than 10 yards by 25 yards. When they saw us, they burst into song and clapped as we sat down on the benches set up so we could speak to all the inmates at once ... Then groups of individuals were asked to stand. Those who were 18 or younger; those who had been in the condemned section for 20 years or more – this group included the "elder", an old man who had lived there for 25 years; those who had not had representation at trial were not asked to stand because there were too many of them.'

Those prisoners were among 417 people in Uganda, including dozens of women, whose death sentences were being challenged by Starmer and his colleagues. In 2005, they secured a ruling from the country's constitutional court declaring automatic – or 'mandatory' – capital punishment for murder to be a breach of human rights because people should be given an opportunity to argue there were mitigating circumstances. The judgment also said prisoners couldn't be held on Death Row for more than three and a half years without their sentence being commuted to life imprisonment. Although capital punishment has not been abolished in Uganda – and the country's parliament has more recently outraged human rights activists by extending it to cases of 'aggravated homosexuality' – at the time of writing, no one has been executed in the country since that landmark legal decision.

Starmer has sometimes tried to imagine what the scene must have been like in that hill fort when they heard the court ruling that saved their lives, and has remained committed to the fight against capital punishment even since entering politics. As recently as September 2018, just a few days after delivering a speech as shadow Brexit secretary to the Labour Party conference, he flew to Taiwan for the sole purpose of lobbying that country's government against reinstating this form of punishment.

Far from serving as a distraction in his development as a politician, this belief and his pursuit of it reveals a lot about the way he operates. It also perhaps gives a hint of how he might pursue foreign policy in any Labour government. Starmer points out that many countries that have more or less stopped using the death penalty in recent years have often done so not because of a sudden conversion to preserving human life but for much more hard-headed reasons. 'They recognised that it was necessary for them to meet the standards required by potential investors, trading partners and military allies,' he says. 'Without their adherence to international laws on human rights, there would be less confidence in the fairness of judicial systems, the security of financial institutions and the accountability of governments.'

For Jabbar, Starmer hasn't changed much over the years: 'He'll walk around a problem, look at it from every angle, almost touch and feel it before working out what to do. If we can't abolish the death penalty altogether, he'll find ways to engage with the prosecutors in that country or the government. There's no point in telling these countries that capital punishment is barbaric just to get some cheap applause – where does that get you?'

This is a pragmatic approach to radical problems. Whether helping vegan anarchists navigate outdated libel laws or using the leftovers of the British Empire's influence over its former colonies to save the lives of inmates in a stinking foreign prison, Starmer was more interested in outcomes than posturing.

If you ask Gavin Millar, who was part of the interview panel when Starmer was starting out and then became a colleague at Doughty Street, this young lawyer was never going to be 'on the barricades' even in those days. 'Keir wasn't as party political as me,' says Millar, 'and nor was he averse to making an accommodation with the Establishment to advance his cause – that's what good lawyers do – they see things from both sides to find a way through.'

13

Seeing both sides

Fair trials for all

In 1991, at the height of the Troubles, Starmer formed part of a fourteen-strong team of Haldane Society lawyers who went to investigate human rights abuses in Northern Ireland. They visited prisons, including the notorious one at Long Kesh known as 'The Maze' or 'H-blocks', and observed the operation of so-called Diplock Courts that sat without juries for terrorism trials.

Their report, published the following year, concluded prisoners had been subjected to interrogation techniques that amounted to torture and that some convictions were unreliable because they hadn't been based on 'properly tested evidence'. It added the Haldane Society was 'in favour of a united Ireland' and wanted 'British withdrawal'.

Starmer went on the trip to gain a better understanding of a place that fascinated him. 'It still looked like the rest of the country,' he says, 'with the same shops and road signs, but had soldiers in armoured cars on the streets and many of the rights that UK citizens usually expect had been suspended.'

His role in that delegation wouldn't have shocked anyone who knew him back then, even though he now emphasises he never supported the 'troops out' movement. He was a young human rights lawyer making his name as someone ready to take on the power of the British state. In one of his earlier cases to attract publicity, he defended a druid called King Arthur Pendragon, who insisted on using his sword 'Excalibur' to take the oath in court, as well as others celebrating the summer solstice at Stonehenge who he argued had been exercising their right to protest without obstructing traffic.

Starmer also went into court on behalf of environment campaigners living in trees to stop bulldozers moving in to build new roads. Later, he represented a Saudi dissident fighting extradition to the US on terrorism charges, a convicted paedophile who feared he would be attacked if his face was shown on a BBC documentary, and a man who had been wrongly convicted of IRA terrorism as he sought damages for injuries sustained in an earlier prison breakout. When he defended a peace campaigner who had climbed over the fence of an American air base and also defaced the flag of the United States, Starmer told the court that protecting 'American sensitivities' had to be weighed against 'what was essential to protect the rights of peaceful protest in a free and democratic society'.

Such examples are no longer half-forgotten episodes from long ago because Conservative Party sources keep telling any journalist who will listen that they plan to make an issue of them at the next election. The standard defence for lawyers-turned-politicians when such cases are turned up is to hide behind the so-called 'cab rank rule' under which barristers are obliged to take on clients no matter what they think of them. But the principle is sometimes 'more honoured in the breach' by successful lawyers who have so much work on offer they can pick and choose their clients. Indeed, given that some of these same cases featured in Starmer's own video when running for the Labour leadership, he can't really complain if his opponents highlight them now.

More convincing, however, is a slightly different argument that says everyone has a right to justice. Ed Fitzgerald, who has gone into court on behalf of everyone from the Moors murderer Myra Hindley to the Muslim cleric Abu Hamza, once said: 'Some people ask, "Why are you spending your life defending terrible people?"

The answer is … it would be terrible if we stopped defending people because they're unpopular. The legal process is an attempt to civilise our emotions of revenge. Anything that's against lynch law seems to me to be a good thing.' Starmer puts it like this: 'I'm proud to live in a country where almost everybody accepts principles about people being free from arbitrary arrest and imprisonment, how they should not be tortured, and – above all – that they should get a fair trial.'

As his career progressed, however, he began to apply that right beyond the liberal left's usual cohort of oppressed victims. In 1999, Starmer was back in Northern Ireland as part of a legal team that successfully appealed the conviction of a British serviceman for the murder of a teenage Catholic girl. The case divided opinion almost as much in London as it had in West Belfast, where the soldier's early release under licence had been met with widespread rioting.

Six years earlier, Private Lee Clegg had been found guilty of killing Karen Reilly, who'd been travelling in a stolen car when it was riddled with bullets as it sped past an army checkpoint. Sections of the press, still smarting over the way former IRA prisoners like the Birmingham Six and the Guildford Four had been found to be victims of miscarriages of justice, were whipping up a political storm to overturn the conviction of the British paratrooper they said had simply been doing his duty. The *Daily Mail* delivered a petition to Downing Street signed by more than a million readers calling for him to be cleared.

But plenty of progressive lawyers were outraged to hear Starmer was helping him. Even today, the case has been cited by the Labour leader's critics on the left as the first sign of his long march towards the British Establishment and the 'security state'.

Clegg's conviction was eventually quashed after several months of appeals and retrials. Starmer remembers working with experts who assessed the trajectory of bullets by shooting at pig carcasses. They were able to show the round that killed Reilly had been fired when the car was still hurtling towards the checkpoint and soldiers were in fear of their lives, rather than after it had gone past.

In helping Clegg appeal his conviction, Starmer wasn't taking sides in Northern Ireland any more than when he acted for convicted IRA terrorists. As he saw it, if human rights were to mean anything they must surely apply to everybody, whether or not they had backing from the *Daily Mail.* The radical human rights lawyers even ended up playing regular games with the British squaddies from the Belfast garrison while preparing for the trial.

A progressive hour

This was a time when Tony Blair had declared 'a new dawn has broken' and what remained of Starmer's scepticism about individualistic legal rights had evaporated with the rising sun of the first Labour government in almost two decades.

Although still well to the left of the party's leadership, he shared in the excitement of May 1997 and stayed up most of the night watching the results. 'The thing I remember most was the morning afterwards with Tony and Cherie walking up into Downing Street, the pavement filled with people screaming their heads off and waving flags,' he says. They all had the sense that change was coming and everything, 'from our food to our football, from our music to our movies', seemed to improve. It felt like an opportunity to make all the things they had been talking about for so long finally happen.

When the government published a consultative green paper on human rights legislation, he rushed out to get it with the kind of excitement others had back then for buying Harry Potter books. Having argued about how human rights could restrain those with the most power or even redistribute it to those with the least, he saw the people in power embracing human rights themselves. It was a progressive hour in Britain's legal system and its most senior judges, led by Tom Bingham, the Lord Chief Justice, were also showing themselves ready to make rulings that opened up further reform. As Starmer later wrote: 'The 1998 [Human Rights] Act did not just give legal effect to rights until then only recognised in international law, it also incorporated the principles that had been developed since the Second World War to give dynamic effect to human rights – to make them practical and effective, not theoretical and illusory.'

And Doughty Street was at the heart of it. The chambers' leading lights included Helena Kennedy, author of *Eve Was Framed*, who had established herself in the vanguard of feminist lawyers exposing the deep-seated sexual discrimination running through British courts. She asserts that although every liberal left-wing lawyer suddenly appeared interested in the way women were 'being marginalised and stereotyped in the legal profession or put on trial in rape cases', not all understood such issues properly: 'The difference is that Keir got it.' Tapping a finger insistently on the table in front of her, she adds: 'Write this down: Keir got it – and he gets it.'

Another side of his character to impress those who knew him in those days was an empathy for people who had felt excluded from, or marginalised by, the legal system. Jonny Cooper, who joined Doughty Street as its first openly gay barrister in the early 1990s and blazed a trail for so many others that he later coined the phrase 'OUT-y Street', said Starmer was the colleague who helped him most. 'Keir looked out for all of us,' wrote Cooper. '[He] wanted to know what my boyfriend and I had got up to over the weekend. Though it may not sound it, this was remarkable. Keir was aware that most LGBT people's private lives were erased; he made sure mine mattered ... He was doing more than just demonstrating his kindness – he was demonstrating that his default position is inclusion.'

Even Starmer's obsession with football seemed to chime fashionably with the times. He remembers watching England's Euro 96 semi-final against Germany at Wembley and 'belting out' David

Baddiel and Frank Skinner's unexpected hit 'Three Lions (Football's Coming Home)'. Although England lost – on penalties again, to Germany again – it remains one of the most vivid nights of his life.

The following year, his Sunday league team, Homerton Academicals, or 'the Accies', won a league and cup double against teams with names like Brixton Monchengladbach, Who Dares Wednesday and Rapid Decline. 'We had a defence made up almost entirely of one family,' he says, 'the Daniel brothers who lived on an estate in Maida Vale. Georgie was the centre back, Ned at right back, Mickey at left back', and sometimes a fourth brother, called Sammy, when he wasn't away working double shifts at IKEA.

The Times coincidentally sent its writer Robert Crampton to do a feature on the team in which Starmer was quoted saying: 'I just love playing football. I love it … I hate losing under any circumstances.' One of his teammates explained to the journalist how their 'captain, midfield engine, motivator, chief scout, alpha male' was always seeking to poach good players from other clubs unless it was someone who might threaten his own place. 'This team would be a bunch of old elephants without my recruiting,' retorted Starmer, who let Crampton play the final fifteen minutes of the Accies' 4–1 win, and kept shouting, 'Let's get Rob a goal!'

The team's other central midfielder was John Feeney, who had been a painter and decorator when he first met Starmer on a stag weekend. Before being recruited, he admits to having been 'a bit lazy', but says 'that was not-so-gently knocked out of me by playing alongside Keir … If I wasn't pulling my weight, he'd let me know because he's so relentless.' Feeney still remembers the year the Accies did the double after a cup final played at Motspur Park Athletics Stadium. 'We'd hired an open-top double decker bus so that our friends and families could come to watch us,' he says. 'We drove back through south London waving the trophy at passers-by like we were superstars.'

This was the year that Arsenal, following the arrival of continental players like Dennis Bergkamp and the French coach Arsène

Wenger, also did the league and cup double. Wenger, who would remain at the club for the next twenty-two years, has said football mirrored bigger changes in society and politics because 'from 1997 onwards, England became more open to the rest of the world'.

'The Encyclopedist' or Mark Darcy?

There was time for parties and dancing too. Shortly after Jamie Burton joined Doughty Street as a young barrister, he remembers going to a celebration being held in the downstairs courtyard for a colleague who had just become a QC. 'In the centre of it, dancing away in a state of general dishevelment were Ed Fitzgerald and Keir Starmer,' he says. 'I thought to myself that this place might be more fun than I expected.' Another Doughty Street barrister, Quincy Whitaker, remembers meeting 'this geezer with a flat-top haircut who could dance to northern soul but had also been involved in major victories against injustice'. She admits: 'Keir represented just about everything I wanted to be as a modern human rights lawyer.'

Yet some of his legal colleagues admit privately to having been slightly irritated by him. 'It was all very well Keir doing this "I'm-one-of-the-good-guys' act",' says one, 'but some of us had kids and a mortgage to pay.' That said, the law is a fairly exacting profession and Starmer's reputation was based more on hard work than haircuts. Not only was he fighting and winning cases in court, he was also filling bookshelves with a prolific bout of authorship.

He had already written *The Three Pillars of Liberty* with Francesca Klug and Stuart Weir, two books with his former Leeds professor Clive Walker on miscarriages of justice, and pamphlets for campaign groups like Amnesty International. In 1999, Starmer produced *European Human Rights Law*, a 900-page heavyweight text Whitaker says has become 'a sort of bible' for members of the legal profession. Although there were other such guides, it set out clearly the new protocols for civil and criminal cases in the UK by reviewing 1,500 judgments in the European Court of Human Rights. 'The judges loved him because, case by case, he laid it all out for them and showed them how it worked,' says Whitaker. Three years later, she was herself writing a book with him, *Criminal Justice, Police Powers and Human Rights*. Somehow, Starmer also found time to co-author a 1,500-page tome on human rights in Africa.

Fitzgerald says: 'I used to call him "the Encyclopedist" because he wanted all human rights law to be available, accessible and systemised. His output was extraordinary, and these are books of real scholarship. They might be a bit dry to read if you aren't a lawyer, but animating them all is his deep belief in human rights and dignity.'

There are no grand rhetorical arcs in these books, which were written to be used as practical tools of the trade, just as much as those his father made from metal in his factory back in Oxted. His book on Africa, for instance, is subtitled 'Manual and Sourcebook'.

In similar fashion, Fitzgerald describes Starmer's style in court as that of a lawyer 'who builds an argument slowly step by step in a very methodical fashion until gradually you see the point'. Helena Kennedy agrees: 'He was never a passionate jury trial advocate who liked milking the drama of the courtroom. His forte was legal argument, an appellate lawyer who was great at getting the legal argument right. He would always go down very well with the judges.'

Starmer also based his success on finding out as much as possible about each judge who oversaw his cases and the kind of rulings they had made before. That focus on the audience is something he has carried into his political career, taking the view, unfashionable at times in the Labour Party, that ignoring the opinion of the electorate is not a great way to win elections.

But that method, learned through law, of putting in place building blocks of arguments, can also get in the way of appealing to voters. Philippe Sands, a human rights lawyer and friend of Starmer, is someone who has managed to carve out a second successful career as a writer of books, plays and documentary filmscripts.

He describes how it took him more than ten years to make such a transition. 'As barristers, we develop this special "court voice",' he says. 'We're trained to remove passion, personality and the core of ourselves because, in front of a judge, you have to be as neutral and understated as possible. A courtroom is not a safe place to relax, kick back and be yourself – if you make a mistake, there can be dismal consequences.' He highlights some of the cases Starmer worked on about capital punishment, where getting something wrong could have cost people their lives. 'It took me a long time to find my voice again as a writer,' says Sands, 'and I think Keir's going through the same thing. He will be cautious if he doesn't know he's in a safe space. A court room is not safe. Standing in front of the media is not safe, so the barriers go up. I think sometimes he sounds too defensive and he just needs to be himself.'

Ken Macdonald, later director of public prosecutions, watched Starmer's rise from a distance and suggests the stiff public image of the Labour leader may be more reflective of him than some accept. 'I've never really believed accounts of Keir being some sort of hell-raising party animal,' he says, 'because all I saw was a very serious, unshowy person – friendly enough – but very contained.' In one case they were both working on, he remembers thinking, 'Keir, for god's sake, spice it up a bit', but says Starmer wasn't interested: 'He just wanted the judge to understand the law and win the argument.'

Someone who has known Starmer both as lawyer and politician is Charlie Falconer, a barrister who became lord chancellor and justice secretary under Labour. 'Everybody who knows Keir seems to like him,' he declares. 'He is very impressive, but he never strays too far beyond the bounds. Even when he was a radical lawyer, he was one of a conventional sort. I think what you see is what you get. He is a good, solid, determined sort of bloke.'

Gavin Millar, who shared an office with him at Doughty Street for several years, says: 'Keir has always been funnier and more of a laugh than he looks but he has also always been serious in the way he went about work.' Recalling an occasion when, as chair of the management committee he was being deluged with complaints about the 'nasty red' chairs and cheap desks they had been given, he was dreading having to draft a reply: 'Then, up popped a message to the entire chambers from Keir. It said: "I would remind you all that we are human rights lawyers. We're here to defend the rights of vulnerable people to best of our ability. We're not here to be concerned about the colour of chairs." That was the last I heard of the complaints. To me, that sums Keir up.'

For a time, Starmer's office in these chambers was next to that of another rising star, Ben Emmerson. But according to Millar you couldn't have two more different characters: 'It was like Keir was the Roundhead and Ben was the Cavalier,' he says. The brash, colourful, risk-taking Emmerson was everything Starmer was not. They clearly got under each other's skin, with one colleague remembering them circling round each other 'like great white sharks'. Emmerson won Human Rights Lawyer of the Year in 1998, Starmer two years later; Emmerson became a QC in 2000, Starmer in 2002.

At least one expression of this duel rumbled on for decades. An *Observer* article published during the time under the headline 'The New Legal Crusaders' described a trip to the Duke of York with a group of young human rights lawyers for whom 'terrorist suspects, transsexuals, protesters – society's dissidents and outsiders – are their meat and drink'. They included Emmerson and Starmer, with the former posited as the possible model for the dashing-but-awkward Mark Darcy in *Bridget Jones's Diary*. A decade later, the *Sunday Times* set off another round of rumours by suggesting the real inspiration might have been the 'chisel-jawed' Starmer. Only when he became Labour leader did Helen Fielding, the book's author, say she'd never even met him, even though he was 'very similar' to Darcy. 'He's so good and decent and intelligent, but so buttoned up. I always want to say: "Come on, Keir, loosen your tie, ruffle up your hair."'

Emmerson has acknowledged that Starmer 'is not a guy I love on a personal level' and that their styles differ. While describing his own approach as 'guerrilla warfare', he calls his old rival a 'real details person', but then adds: 'Isn't that what you want as a prime minister? Somebody who's on top of the detail, who's not going to make a crazy decision for purely ideological reasons.'

Home and Abroad

By all accounts, Starmer could have earned a lot more with his legal skills than he did. His friends say he had no real desire to get rich and spent much of his money subsidising the upkeep of those donkeys at the back of his parents' home or sometimes helping his siblings out.

Nonetheless, he saved up enough to move out of his flat in Islington in 1997 and buy a house in Hackney with his barrister colleague and then girlfriend, Phillippa Kaufmann. A rising star at Doughty Street herself, she describes a heady time when progressive lawyers like them felt they were 'driving forward the vehicle of change' provided by the new human rights laws.

'We were young and would go off at weekends to meet up with mates where we'd all enjoy ourselves,' she says. 'But Keir's ability to work is absolutely phenomenal and why he has a productivity rate about two thousand times higher than me. He can just go on and on with all the details at his fingertips and ridiculously small amounts of sleep. I've never known anyone like him. He can store up the need to recharge until he gets a break like a holiday when he just collapses and sleeps for ages.'

Kaufmann remembers preparing for one such trip when Starmer felt he had to write two chapters of a book on the night before they left. 'I offered to help him type it up and so we worked into the small hours with him bringing in handwritten page after handwritten page. What struck me was, even though this was very difficult law, there was not a single crossing out and they had no need of editing because it was so crystal clear.'

After being together for more than six years, they split up in 1999. Yet their friendship has survived, with Kaufmann attending his wedding and donating to his Labour leadership campaign a couple of decades later. Along with her two children from a subsequent relationship, she still lives in the house bought with Starmer. Over a cup of tea in its kitchen, she talks about her 'ex' with fondness and admiration but also 'great relief' that she does not share her life 'with someone who has chosen such an unrelenting and public path in life'.

She says: 'If you'd told me back then that Keir would be prime minister, it wouldn't have surprised me one little bit.' Then she lists her reasons: 'One, he is very capable. Two, he is utterly driven. Three, his values and principles are so important to him. Four, law was never going to be enough for him.'

Kaufmann reckons there's little of the vanity or desire for self-aggrandisement that sometimes characterises successful people in law and politics. 'What he does have is this attitude that there's absolutely no obstacle that will get in his way and defeat him. Take one step forward after another – and you don't complain.' She says: 'That is embedded in his soul – never complain.'

Much of that 'resilience' comes from Jo Starmer who she remembers as 'the complete crucible of the family'. Kaufmann says: 'His mum came across as this diminutive smiling wife of the domineering Rod but I got the sense that for all her vulnerability, she was the strength which held everything together.

'Like Jo, Keir gets up and keeps going, he just does what he needs to do. But there's not much reflection and no stopping, which can make life difficult for others around him because there really aren't many people made of that kind of stuff.'

Some of those around him in those days have since joined the legions of critics decrying what they see as his drift away from their principles since entering politics. 'Keir is getting a lot of criticism from people, from the left, right and centre – and from some of his friends too,' says Kaufmann. 'I want to be encouraging and I don't want to change him. But I'm not going to be his spokesperson and some things that are happening are extremely difficult for me. He's on his mission and he needs to win this election. But yes, sometimes, this is quite tough.'

Back in the 1990s, however, Starmer appeared to relish the way this golden age for human rights law under Labour allowed him to challenge and sometimes infuriate that government. One on behalf of the Refugee Legal Group in 2003 overturned a Home Office rule designed to stop asylum seekers getting work or claiming benefits, with Starmer telling the court some of them had been left sleeping rough and were so 'cold, hungry, scared and sick' they were mentally distressed. 'It is inhumane to subject someone to that sort of destitution.'

Undoubtedly the biggest issue on which he disagreed with the Blair government was the Iraq War. Writing in the *Guardian*, two days before the invasion in March 2003, Starmer set out why he believed this military action didn't pass the legal test. The article is typical of his prose, with none of that purple shade that characterised so much of the debate at the time. It shows a meticulous mind working, examining the case for war using different United Nations articles and resolutions.

Although he dismissed the notion that Blair could be hauled before the international criminal court for ordering military action, he added: 'If the attorney general's advice is that force can be used against Iraq without a further UN resolution, he must explain fully how the legal difficulties set out above are to be overcome … Flawed advice does not make the unlawful use of force lawful.'

He later backed a Freedom of Information request for the government to release the full text of the attorney general's advice, as well as representing fourteen human rights organisations which won a ruling that evidence against terror suspects obtained through torture was not admissible in British courts. Starmer hailed the latter as 'a landmark judgment' on torture that would ensure the 'fruits of US rendition' could never be used in British courts.

As late as 2007, he was still chipping away at the government over the war, winning a series of court victories against the Home Office that prevented control orders being imposed on terror suspects the security services believed might travel to Iraq to fight against coalition forces.

Remembering the rows over Iraq now, Starmer says: 'The more I looked at it, the more I realised war could not be justified. I thought that this war in Iraq was a huge mistake. I still do.'

He had been one of the million people who marched through London in February 2003 against the invasion, but not the kind of opponent calling Blair a liar – or 'B-Liar' as the placards at that march put it. Starmer says he never doubted the then prime minister's sincerity, adding he had supported the decision to deploy Britain's military in Sierra Leone, Kosovo and Afghanistan. He would also have backed a 'liberal interventionist' military operation in Rwanda ten years earlier to prevent a genocidal massacre in which half a million people were slaughtered.

Indeed, in the same month he took part in the demonstration against Blair sending British troops into Iraq, Starmer flew back to Northern Ireland hoping to play his part in that same prime minister's effort to end a much older conflict. For the next five years, he and his Belfast-born colleague, Jane Gordon, would return there every month or so as the officially appointed human rights advisers to the Northern Ireland Policing Board.

Once again, critics on the left regard his work with the police as further evidence of betrayal or as described by Oliver Eagleton's biography of Starmer subtitled 'A journey to the right'. 'This was an opportunity to implement the reforms recommended in the 1992 Haldane document,' the author wrote, 'yet by this time Starmer's priorities had changed.'

Given that the prospect of a lasting peace had opened up in the decade since he had first travelled to this most troubled part of the UK, however, it would have been a bit odd if those priorities had not changed with the times.

Back to Belfast

The Good Friday Agreement of 1998 had mandated the transformation of the Royal Ulster Constabulary. Instead of it being a 'police force', the idea was to create a 'service' with more transparency and better representation of Catholics, commanding the confidence of both communities. Starmer's role wasn't about using human rights as a battering ram against state power, but about helping this new Northern Ireland Police Service (PSNI) balance different interests.

He remembers getting a sense of this centuries-old and blood-stained sectarian conflict as soon as he arrived in Belfast, where the most innocent-sounding questions turned out to be loaded. This is a city where whether he spelled his first name with an 'i-e' or with an 'e-i' mattered much more than it ever had before, because 'Kier' is seen as having Irish roots while 'Keir' is more Scottish and therefore possibly Presbyterian Protestant.

Even as he tried to tip-toe over such cultural tripwires, Starmer detected a certain amount of suspicion towards him for other reasons. The lawyer arriving from London heard some talk of human rights being 'a charter for criminals and terrorists'. Phil Shepherd, the PSNI inspector who acted as his liaison officer during these visits, was aware of it too. 'Police are conservative – small c – people by nature and there was some resistance,' he says, 'but Keir never came across as one of those "lefty campaigners" who just want to attack us; he was always very approachable and that made it much easier.'

This police officer remembers their first proper meeting at 'quite a posh affair' in the Harbour Commissioner's office. They ended up standing in a corridor having a pint while arguing about who was the better footballer – Paul Gascoigne or the Belfast-born George Best. 'I kept telling him Bestie is best, so I think the Guinness may have won the argument in the end.'

Shepherd, who comes from a Protestant background and had been part of the Royal Ulster Constabulary, had studied human rights law at Queen's University, Belfast and even before Starmer's appointment, watched him give a speech in London on the subject. The two men became friends, going on trips to pubs and Indian restaurants across the city in the evenings because, as Shepherd puts it, 'I wanted to show him a bit of the place.'

On one occasion, their work became properly dangerous. Shepherd took Starmer to the Ardoyne shopfronts next to the Crumlin Road for the 'twelfth'. This is a flashpoint date in July's marching season when the Loyalist Orange Orders parade through Nationalist areas with pipes and drums to celebrate the seventeenth-century Battle of the Boyne which confirmed 'Protestant Ascendancy' in Ireland. 'I was there to monitor what was going on,' says Starmer, 'but before I knew it, golf balls and rocks started being chucked. They were pinging off the wall next to me. Next thing I knew Phil had grabbed me by the scruff of the neck and more or less carried me into a Land Rover.' That night in the summer of 2005 saw blast and petrol bombs being thrown, leading to 105 police officers and eight members of the public being injured.

'This could easily have gone wrong,' says Professor Desmond Rea, chair of the Policing Board that appointed Starmer. 'But Keir is no fool, he understood the importance of building relationships and I think was surprised by the degree of acceptance that he got as a result. I thought then that he's tough and no soft touch.'

Hugh Orde, the then chief constable, recalls that while some police officers thought the presence of a human rights lawyer would be the end of the world, he welcomed Starmer's presence. 'Human rights are not an impediment to good policy but the opposite,' says Orde. 'I found him and Jane Gordon to be completely straight. There was no indication of political bias or ambition. They were there to do a job and the reports they produced were really balanced.

'I told them to look at whatever they wanted. It wouldn't be unusual to have them in the control room during major incidents. If they had tried to interfere, I would have kicked them out, but they didn't, they just went out of their way to understand what was really going on.'

Starmer remembers one such occasion watching a man carrying a gun towards the line of police separating groups of marching Orangemen from protesters. The senior officer in charge said he could see this man preparing to fire the weapon and had to decide whether to authorise the use of live rounds, says Starmer. 'He was pacing up and down, trying to take in all the information. We could feel the tension of this real-time life-and-death decision. We couldn't fail to be impressed by how seriously the policeman took his responsibilities.'

The new PSNI ended up a model for other parts of the UK, particularly in its emphasis on becoming a 'service', accountable to local people, rather than a police 'force' imposing state power. Starmer saw his belief in human rights tested in fire. He recalls: 'Different groups of people had different rights, all of which needed to be respected. Loyalists had a right to freedom of expression and assembly by marching, as they had for generations. Nationalists had a right not to have the peaceful enjoyment of their homes shattered by sectarian parades. Local communities had a right not to have rioters setting fire to their cars or businesses. Police officers themselves had a right not to have their lives put at risk unnecessarily. And everybody had a right to walk the streets of Belfast, as in any city of the United Kingdom, free from fear.'

But it still took Sinn Fein four years to recognise the new Policing Board and even then it refused to endorse Starmer's 2007 report on human rights because he had rejected their demand for an outright ban on tasers and plastic bullets. He had instead recommended new guidelines saying these weapons should not be routinely issued to police officers but used only when they were the last remaining alternative to 'lethal force'. It was another pragmatic compromise and one that has, so far, stood the test of time.

He describes the 'practical framework' human rights provided for balancing the interests of different communities that played their part in building confidence about the peace process. 'At meetings of the Parades Commission, for instance, the police could say they were legally obliged to let the march proceed but that it would only be lawful if it went by a certain route or under particular conditions,' he says. 'It showed the police what was necessary and proportionate action to control trouble with the least impact on people living there, the shopkeepers trying to run their businesses, or the officers caught in the middle.'

The five years he spent working with the PSNI left a deep impression on him, and his affection for Ireland and the Irish endures, so much so that he still plays his football in the Donegal County shirt of the Gaelic version of the game. After he got married, he took Vic for a visit, staying a couple of nights with Phil Shepherd and his wife at their home south of Lisburn.

Shepherd says Starmer asked him to take them to some of the places whose names had been famous for all the wrong reasons during the Troubles. They drove down to Crossmaglen, where the last British Army watchtower had only just been removed. 'We parked and walked around the square for a bit, looked at the memorials and noticed the silence. I had never visited it before without being in an armoured car or having a helicopter flying overhead,' says Shepherd, who adds that they didn't 'push their luck' by stopping at the pub for a drink.

He has been over to London since, where Starmer's son asked a lot of questions about what it was like being a police officer. On his return, he sent the boy his old RUC baton that, he proudly points out, had never been tested in action. 'My idea of policing wasn't really about hitting people on the head with a wooden stick.'

Shepherd is slightly amazed the leader of the Labour Party still stays in touch. 'I'm just an old retired "Peeler" now, picking up my pension and doing the garden, while Keir might be the next prime minister. But he's a very loyal friend and that's indicative of the fella – if you're his friend, you're a friend for life.'

Did getting to understand the police and meet people like him change Starmer? 'I don't know but I hope so,' replies Shepherd. 'Seeing things from someone else's perspective does, doesn't it? Just as autumn changes summer.'

The solicitor Mark Stephens recalls the torrent of criticism from what he calls 'the unthinking left of the legal village' that Starmer got for taking on cases like Lee Clegg and then going to work for the PSNI. He says: 'A lot of lawyers didn't understand human rights in the way Keir did. When he started out as a radical barrister, this was a fairly niche area, but he had written the book on it before the HRA was introduced. He knew where the gaps were and how, in the end, you had to work with the state if you're going to solve otherwise intractable problems.'

But Stephens, who had worked with him on cases from McLibel onwards, also saw 'a maturing with experience' in Starmer over the course of almost two decades. The most lasting impact of time spent in Northern Ireland was that it showed him how bigger and faster change could come from working on the inside with those, like the police, against whom he had, by his description, once been 'railing against from the outside'.

Seeing both sides of an argument usually takes you halfway towards changing your opinion or, as Starmer says now: 'If you had asked me when I was twenty years old whether I would ever work with the police, I would have said no way. But I was on a journey and I'm happy to admit I changed my mind about some things.'

When his term in Northern Ireland ended, he got a new job; one that took him further on that journey and right into the heart of the British state.

14

On the inside

'The curveball'

A lot of people were taken by surprise when Starmer was appointed the chief prosecutor of the nation's criminals in 2008. Almost his entire career had been spent as a defence barrister and what experience he had of being a manager didn't extend beyond the handful of people employed in his office. Now, as the Director of Public Prosecutions (DPP), he would have responsibility for eight thousand officials spread across England and Wales, as well as hundreds of thousands of criminal cases every year.

His friend John Murray was among those to be blindsided. 'I hadn't seen that coming,' he says. 'That was a real curveball.' David Renton, a fellow radical barrister, recalled being at a meeting of socialist lawyers when the news broke. 'We couldn't understand why he'd taken the role,' wrote Renton later. 'He was a principled opponent of state power. He was one of us. But the DPP's role is all about exercising power: prosecuting defendants so that they are fined or jailed.' Starmer himself has acknowledged that going from a defence lawyer whose work had been as much civil as criminal to running the Crown Prosecution Service (CPS) was not a natural transition.

As ever, however, he had prepared his ground. He received encouragement from Ken Macdonald, whose five-year term as DPP was coming to an end and was seen as having blazed a trail for progressive lawyers in the post. Starmer consulted his mentors at Doughty Street, Ed Fitzgerald and Helena Kennedy, both of whom urged him to go for the job. The latter told him it would be good to have 'enlightened about the law's failings someone with his hands on the levers of power'.

He also went to see Charlie Falconer, perhaps to seek his advice or possibly just to make sure he had the support of this lawyer-turned-politician. 'I said to Keir that I thought he was the outstanding candidate – and he was,' says Falconer now. 'He wasn't the biggest star QC at the time, even though he was always very good. Just like becoming leader of the Labour Party a few years later, he managed to be the obvious choice at the right time.'

But some of Starmer's old allies worried moving to a post such as this would change him. Helen Steel, with whom he'd once taken on the corporate might of McDonald's, told him he should stick to fighting injustice from the outside. According to her, he replied: 'Is it the job that makes the man, or the man that makes the job?' If that was an answer that reveals a lot about Starmer's confidence in his ability to make a difference, it didn't entirely convince Steel. 'The reality is,' she said, 'the Establishment shapes you more than you shape the Establishment.'

Others were more concerned about what this man might do in his new Establishment job. 'The country's new top prosecutor was unveiled yesterday – a human rights lawyer who defends the rights of paedophiles' was how the *Sun* reported Starmer's appointment. The newspaper described how this 'Oxford-educated' forty-five-year-old 'liberal' had also 'battled for the rights of asylum seekers to claim benefits, helped two terror suspects overturn control orders, questioned the legality of British forces fighting in the Iraq War' and worked 'to save brutal killers from being executed in the Caribbean'. It quoted unnamed senior police officers as being dismayed at Starmer being put in charge of the CPS, as well as a former Flying Squad commander who said the criminal justice system didn't need 'a human rights lawyer going on the offensive for defendants'.

The editor of the *Sun* in those days was Rebekah Brooks, who would later become a defendant herself during Starmer's term as DPP, facing criminal charges of conspiracy to pervert the course of justice in a hugely expensive trial that eventually resulted in her acquittal. At one stage, Brooks' lawyers felt the need to cite Article 6 of the European Convention on Human Rights – which guarantees a fair hearing – to prevent damaging material emerging during a public inquiry into newspaper phone-hacking.

The year before Starmer's appointment, a journalist from the *News of the World*, part of the stable of newspapers owned by Rupert Murdoch that included the *Sun*, had been jailed for illegally intercepting phone messages from the royal household. Although his position on this would later change dramatically, the new DPP initially resisted demands from Labour MPs and other parts of the media for a deeper probe because he accepted at face value assurances from the Metropolitan Police that there was no need to go further.

Much of his work in that first year at the CPS was behind the scenes. He visited all forty-two regional divisions, personally met about a third of his staff and made a point of asking senior managers to leave the room so that other members of staff would get the chance to speak. 'Many of the best ideas came from them because they understood the systems we used better than anyone and knew the "work-arounds" that could make it more efficient,' he says.

His reforms were outcome-orientated and unlikely to generate any headlines. He pursued a strategy of improving the transparency of decision-making, as well as implementing new national standards and performance benchmarks. One of the measures of which he is proudest could almost be part of a Starmer parody sketch today: the replacement of old paper files with digital ones. This measure would, he proclaimed in an interview with *Civil Service World*, be 'one of the defining moments in the history of the criminal justice system'.

Equally typical, however, is how he seeks to suffuse such apparently numbing bureaucracy with progressive values. He still cites his eradication of paper files as an example of how 'getting the boring stuff right' in an organisation can improve lives. 'I wanted fewer prosecutions abandoned due to lost paperwork – which happened too often – or because we had run out of time,' he says. 'The consequences of such reforms were far from boring to the family of a child that had been injured by a drunk driver or an elderly victim of burglary. Losing the paperwork for their case or failing to deal with it properly meant it would be harder for them to get over what had happened; it was like rubbing salt in a wound.'

Controversy, however, had a habit of cutting through technocracy at the CPS. An early episode revolved around the transatlantic terror plot by al-Qaeda to blow up airliners. These days, it's best remembered as the reason why airport passengers cannot bring more than 100 millilitres of liquid on a flight and have to put items in see-through plastic bags when they go through security.

In September 2008, just a few weeks before Starmer started at the CPS, a jury failed to reach verdicts in the case of several of the accused. A retrial, similarly, couldn't decide if some were guilty. Starmer took the decision to seek permission from a judge for a second retrial. 'It's something that happens very rarely and it ran the risk of seeming oppressive if they were acquitted,' he says. 'But we got them back into court where they were convicted for conspiracy to murder. Britain is a safer place for it.'

Since he became a politician, he has frequently cited this case to show he can be tough on security issues. But talk to Starmer at length about it and he makes a deeper argument that the prosecution was successful, not in spite of human rights laws, but because of them. None of the suspects had been tortured or had their trial compromised by evidence tampering. 'The care that had been taken to treat them properly was why defence lawyers couldn't challenge the prosecution as unfair – and why those terrorists are still serving their jail sentences now,' he says.

'Rights are important for innocent people falsely accused of crimes. But we also have a right to board an aircraft for a holiday without someone trying to blow us up in mid-air. The biggest danger to our freedom comes when we ignore any of those rights or get the balance between them wrong.'

Another challenge came via the fallout from the *Daily Telegraph*'s investigation into parliamentary expenses, which had generated a level of public fury towards elected politicians probably not matched until the final months of Boris Johnson's time in Downing Street. It was entirely new territory because it meant using the law to prosecute lawmakers on a scale that was unprecedented, with the result that four Labour MPs and two Conservative peers were jailed. Once again, the approach he took revealed quite a lot about how he tackles such delicate tasks. 'It was really important that decisions were taken on the simple basis that politicians should be treated in exactly the same way as anyone else investigated by the police,' he says. 'We would not seek to make an example of them just because they were MPs. But nor would we be put off from prosecuting them because of who they were.'

All that might sound obvious now but none of it was straightforward at a time when the scandal appeared to have left Britain's democracy rocking on its foundations.

Starmer says now that many of the expense claim allegations were more about partisan politics than genuine wrong-doing and yet, he says, some of these cases were breathtaking: 'One MP had fabricated tenancy agreements, another had created a whole pile of fake invoices from firms in their constituency. These were really serious cases of fraud. We couldn't shrug our shoulders at such dishonesty on the basis that it is "priced in" because people expect politicians to behave badly.'

His five years at the CPS included having to make decisions about other politicians too. He chose not to prosecute a Tory opposition frontbencher, Damian Green, whose parliamentary office had been raided by police seeking the source of leaks from the Home Office. But his decision to take court action against the then Liberal Democrat cabinet minister Chris Huhne and his ex-wife Vicky Pryce saw both jailed for perverting the course of justice after giving the police false statements to avoid a speeding ban.

Huhne insists he doesn't bear a grudge against the former DPP. After all, he was guilty, even though he says much of the prosecution was largely based on the flawed testimony of a former judge and barrister who herself was later jailed for lying to police over the case.

They have never met properly nor spoken about it since. Huhne says, 'We eyed each other warily across the room,' when, after his release, he found himself at a birthday party for a mutual friend. 'At the time of the case my lawyers were outraged that Starmer announced his decision to prosecute me in a press conference, which they thought might be prejudicial to the case,' he says. 'But my sense is that he was already thinking about what to do next and having the scalp of a cabinet minister wasn't bad for him if he was looking to move into politics. In truth, I would probably have done the same thing. I don't think you can get to the top of politics without a certain streak of ruthlessness in you.'

There were some unexpected consequences of developing a higher public profile as the country's chief prosecutor. A conman called Paul Bint started pretending to be him in order to have sex with women and steal from them. Starmer only found out and called in the police after a taxi driver turned up at his offices saying he was owed £60 because a man claiming to be the DPP had told him to charge the bill to the CPS. At his trial, Bint was revealed to have cheated people out of almost £2 million and tricked dozens, if not hundreds, of women using a variety of false identities. A woman who had believed she was dating Starmer said she had looked him up online and later said, though Bint didn't look much like him, 'You can't always tell with pictures, can you?'

In the midst of all this, Starmer felt it necessary to criticise the then opposition Conservative Party over its plan to replace the Human Rights Act with a 'British' law that did not incorporate the

European Convention. At the CPS's annual lecture in October 2009, he said it would be to this country's shame if Britain lost these 'clear and basic statements of our citizens' human rights … on the basis of a fundamentally flawed analysis of their origin and relevance to our society'. He suggested the idea that human rights should somehow stop in the English Channel was odd and impossible to defend, adding – in a scarcely disguised reference to the Tories – that it was often in the interests of those who wanted to debase a principle to 'chip away at it by citing examples of its occasional misapplication'.

As a public official, Starmer was straying beyond his remit by making such remarks and it led Dominic Grieve, then the shadow justice secretary, to issue a fairly stern rebuke. 'The Human Rights Act is not the only way to implement human rights in Britain,' he said. 'The Conservatives believe a bill of rights will deliver a better balance – and it is a matter for Parliament to decide.' Other Tory MPs called directly for the DPP to be sacked. David Davis, then a backbencher, said: 'We should tear up the Human Rights Act and replace it with something that protects law-abiding citizens from violent criminals. And we should tear up [Starmer's] contract as well.'

An editorial in the *Daily Mail* asked: 'What has our beleaguered criminal justice system done to deserve a Director of Public Prosecutions using his powerful role to promote his own left-wing agenda?' It went on: 'Keir Starmer knows only too well that he has an absolute duty to remain politically impartial. The Act gives lawyers far-reaching powers to overrule the decisions of elected politicians. Now Mr Starmer is saying that those politicians don't even have the right to question whether this is a good thing.'

Bleeding liberals and blind justice

This was probably the first significant political bombardment Starmer had faced, but in those days he could still rely on some covering fire. He had backing from campaign groups like Liberty, as well as Labour and Liberal Democrat MPs, while the *Guardian* ran an editorial entitled 'In Praise of Keir Starmer'. A profile of him in that newspaper around the same time began by declaring the DPP 'a good bloke – a radical lawyer who has spent twenty years defending the downtrodden and working to outlaw the death penalty in Africa and the Caribbean' and went on to warn readers the rest of it might be a 'bit of a love-in'.

Such a relationship with any section of the media, however, is usually a fickle affair. In that same *Guardian* profile, he was quoted saying: 'I wouldn't characterise myself as a bleeding heart liberal, whatever that is. I don't think the agenda of protecting people against crime, making sure things are properly investigated, that people are treated with dignity both as victims and as defendants, is something you can reduce to those terms.'

And, in the next couple of years, he would go on to break a few of those bleeding liberal hearts.

Starmer had already upset some former allies by reaffirming his predecessor's decision that there was insufficient evidence to prosecute the police marksmen who had killed Jean Charles de Menezes at Stockwell station in 2005 after mistaking him for a suicide bomber. But it was the death of Ian Tomlinson in April 2009 during anti-capitalism protests at a G20 summit, that put him on a collision course with his fellow human rights lawyers.

An initial post-mortem attributed the newspaper vendor's death to natural causes but subsequent video footage showed Tomlinson being struck with a baton and pushed to the ground by PC Simon Harwood. Starmer describes how a lot of people he respected were urging him to go ahead with a prosecution on public interest grounds, even without sufficient evidence. There was an open letter warning that delays in a decision on the case called the CPS's credibility into question, signed by Tomlinson's family, politicians and barristers, as well as Shami Chakrabarti, then the director of Liberty, an organisation Starmer had so often represented.

When doubts emerged about the post-mortem's finding that Tomlinson had died of a heart attack, Starmer contacted the pathologist, Freddy Patel, to say he was ordering a new analysis of crucial fluid samples taken from the body. Back came the reply, 'You can't. I've thrown it away.' Starmer told him: 'Well, I know you throw most of it away, but you'll have kept a sample, and we only need a sample because we need to know what the composition is.' 'I chucked it all away,' replied Patel. Throughout this conversation with the now-discredited pathologist, Starmer admitted, 'I had my head in my hands.'

There were protests outside his offices when the CPS announced there would be no charges against Harwood in July 2010. Paul King, the stepson of Tomlinson, said: 'It's been a huge cover-up … [Starmer] has just admitted on TV that a copper assaulted our dad. But he hasn't done anything … why hasn't he charged him?'

Looking back at the episode now, Phillippa Kaufmann, his ex-girlfriend, says: 'It was very difficult for Keir. He was now moving in these Establishment organisations that, historically, the left would not go near. He was hurt by the criticism over Tomlinson because some of it was coming from people who knew him and they were questioning his integrity. That goes to the core – it goes right through him – this need to act with integrity is a very powerful thing for him.'

Among those bending Starmer's ear about the case was Jane Winter, a human rights activist he'd known for years, who called him up to ask what the hell he thought he was doing. He took the time to explain the facts that lay in the way, saying, 'We tried, but we really couldn't make it stand up.' 'I admired him for that,' she says. His caution was vindicated to some extent because, even after a prosecution eventually did take place when new evidence emerged, Harwood was acquitted on charges of manslaughter.

'When you sit on the outside, you can have any views you like because you're only responsible for yourself,' says Ken Macdonald. 'You're wondering, "How the hell did they decide not to prosecute?" But that's because you have much less information and a much narrower range of accountability. When you're on the inside, everything changes because the decisions you take matter to a vastly greater number of people including the police and the general public. When I see a police shooting or death in custody now, I'm much more sceptical about the knee-jerk reaction than before.'

As DPP, he explains, you are cleared to see everything and get visited by MI6 officers carrying a briefcase cuffed to their wrists. Macdonald came out of the job with a much more benign view of the police than before he went in: 'The people doing these jobs are generally a good thing and generally do a good job.' In response to the charge that this was when Starmer was corrupted by the British Establishment and became a 'collaborator' with the security services, Macdonald sighs and says: 'I think, to be honest, that's quite a childish point of view.'

Now a crossbench peer, he is largely complimentary about his 'meticulously independent' successor, but points out Starmer was a relatively conventional DPP. 'I had been quite challenging to the government on issues like twenty-eight days' detention [of terror suspects],' says Macdonald, 'but Keir didn't want any of that stuff. He wanted to run a competent and efficient CPS.'

In the view of Starmer's left-wing critics, he did much worse than that. After David Cameron became prime minister in May 2010, they say, Starmer turned into a willing accomplice of a Tory-led government and an instrument of an authoritarian security state. Such an account usually starts with the riots, looting and arson that began in Tottenham on August 6, 2011, before spreading across London to eight other cities over the following days. For a time, it seemed as if the police might lose control of the streets. There was widespread public support for the use of water cannons, arming police with baton rounds or sending offenders to live on remote Scottish islands. Cameron declared those responsible would face the full force of the law, adding: 'If you are old enough to commit these crimes, you are old enough to face the punishment.'

As head of the CPS, Starmer was obliged to process thousands of suspects but he, too, had felt some of the fear that gripped so many at the prospect of public order breaking down. He remembers walking home from Kentish Town tube seeing shops being boarded up along the streets where he lived and elderly neighbours telling him they were scared to leave their homes.

Starmer co-operated with a judge's order for hundreds of cases to be fast-tracked by having courts sit all night. 'Justice needed to be swift and to be seen to be done,' he says. In the small hours of one morning, he walked from his home to watch proceedings at Highbury Magistrates' Court and remains proud of the way the CPS rose to the scale of this 'unprecedented challenge'.

Over the months that followed, however, came claims that due process had been sacrificed, that children and vulnerable people had sometimes been remanded in custody. Defence lawyers complained trials had been conducted in 'kangaroo courts' and 'conveyor-belt justice' had seen overly harsh sentences such as that of a man jailed for sixteen months for stealing a box of doughnuts.

Although Starmer wasn't responsible for judges' bail decisions or the length of sentences, he maintains it would have been irresponsible to release hundreds of people back into communities while the disorder continued. He has suggested it wasn't the harsh sentences being meted out that helped quell the unrest so much as the speed with which offenders were prosecuted, which 'acted as a deterrent to other people tempted to join in the destruction'.

As DPP, Starmer has also been criticised by the left over the prosecution of so-called 'benefits cheats', who had become an outsized symbol of what was wrong with Britain for Conservative politicians and media during the austerity years. In 2013, he announced new guidance that meant perpetrators of the most serious examples could be charged with fraud and face prison sentences of up to ten years. Such cases included professionally planned or multiple frauds over a significant period of time, as well as those carried out by using a false identity or abusing a position of trust.

Asked about the guidelines now, he says, 'I'm not going to make any apology for toughening up the approach to those defrauding millions of pounds from our benefits system.' Starmer says cases he dealt with involved children as young as three months old being trafficked into Britain from Romania and used to defraud the benefits system. 'This was never about targeting desperately poor people claiming a few extra pounds a week or those who had made a genuine mistake,' he says. 'I had no interest in making out almost anybody getting benefits is cheating the system – I know that's not the case. But this is a system of support designed to enable people to live with respect and in dignity. And those who systematically defraud that system of large chunks of the money deserve to be punished.'

Perhaps the most persistent attack on Starmer's record as DPP has been over the extradition of people alleged to have committed crimes abroad, one of the most prominent cases of which was that of Gary McKinnon, accused of hacking into ninety-seven Pentagon and NASA computers, deleting files and shutting down the networks of entire military bases. Another was Julian Assange, founder of WikiLeaks which had published hundreds of thousands of secret US documents, who faced charges of sexual assault in Sweden. Both became celebrated causes among their supporters, many of whom vented a particular kind of fury on Starmer after assuming he would be on their side. McKinnon's mother confronted him outside a meeting in Parliament and was taken aback when he told her it was inappropriate to discuss the case and walked away. 'I couldn't understand it,' she later wrote. 'Keir Starmer had written six books on human rights. I had such faith and expected so much more of him as DPP.'

Thin threads

In the years since, Starmer has tried repeatedly to explain that such criticism fundamentally misunderstands the role of the CPS. 'People thought I had discretion to choose whether to extradite people according to what I was feeling,' he says, 'but that discretion just doesn't exist.' In these cases, the CPS can only decide if a threshold of evidence has been met for the accused to go in front of a judge, who will then determine whether or not they are extradited. 'Unlike decisions about prosecutions,' he asserts, 'the public interest does not come into these cases – that's up to politicians.' Indeed, McKinnon's extradition to the US was eventually blocked by the home secretary Theresa May on the grounds, she said, it would be incompatible with his human rights because 'he has Asperger's syndrome and suffers from depressive illness'.

All these controversies have nonetheless been woven together with some thin threads into a left-wing conspiracy theory in which Starmer is presented as an agent of the security state or even Anglo-American intelligence organisations. Such claims are, of course, impossible either to prove or disprove completely, which is why they make insidiously effective smears. If you try to deny being part of a secret organisation, a dedicated conspiracy theorist will reply with the time-old, 'You would say that, wouldn't you?'

The claims have flickered across a mainstream media still largely reluctant to publish allegations that are obviously untrue. If they appear in newspapers or broadcast media, it is usually obliquely, followed by phrases like 'go look it up'. But they nonetheless continue to find their full expression online.

Starmer's mutually respectful relationship with Eric Holder, US attorney general in Barack Obama's administration, has been portrayed by some as being at the heart of a sinister Establishment plot. As a veteran of the civil rights movement and the first African American to hold the post, Holder seems an unusual villain for the left, but that hasn't stopped a precarious connection being drawn between his regular meetings with Starmer, the CPS's handling of Assange's potential extradition to Sweden and the WikiLeaks founder's decision to spend much of the period holed up in Ecuador's London embassy as a political refugee from alleged US persecution. There has been talk of files going missing and still more about why a document on Starmer's meeting with Holder in November 2011 was redacted. Patrick Stevens, head of international at the CPS during that time, was in most of Starmer's meetings with Holder. 'They were focused on improving how we each worked and exploring the latest developments or priorities in prosecuting serious crime. It was just good and sensible core business with one of our most important international partners,' he says. 'The idea that Keir flew to the US to carve up some grubby little deal is ludicrous … it's also just not who he is or how he would operate.'

It is a claim corroborated by Amy Jeffress, the US Department of Justice official who liaised with Starmer and was present at the November 2011 meeting. She says an extradition request for Assange was not discussed in 2011 – or at any time 'during Keir's tenure as DPP'. She adds: 'Julian Assange was not indicted by the United States until 2018, well after Keir Starmer left his position.'

In any case, for an Establishment plot to frame someone like Assange to work, it would have had to involve not only Starmer and Holder, but the judge who heard the evidence, an independent CPS inspectorate, the Court of Appeal and the Supreme Court in Britain, not to mention the American judges and juries for any eventual trial in the United States. As Starmer himself points out drily when asked about the allegations, 'That would've had to be really quite a big conspiracy, wouldn't it?'

Another element to heat the depths of the internet has been the CPS's decision not to prosecute MI5 and MI6 personnel for their alleged role in helping torture terror suspects held by the American military at sites in Afghanistan, Pakistan and Morocco. The not-quite smoking gun appears to be the disclosure that Starmer went to a 'networking reception' for Foreign Office ministers and later attended a farewell party for Jonathan Evans, who was retiring as head of MI5. Evans has no recollection of even speaking to the DPP on that occasion, which has not stopped one website recounting the event in a style usually reserved for meetings among spies in murky underground car parks. 'The fact the drinks were listed in Starmer's hospitality register also indicates they were paid for by MI5,' it says, and – drum roll – 'Starmer states that the value of the drinks bought for him is "unknown".'

One of the few hard facts to appear in such theories is that he later delivered a speech to the Trilateral Commission, an organisation the fringes of both far right and far left politics allege has links to the CIA and represents an undemocratic global elite. More than one exponent of the so-called 'Truther Movement' has accused it of staging the 9/11 attacks on America to bring about a 'new world order'.

The reality, once again, is less dramatic. John Kerr, the man who ran the British end of the commission at the time, and a crossbench peer and former head of the Diplomatic Service, says it is a rather benign institution set up in the 1970s by Zbigniew Brzezinski, national security adviser to President Jimmy Carter, a Cold War project to foster better understanding between Japan, America and Europe. 'If there was some secret slush fund from the CIA or any other intelligence service, I'm afraid I never saw it,' says Kerr. 'I was always having to beg the business people who came along to pay for our events.' He remembers inviting Starmer to be a guest speaker on the subject of Brexit in 2017 and him doing a very good speech, but he says the idea that Starmer is 'part of some sort of secret society for world government is, quite frankly, bollocks'.

Such an epithet might also be applied to another ingredient in the left's conspiracy soup about Starmer's time as DPP. According to one writer, he developed 'a particularly close relationship with *The Times*', described as a newspaper owned by Rupert Murdoch that would later play 'a key role in sabotaging Jeremy Corbyn' with leaks from intelligence agencies. The claim seems once more to be based largely on the register of hospitality Starmer diligently filled in when at the CPS, revealing he met the newspaper's crime and legal correspondents for lunches in 2011, and went to its Christmas drinks party. But few are really going to be shocked he would meet such journalists, go to one of the endless parties that media organisations host, or write occasional articles for *The Times*.*

And it is difficult to ignore one particular fact about Starmer's actions that same year of 2011 suggesting that, far from getting into a sticky embrace with Murdoch's newspapers, he was about to go into battle against them. After losing faith in the Metropolitan Police investigations, the DPP ordered a complete review of thousands of pages of evidence about the 'illegal interceptions of communications'. Within days, Andy Coulson, the former *News of the World* editor who had latterly been David Cameron's head of communications in Downing Street, resigned, along with the commissioner of the Met.

The subsequent police investigation became the biggest in history and the scandal rolled on for the rest of Starmer's term as DPP amid disclosures that the murdered teenager Millie Dowler, as well as victims of the 7/7 terror attacks on London, had been the target of hacking. Murdoch closed the *News of the World* and made a humiliating public apology for a scandal that is said to have cost his media group more than £1 billion in compensation and legal fees. So many journalists were arrested that Starmer had to publish new guidelines saying prosecutors should take a 'broad approach' in deciding if it was in the public interest to put them on trial.

More than half a dozen of Murdoch's former employees, including Coulson, together with nine police officers, were eventually convicted for phone hacking or bribing public officials. Rebekah

---

* For the sake of full disclosure, this book is being published by HarperCollins, a subsidiary of Rupert Murdoch's NewsCorp, while its author worked for *The Times* between 1999 and 2010.

Brooks, however, was among those acquitted. After an expensive trial she was then swiftly re-hired by Murdoch to run his media operation in Britain.

Since then, there have been claims that the prosecutions were politically motivated. Neil Wallis has said the charges formed part of an organised Labour Party attack on Murdoch and his Conservative-supporting newspapers. A former *News of the World* executive editor, himself cleared of phone hacking, Wallis has alleged this was spearheaded by the party's future deputy leader Tom Watson and linked to Starmer as DPP who would soon be a 'rising star' in Labour.

In the wake of Brooks' acquittal, Starmer said he respected the jury's verdict but defended the decision to prosecute her, saying: 'Before this trial, there was a feeling that journalists were above the law. I don't think there is that feeling any more … There was a case to answer, so it was a perfectly good case to bring.'

His subsequent interactions with at least a few of the journalists working for Murdoch's newspapers have, however, had an air of threat hanging over them. Jonny Cooper once suggested that Starmer felt he had become a target following the phone-hacking scandal. 'He wasn't going to be intimidated or knocked off course,' said his friend from Doughty Street Chambers, 'but he was aware of the fact that there would be people who then became much more interested in him.' Indeed, it's not too hard to pick up a sense of lasting resentment, even enmity, towards Starmer from some senior figures at News UK. One executive who has since left the organisation went into print to urge Labour to remove him as party leader and make clear Starmer had not been forgiven for being in charge of the CPS when journalists from the *Sun* were put on trial. This was Tom Newton Dunn, who used a newspaper column in 2021 to imply Starmer had made matters worse for himself by failing to accept terms for peace.

'Just after he was elected to Parliament in 2015, two senior *Sun* executives offered Keir lunch in Westminster to suggest a truce,' wrote Newton Dunn. 'It was suggested to him that he might like to apologise to the journalists whose lives he'd unlawfully turned upside down. Starmer said he would consider it. The apology never came.'

Asked about the prosecutions now, Starmer says: 'When we decided to prosecute journalists over phone-hacking and the practice of paying police and public officials for information, we once again applied a strict test of whether there was a realistic chance of securing a conviction. To do anything else would have been to embark on a very slippery slope. We were trying to balance the right to privacy with the freedom of the press. But it was clear we were dealing with vested interests who were very used to getting their way. Some of the individuals involved were among the most powerful people in the country.'

Indeed, the CPS felt pressure to remove Alison Levitt, his principal legal adviser, from overseeing the prosecutions on the grounds she might be biased because her private life had already been trawled over in the newspapers. 'It got quite heated,' says Starmer. 'I would not alter those decisions. The rules should not be bent for anybody, whatever they do and however important they are.'

There are plenty of campaigners for press reform who have been disappointed since Starmer became leader that he hasn't taken a stronger stance in favour of greater regulation of the type suggested by the 2012 Leveson Report. Some of them have cited his attendance at News UK's summer parties as evidence of him reaching an accommodation with the Murdoch empire. A close ally of the Labour leader, however, points out he did not fly 'halfway round the world to bend his knee to Rupert', as Tony Blair famously did in 1995. Starmer doesn't show any sign of wanting to spend the election having a fight with the *Sun*, not least because it's a newspaper that has a record of supporting political leaders who win. In any case there are now probably bigger issues to do with the media, including the future of the BBC and how to stop the most harmful aspects of social media, than the exact system for newspapers handling complaints.

Perhaps the most substantial element in the left's conspiracy soup concerns the CPS's work in other countries during his time as DPP. The allegation is that he pioneered a form of 'lawfare' by building up the legal apparatus of authoritarian regimes around the world that were allied to the United States.

Patrick Stevens, who ran this programme and became a friend of Starmer, finds these claims as baffling as those about the then DPP's dealings with President Obama's administration over extraditions. He says the primary purpose of the network established across more than twenty-five countries by the CPS was to ensure serious crime abroad was more likely to be prosecuted and dealt with in fairer fashion.

'This helped protect Britain from cross-border criminals such as drug smugglers, people traffickers and terrorists. Serious crime almost always has an international element so working together is essential. We changed our organisation from one that simply reacted to crimes committed here to one that acted strategically and so reduced threats – or helped others deal with them where they occurred – before they reached our shores,' says Stevens.

As so often, the heat generated by conspiracy theories may have served merely to distract attention from what Stevens believes is a much more significant insight into the Labour leader. Starmer's record at the CPS not only shows that, unlike most opposition leaders, he has real experience in dealing with overseas governments, but also real evidence of the approach he might take to foreign policy in government. 'We weren't only reducing the threat to the UK, we were extending Britain's soft power by forging partnerships and spreading influence, as well as strengthening human rights globally, which I think is a good thing,' says Stevens. 'Our work was based on fundamental principles about justice and increasing transparency. By helping improve justice systems and develop the rule of law, we achieved things that were genuinely transformative and will stand the test of time. I'm really proud of that.'

He cites the way the CPS helped prevent suspects being subject to arbitrary arrest and facing trials based on forced or fabricated confessions by prosecuting them according to clear and consistent rules. 'We learned from the reforms that had made a difference in the UK over the last thirty years or so. Having independent prosecution services and agreed standards for charging people will improve things in those countries for generations to come. Even simple measures, like recording of interviews in the Caribbean, helped both convict the guilty and stop the innocent going to jail,' says Stevens.

Another example cited by him involves a visit to Albania, where Starmer demonstrated support for the country's prosecutor general who was under intense pressure from that country's government at a time when it was mired in allegations of corruption and links to organised crime. Stevens says the then DPP used a meeting with an Albanian minister and a live televised press conference to assert – 'respectfully but clearly and unequivocally' – the importance of prosecutors being independent from political interference. Stevens describes how the minister was 'furious' and 'it was without doubt the most explosive reaction to any meeting that we held internationally'. He adds that the British ambassador who was present had been 'delighted' by Starmer's intervention.

Ironically, this same example is used by Oliver Eagleton, in his biography of Starmer, to show that Keir was acting almost as a diplomatic representative of David Cameron's government in the pursuit of its political objectives back in Britain. The writer says later work by the CPS international division to tackle people-trafficking gangs and 'stem the flow of refugees into Britain' is also part of Starmer's legacy.

On this, Starmer's allies can justifiably reply, 'So what?' Being opposed to organised crime in Albania and people-trafficking gangs did not make him a patsy of Britain's Conservative government. Indeed, it forms a large part of a set of Labour policies for tackling illegal immigration which, compared to the current Tory proposal of flying asylum seekers to Rwanda, offer significantly better value for money and have the advantage of being within the bounds of Britain's international treaty obligations too.

Did Starmer become more sympathetic to institutions of the British state such as the police and security services than many people, including himself, had once expected? Undoubtedly, yes. But does that make him the pawn of some sinister and secret right-wing spy network? No.

There are valid arguments to be had about whether Starmer was too hard or soft at different times on crime. And there are plenty of criticisms that can be fairly levelled at him over this period of his life. Some suspect his political ambition meant he sought a higher media profile in certain cases than his role in them deserved. At the same time, his former allies on the left complain he let them down and changed his position on some issues. But too often such critiques are so blinkered about his motives, they miss other factors that altered his outlook.

There was, after all, another new and very real influence on his life during this period that changed him in ways no intelligence agency, police chief or newspaper proprietor ever could: he fell in love, got married and had children.

15

Family values

Love and Marriage

Before he met Victoria Alexander, Starmer had been through a series of serious and long-term relationships without ever fully settling down.

At university, and for a good while after, his girlfriend had been Angela O' Brien. Then there had been the Doughty Street barrister Phillippa Kaufmann, with whom he bought his first house. Later, he went out for more than three years with Julie Morris, an employment lawyer and former gymnast, who his friends remember performing handstands at parties.

'Keir was always so driven by work and questioned whether he would be able to give children the time he knows they deserve,' says John Murray. 'I thought this was a real shame because he is great with children. Then, when Vicky came on the scene, I knew this was different.'

Starmer prefers to call her Vic, but their first conversation, on the telephone, resulted in her calling him every name under the sun. She was a solicitor and he was a senior barrister obsessively checking if some documents prepared for a court case were accurate. 'Yes, of course, they are,' she told him. 'But are you sure?' he asked again. 'Yes, I'm certain,' she replied. Exasperated, she turned to colleagues sitting next to her as she put the phone down and said: 'Who the fuck does he think he is?'

There was an opportunity to find out a few weeks later when they were placed next to each other at a legal dinner. This time the conversation went well enough for Vic to share her vegetarian food with Starmer, who had been served meat. Later, they arranged to go for a drink sometime and, when they eventually got round to arranging something, Starmer not untypically suggested they meet in a pub.

These days, the Lord Stanley in Camden is known for doing decent food at a weekend. Back then, it really was just a pub. Their now-teenaged son has denounced it as the least romantic location for a first date he can imagine, but Starmer claims that Vic has come to his rescue with some faint praise: 'At least he walked me to the bus stop afterward and waved at me when it left, so he got a tick for that.'

She got used to his ways in the weeks that followed, with a courtship largely spent in a variety of other north London drinking spots. A highlight came at what Starmer termed one of the 'notorious parties' hosted by Jonny Cooper's father in his flat off Shaftesbury Avenue. When he introduced her to his friend, Jonny immediately took to Vic – he held her hand and took her into the front room to dance. 'I followed through about twenty minutes later,' says Starmer, 'to find Jonny standing on a glass coffee table, throwing Vic in the air and catching her.' Later, when Cooper had got to know her, he would tell Vic she had made Starmer complete.

Vic is about ten years younger than Starmer and grew up in the same corner of north London where they live now. Her mother was a community doctor who everyone seemed to know. Her sister is a teacher who once taught at Gospel Oak primary where Vic went before going to the nearby private day school of Channing.

Her father was born in England as part of a Jewish family who arrived from Poland before the Second World War. Although he doesn't talk much about what happened, she went on her own to the village near Kolo where the Jewish population had represented almost half of the local inhabitants before the Holocaust and met some people there who still remembered her family.

At Cardiff University, she studied law and sociology, then became president of the students' union, following in the footsteps of Neil Kinnock thirty years before, then worked as a volunteer at Tony Blair's campaign headquarters in 1997. Although someone often portrayed as a 'reluctant leader's wife' who pops up into the public eye once a year at party conferences, it's worth pointing out that she has a longer record of Labour Party activism than her husband. That doesn't mean she hankers after being a politician herself or wants to start doing media interviews or be seen 'hanging off Keir's arm' all the time for the photographers. She prefers to help in other ways and remain behind the scenes.

As a lawyer, Vic first worked at a firm in Soho that specialised in street crime and remembers meeting clients in police stations during the small hours of the morning but, by the time her relationship with Starmer began, she had moved into calmer and less emotionally draining work on fraud cases.

Yet, by all accounts, in those first months of their relationship they didn't talk much about politics or the law. Starmer realised he had found someone 'grounded, sassy, funny, street-wise – and utterly gorgeous too'. Pretty soon, they were together the whole time. On holiday in Greece, he spontaneously asked Vic to marry him, for once in his life not properly prepared. 'Won't we need a ring, Keir?' she answered. It was her way of saying yes.

They phoned her mother who shouted: 'Bernard! Get me a gin and tonic!' Starmer remembers going out for a pizza washed down by a bottle of pinot grigio that night, Vic's wine of choice and not the easiest to find in Santorini, he says, a touch defensively. The next morning, they went out and chose a ring together.

He brought Vic down to see his parents in Hurst Green a few days later, and she remembers Rod immediately asking his son the route they had taken. 'Why did you use the M25, Keir? Didn't you know that's always slow at this time of day?' Jo turned to her, eyes twinkling, and asked: 'Are you sure you want to marry a Starmer?' She was.

His friends organised a stag weekend at a hotel near Glastonbury, where one of them – Gordon Young – claimed they could get a discount because he knew the owner. For all the high-end hippy connotations of this part of Somerset, those present at this event say it mostly consisted of endless games of football. 'Some local kids asked whether we were okay because they thought we were too old to be playing,' says Murray. On the last night, they tried to find a nightclub but it turned out to be 'more like a village hall disco'.

They got married on May 6, 2007 at the Fennes Estate in Essex, a big affair with a couple of hundred guests including no fewer than four best men and the almost unprecedented sight of his father in a suit instead of his usual shorts and sandals as he wheeled Jo round. Ed Fitzgerald brought the house down with a gently mocking speech, apparently in the style of a Roman poet, that described dolphins dancing with joy in the Thames at the union of these two vegetarians. Vic welled up during her own, but got through it with everyone cheering and clapping her on. The groom addressed his speech just to his bride. 'I wanted Vic to know how much I thought of her, what I could see in her, the love I got from her,' he says.

There was a honeymoon on the Amalfi coast in Italy and, barely a year later in July 2008, a baby, their son, weighing a little over 8lb, screaming his head off and, 'for once, bang on time'. Although he'd been in a strictly supporting role during Vic's labour, he remembers afterwards the nurse plonking their boy in his arms and walking off, 'assuming I had some idea of what to do'. He had a baby outfit and some nappies ready, but says it must have taken him an hour to put them on him. 'My hands shook and my back was covered in sweat. There were a lot of buttons. Every time I moved one of his limbs, I thought I was going to break it or that social services would arrive and declare me an unfit parent.' He did things that first-time dads do, like driving home 'at about two miles per hour', putting him to sleep in a basket in the bedroom then 'waking up every thirty minutes to check he was okay'.

Three weeks after the birth Starmer was standing in his kitchen rehearsing the presentation for his final interview to be the next DPP, in front of his wife and son. Halfway through, the latter was copiously sick. It was, says the Labour leader now, some of the most honest feedback he has ever had from a live audience. He still got the job and had a three-month break before starting. They spent much of the summer pushing a pram round different London parks, taking delight in discovering new ones they had never heard of before, and using Vic's parents as a free baby-sitting service. She tells people that Starmer deserves credit for doing his bit with bottle-feeds and nappy-changing rather than 'pretending he was too important or busy'.

Other people's sons

Starmer remembers how, when his son was born, a friend sent him a celebratory card inscribed with the words 'and in that moment, everything changed'. It stuck with him because, in a way he could not have understood before, his life was different.

'There was now someone for whom I would unhesitatingly – without even thinking – throw myself in front of a speeding truck to protect' is the way he puts it. In contrast to his own distant relationship with his father, Starmer has repeatedly expressed his determination to know his children, 'to be around while they grow up'. And, if that might sound a bit banal to some, he also talks thoughtfully about the choices other parents have had to make or the pain they have gone through and how being a father has some-times given him insight into the decisions he has to make.

An early example, shortly after the birth of his son, involved a young rugby player called Daniel James, who had played for England as a teenager and looked set for a professional career until a scrum collapsed on him while training for Nuneaton. Paralysed from the chest down, unable to feed himself or go to the toilet, he couldn't face the prospect of living for another sixty years in a body he had decided was 'a prison'. But, as a quadriplegic, the only way he could end his life was to starve himself to death or go to Dignitas in Switzerland.

His parents tried to change his mind, promising to take him to watch rugby matches and making a chart listing something worth living for every day. In the end, though, none of it worked and they decided they had no option except to abide by his wishes. A month before Starmer started as DPP, Daniel's parents took him to Switzerland and were with him when he died. On their return home, they were questioned at length by the police and told they might be charged with the offence of assisting suicide, for which the sentence was up to fourteen years.

'I thought about what that must have been like for them and wondered what I would have done if that had been our son,' says Starmer. He found the transcript of the police interview with James's mother particularly hard to read. 'Didn't you think you might be committing a crime?' they asked. 'You just don't get it, do you?' she kept saying, 'he didn't want to live.'

Explaining his decision whether or not to prosecute, he says: 'The question that needs to be answered first is, do you have enough evidence for a realistic chance of a conviction? Then you ask, is it in the public interest to do so? In this case, there was plenty of evidence, but I didn't think Britain would be a better place if Daniel's parents were put on trial.'

This triggered a hotly contested debate as subsequent decisions not to prosecute in similar circumstances were condemned by everyone from faith leaders to Nadine Dorries. The DPP was accused of applying a new definition of the public interest and Starmer says he remembers getting 'all kinds of letters' with 'some accusing me of acting like a Nazi, others saying I was trying to be God'. He eventually published new guidelines for prosecutors that struck a balance between protecting vulnerable people from coercion at the end of their lives and allowing compassion for friends and families helping people take control when their life ends. Even so, he still thinks new legislation is needed and has indicated that a Labour government would make room in the parliamentary timetable for an 'Assisted Dying Bill'.

Another family's son whose case had tested Britain's system of justice, in very different fashion, was Stephen Lawrence. When Starmer took over as DPP, fully fifteen years had passed since an unprovoked racist attack had left this teenaged boy bleeding to death on a south London street. Some of the suspects had been put on trial but no one had been convicted of killing him. A glimmer of hope came after a team of police investigators reviewing the murder file discovered new forensic evidence involving tiny specks of blood and microscopic fibres missed in the original investigation. Starmer decided to make use of a new law that allowed, in exceptional circumstances, the CPS to prosecute someone cleared of an offence a second time. Much of the liberal left, including esteemed human rights colleagues, were up in arms about this breach of the so-called 'double-jeopardy principle'. But Starmer says: 'If ever a case proved the need for this reform, it was surely the Stephen Lawrence murder. It meant we had a chance to go after his killers again.'

He remembers having 'agonised discussions' with Doreen Lawrence, who'd been campaigning for justice ever since her son's murder, before deciding whether this was the right moment to use her one shot at getting it. In the end, they decided they had enough evidence to justify a fresh prosecution and Starmer himself made the application to the Court of Appeal, asking a judge to quash Gary Dobson's previous acquittal. Together with David Norris, another of the original suspects, Dobson was put on trial again and – finally – found guilty of Stephen's murder.

Other people's daughters

By then, Starmer's own family had expanded again, with the arrival of a baby girl in November 2010. 'From the get go,' he says, 'it was pretty obvious she was going to have me wrapped around her little finger, and that grip has only tightened with every day that has passed since.'

Vic's waters had broken a week earlier than expected and he remembers racing to get her to hospital, then frantically running along corridors trying to find doctors and nurses.

An immediate consequence of this last-minute scramble was that he'd had to cancel a string of meetings at the CPS, one of them with the parents of a girl called Jane Clough. Like his own daughter, she was a second child. Like her mother and his, she had worked as an NHS nurse. And like him now, she had a baby daughter.

In July that year, she'd turned up for the night shift at Blackpool's Victoria Hospital to find her violent ex-partner waiting for her in the car park. After he stabbed her seventy-one times, witnesses said they saw Jonathan Vass walk away, then come back to slit her throat.

Penny and John Clough were angry and blamed the legal system for letting their daughter down. Starmer had agreed to see them despite the reservations of his officials, who feared meeting a family upset over the way their case had been handled was setting an unhelpful precedent. But he insisted on the appointment being put back in his diary when he returned to work. The meeting lasted more than two hours and, he recalls, 'I didn't say much.'

Starmer describes the story they told him that day as 'horrifying'. Jane had been heavily pregnant when Vass raped her, two months before her baby was due. He raped her again repeatedly, even with her six-week-old baby daughter in the same room. After she summoned up the courage to report him to the police, Vass was arrested and charged but released on bail just twelve days later, despite both police prosecutors telling the judge there was a real risk he might harm Jane and her baby.

Vass proved a threat to her whole family. After murdering their daughter, he was found by police near the Cloughs' home with a car full of cans of petrol. He pleaded guilty to murder and was jailed for thirty years, but the Cloughs faced a further injustice. When sentencing Vass, the judge had taken the rape charges into account and so, at least in a strict legal sense, there was little point in going ahead with his trial for those offences. However, it made no sense at all to Jane's parents to be told the rape charges would 'lie on the file'. Her mother said: 'We were told he felt it wasn't in the public interest. How can that be so? If someone is a rapist, it is very much in the public interest. Jane paid with her life for the right to have these charges heard. For her sake, justice should be seen to be done, and he should stand trial for rape.'

Starmer promised to help, even though it meant disturbing the equilibrium within the CPS. 'The first instinct of an organisation when it's challenged in this way is often to defend what it's done so far,' he says. 'But this was one of the occasions when something wrong needed to be put right.'

It was far from being the first time he had seen the impact that rape and murder have on families. Years earlier, he and Jonny Cooper had fought a case on behalf of Irene Ivison whose daughter, Fiona, had been horribly manipulated by pimps as a fourteen-year-old before being killed by one of her abusers. Starmer admits he doesn't know if being a father himself was why he pushed so hard on the Clough case, but says: 'My meeting with the Cloughs came so close to the birth of our own daughter that it left me feeling torn up. And, in contrast to when I was a young lawyer working with Irene Ivison, this time I was in a better position to do something.'

He issued new guidance to prosecutors so that what went to court reflected the true depth of the criminality and that legal deals to let rape charges 'lie on file' would be the exception rather than the rule. Giving prosecutors a way of appealing against potentially dangerous defendants such as Vass being allowed out on bail, however, required – in Starmer's words – 'us to roll up our sleeves' to change the law. He is careful not to exaggerate his role in the Cloughs' subsequent campaign, although after Parliament wobbled over whether the CPS really needed this new power, he intervened directly to tell MPs it was both necessary and would not be misused.

Every year, on his daughter's birthday, Starmer marks that first missed meeting with the Cloughs by sending them a message to say he's thinking of them. For a Labour leader often said to lack passion, there was some real emotional connection in the room when he told their story to his party conference in 2021. When he then pointed out his 'good friends' the Cloughs sitting at the front of the audience, who by then had tears streaming down their faces, the hall rose as one for a standing ovation.

Their experience crystallised what he has since said was a growing realisation in him that the criminal justice system was failing victims. In the face of stiff resistance from officials at the CPS, he introduced a 'Victims' Right to Review', enabling thousands of people each year who were unhappy with a decision not to proceed with a prosecution to demand a second opinion without having to go through a long and costly legal challenge.

The injustice faced by victims was also beginning to alter his view about the role of the state. Instead of human rights and civil liberties merely protecting the individual from abuses of power like false imprisonment or torture, he emphasised that victims had a right to 'call on the state to take steps to protect them'.

This new belief found expression again a few months after his meeting with the Cloughs, with the prosecution of a dozen Asian men who had sexually exploited or raped young girls in Rochdale. Given some of the racially charged commentary about 'grooming scandals' since, it's worth pointing out that the impetus for these prosecutions came from the CPS team for north-west England led by Nazir Afzal, a British Muslim of Pakistani descent. But the story's relevance here is what it shows about the way Starmer takes decisions.

Afzal initially needed to talk to him about the prosecution because it was almost unprecedented in its scale and would mean reversing a previous decision in the case of one defendant. He was worried that the head of the CPS would be defensive or concerned it would embarrass the organisation, but says Starmer's priority was to rectify mistakes. 'Look, that can't be the only one we got wrong,' he told Afzal. 'What about the other cases that didn't get to the stage where we prosecuted?'

A panel comprised of police and prosecutors looked at dozens of cases dating back ten or even twenty years, extending out across other towns and cities, from Rotherham to Swansea and Oxford to Glasgow, and revealed that when women and girls had gone to the police, too often they were not being taken seriously.

'As I started reading through the files,' says Starmer, 'it became clear to me that the system was not working properly. We had good prosecutors and decent police officers. But they were asking, "Will this case succeed in front of a jury?" or "Will they make convincing witnesses?"' Usually these girls were from working-class backgrounds. Some had been in trouble with the police and had problems with drugs or alcohol. Often they had not reported rapes to the police immediately or had gone back to their abusers. 'The police were saying, "They will get slaughtered if we put them up to give evidence in the witness box." The problem was we were looking for "the perfect victim" and, almost always, that was not going to include the most vulnerable people most in need of protecting.'

The injustice didn't stop when the cases got to court. Afzal has described how one of the girls in the Rochdale trial had to give evidence for six days, during which she was cross-examined by eleven barristers, nine of them calling her a liar 'over and over again'. Starmer illustrates the point with a story about an event he attended organised by the charity Rape Crisis. 'We were told to shut our eyes and think about the best sexual experience we'd ever had. It was a bit awkward but most of us did it,' he says. When the participants were allowed to open their eyes again, they had to tell the person sitting on their left what they had been thinking about. 'The consternation that ensued showed us all that, if we couldn't tell a colleague about a positive experience, it must be a hundred times harder telling someone you've never met before about the worst and most degrading experience of your life.'

The other difference, as Starmer swiftly goes on to say, is that 'rape is not about sex, it's about violence, control and power'. And the grotesque, gold tracksuit-clad embodiment of that was Jimmy Savile: a star presenter at the BBC; treated as a national treasure for his charity fundraising, a personal friend of Margaret Thatcher, senior police officers and the future king. He used this celebrity status to hide his predatory campaign of rape and sexual assault against hundreds of people, including dozens of children, some of them under ten years old and often the most vulnerable or power-less – precisely the kind of people ignored by the police or disbelieved by a jury.

When the horror of what Savile had done was exposed after his death in 2011, Starmer was still at the CPS. 'It was like a dam had burst and people rightly wanted to know why he had been able to get away with it for so long,' he says. It was then that he found out there had been four complaints made against Savile to police in Surrey and Sussex about his past abuse during 2007 and 2008. A decision had been taken against prosecuting him on the grounds that his victims themselves did not support court action and there was insufficient evidence. 'It never came close to crossing my desk and the local CPS lawyer who looked at the case did not even mention the decision to his immediate boss because, to him, it seemed routine,' says Starmer now.

This was precisely the kind of culture among prosecutors he had been trying to change. Alison Levitt, his chief legal adviser at the CPS, had designed a new approach for rape cases that focused more on the credibility of the allegation rather than that of the witness. Designated units staffed by specially trained officers were set up to deal with these cases and the cross-examination of victims in court had been made less adversarial, with time limits introduced on how long a witness had to give testimony.

When it emerged that investigations into Savile had not resulted in prosecutions, Starmer asked Levitt to conduct a full inquiry into what had gone wrong and whether further measures were needed. The story she uncovered showed police had warned victims that Savile was a powerful man whose lawyers would put them through the mangle if they went to court. One of the complainants was wrongly warned that her name would be in the newspapers; another was incorrectly informed she was 'the only one' making allegations. None were told, as they should have been, that there were other complaints against Savile being investigated.

Levitt didn't point the blame at any particular police officer or prosecutor. The problem was the system that, Starmer says, 'still had a blind spot when it came to protecting some of the people most in need of justice'. He published Levitt's report at the start of 2013 as he entered his final year as DPP, along with an apology on behalf of the CPS 'for shortcomings' for not doing enough to bring Savile to justice. He said it should be a 'watershed moment' and issued new guidance for prosecutors in sexual assault cases.

'We told prosecutors they should seek to build a case by looking harder at the credibility of the person accused and proceed with a prosecution if there was a reasonable chance of conviction,' says Starmer. 'It meant fewer vulnerable voices would be ignored and other victims would be given the chance to speak.'

Falsehoods and truths

In the years afterwards, high-profile members of the Establishment, ranging from former cabinet ministers such as Leon Brittan to the retired army general Edwin Bramall, found themselves falsely accused of being part of a murderous and child-abusing sex ring.

One, the ex-Tory MP Harvey Proctor, contemplated suicide and has since sought to lay the blame for his ordeal at Starmer's door: 'As DPP, Sir Keir's job was to uphold the law. Instead, he overturned the basic principle of innocence until proven guilty. He did not just overturn it; he shattered it and contributed to the inducement of a moral panic.'

Given that Proctor is concerned about truth, it is a big charge to make. Starmer was no longer the DPP at the time and the allegations, which were only ever investigated by the police, did not even reach prosecutors. When asked about them, Starmer slightly wearily emphasises that the guidelines he issued at the CPS 'never said the accuser should always be believed'. But he also acknowledges that 'unfair and unjustified harm' was inflicted on Proctor because police investigators had 'oversteered' to correct mistakes made in the past.

Nonetheless, the decisions made during his time at the CPS will remain both a subject for justifiable scrutiny and a likely source of more scurrilous claims in the lead-up to the next election. In the summer of 2023, for instance, *The Times* was briefed that Rishi Sunak planned to be 'more personal in his attacks on Sir Keir Starmer, particularly over his record as Director of Public Prosecutions [and] the failure to prosecute Jimmy Savile'.

On the face of it, this would be a bizarre course of action for Sunak to take, not least because he publicly criticised one of his immediate predecessors for trying to do just that. In the latter stages of his premiership, while beginning to slip and slide on his own contradictions, Boris Johnson used a House of Commons debate to say Starmer had spent his time as head of the CPS 'prosecuting journalists and failing to prosecute Jimmy Savile'. The then prime minister had every reason to know this to be untrue because he had been told so by his advisers, one of whom promptly resigned after he failed to issue a full apology. Asked about Johnson's remarks at a press conference, Sunak, who was then still chancellor in Johnson's government, replied: 'Being honest, I wouldn't have said it.'

And yet the reason this smear may yet resurface is that subsequent polling showed 87 per cent of voters had heard Johnson's claim, with one in five members of the public saying it was 'probably true'. Although twice as many thought the claim 'probably false', a similar proportion of voters said they were 'unsure'. Nor was Johnson's attack the first of its kind. Conservative MPs had previously been criticised for sharing a video that had been doctored to make it look like Starmer endorsed the old guidelines for prosecuting grooming gangs instead of reforming them.

The rougher end of political strategy has always held that if 'you fling enough mud some of it will stick'. And, these days, the most toxic forms of it lodge in the crevices of social media platforms that seem either unable or unwilling to remove it.

Just a few days after Johnson made his remarks about Starmer failing to prosecute Savile, the Labour leader was walking past a group of 'anti-vax' protesters. On seeing him, some started climbing over security barriers and, for a few seconds, he was surrounded, before being bundled into the safety of a police car. In the way that conspiracy theories cross-contaminate each other, some were heard shouting about Julian Assange and others about Jimmy Savile. A few screamed 'Paedo protector!', words Starmer had never heard hurled at him before Johnson himself effectively had done so from the government dispatch box in the House of Commons.

The Conservative Party has made no secret that it will continue to dig for dirt in Starmer's record at the CPS and, to some extent, that is just politics. If a former head of criminal prosecutions was Tory leader, Labour would probably do the same. In January 2024, there were demands he should apologise for failing to intervene against private prosecutions brought by the Post Office in the Horizon scandal, even though he didn't have such a power. In three cases of sub-postmasters prosecuted by the CPS when he was in charge, Starmer has said he wasn't aware of them and doesn't know if they had anything to do with Horizon. And on it goes. But the former DPP points out that it's hard to hide a mistake. Every prosecution goes to court, where judges will throw out cases if they find there is insufficient evidence, so there is a judicial test at the start of every trial – whether or not it results in a conviction

– about whether the CPS was justified in deciding to prosecute. Starmer considers this just one of a number of 'auto-corrects built into the system'. Others include the right of offenders to appeal, the right he introduced for victims to demand a review if there isn't a prosecution and, on top of all that, the CPS being subject to an independent inspectorate which can call in any case at any time.

'I'm not saying we never made a mistake because, of course, there will be poor decisions in an organisation dealing with hundreds of thousands of cases,' says Starmer. 'But I never took one in bad faith. I certainly don't lie awake at night worrying they will find a file where I said, "Don't prosecute him because he's my mate or something" because it just doesn't exist.'

A more nuanced argument put forward by some Conservatives is that, although he wasn't involved in decisions such as Savile, he should still be held to account for the culture of the organisation he ran. The Labour leader is on record as saying he takes 'full responsibility for every decision of the Crown Prosecution Service when I was director of public prosecutions'.

One Tory MP has said that, just as Johnson was held responsible for the lockdown parties held in Downing Street when he was prime minister, the Labour leader now 'can't feign outrage at the same standards being applied to him'. The problem with this line of attack is that his term as DPP was judged to be very successful by the Tory government. Ministers signed off a report from the House of Commons Home Affairs Select Committee – then chaired by a Labour MP but with a government majority – commending the work he had done on grooming scandals. 'Mr Starmer has striven to improve the treatment of victims of sexual assault within the criminal justice system throughout his term,' it said. Theresa May, then home secretary, took him out to dinner to thank him for his service. Dominic Grieve, the Tory attorney general who at the start of Starmer's tenure had rebuked him for being too political, was pouring praise on him by the end of it, and gave a speech at his

leaving party that described him as 'one of the most successful
directors of recent years'.

He says: 'I found him to be highly effective and someone who
always behaved with great integrity.' Grieve points out that his
cabinet colleagues were not 'complaining about what an awful DPP
we've got'. Although Starmer had made clear that he would not
seek a second term at the CPS, Grieve says: 'I would definitely have
reappointed him, of course I would. And I don't think anyone else
in government would have had any basis for taking a contrary view.
For them to turn around now and attempt to muckrake his time as
DPP is really infantile behaviour, completely unjustified and just a
load of rubbish. It won't work and I fear attacking public servants
in this way will backfire badly on the Conservative Party.'

Grieve is an old-fashioned, patrician Tory who subsequently fell
out with both his government and his party over Brexit. Although
disagreeing with many Labour policies, he has not ruled out voting
for Starmer whose 'personal integrity', he thinks, stands in stark
contrast to 'what we've seen in recent years'. And, if his former
DPP lacks some of the star power of other politicians, Grieve says:
'So did Clement Attlee, of course. And he turned out to be a very
good prime minister.'

Yet some of the admiration Starmer attracted from Conservative
ministers like Grieve can be attributed to the way he implemented
austerity cuts of almost 27 per cent in the CPS's budget, reducing
the workforce by a quarter. Starmer himself set an example two
years into his term by getting rid of the chauffeur-driven government car that came with the job and which officials had previously
insisted was necessary for his personal security.

'In some ways, that focus on saving money helped us become
more efficient and spurred on modernisation,' says Starmer now.
The problem was that after they had trimmed out any remaining
fat, the government 'took out the bone saw'. He thinks the criminal justice system and the courts probably seemed a soft target.
'They began to tear up lots of things I thought were pretty funda-

mental, in terms of how the country had been run since the Second World War, without trying to make them better in any way.

'It meant people couldn't afford representation in court after budgets for legal aid were slashed. They couldn't get a court date because of a huge backlog of cases. They saw people who had committed crimes against them walking around their communities because justice had been delayed – and they felt that meant justice was also being denied.'

Starmer once said the law shouldn't be regarded as a 'rigid framework', but as something that should 'bend to justice', yet by the time his five-year term as DPP was over, he had become convinced that being on the inside of government still wasn't enough to bend that long arc if he was on the outside of political decisions.

'I saw the limits of legal justice,' he says. 'I wanted to move on from arguing about, interpreting and implementing the law, to being part of the Parliament – and hopefully the government – that makes law. I had a sense that to fix problems you had to pull levers only politicians could do. I wanted to be part of making social justice.

'I wanted to be a Labour MP.'

Part IV

Standing

From becoming an MP to
becoming leader

16

Putting the rubbish out

At around seven most Wednesday mornings, the leader of His Majesty's Opposition can be seen barefoot in a T-shirt outside his house, carrying out bins filled with rotten vegetables, old newspapers, plastic wrappings and an empty bottle or two.

Five hours later the same man is at the dispatch box in the House of Commons buttoned up in a suit and tie for Prime Minister's Questions – 'PMQs'. Neither task, at opposite ends of his morning, is the kind he relishes. But Starmer acknowledges they both serve a purpose.

Like most leaders of the opposition before him – and, for that matter, prime ministers – Starmer admits he doesn't much look forward to these noon-time confrontations on Wednesdays.

This one is on November 9, 2022. Even after Starmer has done the bins and downed his first cup of strong tea, it's still dark outside. Last night, Gavin Williamson quit the government over leaked messages showing he'd berated a colleague for not getting him an invite to the Queen's funeral and told a civil servant to 'slit his throat'. It's the first resignation from Rishi Sunak's cabinet but the third time Williamson has been forced out, for a variety of misdemeanours under three different Tory prime ministers in as many years.

On Starmer's glass kitchen table, next to a fresh pile of that day's newspapers, is a printout of the six questions he was planning to ask Sunak, intended to open up a debate on the direction of the economy. But Williamson is the biggest political story of the day and Starmer knows he can't afford to spurn a gilt-edged opportunity to insert himself into the lunchtime and evening news bulletins.

Before long, the sound of feet on floorboards can be heard from upstairs. First down is Starmer's son, who waves one arm at his dad and uses the other to switch on the TV. Vic arrives next, fries an egg and hands it wordlessly to the teenager, who is now watching *The Simpsons*. With a little roll of her eyes, she points out how breakfast on the sofa had been a privilege allowed during Covid that now seems to have become 'a right'.

Last to appear in the kitchen is their daughter with her hair in new plaits. 'Did you do them yourself?' asks her father. 'No,' she replies, frowning. 'Who does that?' There is a brief conversation about her pet hamster who is called Bear and has been a recent gift from her parents in an effort to appease growing demands for a dog. Starmer finds some of her homework in the middle of his own papers, leaves it on the table, and goes upstairs to change. When he re-emerges, it's pointed out he's wearing his son's school blazer. 'I thought it felt tighter than usual,' says the Labour leader as he hands it over and adds: 'That could have gone badly wrong for both of us.'

At 7.40, he is out of the house and the cocoon of family life. The photographer who was outside earlier has gone by the time Starmer climbs into the back of a waiting SUV, its front seats filled by personal protection officers. They were assigned to him by the Home Office in 2020 because of unspecified but credible threats. They go everywhere he goes, including on holidays or even down the pub. When he takes Vic out to a restaurant for their wedding anniversary, they're sat at the next table. But they also act as a bridge between his old life and the one he has now. Some of Starmer's aides suspect he gets on better with these 'PPOs' than with them.

On this Wednesday, he is being guarded by a pair of football fans he's got to know well. One supports Chelsea and Starmer talks to him, with sympathy rather than triumph, about top-of-the-table

Arsenal's one-nil victory last Sunday at Stamford Bridge, where they were both in the directors' box. The other is a Spurs fan who, Starmer says, 'has been giving me no trouble this season'.

The journey into Westminster takes him through his constituency and Starmer puts his notes to one side and starts enthusiastically pointing out blocks of flats where he has taken on cases, first as a lawyer and only later as a politician. Within a few minutes, the car is in Trafalgar Square and heading down Whitehall past Downing Street on his right. Starmer allows himself a sideways glance at the prime minister's residence, 'more out of habit than anything'. Then the gates of Parliament swing open and, once out of the car, he slips more fully into politician mode, saying hello to anyone walking by and, as he grabs a takeaway coffee from Portcullis House, waving at his friend in the 'vote office' who stands behind a high stack of that day's *Hansard*.

After bounding up two flights of stairs to the leader of the opposition's suite in the Norman Shaw South Building, formerly the home of Scotland Yard, Starmer shuts himself away again. He likes to spend thirty minutes on his own in his office at the start of each day to think things through. 'It's the lawyer in me, wanting to be sure of what I'm doing, I suppose.' He keeps an immaculately tidy desk. There are no mounds of paper, just a few family photos and whatever the task is in hand. On the walls are a picture of the black cat statues that guard the entrance to the old Carreras Cigarette Factory at Mornington Crescent in his constituency, as well as a landscape that reminds him of childhood holidays in the Lake District. There are a few books on the shelves behind him but he insists not too much can learned from their titles. From his window he can see the brown water of the Thames flowing fast under Westminster Bridge and out towards the sea.

On this Wednesday morning, one of his senior advisers, Paul Ovenden, has sent through the draft of a new set of questions. He has spotted that the letter Sunak sent last night expressed 'great sadness' to Williamson over the resignation, before thanking him for his 'loyalty'. One question is about how the civil servant who was told to slit his throat should feel about Sunak feeling such a deep sense of loss over his 'loyal' friend. There is another line Starmer likes because it tries to move the debate from Westminster into the real-world experiences of people at work. It says everyone knows someone like Williamson, 'a middle manager getting off on intimidating those beneath him' – then adds they also know someone like the prime minister, 'the boss who is so weak and so worried that the bullies will turn on him that he hides behind them'.

All of which will play well into what the media has been saying about the resignation. Starmer worries, though, that it's still too knockabout and wonders aloud if this is a chance to tell a 'bigger story'.

Just after 9 a.m. he goes into the office boardroom to work on the questions with his team. On one side of the room is a fireplace flanked by Union flags besides which Starmer does many of his TV interviews; on the other are more windows looking out across the river. Running down the centre of the room is a long table lined by high-backed chairs.

Sitting on the left is Stuart Ingham, his policy director. Next to him is the head of domestic policy, Muneera Lula, a 'defector' from the civil service, then Jenny Chapman, a long-time parliamentary ally who is now in the House of Lords and says she takes pride in not 'sugar-coating' her advice. Opposite are Ovenden and Kate Robson, who works for Angela Rayner. The Labour leader himself stands in shirtsleeves at a lectern at one end of the table; at the other is Tom Webb, the deputy policy director, who plays the part of Rishi Sunak in rehearsals.

At 10.30 they practise some rebuttals and do a run-through of the final questions, but he doesn't like to rehearse too much. One of his aides tells him to put more dramatic emphasis on the words 'slit their throat' because that's the quote the news bulletins will pick up. Starmer pauses, frowns slightly, then nods as he makes a note.

At 11.50 he heads off to the Commons chamber with Rachel Reeves and Angela Rayner, passing through Portcullis House then up the back stairs into the chamber entrance behind the Speaker's chair. 'I don't have any superstitions, just habits, and one of them is to make sure I'm in place before the prime minister so that I can watch him come in,' he says.

These days, he's up against Sunak, who he thinks is probably a nice enough person but too weak to stand up to the urges of his party. He's noticed how often the prime minister turns away at the dispatch to address Tory MPs 'as if they're the only audience that matter'.

The mayhem begins with Starmer's first question and usually lasts for about ten minutes, amid the noise of the orchestrated barracking that has been known to reach decibel levels higher than those hit by Deep Purple when they were 'the loudest rock band in the world'.

Starmer admits that sometimes neither he nor Sunak can hear what the other is saying and their exchanges become a kind of dialogue of the deaf. Most of this isn't picked up on TV because broadcasters have microphones suspended from the ceiling that amplify the voice of whoever is speaking and cancel out some of the shouting. 'If someone's screaming at you, your instinct is to pause and stare at them,' he says. 'But you have to learn to keep talking, otherwise it just looks like you've stopped for no reason.'

The Labour leader's dislike of PMQs is not just because of the ordeal of having to stand in front of a bank of rival MPs, some of whom seem so hostile they might be insane. He goes further than most party leaders in pointing out he's not a career politician and says he feels an aversion for what he has called the 'shallow men and women of Westminster'.

At first glance, such a stance might resemble that of populists from both left and right who spend their time railing against out-of-touch elites or claiming to be outsiders who will clean up the mess and 'drain the swamp'.

But Starmer is no populist. Instead, his distaste for certain aspects of politics appears to have more to do with the lack of seriousness in the way it is conducted or how often posturing is mistaken for principles and fandom for action. The weekly theatrics on display at PMQs, accompanied by noises that other functioning systems of democracy around the world manage to do without, mean anger and drama generally get reported ahead of substance, says Starmer, as well as symbolising what he calls Britain's 'tribal' and 'adversarial' political culture. 'I still find very hard to understand why so many people think it's so important to be shouting very loudly to impress other people who think, Wow! That's really passionate! They all go home saying that's been a huge day while I'm left scratching my head because none of that has changed anything.'

Starmer particularly despised the way Boris Johnson used to catch his eye with what he calls an 'it's-all-a-bit-of-a-joke expression' and challenges the notion that politics is a game. 'It isn't,' he says, 'because livelihoods – and sometimes even lives – are at stake … Twelve o'clock every Wednesday we have this slanging match but people watching at home must sometimes think, What's the point of this?'

Although opinion polls suggest the public seem to agree with his view about such antics, they also seem to know enough about these weekly clashes to form an opinion. According to one such survey, 54 per cent of voters had watched at least a clip of PMQs on the news or social media in the previous twelve months. Nothing else that happens in Parliament has that kind of consistent impact and, as such, Starmer accepts this weekly duel remains a crucial tool for the opposition to hold – or at least to be seen holding – the government to account.

And he really isn't bad at it. He has learned how to grab, hold and maybe sneak in a punch around the kidneys.

In his five-year transition from standing to be an MP to standing for the Labour leadership, practice and dutiful hard work have enabled him to become proficient at some of what he professes to dislike.

Indeed, he's become good enough at some of the baser forms of politics, you might be forgiven for thinking he's part of it. But he hasn't always been and, in his own mind at least, he still isn't.

This is another conundrum about Starmer. He sometimes seems to be reaching for something higher and more respectful. But he also knows that is both beyond his grasp and difficult to define, so he frowns and just gets on with the job.

'It is what it is,' he says grimly of the Wednesday PMQ ritual, 'and I don't see any prospect of it changing any time soon.'

In the same way that he dutifully puts some rubbish out on those mornings, he'll also deal with the side of politics that doesn't smell that sweet. He just does what has to be done.

17

Starting over

'Mr Everywhere'

When he decided against seeking a likely second term as director of public prosecutions in 2013, Starmer was already the wrong side of fifty. He had a mortgage to pay off and two small children to support. There really was no pressing need for a complete career change.

For a while, he resumed his career as a successful barrister back at Doughty Street, where there was talk of him going on to become a judge. With a knighthood about to be attached to his name and a blue-chip reputation in his field, Starmer could also have sought out some boardroom directorships or consultancies. All these options, as those closest to him gently suggested at the time, would mean a more comfortable life and less pain than that offered by politics.

He also knew that merely wanting to become an MP offered no guarantee of success. There are hundreds, if not thousands, of well-qualified people alive today who at some point have had parliamentary ambitions only to see them come to nothing. One Labour frontbencher says he would 'never have thought of quitting politics and becoming the chief prosecutor, but Keir thought nothing of doing that in reverse', before remarking with eyebrows arched, 'That takes quite a lot of self-belief.' Even some of Starmer's loyal and admiring friends wondered if he knew what he was doing.

'If this was a mid-life thing,' says one of them, 'he could have just bought himself a motorbike.'

As is so often the case with Starmer, however, he was already nearer his goal than it might have seemed. His time as DPP had given him the kind of public profile that has not only largely eluded his successors but also is a rarity among first-time political candidates. And he had established some very good connections too.

Quincy Whitaker, his colleague at Doughty Street, had introduced him five years earlier to an old friend of hers from school as 'someone who might want to be a Labour MP one day'. That friend was Ed Miliband, then a high-flying minister in Gordon Brown's government who would soon go on to be elected leader of the Labour Party. Recalling this first meeting with Starmer in 2008, Miliband says: 'He struck me as someone with deep values of integrity, decency and seriousness … he was a progressive who happened to be a lawyer not a lawyer who happened to be a progressive.'

They stayed in touch, not least because they live barely half a mile from each other, and Vic got on well with Justine Thornton, Miliband's barrister wife. In the years since Starmer has himself become Labour leader, there have been repeated reports that he is at loggerheads with him over the direction of the party, and that they have 'no great personal history or affinity'. This annoys them both because Miliband has probably known him for longer than almost any other MP and describes how his Arsenal-mad sons love discussing football with a man who definitely has a better understanding of the sport than he does. The ex-leader is close enough to the current one to echo a persistent complaint from Starmer's oldest friends that the media caricature is unfair. 'One of the things people don't see is his sense of humour,' says Miliband. For instance, in the summer of 2023, they met up for the York Rise street fair in Camden where, to the possible embarrassment of all involved, they found themselves watching the debut of a middle-aged punk band called Centrist Dad fronted by ITV's political editor Robert Peston, with Ed Balls, the former cabinet minister

and *Strictly Come Dancing* star, on drums. As Peston launched into
a Sex Pistols cover, screaming 'I am an Antichrist!' into the microphone, the Labour leader turned to Miliband, who had begun to
sway more or less in time with the music, and said: 'Ed, you're
really not allowed to sing along to this one.'

A decade earlier, back in 2013 when Starmer left the CPS, there
was speculation he might be given a Labour peerage in the House
of Lords, but Miliband had encouraged him to stand for election.
And it just so happened that Frank Dobson, the long-serving
Labour MP in the Holborn and St Pancras constituency where
both Starmer and Miliband live, announced in the summer of 2014
he was stepping down at the next election.

If that seemed like a stroke of good fortune, there were some
equally large obstacles still in Starmer's way. Labour's rules stipu-
lated that anyone seeking selection as a candidate must have been a
member for at least twelve months. Starmer, who had to be politically neutral and give up his party membership when running the
CPS, would therefore have been ineligible had the process got
under way promptly. Officials dragged their feet through several
meetings of the party's National Executive Committee that organ-
ises such matters, so that the timetable didn't start until the
autumn. It was also notable that, unlike many other safe Labour
seats at the time, Holborn and St Pancras wasn't a constituency
that had to pick a candidate from an 'all-women shortlist'.

But no one can really claim Starmer was imposed on this seat
against the wishes of activists or that the selection was fixed. He'd
lived in the constituency for the best part of twenty years and it
would have surely been a bit unfair to prevent him from standing
just because the last Labour government had appointed him as a
public servant. Compared to some of the interference in local selections before and since, this was very small beer.

'I didn't want to get parachuted into some constituency
with which I had no connection,' says Starmer. 'When Frank said
he was retiring, I joined the queue with some very strong local

candidates all hoping like me to represent the place in which they live.'

It was his first electoral contest of any sort and victory was far from a foregone conclusion. He was up against Raj Chada and Sarah Hayward, the well-respected past and present leaders of Camden Council, as well as Patrick French, a popular local NHS doctor. All of them had become well known in the constituency party during Starmer's enforced inactivity during his years at the CPS.

The contest, however, proved to be another example of his unrelenting approach to overcoming anything that might stop him. Jamie Burton, his colleague at Doughty Street, remembers Starmer phoning him because he vaguely knew a potential rival candidate. 'He wanted to know everything about someone who had probably a 0.1 per cent chance of beating him. This is someone who leaves absolutely nothing to chance.'

Asked about how he went about getting selected with such little political experience, Starmer replies: 'If you are going to do something, you do it properly. And I was ruthlessly focused on what members care about.' Substitute the word 'members' for 'voters in target seats' and – in his ruthless focus – this is pretty much the same strategy he is likely to deploy in the general election a decade later.

He also recognised his own limitations, then went out to rectify or mitigate them. This political novice got himself an organiser, Elliot Chappell – who would later become a journalist for *LabourList* – to guide him through the maze of nominations, branches and affiliates. He got an insight into Camden Council through some of its longest-serving members. A link to Dobson came from Robert Latham, who had not only been friends with the local MP for years but had also been a colleague of Starmer's from Doughty Street and his sometime squash partner on Friday afternoons. 'When Keir was DPP, he always hit the ball with some venom if he had just been in a meeting with [former Justice Secretary] Chris Grayling,' says Latham. 'I could tell he has some real politics in him.'

And then there was Fiona Millar, a journalist and education campaigner who had quietly served the last government as a Downing Street adviser at the same time as her partner, Alastair Campbell, had been more noisily running its communications. Her barrister brother, Gavin Millar, had once shared an office with Starmer just as he had with Tony Blair. And, when she went to meet Starmer, it turned out the two families had other links too. 'Vic's mum had been the local doctor for our children,' says Millar, 'and I was part of the selection panel that gave her sister a job as a newly qualified teacher when I was vice-chair of governors at Gospel Oak primary school.'

Although a certain sort of lip will instinctively curl at such tales of north London folk, where lawyers, doctors, school governors and teachers – not to mention politicians, journalists and advisers – are all connected to each other, Millar observes: 'Vic and I both grew up around here, so I instantly recognised her as someone very like me. But Keir himself is a bit different, he obviously loves this part of the city, but he retains that sense of coming from somewhere smaller, less metropolitan. He's slightly outside it all. That "north London lawyer" label they try to pin on him is not quite right.'

In 2014, however, access to those networks was just what a first-time candidate needed. 'We had about 1,200 members, which was a lot back then, and I must have known at least a quarter of them,' says Millar. 'Keir was very organised and quite a hard taskmaster. We would have regular meetings, usually at Robert Latham's house, where he would want to know how many each of us had contacted. He was always keen on numbers and data.

'The plan itself was not so complicated. I would phone up my friends, then friends of friends – even friends of my mother who was in her eighties – and invite them to meet Keir for coffee. I remember asking him, "How many coffees can one man have?"' The answer, it turned out, was a lot.

By Starmer's own account of the campaign, he drank 'literally hundreds' of cups of the stuff with local Labour Party members, having meetings, one by one, with trade union members, local business owners, public service workers, young and old, rich and poor. He was methodical about it and it gave him what he calls a 'deep dive into local politics'. Even before he'd formally announced his candidacy, he had become so omnipresent at meetings and events the *Camden New Journal* dubbed him 'Mr Everywhere'.

One of the members' doors he knocked on was that of Martin Plaunt, a former BBC journalist specialising on Africa, who lives nearby in Kentish Town. Plaunt had heard 'this person called Keir Starmer' was going to stand but he'd hardly been a member of the party for that long so, as far as Plaunt was concerned, this late arrival into the field would be just an also-ran. 'Within ten minutes of him sitting down for a cup of coffee, however,' says Plaunt, 'Keir had convinced me he was not only our next MP but also our gift to the Labour Party.'

Asked why, however, and Plaunt hesitates. 'I can't really tell you,' he says. 'There's something intangible about him which I've never quite been able to put my finger on. But I've met dozens and dozens of politicians in my life and I know he would be able to walk into a room and hold his own with any of them. He has a certain integrity.'

By the time the Kentish Town branch of the constituency party met for its selection meeting, the room was packed with more than a hundred people, most of whom had never been to a meeting before. 'These were all the members who Keir had been to see personally and they all voted for him,' says Plaunt, who took his support for Starmer so seriously he even did a bit of part-time work for him later as a media adviser.

Aside from his endless cups of coffee, Starmer was being presented as a heavyweight who would inevitably become a minister if Miliband won the election. He launched his campaign with a dinner at the Salaam Namaste restaurant near Doughty Street and a slogan of 'A National Voice for Local People'. He was given the kind of star billing from the press that Labour politicians rarely get, let alone aspirant candidates who haven't even secured their local party's nomination. The *Evening Standard*, which at time was still in thrall to the then London mayor Boris Johnson, ran a double-page spread decorated with pictures of a tieless Starmer gazing deep into the camera under the headline: 'Hot, ready, legal'.

Raj Chada, one of his opponents, sensed the game was up. 'Keir was just more organised and more focused than anyone else. He was meticulous in how he approached this. We all sort of knew he was going to win. Frankly, there were times he almost convinced me to vote for him. Although he wasn't then – and still isn't – some blazing orator, he was always the grown-up in the room.'

On his website were endorsements from big Labour names like Tessa Jowell, Trevor Phillips, David Miliband and Robert Gavron, as well as supporters in the media such as the broadcaster Joan Bakewell and Liz Forgan, then chairing the trust that owns the *Guardian*. Starmer also had public backing from fellow lawyers like Geoffrey Bindman and Helena Kennedy, human rights academics including Francesca Klug and Conor Gearty, Mohammed Gofur, the chair of Kings Cross Mosque, and a sprinkling of some of the British-Bangladeshi business owners who represent a significant section of the local party. Rather more incongruously, he had endorsements from Mick Whelan, general secretary of the train drivers' union, ASLEF, and Ken Livingstone, who had run as a left-wing independent and beaten Dobson for the post of London mayor in 2000.

Notably, there was nothing from Alastair Campbell, who was giving Starmer some informal media advice, even though there were messages of support from both Fiona Millar and their comedian daughter, Grace. This was because of concerns that Campbell's role in making the case for the Iraq War had made him a polarising figure among some party members. Nonetheless, there was a certain amount of 'shock and awe' in the scale of all these endorsements, with Starmer saying, 'People were taken by surprise over how much support we had got and it had the desired effect.'

Millar felt Starmer was helping to turn the page on the bitter battles of the last government and its 2010 election defeat. 'The Labour Party was still a bit lost at the time and there was a sense that a big public figure like Keir wanting to be a local MP instilled a sense of confidence in the future,' she says. 'I think the subtext to some of our campaigning was that we were selecting someone like Tony Blair, a brilliant lawyer with some glamour attached to him. Like Tony, Keir was coming into politics from left field; he felt like someone with a real chance of being prime minister.'

By the time of the final selection meeting, which was packed out with seven hundred people at St Pancras Church, however, Millar had begun to notice that 'he didn't really have Blair's panache'. Although his speech that night included a long personal passage about his mother's illness – the first time he had talked about her publicly in that way – some of those present were left feeling underwhelmed by the former DPP who they had heard so much about. It didn't matter much because Starmer's endless cups of coffee had already secured him the votes he needed. And that, perhaps, is the real point of this story. 'He's not Tony, he's Keir. There's nothing eye-catching about it, but he gets there in the end,' says Millar.

A few years later, in the middle of the rows over Brexit and anti-semitism under Jeremy Corbyn, she got so fed up she very publicly resigned from the party. Even now she finds it 'a bit strange' Starmer never discussed her reasons for leaving, even though she and Campbell still see him socially from time to time with Vic.

Her puzzlement over why Starmer is not more obviously political is shared by many who have worked with him in the decade since. Some of those who know him complain he lacks the political instinct to see how emotional connections rather than rational calculation can bring change.

Starmer's own explanation is more straightforward: he did not – maybe does not – want to be seen as a certain kind of politician. Shortly after becoming the official Labour candidate, he gave an interview that hinted at this tension within him. 'One of the things

I did not like from the last few months is that I did not feel I was solving a problem, I felt I was self-promoting and I find that really uncomfortable,' he said.

Just as in his selection, however, none of it affected his chances of becoming an MP. Starmer's was one of those constituencies in which Labour piled on votes in 2015 while losing them elsewhere. The party's candidate was new enough to all this to believe the reaction he was getting on Camden doorsteps was being replicated in other seats and that meant his party was heading back to government.

Then, in the middle of the campaign, his mother died. An earlier chapter has described the final years of Jo's life, as well as how her eldest son's grief was mixed with a sense of relief that her suffering was over. But one of the features of Starmer's political career is the way events like these have repeatedly drawn him back towards his inner emotions just when he might have been expected to be projecting himself outwards. 'I stopped the campaign and went down to see Dad and they hadn't yet taken her body away. She was still there in the house,' he says. 'It was the weirdest day of my life. I think I just held her for a bit.'

After taking some time off to arrange the funeral back in Surrey, he returned to the election campaign and swiftly got another shock from the world beyond politics. All day, there had been missed calls from John Murray, which Starmer had assumed was just an old friend checking up on him after his mum's funeral. Only later that evening did he get a chance to phone back. Murray told him his wife had just died, within hours of a massive and sudden brain aneurism.

'Debbie was in her vital prime, a teacher in Bingley and I had known her ever since she had started going out with John. She had become a huge part of our family's life,' says Starmer. The next morning, he climbed into the car with Vic to drive to Murray's home in Leeds. 'Her phone was still on the table, her jewellery in the bathroom, John just hollowed out. We all hugged each other, cried a bit. We didn't know what else to do so we went for a walk with their dog,' recalls Starmer. 'On that day, the idea of knocking on a door and saying, Hi, I'm Keir Starmer, your local Labour candidate, seemed about as removed from who I was as it was possible to be.'

That evening, however, they had to drive back down the M1 towards more mixed emotions. The general election was on May 7 and it was obvious from the exit poll at 10 p.m. that Labour had done far worse than expected, with David Cameron leading the Tories to their first parliamentary majority in twenty-three years. At around five the next morning in Somers Town sports centre, Starmer was announced as 'duly elected' for Holborn and St Pancras with a significantly increased Labour vote. He remembers feeling both proud and crestfallen. The downbeat tone was apparent in his victory speech in which he said the challenges facing the poorest and most vulnerable people in his constituency 'have got bigger as the results elsewhere tonight have become better known'.

The new MP

Starmer was certainly proud of being elected to Parliament but he had given up the law at the top of his profession in the belief he could use his experience to be a minister, maybe attorney general, in a Labour government led by Miliband. Cameron's victory meant none of that would be possible for several years at least and, by then aged fifty-two, the new MP for Holborn and St Pancras was all too aware the clock was already running down on his prospects of making a real impact.

'I never wanted to become an MP for the sake of it,' he says. 'I thought Ed was going to win. Five years of opposition felt a very long time, it's like a prison sentence. There is nothing that reduces you so much as knowing you can only make noise and not change.'

Instead of propelling him into ministerial office, Starmer's experience as DPP, together with his name recognition in the media and heavyweight reputation, were proving to be oversized baggage to carry into opposition. This became clear a week after the election, when he was back in Leeds with John Murray for Debbie's funeral. He had kept his phone off all day and it was only later at the wake that he saw a #Keirforleader campaign had begun on Twitter and Facebook. It was being backed by at least one former minister and his name was also mentioned as a possible candidate by *Guardian* columnists like Polly Toynbee or Michael White, the latter describing him in glowing terms as 'a battle-hardened barrister and ex-director of public prosecutions, with a tough reputation untainted by political failures of the past decade'.

Starmer squirms at the mention of all this now and insists it had nothing to do with him. 'I hadn't even turned up or been sworn in at the House of Commons yet. I could imagine some old hands thinking I must be an arrogant dick,' he says. Hasty denials were issued with a tweet that said while he was very flattered by the attention, the next Labour leader should be someone with more political experience.

He says, 'I needed to graft and learn the ropes.' One of his early decisions was to tell the parliamentary authorities to refer to him as plain 'Keir Starmer' without the 'Sir' prefix awarded for his glittering career outside Parliament. Indeed, neither that, nor mention of him being a KC, appears on his House of Commons letters, where the only title and letters before or after his name are 'MP'.

But finding his feet in Westminster turned out to be more difficult than many people, including him, had expected. Just as when he first went to university, or became a barrister, it took time to settle in the new environment. Although he had often appeared as a witness at parliamentary committees, Starmer was used to working in the relatively narrow confines of the law and being on top of his brief. 'As an MP, I had to have opinions on everything while learning all kinds of new rules; it was like going into court for the first time,' he says, recalling his embarrassment as someone who usually prides himself on being a master of process, at having a proposed amendment blocked because he hadn't filed it properly.

As a consequence he describes withdrawing into what he calls his 'defensive armour' during those early months as an MP and beoming 'more of a caricature lawyer than I had been before'. He says: 'I had learned how to present an argument in court where judges and juries expected me to be professional but did not want to hear my life story or find out what I'm like down the pub. I did the things I knew I could do and got across the detail.'

So much so that some of his early constituency surgeries would go on for four or five hours, with his staff suspecting that word had got around Camden that people could get thousands of pounds' worth of free legal advice from a leading QC. He also continued to do some well-paid consultancy work with the legal firm Mishcon de Reya, which briefly gave him unwelcome publicity when details of his earnings were disclosed in the MPs' Register. The role came to an abrupt end when he later became a member of the shadow cabinet amid stories suggesting it might be a conflict of interest.

The new MP showed little interest in the Tea Room gossip or late-night Strangers' Bar drinking sessions that some old hands in the House of Commons regard as an essential part of the political process. At first, the perception of him being a bit distant may have been explicable by the reputation he had already earned for himself outside Parliament. One of his new colleagues was the Welsh politician Carolyn Harris, who had heard so much about this famous human rights lawyer that she says: 'I didn't know whether I should shake his hand or curtsey when I met him.'

It's part of a now familiar paradox about Starmer, because he enjoys a drink and other people's company probably more than many other politicians. Aides says part of the answer is that he doesn't want to be in 'a club culture' many voters despise, but they also suspect he likes to travel light, unburdened by obligation to this or that group. Asked about this reluctance to 'play the Westminster game', Starmer says: 'I'm not sure that's a deliberate strategy, it's more instinctive. I mean I've got good longstanding friends outside politics who I want to make time to see. And quite

a lot of political friendships seem to me fairly thin and transactional
– you know, people are your friend and loyal until they're not –
there's a lot of that going on and I want to keep away from it.'

Harris later broke through his barriers to become one of the very
few close friends Starmer has made in Parliament, but says he still
resists her efforts to make him 'more clubbable' and build alliances
on the backbenches. Instead, when his family comes on holiday
with her in the Gower, Starmer will head off to the pub with her
husband, David, who voted for Brexit and supports Chelsea – with
a tattoo to prove it. He calls this railwayman 'my sounding board'
and, unlike some of the people he meets in politics, says that when
David 'tells me something at least I know he's not blowing smoke
up my arse'.

As a new MP, Starmer swiftly delivered his maiden speech in
the House of Commons, focusing, as so often before and since, on
defending the Human Rights Act. He warned the poorest in his
constituency would be the losers 'if we abandon the guarantee of
equal rights for all'. He also campaigned hard against HS2, opposing it on grounds of 'cost and merit', as he repeatedly attacked the
project's mismanagement and the disruption caused to his constituents around Euston station. He is generally in favour of big
infrastructure programmes and, after so much had already been
spent on this one, has been critical of the way Rishi Sunak's
government abandoned it with the job less than half done. Even
so, Starmer still thinks HS2 should have started in the north and
the only occasion he has rebelled against his party's official line in
the House of Commons was when he refused to vote on proceed-
ing with it in 2015.

Another statistic – one he has probably quoted more than any
other in the years since – is that in his first twelve months as an
MP, he voted against the government on 172 occasions and was on
the losing side 171 times. Just because he repeats this so often should
not detract from its meaning. Some MPs gain a sense of achievement from a voting record showing they stood defiantly against the

Tory government. Others boast about how often they defied their party as proof of their rebelliousness and independence. Starmer thinks both are pointless, saying: 'I have achieved less in opposition than at any other period in my life. It is noise but not change. Arguing, losing and then tweeting about how unfair everything is does not do anything for anyone.'

Ironically, the one area from which he derives some pride – or at least a sense of absolution – during those first few months relates directly to a mistake made while he was DPP before he even became an MP. In 2013, Miliband had commissioned him and Doreen Lawrence to produce policy proposals for the party on supporting victims of crime, and Starmer held a series of consultative meetings on this subject, including one in Camden. At first, he didn't notice a woman sitting at the back with her arms folded.

This was Claire Waxman, a victim of a serial stalker who had terrified her and stolen much of this mother of two's life over a decade-long campaign of harassment. The case is complicated but, in essence, this man had been bringing malicious and vexatious legal cases against Waxman to force her to engage with him. The CPS initially decided to prosecute him for disobeying a lifetime restraining order against contacting her in any way, but then officials changed their mind amid concerns that stopping someone taking legal action was a breach of human rights. Waxman eventually had to go to court herself to overturn their decision and won £3,500 in damages from the CPS in 2011. She had written to Starmer several times while he was DPP, saying she held him responsible for re-opening her ordeal but had never received a reply. She doesn't know if he even saw her letters.

'To tell the truth, I had only gone to the meeting because I really didn't like Keir Starmer,' says Waxman now. 'I listened to him talking about victims' rights and didn't believe a word he was saying. So at the end of the meeting I went up to him and was pretty aggressive and rude. What was amazing was he then listened to me, then said, "I'm really sorry. Hands up. I got that wrong."'

From such unlikely beginnings, a working partnership flourished. Waxman met him in his Doughty Street lawyer's office and he asked her to help him and Lawrence on their report. And when he became an MP the following year, he enlisted her again when tabling backbench legislation to strengthen victims' rights.

She says: 'We had an interesting collaboration because we would still often disagree but he does listen and, if you present him with a good argument or new information, he will change his mind.' She has since gone on, with Starmer's recommendation, to become the victims' commissioner for the mayor of London and is credited with helping bring about legal reforms that recognise stalking as a criminal offence. But their backbench Bill never made it to the statute books. Despite promises of cross-party support, it ran out of time and became another of those votes Starmer lost in his first year.

He was on the losing side too in the Labour leadership contest that ran through the summer of 2015 after he backed Andy Burnham, only to see Jeremy Corbyn, initially dismissed as a no-hope candidate from the fringes of the party, storm to victory. In his public utterances, Starmer insisted the new leader be given a chance. But his ranking, in a notorious leaked analysis of Labour MPs drawn up by Corbyn's aides, placing him in the second tier of loyalty – called 'core group plus' – was over-optimistic on their part.

The new MP was already wary of the fanaticism displayed by parts of the left, telling a meeting at the party conference in Brighton that Corbyn 'is not the Messiah ... and if you touch Jeremy you are not healed'. In a subsequent interview, he went further, saying: 'It's a big mistake to think that bundled up in one person, whether it's Jeremy or anyone else, are the answers to all the world's ills and you just have to sit at the feet of that person and wait for the pearls of wisdom. It doesn't work like that.'

The frontbencher

When Starmer offered his first key adviser a job at the end of 2015, Chris Ward was in two minds about taking it. 'I told Keir that, even with the best will in the world, we weren't going to be winning power any time soon, and I was pretty fed up of losing,' he recalls.

But over a long cup of coffee, Starmer talked to him about how the party had to change, how it didn't get the chance to form a government very often, and how it only did so when it faced the public and looked to the future. 'It was the same strategy Keir has now as leader,' he says. 'It was a twenty-five-minute conversation that would hook me up for the next six years.'

Asked if Starmer already saw himself as a potential successor to Corbyn, Ward pauses before he replies: 'I believe him when he says that wasn't in his head when he first got elected. But by the time I started working for him or even talking to Keir over that first cup of coffee, I could see he was someone thinking this whole thing is dysfunctional and it's got to change. He had just come out of a really senior leadership role, and I think he came to realise he might have to do one again.

'Right from the start, he was continually thinking how he would have done something or gone about it differently if he was leader,' says Ward. 'We'd book afternoons out to practise. There would be a Budget and I'd say to him, one day you might have to respond to this, so we'd sit down, go through the Treasury's figures together, and work out what he would have done if he had been leader. Some of our first efforts were probably terrible but step by step it got better. That's why he ends up at the top of whatever he does. He learns, he improves, and he works at it until he becomes comfortable.'

Starmer wasn't asked to be in Corbyn's first shadow cabinet but, among those that had been, there was real competition about who would get this high-profile former DPP to join their team of spokespeople. Andy Burnham, the shadow home secretary, proved the winner and is said to have compared signing Starmer to US sports teams who 'get the pick of the draft'.

Within a few weeks as a junior shadow minister, Starmer began to repay some of that confidence by showing he not only had learned the ropes of Parliament but could tie knots in them. In his first frontbench task – scrutinising legislation that would give controversial new surveillance powers to intelligence agencies – he wrung enough concessions from the government, and his very right-wing opposite number John Hayes, for the Bill to be approved by MPs with Labour's support. No small achievement in the sharply polarised atmosphere that surrounded Corbyn's election as leader. When Starmer talks about those 171 defeats in 172 votes in his first year as an MP, the exception had been a cross-party compromise he himself negotiated.

But he kept his primary focus on being Labour's spokesperson on immigration, an issue that had proved so toxic for the party during the 2010 and 2015 elections some worried it might contaminate his reputation too. 'I did tell him that this wasn't the wisest launchpad for trying to endear himself to the party,' says Ward, 'but Keir saw it as important because he thought Labour had always walked past the problem before without ever properly confronting it.'

Starmer was asked to draw up a report on immigration policy and undertook the task with his usual intensity. He visited around thirty towns and cities to produce a report, relishing the opportunity to get out of Westminster for the day with just his laptop and a few sandwiches. Paul Ovenden, who later became one of Starmer's senior advisers, was then working as Labour's regional organiser in the south-east and remembers warning him Dover might be difficult because of 'rising far right activity' trying to exploit local concerns. 'I was fully expecting them to say "Ah, thanks, can you recommend somewhere else?" But Keir said: "Well, I want to speak with people, not hand-picked audiences."' The event ended up going ahead and, despite being Ovenden's only meaningful interaction with him for several years, he says, 'It stuck with me that he was really serious about an issue that the party at the time just wasn't interested in.'

Ward thinks the project was a genuine effort to understand both sides of the argument, separate the debate on immigration from that around asylum seekers and move on from the simplicities of a strict cap on numbers. Manufacturing businesses in Wolverhampton and farmers in Rochester were telling him they were frustrated they couldn't get the workers they needed. He went to refugee camps at Calais, where children the same age as his were sleeping in freezing cold and flimsy tents, as well as a refugee project in Stockton whose volunteers voiced fears that demonising vulnerable people would deprive them of basic support and dignity. He heard from universities drowning in bureaucracy and frustrated they couldn't attract the best and brightest international students. And he also spoke to trade unions and workers worried about stagnating wages, pressures on public services and the failure to protect migrant and local workers from exploitative employers.

This report, entitled 'Reshaping the Debate: Toward a New Deal on Immigration', never saw the light of day and no one can lay hands on the final document. Indeed, it's only being quoted here because Chris Ward found sections of the draft copy on a disused computer in his shed. It proposed a comprehensive immigration review, conducted by an independent body every five years, to match the needs of the economy with the provision of public services. Starmer suggested 'money should follow the movement of people' so communities could see migration was accompanied by additional resources, and that the EU itself should do more to protect the wages of the lowest paid. He also wanted a faster and more compassionate system for dealing with asylum claims.

His main recommendation, however, was for changes in European free movement rules 'to make it work better for the UK'. This idea would have been controversial with some of the more left-wing factions in the Labour Party, for whom freedom of movement and mass immigration were the least objectionable aspects of EU membership. At the same time, there must be doubt about whether it would have succeeded with the EU implacably opposed to watering down the 'four freedoms' of the single market.

But the report is of more than merely historic interest because immigration is almost certainly going to be one of the bigger election issues in 2024. It provides evidence to suggest Starmer was never uncritical about every aspect of the EU and, in his first year as an MP, was already thinking about ways to win back Labour votes in its former heartlands. More significantly, the report provides insight into the approach of a future Labour government towards immigration. What's most striking about this document is that there was no sense of him trying to make a name for himself by engaging on either side of a cultural battle about immigration and asylum seekers which was generating such heat at the time. Instead, the emphasis appears to have been on piecemeal answers to two very separate problems. Just as Labour's position on immigration now is attacked for being managerial and technocratic, his first effort at political policy-making was more focused on outcomes than newspaper headlines.

Yet the reason this report received no publicity at all back then was, of course, because it was written in the expectation of Britain remaining in the EU and using the scare of near-defeat in a referendum to go back to Brussels and seek negotiated concessions on issues such as this.

And, on June 23, 2016 – just a few weeks before the report was due to be published – the UK voted to leave.

18

Brexit's shadow

Detailed questions

Starmer spent much of the morning after that referendum in his garden discussing what had just happened. The bright sunshine of the day mocked the mood of an MP who, barely a year after being elected, remembers feeling devastated and empty at the result. Like most people in politics, including some leaders of the Leave campaign, he had not seen this coming.

Earlier that morning David Cameron had resigned and the pound had plummeted as soon as markets opened. Later, Starmer had to call Camden Council to remove some far-right stickers that had appeared overnight on lamp posts across multicultural Kentish Town. Not only did he believe being part of the EU was vital to the interests of the UK economy, he had also seen first-hand the way it had helped to deliver peace in Northern Ireland, and had worked with European partners on cross-border crime when DPP. His big fear, he said later, was that the nation might turn in on itself and become intolerant, going against everything he had believed in all his adult life. When his children went off to school that morning, he says: 'I sort of gulped and thought about what kind of world they were going to grow up in.'

Speaking about those feelings now, Starmer says: 'I had come into politics with the belief Labour would be in power and that got shattered. Then Jeremy Corbyn becomes leader – and now we had left the EU.' On top of that, Leicester City who had been one of the pre-season favourites for relegation had just won the Premier League ahead of Arsenal in second place. 'What the hell did we know about anything?' he asked. A few months later, Donald Trump would be elected president of the United States. That year, 2016, was when Starmer's world turned upside down.

The referendum had also been more divisive than any campaign in living memory and Labour MPs like him had their own reason to feel shocked. A week earlier, Jo Cox had been murdered on the streets of her constituency by a far-right nationalist. 'She had been elected at the same time as me, her kids were the same age as mine, and we met up over weekends,' says Starmer, who had not made many friends among his parliamentary colleagues but counted her as one. 'I had been with her just a few days before she died when she hosted drinks on her houseboat,' he adds. 'It was awful.'

Along with Cox and the overwhelming majority of Labour MPs, Starmer had backed Remain. He says the 'Stronger In' campaign was too negative, as well as being 'lop-sided', because it was dominated by David Cameron and George Osborne who didn't connect with Labour voters.

Chris Ward recalls how the conversation that rolled on through that morning in Starmer's garden slowly changed, from grim post-mortem analysis to questions that revolved around practicalities and detail about what happened next. Starmer wanted to understand better how the Brexit slogan of 'Take Back Control' had resonated with people who felt politics had been too remote and had failed them. He asked: 'What does a bad Brexit look like?' 'How about a better one?' 'What should the Labour Party do?' 'What should I do?'

Corbyn, who had already been criticised over his lukewarm support for Remain during the campaign, had gone on TV at breakfast to say the UK should immediately trigger Article 50 – the 'exit clause' from the EU – and start the two-year countdown for departure. This had dismayed Starmer, who says: 'The speed with which Jeremy was willing to toss away the strongest card this country had to play in a negotiation convinced me that he was never really engaged on this issue.'

And yet Starmer hesitated to join the stampede among his party's MPs demanding Corbyn's removal in the days that followed. 'I thought Labour should have been focused on finding solutions to the new issues thrown up by Brexit, not staring at its navel,' he says. Only when forty frontbenchers quit in as many hours did Starmer reluctantly decide to join them. His resignation letter to Corbyn on June 27 began by stating: 'I have never spoken out against you publicly and I do not intend to do so now', before going on to add that they needed 'a much louder voice' on the critical issues facing Britain after the referendum.

He was unsurprised, however, that Corbyn easily saw off the centre-left challenge from Owen Smith to win the leadership for a second time in a year. 'It always seemed inevitable to me that party members who had only just elected Jeremy as leader would give him another chance,' says Starmer now. 'As uprisings go, it was ill-thought-through, too early and a mess.'

According to Ward, Starmer reached two conclusions from what would later be called 'the chicken coup'. The first was that no attempt to oust Corbyn would succeed under the existing rules; the second was the next Labour leader would come from within the shadow cabinet. Both factors probably played their part in his thinking about whether to rejoin the frontbench.

Andrew Fisher, Corbyn's policy director, has claimed Starmer was pushing to be given a job even before Smith's defeat was official. Starmer, for what it's worth, insists that they approached him. What no one really disputes, however, is that there were some in the leader's office who were already suspicious about him. Seumas Milne, who'd first met Starmer back in the 1980s during the Wapping printworkers' dispute, warned colleagues this MP never quite seemed to 'act or think like other people around at the time – he always seemed a bit too stiff and weird'. But John McDonnell, the shadow chancellor and long-time ally of Corbyn, is said to have championed Starmer's appointment, saying the former DPP was competent and had 'an eye for detail'. In any case, he later added, 'We were desperate [for] anyone who was willing to serve.'

Starmer had flown out to Taiwan for work opposing the death penalty when the call came from the then Labour leader's chief of staff, Karie Murphy. He told her the only posts he would consider were those of shadow home secretary or shadow Brexit secretary. The former was already earmarked for Diane Abbott, so he was offered what some thought of as the poisoned chalice of Brexit.

But Starmer saw it as an opportunity to get into the thick of the action. 'I wasn't going to take a job just to make up the numbers,' he says now. 'The referendum vote was the biggest decision our country had taken in a generation, the Labour Party had a duty to get involved in what happened next. And it was becoming abundantly clear that answering specific questions was not a priority for those running the government.'

Awkward answers

Starmer says he always got on pretty well with his opposite number, David Davis, even though just a few years earlier this had been the Tory MP calling most vocally for him to be sacked from his role at the CPS. He says the then Brexit secretary is someone who can at least 'laugh at himself' and never took it too personally when they clashed. He had also worked with Theresa May, the new prime minister, while at the CPS and she was home secretary. Although their relationship had never been warm, she had taken him out to dinner at the end of his term as DPP, which he remembers as both a 'slightly awkward' occasion and a kind gesture from a serious person for whom he has 'always had a lingering respect'.

But he also despaired of the way they had reduced deeply complex issues about leaving the EU to simplistic slogans like 'Brexit means Brexit' or 'No deal is better than a bad deal'. On one occasion, when he was leaving the House of Commons chamber, he remembers Davis taking him aside and offering him some advice: 'It's a bad idea to get bogged down too much in the detail.' Starmer replied tersely that it was precisely 'the detail' on Brexit that mattered most.

Davis just laughs when this anecdote is put to him. 'I can't really remember, but I may well have told him something like that because Keir wasn't getting very far with all his legal points,' he says, before describing his Labour shadow in those years as 'an intelligent and decent man' if not in the 'first rank of politicians'.

Starmer's first appearance as shadow Brexit secretary in October 2016 saw him asking politely enough whether Parliament might have any say in determining the way Britain left the EU. The eye-bulging reaction the question provoked was a hint of what was to come. Iain Duncan Smith, a former Tory leader, declared Starmer should be ignored because he was 'a second-rate lawyer who doesn't even understand the parliamentary process'. Davis generously defended his opposite number's legal credentials. Duncan Smith went on live television to deny having said any such thing before returning to the House of Commons a couple of days later to admit that, while he had used those words to describe Starmer, they were 'not meant about him'.

By then Starmer, together with the shadow foreign secretary Emily Thornberry, had sent Davis a list of 170 more questions – one for every day until the deadline it had set itself for triggering Article 50 – asking for details on what leaving the EU would mean in practice on everything from fishing to reciprocal healthcare and chemicals legislation. That same morning, the Brexit-supporting *Daily Mail* launched a fresh campaign against what it called 'whingeing' and 'contemptuous' Remainer MPs intent on subvert-ing 'the will of the people'.

Such exchanges set the tone for the months that followed, as the polarisation of the referendum campaign showed no sign of abating. Hardcore Brexiters railed against anyone they thought were getting in their way. Judges on the Supreme Court who confirmed Parliament needed to vote on a final deal were branded 'Enemies of the People' on the front page of the *Daily Mail*. Starmer, meanwhile, continued asking his detailed evidence-based questions and began to be lauded by liberal commentators as a rare example of effective, forensic opposition. When attacked by an SNP MP in Parliament for not being more full-throated in his opposition, he defended his tactics, saying what might just seem to be 'nagging away' had already secured concessions from the government over giving MPs a 'meaningful vote'.

All this meant there was more media attention than might have been expected for Starmer's foreign policy speech at Chatham House on March 27, 2017. Although the British people had voted in principle to leave the EU, he said, Brexiters had made all kinds of contradictory promises and none of them had been on the ballot paper. 'June 23 last year answered one question but opened up many more – particularly about the UK's future relationship with Europe,' he told the audience. In the absence of any form of democratic accountability for the Leave campaign's leadership, he served notice on ministers that the Labour Party would make them take responsibility.

Starmer set out six tests based on some of the boasts they'd made about what Brexit could deliver and designed to protect what he called 'core progressive values', saying Labour couldn't support a deal unless it met all of them. The second proved the most controversial. Echoing what the government's Brexit secretary had told MPs negotiations with Brussels would achieve, it must deliver 'the exact same benefits' the UK currently had as member of the single market and customs union.

Some of Corbyn's allies now believe the tests were set up to be failed as part of a long-term strategy to push Labour towards a Remain position. After all, they say, it would be impossible to have the 'exact same benefits' without staying in the EU. Barry Gardiner, the shadow trade secretary, was secretly recorded branding Starmer's tests as 'bollocks', while Ian Lavery, a former coal miner who would later become chair of the Labour Party, said, 'They were never meant to be achieved … they were meant to make sure we didn't have a deal.'

Not only had Corbyn agreed to the tests, however, many of his staff also saw them as a useful device to get Labour through the next few months without a damaging split. In the days of Tony Blair, this kind of politics would have been called 'triangulation', in which New Labour positioned itself as being above or between two opposing opinions. For all that the Corbynites promised a bolder and more principled politics, their position on Brexit was deliberately ambiguous. They wanted an excuse to vote against any proposed deal while still maintaining they would honour the result of the referendum. The calculation was that, because the Conservatives still had a majority in the House of Commons, they didn't really need to do anything more.

Starmer was useful to them too, in helping corral most Labour MPs into voting for Article 50 that year and showing no sympathy for an increasingly noisy, if still minority, faction among Labour MPs who wanted to reverse Brexit. One newspaper profile at the time said he had visibly 'winced' when introduced as 'the man who'll make sure we stay in the EU'. Where the left's suspicion of Starmer had more justification, however, was over his efforts to go beyond this position of 'constructive ambiguity' and begin to clarify the relationship Britain should have with the EU after it left.

Many of Corbyn's key supporters saw the result of the referendum as the moment to conjure up their own 'left populism' with an anti-capitalist 'Lexit'. Jon Trickett, a Yorkshire MP and shadow cabinet office minister, is reported to have complained bitterly to Corbyn about these 'bloody tests', saying: 'Look at them. They're the status quo … That's fine if you live in Camden or Islington [but] we're not interested in the status quo. We want rid of it!' He advocated a radical 'anti-racist Labour Leave option' in which the UK would spurn the free-market EU with its competition rules

against subsidising nationalised industries, then forge a new inter-
national alliance with fellow socialists from the Global South.
'Jeremy,' he pleaded, 'pick up the phone and speak to people like
Lula in Brazil or Correa in Ecuador.'

By contrast, Starmer wanted the UK aligned with its biggest
trading partner so that it could salvage many of the benefits – if not
the 'exact same' ones – it had in the single market and the customs
union. This would have meant keeping most of the EU's rules,
including social and environmental protections, in return for unfet-
tered free trade. Starmer wasn't an unthinking enthusiast for every
aspect of the EU and believed remaining in the single market was
impossible if that meant accepting freedom of movement rules. But
his overall stance was for a 'soft' deal that mitigated the damage to
the economy from Brexit, rather than one that saw it as an opportunity for a radical incoming Labour government to do whatever it
wanted.

Chris Ward describes how the diagram-loving Starmer would
draw concentric circles showing the Eurozone, the EU, the single
market and the customs union. 'He'd say he wanted Britain on the
outside but right next to it, here, at the very edge of this big circle.'
The language Starmer used at the time is also noteworthy because
it was consistently aimed less at the Labour Party, or one side of the
Brexit divide, than at the public as a whole. In one speech, he
referred to 'conversations I have had with hundreds of businesses
and trade union members in recent months' showing there was
'widespread consensus' against any divergence from the EU on
tariff-free trade, regulation or competition rules. A responsible
government, said Starmer, would be trying to bring the 52 per cent
who voted Leave together with the 48 per cent who voted Remain
by setting out a future that worked for the 100 per cent.

Today, he still thinks such a 'soft Brexit' could have been agreed
if May had sought a cross-party deal early on in the process. 'I was
very clearly in the camp where we try to make this work as well as
possible and have a close relationship with the EU,' he says, 'but

this was always bigger than one political party and if she had reached out at the beginning it could have been different.'

Instead, in the spring of 2017, May called a snap general election, believing it would give her a mandate to secure her leadership of the Conservative Party and drive a Brexit deal through Parliament. Starmer acknowledges he was initially pessimistic about Labour's chances, not least because polls suggested the Tories were headed for a hundred-plus majority.

Ward began making what he calls 'putative plans' for a possible leadership contest afterwards. 'I was thinking if Corbyn went down in flames, Keir would be under pressure to stand,' he says now. 'We had got as far as having a spreadsheet of MPs we might approach for a nomination, but it hadn't really been thought through. There were probably half a dozen potential candidates doing the same thing, some of them probably better prepared and placed to win than Keir.'

None of it, however, proved necessary. For the third time in two years, Britain's voting public surprised both Starmer and just about every pundit in Westminster. Although Corbyn's Labour Party did not – as is sometimes suggested – 'almost win' the 2017 general election, it outperformed all expectations by depriving the Conservatives of their overall majority in the House of Commons.

Starmer thinks the reasons included a truly terrible Tory campaign and some equally genuine excitement about the radicalism of Labour's manifesto, which got more traction than such documents usually do thanks to it being leaked prior to publication. Even now he pays what is, for him, a high compliment by saying the manifesto 'cut through with some of the guys in my eight-a-side football games who aren't much interested in politics'.

But he also viewed the result as a repudiation of May's effort to secure a blank cheque from voters on Brexit. Labour's surge had been fuelled by Remain supporters who wanted to stop total power being handed to the Tory party as much as, if not more than it had been by any Corbyn-inspired 'youthquake' of radical left energy.

In the immediate aftermath, Starmer was convinced May would try to find cross-party compromise on the terms for leaving the EU. On the morning after the election, having increased his own majority in Holborn and St Pancras to more than thirty thousand, he was at home when his phone flashed up with David Davis calling him. 'This is it,' he said to Vic before answering, 'we're going to get joint talks.' It turned out the minister was merely getting in touch about joining the Privy Council, an offer Starmer thought was a long way from being either as important or urgent as that moment demanded.

Instead of trying to make a deal with Labour, May locked herself into a toxic relationship with the most ideological Brexiters in her own party. As the shadow Brexit secretary put it that September, in his first speech to the Labour Party conference, she was 'robotically marching towards an extreme Brexit – focused on her own survival not the national interest'.

At the same time, Remainers on the other side of the House of Commons had been emboldened and empowered. There was no prospect of getting a soft Brexit deal over the line without their help but Labour, sensing May's weakness, didn't want to bail the prime minister out by enabling her 'Tory Brexit'. Far from being a chance to find consensus, over the next two and a half years this hung Parliament would be one in which rival groups of MPs fought themselves to a standstill.

In 2017, the ground on which Starmer was standing had changed and – as so often before in his legal career – slow-step by slow-step, so did he.

On the edge

When formal talks on Brexit began in Brussels between the British government and the EU's negotiating team shortly after the 2017 election, Starmer recalls how the television news became embarrassing to watch. 'Michel Barnier turned up with a van load of papers in colour-coded ring binders, while David Davis wandered in with nothing more than his glasses case,' he says.

Within five months, Davis was sidelined by May in the negotiations and eventually he resigned from the cabinet in protest at her withdrawal agreement. Speaking about that time now, he says Starmer's claims a soft Brexit deal could have been got over the line with Labour support only go to show 'he didn't understand the internal dynamics of the Conservative Party – no Tory prime minister would survive doing that'.

But as the prospect of a compromise became disappearingly remote, Starmer demonstrated he did understand the changing dynamics of his own party – perhaps better than most. In the spring of 2018, the People's Vote campaign had been launched with the backing of barely a couple of dozen MPs, calling for a new referendum that might keep Britain in the EU. In the eighteen months that followed, it rapidly gained momentum, with the support of growing numbers of Labour backbenchers as well as the Liberal Democrats, the SNP and a handful of Tories, including the former attorney general Dominic Grieve, with whom Starmer had worked so closely at the CPS.

Whereas the Remain campaign before the referendum had been soulless and negative, the People's Vote was bursting with energy and life. It staged four enormous demonstrations at which hundreds of thousands of people marched through London, deployed teams of young activists in eye-catching stunts and to lobby MPs in Parliament, as well as generating millions of pounds online in small donations. In a sign of the campaign's reach, at a rally in the capital *Match of the Day* presenter Gary Lineker welcomed Boris Johnson's brother, Jo – who had just resigned from the government to support a new referendum – onto the stage.

Corbyn's team, who thought they owned the franchise on appealing to big crowds and mobilising youth, did little to conceal their loathing for the People's Vote. Seumas Milne, Labour's strategy chief, described the campaign as a 'mortal threat' to the coalition of support they had assembled in the 2017 election. Many of them saw it as a proxy for a breakaway centrist party and the ambitions of the then Labour MP Chuka Umunna.

But Corbyn's political project had been built on, and sustained by, giving more voice to Labour's grassroots. And, by the summer of 2018, it was being presented with polling showing 86 per cent of party members backed a new referendum and fully 90 per cent would support Remain.

A fault line was opening up. For much of that year, however, Starmer continued trying to straddle it. After travelling to Norway and Switzerland to see how their systems worked – outside the EU but still aligned with its rules – he left unconvinced that either would be a good fit for the UK. At the same time, Tory hardliners were pushing Britain ever closer to the cliff edge of leaving the EU without any deal at all.

Trust levels between Starmer and Corbyn's team were sinking fast. In a fractious meeting of the shadow cabinet's Brexit sub-committee in January 2018, Starmer refused to even read a policy paper for a Lexit-style deal with Europe he felt had been sprung on him. Although he later agreed a compromise for a form of customs union that allowed some leftish variation in EU rules, the leader's office was furious he had revealed the new position in an interview the day before Corbyn could announce it himself.

One Corbyn aide at the time says: 'Keir was very good at staying just within the margins of what was agreed but was pushing it as far as he could and was always at the Remainer edge of that envelope.' The former Tory minister David Lidington has recalled a 2018 meeting with Starmer to discuss Brexit where Milne was sent along as a minder. 'I saw Seumas sort of looking from one to the other of us … I always felt that when the revolution came, in Seumas's mind, both of us were going in front of the firing squad, it was just a question of sequence.'

Starmer also began holding faintly clandestine meetings over coffee and eggs with Alastair Campbell, the People's Vote campaigner and former Downing Street strategist, in cafés dotted across Kentish Town, but repeatedly, even stubbornly, underlined his caution about a new referendum. 'My memory of that whole time is of feeling incredibly frustrated,' says Campbell. 'I mean, I got kicked out of the Labour Party in the end because I was so bloody frustrated. Labour should have been moving so much faster to seize this chance to stop the madness. When I hear Tories now saying Keir was always this liberal Remainer, they're well wide of the mark. He'd always be going on to us about how he wouldn't even countenance a new referendum before every option for a soft Brexit had been exhausted.'*

But those options weren't the only thing being rapidly exhausted. The entire political system seemed to be creaking.

Starmer remembers it as an awful time to be in Parliament. 'MPs were really jumpy. Jeremy would walk into the chamber and our benches were eerily silent.' He was still immersed in 'the stuff of technical detail' but found the Labour leader curiously disengaged. Sitting next to him on the frontbench in a big debate about Brexit, Starmer recalls 'listening carefully to what the prime minister was saying – every word mattered. I glanced over at Jeremy and saw he was fully engrossed reading the *Hansard* record of a Westminster Hall debate from the previous Friday about cycleways or something. This was probably important in its own way, but it wasn't what he should have been doing when our chance of getting a half decent Brexit deal was slipping away.'

As summer turned to autumn, it was getting harder to avoid the conclusion that a new vote might be one way to break the log jam, says Starmer. One of his closest colleagues, Jenny Chapman, his deputy in the shadow Brexit team and MP for Darlington, had been telling him how difficult it would be to reconcile a new

---

* For the sake of full disclosure, the author of this book was present at some of these meetings in his capacity as director of communications for the People's Vote campaign.

referendum with her constituents. 'Some of the Remainers came across as so patronising to people who voted Leave, saying things like they had been lied to or did not know what they had voted for,' she says. 'I thought that was very damaging. But in the end, even I conceded we had run out of options – there was nowhere else to go.'

'No one is ruling out Remain'

In the run-up to Labour's annual party conference that September, the supporters of a fresh referendum who were the least tainted by their past within the Labour Party – young campaigners from For our Future's Sake (the acronym of 'FFS' was very deliberate) and a group of otherwise impeccable Corbynites called Another Europe is Possible – organised a blizzard of motions from local parties. Even unions like the GMB and Unison were moving on the issue.

On the first day of the conference in Liverpool, the People's Vote campaign marched in its thousands through the city to a dockside rally addressed by left-wing trade union leaders and Peter Reid, the former Everton footballer. Umunna was told to stay away, while Starmer – who would have been welcomed – made sure he was somewhere else. Making waves was not his thing.

But later that Sunday evening, he had to dive headlong into the turbulence when delegates met for their so-called 'compositing meeting', to synthesise different motions into a single resolution. What happened that night and over the next couple of days has become one of the most bitterly controversial, as well as pivotal, moments in Starmer's political career.

At 6.30 p.m. on September 23, 2018, perhaps as many as three hundred delegates were packed inside a stiflingly warm room at the conference centre, allowed neither tea nor anything stronger in the hope this might encourage an early consensus. But the chances of that were so remote an impassioned argument broke out at one point even on the meaning of the word 'consensus'.

Starmer sat at the front, flanked by his aides. After several hours of debate, a compromise seemed to be inching towards agreement, with a motion saying that, in the absence of a general election, 'Labour must support all options remaining on the table, including campaigning for a public vote on the terms of the Brexit deal.' Remainers were insisting a public vote shouldn't just be about how the UK left the EU, but also about whether to leave at all. They were resisted by a rearguard action from the leader's office and its allies. As the clock approached 1 a.m. and tempers frayed, Starmer proposed a compromise motion that would commit the party only to 'campaigning for a public vote', with the question of what was on the ballot paper of that referendum left deliberately open.

He says: 'I looked them in the eye and said there was only one way to get this over the line. I told them I knew they wanted the option to Remain and promised that, if they signed off this motion, I would faithfully recognise what everyone in the room knew was the basis on which it had been agreed – I gave them my word.'

But this was always going to be a fragile truce at best, and was broken shortly after dawn by John McDonnell in a round of broadcast interviews where he said any 'people's vote will be on the deal itself and whether we can negotiate a better one' – in other words, not about reopening the question of Brexit itself.

The shadow Brexit secretary spent much of the day being chased through fire exits, down concrete staircases and along corridors by Michael Crick from *Channel 4 News*. 'Isn't this a betrayal, Mr Starmer?' asked the veteran reporter. Starmer decided to stop for a moment and give a brief interview in which he emphasised, 'All options are on the table.' 'Oh, come off it!' shouted Crick, who resumed his chase through another set of swing doors.

Although, by then, McDonnell had backtracked on his comments, the leader's office was very keen that Starmer not stoke the row. In the conference speech he submitted to Milne for approval that night, there was no reference to the possibility of staying in the EU. Nor was there any hint of it in what was briefed out to journalists the following morning on September 25. It most certainly wasn't on the autocue version from which he was expected to read.

Minutes before he was due to speak, however, Starmer scribbled a sentence on a sheet of paper he slipped into the text as he entered the hall. Towards the end of his address, after some standard lines about the need for an election to sweep away the 'failed Tory government', he got to the composite motion agreed on Sunday night. 'If that's not possible we must have other options. And, conference, that must include campaigning for a public vote.' There was a smattering of applause. 'Conference, it's right that Parliament has the first say,' he continued, now looking down at his notes instead of the autocue. 'But if we need to break the impasse, our options must include campaigning for a public vote.' Then he read out the eight words he had scribbled on the piece of paper: 'And nobody is ruling out remain as an option.'

There was momentary silence, followed by cheering. Delegates began rising to their feet, not so much in an ovation as an act of defiance. The applause rumbled on, with two-thirds of the hall eventually standing, while the rest sat on their hands. No one could accuse Starmer of rousing oratory. The language had been convoluted and repetitive, to the point where it had all become difficult to comprehend. But for anyone there, they knew what he meant and that they had witnessed a real moment, the unexpected kind you rarely see at any party conference these days; one when politics changes.

Starmer blinked a few times and stumbled through the rest of his speech, then sat on the platform behind the lectern for twenty minutes listening to other speakers and, in his words, 'glowing a little bit', because he had never had one of his speeches received in this way.

When he went backstage, however, Amy Jackson was waiting for him. Corbyn's political secretary had her phone out, showing a social media graphic the Tories had put up within minutes of his speech, declaring: 'Confirmed: Labour will not respect the result of the referendum.' She waved this in Starmer's face, shouting: 'Look at what you have just done!' They were bundled into a side room to avoid a camera crew, but the shouting carried on, with Starmer countering that he was reflecting the resolution agreed on the Sunday night. 'You know the position!' she said. 'You've made us look like a Remain party.' Since then Jackson has described her immediate thought when she heard that part of the speech: 'He wants to be leader.'

Reflecting on it now, Starmer declares: 'I didn't add those words to my speech to be difficult. I wasn't trying to ingratiate myself with the membership. I did it because I knew what we had agreed on the Sunday night to get the resolution over the line. I was trying to fix the problem.'

Nonetheless, the drama represented a turning point. Starmer moved from being someone wrapped up in a byzantine legal and parliamentary process to a politician who had connected with the party outside Westminster, as well as large swathes of the public.

The charge levelled at him now by pro-Brexit critics from both left and right is that his position shifted either because he was a political opportunist or because he was always an ideological Remainer. One version has it that Corbyn, having almost won in 2017, was undermined by a pro-Remain Establishment so they could replace him with 'one of their own': Starmer.

The problem with such an analysis is that, far from being a wrecker, he was probably more disciplined than most of the party's frontbench. It's why Corbyn himself shrugged off the rows and there never was much question that his shadow Brexit secretary would be sacked. And, as we have seen, Starmer wasn't in the vanguard of those calling for another referendum. Instead, he had been one of those following truculently behind shadow cabinet colleagues like deputy leader Tom Watson, whose 'grandstanding', say Starmer's advisers from the time, was a frequent source of annoyance to him.

Michel Barnier, the EU's chief Brexit negotiator, had watched the smoke rising from Westminster with more interest than most. Despite this veteran French politician spending most of his time trying to agree a deal with the Conservative government, he also held talks with the Labour Party, writing in his diary in 2018 that Starmer was without doubt the figure in Labour's hierarchy 'who impresses me the most for his ability to grasp in detail what is at stake in the Brexit negotiations'. He added: 'Listening to him, I get the feeling that Keir Starmer will one day be UK prime minister.'

'Starmer is clever,' says Barnier. 'What I saw over those years was how he was always learning. He improved, day after day, year after year. At the beginning he was wise enough to stay close to Corbyn and, while everyone else made mistakes, he was careful. From the first time we met, I thought there was something about him.'

Towards a certain end

'Mayday'

Keir Starmer's name appears just once in Theresa May's memoirs and her verdict is characteristically terse, saying she 'would leave it to the reader to decide' whether he took his stance on the second referendum 'purely through conviction or with an eye on his own leadership ambitions'.

At the start of 2019, her plan for leaving the EU was rejected by Parliament three times in as many months because MPs saw it as either too soft or too hard. May announced she would step down as prime minister before the next election. Boris Johnson became the favourite to succeed her, even as Nigel Farage's Brexit Party began to surge in the polls.

The whole political system seemed in danger of capsizing and some were running for the lifeboats. A small group of Labour MPs, including Chuka Umunna, joined up with an even smaller rump of Remain-minded Tories to form an ill-starred new party called Change UK. At the same time a larger faction of perhaps sixty or seventy Labour MPs, coalesced around Tom Watson, were rumoured to be considering forming a separate group – if not a new party – in Parliament.

Although Starmer made plain he would have nothing to do with any breakaways, he was becoming the object of scorn or even loathing within Corbyn's office. Some aides mocked how, at shadow cabinet meetings, he often used the phrase 'moving through the gears' while making mechanical lifting motions with his hands. Colleagues remember Andrew Murray, the former communist by then part of Corbyn's team, telling them his son – at one time a street artist with experience of run-ins with the police – always thought Starmer had a 'cop's face'.

Murray's daughter, Laura, who also worked for Corbyn, told them for all Starmer's expressions of loyalty he had behaved in 'factional' fashion in their constituency party, spending more than an hour trying to persuade her to back Owen Smith's leadership challenge in 2016. Having failed, Starmer and his wife turned up at the Kentish Town branch meeting – usually attended by just a few people – to vote against her in an election for the lowly post of ward secretary.

Even so, when May played one last card in the dying days of her premiership by announcing the cross-party talks on a deal that Starmer thought should have been offered two years earlier, he was still chosen to head the Labour team of negotiators. Formal meetings began on April 4, 2019 and alongside him at different points were John McDonnell, by then an advocate of a fresh referendum, as well as the more sceptical Rebecca Long-Bailey and Seumas Milne.

The short walk they had to take from Parliament along Whitehall towards the Cabinet Office saw them surrounded by photographers and camera crews. Starmer, often with files of documents pressed to his chest, would usually be striding ahead of the others while Milne eyed him warily, as if poised to leap in front of the cameras should the shadow Brexit secretary try to brief the media before him.

There are different accounts of what happened inside those talks. According to Gavin Barwell, Downing Street's then chief of staff, it swiftly became clear Starmer had set his face against an agreement. 'Jeremy Corbyn wanted to do it, but Keir Starmer stopped it,' wrote Barwell, who has described handing out a first draft of a deal and the Labour side responding, 'We don't like this. We don't like that. Change this to that.' When Barwell came back with a revised version, he says: 'Keir picked it up and looked at it, and said, "Well, I don't like this wording on customs at all." I was like, "We literally put in the wording on customs from Jeremy Corbyn's letter. You've just criticised your own language." He looked slightly po-faced.'

This isn't the sort of accusation usually levelled at Starmer and it rankles a former barrister who takes pride in knowing the detail. 'I'm not an idiot – I mean – I know my own case,' he says. 'Barwell took our documents and tried to synthesise them into something both sides could accept. He wasn't acting in bad faith because that's a perfectly reasonable thing to do, but he had misunderstood what we were saying.'

A bigger sticking point was Labour's position on a second referendum. Starmer had become increasingly convinced any Brexit deal would be inherently unstable because so many Tories preferred not having any deal at all. He also believed Labour MPs would oppose an agreement that was not subject to a 'confirmatory referendum' with Remain on the ballot paper. He told the government team the task of 'trying to sell an outcome' to MPs was one that 'we are going to find hard'. Although a new referendum had been shown to be the single most popular option among MPs across the House of Commons, a majority – including the prime minister herself – were implacably opposed.

The government's negotiating position had been fundamentally weakened by May announcing she was leaving. Her likely successor Boris Johnson was clearly someone more than capable of ripping up any agreement with anyone. McDonnell is said to have likened trying to do a deal with May to a trade union negotiating with a company going into liquidation.

'Any opportunity to find consensus on a Brexit deal had long since disappeared. Different camps had become too entrenched,' says Starmer now. Even the refreshment they were offered at the negotiations seemed to symbolise the downgrading of expectations. At the start, they'd been given plates of freshly made sandwiches but, by the final meeting, all they got were a few plastic-wrapped biscuits. He suggests: 'The Whitehall caterers clearly knew the game was up.'

A week after the talks collapsed in May, voters themselves showed they weren't much interested in any compromise deal stitched up by the two main parties in Westminster. At the elections for the European Parliament, Nigel Farage's Brexit Party, campaigning for 'no deal', proved the clear winner, followed by the Liberal Democrats, whose slogan was 'Bollocks to Brexit'. Labour came third on just 14 per cent, while the Conservatives got less than 10 per cent for the first time in a national election and were even eclipsed by the pro-Remain Green Party.

Ultimately, both Tories and Labour were forced to pick a side. In July that year May was replaced by Johnson, promising the UK would leave the EU on October 31 – 'deal or no deal'. Now fearful of an election whose polls showed it faced losing more seats if it backed a deal than if it blocked one, Labour moved ever further behind a new referendum to solve the issue.

By the time of the 2019 Labour Party conference in Brighton in September, Starmer had finally become a standard bearer for the People's Vote. Symbolically, he wasn't at the front of the march when it set off through the town, but turned up for the last bit along the seafront and then told the rally: 'I have to admit I was not sure last year that a referendum was the right way out ... Now I'm utterly convinced it is the only way out.'

Far from being the 'Remainer-in-Chief' who had led a plot to overturn the 2016 referendum he had moved, very carefully and in crab-like fashion, across a dangerous terrain that was in a state of upheaval. As he puts it now: 'In the end we got to that position because the circumstances pushed us there.'

It was all a bit too late to stop that Parliament hurtling towards the end. At the conference, Corbyn's allies ensured the party was saddled with one final incoherence to take into a looming general election. Delegates approved a policy promising a Labour government would negotiate its own Brexit deal, without saying whether the party would campaign in a referendum to leave the EU on that basis, or fight to stay in. Try explaining that while standing on a doorstep in the rain.

Starmer did his best to make sense of it with his speech to delegates: 'I have a very simple message today: If you want a referendum – vote Labour. If you want a final say on Brexit – vote Labour. If you want to fight for Remain – vote Labour.'

By then, however, he also knew there were lots of other reasons why people might not want to 'vote Labour'.

The oldest form of racism

Starmer has compared the final years of being in Jeremy Corbyn's shadow cabinet to a footballer at a club facing relegation: 'You turn up for training. You try to uphold your standards. You pretty much know the manager will be leaving at the end of the season and you just do your best to keep going.'

He considered resigning several times. If he had quit, however, it would not have been over the Brexit battles consuming British politics and most of his attention. Instead, it would have been in protest against what he calls 'a type of racism that festers and to which those who call themselves anti-racist are often the most blind'.

He is talking, of course, about antisemitism. Many of the left-wing activists who joined Labour in the Corbyn years were so hostile to the Israeli government's treatment of Palestinians that their views had metastasised into forms of prejudice against Jewish people that go back through the centuries and some of humanity's darkest periods of history.

Many millions of words have been written about how this meant Labour, a party that had done much to fight all forms of racism, became tainted by the oldest form of it. But it's still worth adding a few more to trace the blurred and often disputed line of Starmer's engagement on this issue because, for very different reasons, antisemitism would later come to mark out his leadership as much as that of his predecessor.

Like many MPs at that time, between the 2017 and 2019 elections, he remembers with a shudder people telling him they couldn't vote Labour because they were Jewish. But he feels it more personally – and viscerally – because Vic's family are Jewish too. Although his wife is no more religious than he is, they give a respectful nod to her roots by occasionally taking their children to the Liberal Jewish Synagogue in St John's Wood near Lord's cricket ground in London. As the outcry over antisemitism in the party grew, so did Starmer's sense of shame. 'People I had got to know a bit at the synagogue would come up to me, asking, "What's happened to your party? Why can't you do something? Are you embarrassed to be a Labour MP?" I would go home feeling angry,' he says.

At times this became – almost – too much to bear. Chris Ward remembers Starmer coming in one morning and saying he was going to have to resign because 'he couldn't defend this to his members, his family or his constituents; it was very difficult for him.'

Asked why he didn't resign from the shadow cabinet, Starmer says: 'I did question myself the whole time about whether I should stay on or leave. But I thought, on balance, it's better to fight it from the inside.' Many of the MPs most vocal in denouncing Corbyn from the backbenches were privately urging him to remain in place as shadow Brexit secretary because the European issue was so crucial to them. He recalls one particularly fiery meeting of the shadow cabinet in the summer of 2019 after the BBC *Panorama* documentary 'Is Labour Antisemitic?' had aired. 'Jeremy wouldn't stick up for the staff who had blown the whistle,' he says, 'and his office was putting out stuff disparaging them.'

Diane Abbott, the former shadow home secretary, has since poured scorn on the notion that he challenged Corbyn over the issue at these meetings. 'I was in Jeremy's shadow cabinet alongside Starmer,' she said in 2023. 'It is nonsense to say he was fighting privately.'

But her recollection is sharply at odds with not only Starmer's – he has said the rows on the issue went on for entire meetings of the shadow cabinet – but also that of several of her colleagues at those meetings. Even one of Corbyn's most senior advisers, someone who had little sympathy for Starmer but is known for making copious notes on what was being said, has confirmed the shadow Brexit secretary spoke out. 'Keir was among several members of the shadow cabinet raising what was being said in the media about antisemitism,' says this aide. 'He was always very procedurally focused. At one point he was asking for weekly reports on how the party was dealing with the backlog of complaints about it.' Formby eventually agreed to monthly reports to the parliamentary Labour Party instead.

Tom Watson, the party's former deputy leader who repeatedly voiced his concern in public, was impressed by the way Starmer tackled the issue behind the scenes. 'I remember this time when Keir sat opposite Jeremy and gave him the full barrister treatment. He stared straight at him and went very calmly through what was happening and what was wrong,' says Watson. 'Jeremy could not meet his eyes – he'd look down and start playing around with his notes – it was a real moment. Keir got into his head and into the sinews of his soul. In many ways, that was better than anything I could do.'

Starmer also spoke privately with Louise Ellman, a Jewish MP who quit Labour in this period, telling her that his test of whether the party had dealt with the issue was whether she could rejoin. He has nonetheless been criticised by those who refused to serve on Corbyn's frontbench or quit the party for not taking a stronger public stand. Ian Austin, an old ally of Watson who now sits as an independent member of the House of Lords, tweeted at the end of 2019 that he had heard 'Keir Starmer is commenting on Labour antisemitism', adding: 'I wouldn't know. He blocked me for asking him to speak about it and Corbyn's dreadful leadership some months ago. Amazing how these people have finally found some courage.'

Starmer was bound by the rule of collective responsibility under which members of the shadow cabinet are not supposed to attack the leadership or the party's positions in public. Others, however, suggest his public loyalty owed less to this than to his previous profession, in which lawyers are still duty-bound to defend a client even if they suspect he is guilty. Charlie Falconer, who also served in the shadow cabinet on the frontbench during Corbyn's leadership, said lawyers are not allowed to say 'my client's the most appalling fuckwit', but that should not be mistaken for Starmer 'thinking that Corbyn was a good thing'.

If his membership of the shadow cabinet in these circumstances was an act of endurance, there were under-reported moments when Starmer did raise the issue of antisemitism in public. One came as early as July 2018, after the party refused to adopt in full the internationally recognised Holocaust Remembrance Alliance's definition of antisemitism. The Labour leadership insisted it wasn't antisemitic to accuse Jewish people of being more loyal to Israel than the country they live in, to suggest Israel's existence is racist, to hold Israel to a higher standard than other countries, or to compare Israeli policies to those of the Nazis. As condemnation rained down from Jewish community groups, Starmer went on the BBC's *Andrew Marr Show* to say the party needed to do more than 'reflect' on what they were saying. 'If we're not in a position of supporting the full definition,' he added, 'we need to get into that position – and sharpish.'

Another came during an appearance at the Hay Festival in May 2019, when Starmer said: 'We have too many people in the Labour Party who want to pretend there is not an issue. To deny there is an issue is to be part of the problem and we have to be as loud on this as we can be.' He went on to advocate some 'straightforward rule changes' by which members would be as swiftly expelled for anti-semitism as if they supported a candidate from a rival political party. 'It should be clear that if you're going to act in that way you are straight out. If there is an appeal to be had, you can appeal from outside. We just need some clarity on this and some strength to deal with this problem.'

His point about the disparity in the party's disciplinary process was underlined three days later when one of the more prominent members of Starmer's constituency party – Alastair Campbell – found himself summarily thrown out of Labour for the crime of having voted Liberal Democrat in the European elections in protest over Brexit. In contrast, it was claimed Labour members who had been quoted denying the Holocaust were merely suspended, pending an investigation that might last up to two years.

Nor were Brexit and antisemitism the only issues causing deep divides within Labour. Many concerned national security. When Russian spies were caught on camera in Salisbury in March 2018, attempting to murder Sergei Skripal and his daughter Yulia with a deadly nerve agent, Corbyn initially refused to blame the Kremlin and instead asked the prime minister whether the government would cooperate with Moscow's request to be sent a sample of the nerve agent for testing. Seumas Milne, Corbyn's spokesman, went even further in a briefing to journalists outside the House of Commons chamber, comparing the intelligence agency evidence pointing to direct Russian involvement with that used by the last Labour government to justify war in Iraq fifteen years earlier.

Many MPs, from every political party, thought Corbyn crossed a line that day. Part of his appeal to idealistic supporters was his long history as a backbencher fighting for anti-imperialist or inter-nationalist causes. Two years earlier, however, Labour had reaffirmed its support for NATO and the UK's possession of nuclear weapons in spite of the party leader's own views. The perception that Corbyn was instinctively hostile to the West and its military power may have been exaggerated by the media, but it was politically toxic. Milne was regarded with even more suspicion by moderate Labour MPs because the sharpest edges of his opinions had all been laid out in the *Guardian* columns he wrote before going to work for Corbyn. One such, for instance, described Russia's annexation of Crimea from Ukraine in 2014 as a 'purely defensive action'.

Contrary to later claims made by the Conservative Party, Starmer did not remain silent about this issue either, and was one of a few shadow cabinet members to publicly – and swiftly – distance himself from their leader's equivocation over the poisonings. In an appearance on BBC 1's *Question Time* the day after Corbyn's remarks, he expressed full-throated support for the sanctions Theresa May had announced against Russia and its diplomats. The attack 'deserves to be condemned by all of us without reservation', he said, repeating the last two words for emphasis. Pointing out that he had done legal work for the family of Alexander Litvinenko, the victim of another Kremlin assassination plot, Starmer added: 'This is not the first time. It needs to be called out with no ifs and no buts, and we need strong action, as set out by the prime minister.'

The Arlington Group

Jenny Chapman, part of his frontbench team on Brexit, remembers that weekend as one when many people in the party said they could not go on unless there was some light at the end of the tunnel. 'I was at home on a Saturday morning and feeling really angry and upset over the way Corbyn had responded on Salisbury,' she says. 'I called Keir, and asked him if he'd ever thought about being leader. I can't quite remember how he replied but it was along the lines of, "Yes, that's something I might want to do."'

From then on, she hosted Monday morning meetings for him and his aides around her kitchen table. They were joined by Tom Kibasi, then director of the centre-left think tank the IPPR, as well as a smattering of MPs including Chapman's husband Nick Smith and Steve Reed. This embryonic leadership campaign team called themselves the 'Arlington Group', which sounds like a generic insurance firm but was in fact named after the road in Camden where Chapman lives.

Coincidently, *Arlington Road* was also the title of a Hollywood thriller starring Jeff Bridges about a sinister right-wing terrorist plot involving seemingly normal neighbours. And, though covert meetings or codewords conjure up the idea of conspiracy, those involved in the Arlington Group insist it wasn't really like that. 'We just thought it best to meet elsewhere to separate this off from the day-to-day work we were doing in Westminster,' says Chapman. The calculation Starmer had made after the failed parliamentary coup in 2016, that any attempt by MPs to oust Corbyn would be futile and that his eventual successor would come from inside the shadow cabinet, still held true.

One of them recalls that for a long time Starmer refused even to acknowledge in private that he was running for the leadership. 'Keir used to have this lawyerly phrase of "I want to be in a position to consider standing – should a vacancy arise",' he says now. Perhaps, to extend Starmer's analogy of being at a football club facing relegation, he was a player getting his coaching qualifications so he could be ready to become manager of the team if the current one quit.

Whatever the exact definition of his ambition, he set about fulfilling it with the same focused attention to detail that characterises everything he does. Over the previous couple of years, he had been putting together a group of advisers. By then, Chris Ward had been joined by Yasmeen Sebbana, who became his office manager, as well Stuart Ingham, hired as a policy researcher.

Then came Ben Nunn, a quietly spoken but effective media adviser who had previously worked on Owen Smith's failed effort to oust Corbyn. He says it swiftly became clear to him that 'Keir might be in the next leadership contest' and part of his job was to 'make sure he could be the best possible contender'. That meant demonstrating Starmer was providing effective opposition to the

Tories, while also raising his profile and status. There are subtle markers for this within Westminster, which often require a certain amount of self-discipline in not accepting every request to pop up on TV or radio. For instance, Nunn would insist Starmer only do interviews on the BBC Radio 4 *Today* programme in the prime slots of 7.50 a.m. or 8.10 a.m. 'Keir was not going to be a 6.50 a.m. slot politician,' he says firmly.

Through much of 2018 and 2019, Starmer was also painstakingly preparing the ground. A key component of the electoral college in Labour leadership elections are the affiliated trade unions. 'MPs and the media hardly ever go to trade union conferences these days,' says Ward, 'but pretty much whenever and wherever one was being held, Keir was there.'

He and Starmer trailed around these regional meetings and executive councils, well out of sight of the press and some of his rivals who, Ward says, 'were too busy trying to get themselves on TV to notice Keir was doing the hard work'. He also became a regular speaker in local constituencies across the country, earning the gratitude of MPs and a measure of respect from activists. Ward says: 'We weren't oblivious to the fact that a big issue with the party membership in those years was Brexit – so going out to talk to them about it helped establish him there as well.'

These trade union and local party events are about as far from the north London dinner party scene or the imagined lifestyle of a 'lefty lawyer' as you can get. They mean long and lonely train journeys on dark nights and getting home in the small hours of the morning. On one occasion, Starmer remembers being handed a box of takeaway food as he left to catch the last train back to London from Sheffield. 'I opened it sitting on a freezing cold station platform and found it was chicken,' says this vegetarian of more than thirty years. 'I wasn't going to get anything else at that time of night, so I ate every morsel – and very good it tasted too.'

But it got much harder to cling to the notion that it was all just a scoping exercise after one Monday meeting of the Arlington

Group in June 2019, when Starmer told Ward: 'We're going to meet a new guy today.' This turned out to be the red-headed, rapid-fire Irishman Morgan McSweeney, who had cut his teeth fighting the far right in Barking and far-left factions on Lambeth Council when Steve Reed was its leader. Ward was somewhat sceptical because he remembered McSweeney overseeing the debacle of Liz Kendall's leadership bid in 2015, which had achieved a mere 4.5 per cent vote share. 'I'm not sure that's really what we had in mind, Keir,' he said. Starmer told him to reserve judgment until he had heard what McSweeney had to say.

'When we got to the meeting, Morgan didn't say anything for about fifteen or twenty minutes,' remembers Ward. 'Then he got out his slide deck. He ran through exactly where the membership was on every question, which bits of it we could get, which bits we couldn't. It was brilliant. Afterwards, when we're walking back, Keir had this little grin on his face and was like, "D'you see what I mean now?"'

In the previous two years, McSweeney had been running a group called Labour Together that was largely funded by pre-Corbyn donors to the party, including businessman Trevor Chinn, hedge fund manager Martin Taylor and the media tycoon Clive Hollick. The organisation was later fined £14,000 for failing to properly declare around £700,000 in donations as a result of what it said was an administrative error, a story that went virtually unnoticed at the time but made front-page news in the build-up to the 2024 election, when McSweeney's political opponents realised he had been running the organisation for much of that time.

Initially, it echoed a lot of the so-called 'Blue Labour' thinking about reviving working-class tradition and community that cut across the usual left–right divides. Starmer had occasionally attended its regular dinners in Soho, along with MPs like Lisa Nandy, Lucy Powell, Steve Reed, Shabana Mahmood and Jon Cruddas. But McSweeney's focus was not so much on ideas as organisation. Through 2018, he had used private polls and focus groups to perform the equivalent of an MRI scan on the party's membership. By the time he joined Starmer's circle, he probably knew more about Labour's internal wiring than anyone alive.

The research had concluded that, far from being entirely in thrall to Corbyn and the hard left, the largest segment of members weren't particularly ideological at all and had joined the party as an expression of much vaguer values. As was sometimes said during the Cold War, they owed more to 'Len-*non*' of the Beatles fame in the 1960s than the 'Len-*in*' of the Russian Bolshevik revolution in 1917. Together with a smaller number of what he called 'instrumentalists' who would back the candidate with the best chance of beating the Tories, McSweeney believed it was possible to put a leadership-winning coalition together.

Although McSweeney later admitted to colleagues that he had doubted whether Starmer 'had enough political instinct to win', he was struck by how much of their conversation had been about not just winning the leadership or running the Labour Party but about being prime minister. None of the other potential candidates vying for his services had mentioned that to him and McSweeney decided that if the shadow Brexit secretary had set his sights on Downing Street, he probably deserved some help with the 'easier task' of succeeding Jeremy Corbyn.

McSweeney's arrival, initially very much behind the scenes, coincided with a step change in activity. Everybody was delegated a particular area of responsibility. He focused on the party's membership while Nunn ran communications, Ward worked on trade union nominations, Chapman was busy lining up support from MPs, Ingham concentrated on policy and Kibasi on strategic messaging.

From a distance, it might seem remarkable such a machine could have flown under the political radar for so long. But these were extraordinary times when political attention was fixated elsewhere, first on the Tory party's leadership contest in the summer of 2019, then the fireworks that accompanied Johnson's arrival in Downing Street.

Within weeks of becoming prime minister, he had illegally suspended the sitting of Parliament and told almost two dozen MPs – including former chancellors Ken Clarke and Philip Hammond – they were no longer allowed to sit as Conservative MPs. There was a brief spasm of speculation amid the mayhem that Starmer might take over as an interim prime minister of a coalition government to stop a No Deal Brexit but this quickly faded with no sign the opposition parties could agree. Instead, Johnson negotiated what he claimed to be an 'oven-ready' deal to leave the EU and then, with the support of Liberal Democrats – who believed polls showing their party were on the verge of a 'historic breakthrough' – got parliamentary approval for another general election that would 'Get Brexit Done'.

Through that strange winter campaign of the last days in November and the early ones of December, Starmer spent much of his time almost entirely out of sight, unless you lived in one of the more than forty remote constituencies where he may have knocked on your door. A politician who had been in the heart of a titanic political battle for the previous three years saw his media profile reduced to posting selfies of himself with small clumps of anorak-clad activists. According to figures compiled by Loughborough University, he appeared in just 0.6 per cent of the election coverage, even though he was the shadow cabinet member responsible for Brexit – the single most discussed issue. A measure of Starmer's invisibility is that Ian Austin, the former backbench Labour MP who wasn't even standing for election, was given three times more airtime during the campaign.

There is no real dispute that Corbyn's team deliberately kept Starmer away from the limelight. In part, this was because they hoped to switch attention away from Brexit to other issues, but they also probably calculated that, with defeat looming and a leadership contest almost certain to follow, denying Starmer the oxygen of publicity might boost the chances of a more left-wing candidate.

And for once, their purposes also suited Starmer. The end was in sight and with Corbyn's leadership heading for an electoral car crash, it made sense to be as far from the scene as possible.

By the end of those overheated years between the referendum of 2016 and the election of 2019, many political careers – left, right and centre – had been turned to ash. Brexit destroyed two prime ministers in Cameron and May, while a string of ministers like David Davis resigned and never returned. Corbyn announced the day after the election that he would step down when a new leader was elected, and most of his staff now no longer even have security passes for Parliament. Owen Smith quit politics, along with Tom Watson, who published a bestselling book on losing weight and eventually re-emerged with his slimmed-down frame clad in ermine as a member of the House of Lords. Chuka Umunna and all the MPs in Change UK were defeated. So too were patrician Remainer Tories like Dominic Grieve who had stood as independents, as well as the Liberal Democrat leader, Jo Swinson.

Of all the main players, only two walked from this burning theatre with their reputations enhanced. One was Johnson, who would self-immolate a couple of years later. The other was Keir Starmer.

Despite his stated disapproval for the profession he had entered fewer than five years earlier, it is hard not to conclude that this was someone who had, usually quietly and always assiduously, got pretty good at politics. Or, at least, parts of it.

20

The candidate

Another Future is Possible

Starmer spent the election night of December 12, 2019 at home with Vic and a few of his aides watching the careers of parliamentary colleagues coming to an abrupt end as the results rolled in. Later, he went over to the count at Somers Town sports hall for his own.

In Holborn and St Pancras, though he still received almost thirty-seven thousand votes, that was down by more than five thousand, with the bulk of those going to pro-Remain parties like the Liberal Democrats and the Greens. The speech he delivered not long before dawn was anything but victorious in tone.

'There is no hiding place from the result of this election,' he said. 'It is devastating for the party, devastating for our members and activists who have done so much campaigning to win this election. It's devastating for the communities that we seek to represent and, frankly, it's devastating for our country too.' The sharper ears present pricked up at the way he placed so much emphasis on the 'members and activists' who had wanted to win – and whose support he would need if he was to win the leadership. The end of his speech was also notable in this regard. 'We as a movement need to reflect on this result and understand it together. We also have a duty to rebuild, starting now,' he said. Starmer's local newspaper duly reported the next day that he was 'one of the favourites to replace Jeremy Corbyn, who has announced he would stand down'.

Johnson's Conservatives had won 330,000 more votes than Theresa May two years earlier, an increase of just 1.3 per cent in the overall share, but he nonetheless gained the big majority she had been denied because his opponents' support splintered in different directions. The Liberal Democrats – far from making their historic breakthrough – had seen their already paltry total of twelve MPs fall to eleven. Labour was left with sixty fewer MPs, its lowest total since 1935.

Some blamed Labour's painfully born pro-referendum position for the demolition of the 'Red Wall' in the party's traditional working-class heartlands. For their part, Remainers said the party had moved too slowly to adopt the policy but would have suffered an even worse defeat if it had still been stuck on the fence.

As for Starmer, his tour of far-flung constituencies had convinced him the reasons for the election disaster included voters' hostility towards Corbyn, the antisemitism row and a manifesto overloaded with less-than-credible promises, as well as Brexit. 'If anybody says they weren't the four issues I'd question how many campaign doorsteps they actually went to,' he said later.

His disappearance from public view during the election had enabled him to prepare harder than ever for what would happen next. The Arlington Group started meeting twice a week during the election. With Jenny Chapman away fighting, in vain as it turned out, to hold her Red Wall constituency in Darlington, Starmer's team swapped her kitchen table in north London's Camden for that of Tom Kibasi in Kennington on the south side of the river.

There was endless debate about a campaign slogan. Some wanted it to be 'I'm Ready', as a way of focusing attention on his competence and experience. Others preferred 'For Justice', because they thought it would highlight the battles for human rights he had fought in his long legal career.

Eventually Starmer himself came up with: 'Another Future is Possible', which might have seemed an echo of a book John McDonnell had written about socialism back in 2007, entitled

Another World Is Possible, or perhaps of the left-wing anti-Brexit group Another Europe is Possible. But Starmer says neither of them, at least consciously, were in his mind. The slogan was meant, instead, to show there was still an alternative to defeat, but also signal how the path towards any victory was narrow; progress was 'possible', not inevitable.

Ben Nunn had scribbled down three words on a Post-it note that later became the frame of the leadership campaign's communications. The first was 'unity', to underline Starmer's desire to end the factionalism many thought had defined the left's attitude towards the rest of the party. The second was 'radical', to reassure the left he remained committed to deep and lasting change. The third was 'win'. A few weeks into the campaign, Nunn began underlining this last word because he realised that for party members the most important component of Starmer's appeal was that he might be able to break Labour's sequence of four successive election defeats.

Even then, however, there was some scratching of heads within his team over another word – 'vision', something political leaders are typically supposed to offer to voters. But Starmer has always disliked the obsession with 'vision' because he is neither given to grand abstractions nor easily located in a particular ideological framework.

Someone who got an early insight into this was Paul Mason, a former BBC journalist who, despite having been a disciple of Corbyn's project, had split with it over Brexit. Along with other pro-Europeans on the left of the party, he found himself being drawn into the orbit of the shadow Brexit secretary. Over a curry and a trip to the pub, he formed the impression Starmer was 'a heavyweight politician with slightly lightweight politics'. At one meeting, where Chapman and McSweeney were also present, Mason says: 'I asked Keir directly what he really stood for. The room went silent for a moment and then he explained, how, if he saw something wrong, he "could not turn away and walk by on the other side of the road".' For someone so versed in Marxist economics as Mason, this may have lacked the theoretical rigour he expected but he nonetheless recognised a 'genuine instinct for justice'.

This became condensed into what Starmer started to call 'the moral case for socialism', an argument that dovetailed with McSweeney's research into Labour's largely values-driven membership and the coalition he was trying to build to win the leadership. It would also provide the basis for the campaign launch video, but was probably best expressed by an article that later appeared in the *Guardian* which began: 'I have always been motivated by a burning desire to tackle inequality and injustice, to stand up for the powerless against the powerful. That's my socialism. If I see something wrong or spot an injustice, I want to put it right.'

A campaign office was set up in Vauxhall where there was a sense of insurgency against what had been presented over the previous five years as the left's domination of the party. Momentum, the grassroots campaign that had propelled Corbyn to the leadership, was said to have the best data. Unite, the powerful union run by Len McCluskey, had the most money. Victory without the backing of either was regarded as very difficult. In the days following the general election, Rebecca Long-Bailey, the 'continuity candidate', was expected to get the support of both as well as that of the shadow chancellor John McDonnell, and was promptly declared by the *Guardian* as the 'favourite to win'. The *Observer* confidently predicted Corbyn's successor was 'likely to be a woman'. *The Times* mused that, while it might not all be plain sailing for the left, 'conventional wisdom' meant Long-Bailey 'had the easiest path to victory' – especially because her flatmate Angela Rayner had decided to stand for the post of deputy instead. The *Sun*, perhaps still smarting over Starmer's role in prosecuting phone hacking eight years earlier, said 'the multi-millionaire human rights QC now posing as a working-class boy' looked like a 'stone-cold loser'.

But much of the data McSweeney needed was available through networks of MPs, while money was pouring in from friends and donors who had turned their back on the party during the Corbyn years. Robert Latham, Starmer's old colleague at Doughty Street, gave £100,000, as did Waheed Alli, who had made a fortune in the TV industry before becoming a Blairite peer. They were among just a handful of people – including three of the big donors to Labour together – Martin Taylor, Trevor Chinn and Clive Hollick – who, by the end of the campaign, had contributed a total of £455,000, twice the amount that Unite gave to Long-Bailey.

Any confidence the left had in retaining control of the party was shaken by the decision of Simon Fletcher to join Starmer's team. Fletcher had masterminded both Ken Livingstone's successful London mayoral campaign in 2000 and that of Corbyn for the party leadership in 2015. His instinct had been to help Long-Bailey but, having seen the dysfunction surrounding her embryonic campaign, he decided it would be better to join someone who 'at least wanted engagement with the left'. Starmer had sounded him out when they met during the election campaign in a Camden café. 'I knew him a bit already but I found myself liking him more than before. He's quite approachable – almost a bit earnest – and, more importantly, he reassured me that he wanted to stay within the broad left framework.'

Fletcher admits to looking askance at some in Starmer's circle of advisers, who by then included battle-scarred warriors from the party's 'old right' who have a tendency to refer to anyone to the left of them as 'Trots'. But he found some familiar faces too. His name-sake and fellow former Corbyn staff member, Kat Fletcher, had been hired to run the campaign's logistics. They were soon joined by others, including Paul Mason who was part of the team assembled to prepare him for hustings and, much to the annoyance of some of his former comrades, publicly endorsed Starmer the following month.

This eclectic campaign drew up a list of the potential strategic and messaging challenges the candidate would face. It included finding a way to appeal to the broad mass of Labour members who had backed Corbyn twice before in 2015 and 2016, showing how a former lawyer from London could understand the party's working-class heartlands, addressing the widely felt desire for Labour to have a woman leader, and recasting a political identity that had become linked to Remain.

As they prepared for 'the soft launch', Jenny Chapman was sent out to roll the pitch for him, telling the BBC Labour should not pick its next leader on the basis of whether they 'have ovaries or a northern accent'. The following day, December 18, still less than a week after the general election, the *Guardian* published an interview that McSweeney declared triumphantly the next day to the rest of the office had been 'pitch perfect' and would now be pivotal to their success. Starmer confirmed, with a large measure of understatement, that he was 'seriously considering' running for the Labour leadership. But much more interesting was how, by addressing each potential negative in turn, he demonstrated he had thought about each with the kind of thoroughness he had shown both in court as a lawyer and dealing with the complexities of Brexit.

Starmer declared that 'the case for a bold and radical Labour government' was as strong as before the election, describing the 'moral injustice' of poverty, inequality and homelessness, an appeal aimed squarely at the expressive values of the Labour membership. But then he added another, for those activists just craving victory who had been identified in McSweeney's research as 'instrumentalists'. Starmer said: 'I want trust to be restored in the Labour party as a progressive force for good – and that means we have to win.'

While acknowledging no one would call him a 'Corbynista', he emphasised he was a socialist and didn't 'need somebody else's name tattooed on my head to know what I think'. Asked if he was too middle class, he replied, 'My dad was a toolmaker and my mum was a nurse,' before adding – in words that these days might induce some form of aneurysm among those who have followed his interviews and speeches since – 'not everybody knows that and that's because I don't say it very often'. He then deftly dealt with the fact of his being a man, saying this was 'undeniably true' and 'there will be very good women candidates', but he would be entering the race 'because of the ideas I want to put forward'.

Yet his answer on Europe proved the most significant because Starmer demonstrated once more a pretty ruthless capacity to extricate himself from a position he believed could no longer be defended. He expressed passing regret over the way the campaign had been fought by Corbyn's team, saying: 'I don't think we tackled the "get Brexit done" slogan strongly enough.' Then he added that this now meant 'the Brexit debate changes – we will leave in January and the argument will have to be about the type of deal that we have with Europe'.

Two of his rivals, Emily Thornberry and Jess Phillips, ran on much more overtly Remainer platforms. Neither of their candidacies ever really got off the ground. By contrast, the shadow Brexit secretary, who had been more associated with Labour's policy than either of them, just drew a line under the issue that had so dominated the first five years of his political career and walked away with barely a glance backwards.

The election had settled the matter. In Starmer's words, it was 'time to move on'.

Points of view

Starmer had talked with Vic during the general election about what would happen afterwards and she knew him well enough to realise a campaign was underway. One former aide points out, 'A married man doesn't disappear off to a USDAW regional conference on a wet weekend without a decent explanation.' But his habit of compartmentalising different aspects of his life meant the prospect of becoming leader of the Labour Party and the consequences for everyone around him had not been properly thrashed out.

As is so often the case, it was Colin Peacock who got straight to the heart of the matter. 'What the hell are you doing, Keir?' asked his old friend over a New Year's Eve dinner in Crouch End. 'Why would you want to take all that on? You'd have a much better life without this.' At one point, when Starmer got up to reach for the potatoes, his daughter decided this was the moment to pull his chair away before he could sit down again. 'Colin had just told me that all political careers end in failure and, as I lay on my back swearing, I could see what he meant,' says Starmer.

What really struck him, however, was that this conversation came from an entirely different perspective than those of people in politics. 'Colin's concerns had nothing to do with whether or not I would win the leadership, the state of the party or the country. He didn't discuss how I would raise money or get nominations. He certainly wasn't after a job on the front bench. Instead, he was worried about the impact on my family, or whether I would still have time to play football and go for a drink.'

Starmer didn't heed his friend's advice that night and, in any case, it came just as his campaign bandwagon was leaving the station. The very next day, he became the undisputed frontrunner in the leadership race, with the publication of a poll of Labour members showing he was the most popular choice across all regions of the UK, age groups and social classes.

On January 5, 2020, Starmer formally launched his campaign, followed by a visit to Stevenage, chosen for its symbolic significance as the kind of constituency the party had lost and needed to win back. Much of his speech focused on why Labour had lost four elections in a row and 'the huge task of forging a way forward to victory'. By most accounts it was a fairly nondescript occasion, but there were a few flashes of passion. The first came when Starmer reminded those present of the experience of knocking on doors and being told by someone they couldn't vote Labour because of anti-semitism. 'Never again!' he declared, consciously using the phrase carved in stone on Holocaust memorials. The second came after a member of the audience attacked his communications director Ben Nunn for having previously worked for a private healthcare firm. 'I won't tolerate that,' replied Starmer abruptly, saying that criticism of any member of his staff should be aimed at him 'because I will carry the can for every organisation I lead'.

Much of the energy flowing into the campaign that day came from the video he launched at the same time, directed by Flo Wilkinson, the filmmaker wife of Nunn, who had driven her around the country in the final weeks of December in search of footage. It opened with a monologue delivered in the strong northern accent of a former miner, Jimmy Haworth, along with news clips from 'the struggles of the 1980s' against Thatcher. He described how 'Keir defended the printworkers in Wapping and was there in the crowd that night when police on horseback charged into the crowd of peaceful pickets.' There was a shot of Haworth next to an old pithead as he praised Starmer for standing up too for 'my union, the National Union of Mineworkers, when the Tories closed the mines'. The next testimony was provided by a veteran peace protester, Lindis Percy, who paid tribute to his legal work for environmental campaigners trying to stop the widening of the M3 and drilling for oil in the North Sea. She carefully avoided any reference to her own campaigns against nuclear weapons, saying merely that Starmer had defended her in court for 'bringing public scrutiny and awareness to the presence of the United States' visiting forces'. Then came Doreen Lawrence who pointed out how, when he was director of public prosecutions, Starmer had shown courage to 'take on the Murdoch press over phone hacking' – a still photograph of Rebekah Brooks was shown – as well as being 'instrumental in getting justice' for her son, Stephen.

Only at the end of the film did the candidate himself appear, for once not wearing a suit and tie, saying: 'I've spent my life fighting for justice and for the powerless against the powerful.' Apart from some vague comments about spreading power to communities, rebuilding the economy and pursuing a human rights-based foreign policy, Starmer didn't make clear exactly what 'future' he believed was 'possible'. The video was instead about showing how someone with relatively little political background fitted into a sentimental version of past battles in opposition as remembered by Labour's members and trade unionists.

Some of the cases highlighted from his legal career are probably not those he would choose now. Alastair Campbell texted him asking why the only mentions of the last Labour government were to highlight Starmer's opposition to the Iraq War and his legal representation of asylum seekers who were being denied benefits. But the story being told wasn't an ideological one in any way. It was about values, tribal identities and feelings. As a piece of political campaigning within the Labour Party, therefore, it was hugely effective and received an almost rapturous reception from many quarters.

When all the nominations were in, Starmer had secured the backing of 374 constituency parties including Corbyn's Islington North, 88 MPs or MEPs, and 16 affiliated organisations, more than double those of Long-Bailey.

A particular source of satisfaction was the support of Unison. As Britain's biggest trade union, it had been one of two key nominations Starmer believed were essential and getting Unison justified the countless hours he had spent over the previous year building up relationships at regional conferences.

The other one he had wanted was Andy Burnham. They had been relatively close when, as a newly elected MP, Starmer had been a member of Burnham's shadow home affairs team. They shared similar politics, a passion for football and a sense of being slightly apart from the Westminster scene. Burnham had left Parliament in 2017 to become the directly elected mayor of Manchester – a post the media insist on calling the 'King of the North' – and his endorsement was seen as a potentially crucial counterweight to perceptions of Starmer being 'too southern', or worse, 'too London'.

Starmer went to see Burnham in Manchester and asked for his support. According to one of those present in the meeting, he said,

'You know what needs to be done and I can't do it without you.'
The mayor apologetically explained why that would be very difficult for him in a contest where other leadership candidates were
likely to include two MPs from the Greater Manchester region,
including not only Long-Bailey but also Lisa Nandy. 'I can't be
seen to be backing a London lawyer against two women from the
north,' Burnham is said to have told him.

The best that he could offer was a promise to stay neutral but
their relationship would turn steadily more sour in the years that
followed, with Burnham since publicly complaining Starmer's
office have briefed against him. One source who knows both of
them says this tension goes back to the leadership contest because
'it took a lot for Keir to ask for help – he trusted Andy and felt let
down'. Friends of Burnham, however, say the Manchester mayor
has only a hazy recollection of the meeting and it was never entirely
clear to him that Starmer was asking for his support. 'Andy gave
him a lot of advice on the leadership campaign and did, towards
the end of the contest, say he'd be voting for him. So to be honest,
he's a bit baffled about all of this.'

Starmer wasn't short of other endorsements. He got public backing from Gordon Brown, the last Labour prime minister, whom he
had been talking to privately for the past couple of years, as well as
another former leader in Ed Miliband. David Lammy, who had
briefly considered running himself, became a co-chair of Starmer's
campaign. But the failure to secure Burnham's support may have
had a long-term consequence by shifting him further away from the
so-called 'Blue Labour' group, much of which has subsequently
coalesced around Nandy.

More immediately, it reinforced Starmer's dislike of the
favour-trading transactional side of politics that comes so naturally
to others. Chris Ward remembers persuading a 'very reluctant Keir'
to have a drink at the Strangers' Bar in the bowels of Parliament as
part of a plan to boost his nominations. 'He stood there for about
half an hour and then decided it was time to go,' says Ward. 'I had

got him down in his diary for a second trip the next day too but, when we got there, most of the people were exactly the same as the previous night and he's like, "We're not doing this." I don't think he went back for another two years.'

This goes deeper than not wanting to hang out with MPs every night. It was reflected in Starmer's language at the time about ending the 'factionalism' he saw as not only a feature of the Corbyn years but also those of the Blair–Brown battles during the last Labour government.

'Keir's instinct is to be wary of any label being pinned on him or being seen to form permanent alliances with one group or another – he prefers to keep them quite fluid,' says Ward. 'If you think of other leading figures in Labour, their social group and their political network are almost the same thing. But Keir's political and personal life don't merge. When he finishes for the day, he goes home to his family or to see his old friends. He's just not a normal politician – that's always the biggest thing I tell people when they ask me what he's really like.'

Perhaps it means he can move faster and more freely than others who carry the expectations of their alliances and factions. Some worry for him, though, and say he will eventually need some closer friends in politics ready to 'die in the ditch for him' during the tough times.

In the end, it may be less of a conscious decision than an expression of his desire to cling to the normality of his old life which means he will still prefer an evening with Colin Peacock than with the people he meets in politics – even if Starmer doesn't always take his advice.

'The measure of us'

Concerns about Starmer's reluctance to build a political network to sustain him in government were the tiniest clouds on the horizon at the beginning of 2020 because he had not yet won the leadership, let alone a general election.

His aides felt a sense of liberation as they prepared for a campaign schedule that would include more than a dozen hustings meetings across Britain and three televised debates with his rivals. Nunn said a set-piece interview Starmer had done on BBC 1's *Andrew Marr Show* for the campaign's launch had been the first time he 'hadn't been shouted at by the leader's office afterwards'.

But there was danger in this too. Starmer knew endless shopping lists of proposals were going to be put to him during the weeks ahead in TV studios or hustings – and he considered these bad places to make policy decisions. His natural caution was already seeing him hedge some answers about how much of Corbyn's programme he would retain. In an interview with *LabourList* on January 12, for instance, he ducked a question about whether he supported the nationalisation of key public services by saying, 'I'm very focused on the fact that the next manifesto is likely to be in four or five years' time and we need to build towards that.' A few days later, Momentum had thrown its considerable weight behind Long-Bailey, who had no hesitation in backing a raft of the most left-wing policies, claiming she had not only supported Corbyn's programme but had also written much of it.

Simon Fletcher, Chris Ward and Stuart Ingham in Starmer's team began work on a list of 'Ten Pledges', based largely on positions he had previously set out or was planning to take. The idea was to give him more definition and neutralise attacks from the left on policy as much as they could.

Then, on January 23, just a few days after the first set of hustings in Liverpool, the sharp spikes of real life once more punctured this political bubble. Starmer was walking towards his office in Parliament, when Nunn approached him with the kind of urgency that meant bad news and told him to speak with Vic. 'Find somewhere to do it in private,' he said, 'but do it now.'

Her mother, Barbara, was in an ambulance. There had been an accident at the hairdressers where she had broken her neck falling down some metal stairs. Vic told him to get to hospital fast. He says: 'Barbara was conscious but, being a doctor herself, knew exactly how serious it was. She needed a massive operation and there was never going to be a perfect outcome. This was a woman who had been in really good health, completely independent, who was really close to her grandchildren. She meant the world to all of us.'

He immediately suspended his campaign and spent many hours with her over the next two weeks, even after he went back out to do hustings events. On one occasion, he remembers being backstage taking a phone call from the hospital and then finding it almost impossible to walk out with 'a big smile on my face' to ask people to vote for him. Although Barbara had her surgery, Starmer says 'she never properly regained consciousness' and died a few days later.

It is still viscerally personal to him and something he finds difficult to talk about. 'To watch Vic lose her mum was even harder for me than losing my parents. I felt completely helpless because I couldn't reach into the space to stop her hurting. There was nothing I could say to make this right. All I could do was show her how much she mattered to me,' he says.

Vic tried to stop her husband suspending the campaign, telling him that her mum wouldn't want him to do that – but he felt he had to do so anyway. He later turned his office in the house into a bedroom for her ninety-year-old dad, so they could look after him at home.

When Starmer was at the hospital with Vic and her mother, the campaign team emailed over the Ten Pledges for him to sign off. Although another example of the political world grinding up against what is very personal to him, he has never tried to use his family's crisis as an excuse for the difficulties these pledges have caused him since. Indeed, he acknowledges that he read and approved them before they were unveiled on February 11, three days after Barbara Alexander died and twenty-four hours before the leadership candidates' first televised debate.

The pledges included measures he has since dropped, such as the common ownership of the Royal Mail, energy and water, defending the free movement of people with Europe, higher taxes for the richest and the abolition of student tuition fees.

Although they did not include some positions which would have marked him out as a left candidate, such as being opposed to the UK having nuclear weapons or the expansion of NATO, it was untypical of Starmer to tie himself to specific policy positions. A few days later in the campaign, for instance, he refused to join Nandy and Long-Bailey in signing a twelve-point pledge card committing the party to expel 'trans-phobic' members who were part of 'exclusionist hate-groups'. More notably, he also declined to follow the other candidates – including Long-Bailey – in describing himself as a 'Zionist', saying only he was 'sympathetic' to the cause.

In some of his interviews at this time, Starmer tried to walk back expectations by explaining the Ten Pledges were only 'an indication of my direction of travel' and he could not be expected to write the manifesto for a general election four years away without knowing 'what the state of the economy will be'.

But the belief among many of his critics that the promises were an entirely cynical manoeuvre has sometimes been reinforced by comments from those running his campaign. Jenny Chapman has suggested the pledges were not his 'real politics', adding: 'There was an understanding of the best issues to talk about if you want to become leader of the Labour Party. There is permission there to say, "this is the kind of country it would be lovely if it could be", because you're not actually pitching to the entire country to be the prime minister.'

The idea that Starmer promised 'Corbynism without Corbyn' to appeal to Labour's left-wing members and then ditched all his pledges after being elected leader has taken root even among the more thoughtful commentators. 'Low politics put Sir Keir in a high place' was how the *Economist*'s Duncan Robinson put it in 2023. Others have pointed out that making different cases depending on the audience is something for which politicians are occasionally criticised but barristers do all the time. In any case, these days, plenty of people across the political spectrum line up daily on social media platforms to denounce what they claim were his outright lies told during the leadership election. Matt Zarb-Cousin, a former spokesman for Corbyn and Long-Bailey, is typical. He has said: 'If Starmer was honest about his intentions, or if there was even some ambiguity, he would not have won the leadership. That is why he felt the need to publish the Ten Pledges, and foreground them on his website and a mass mailout to all members that would have cost tens of thousands.'

Such attacks often come from those who were always opposed to Starmer and never countenanced backing him, so it is harder for them to claim betrayal. For instance, so little did the 'ten pledges' cut through with Long-Bailey that even at the end of the campaign she was still complaining, 'I don't know what Keir's policy ideas are, if I'm honest.'

But those who said at the time that the pledges were the reason they voted for Starmer deserve to be taken more seriously. They include Laura Parker, who had previously been Corbyn's private secretary and Momentum's national coordinator. She had got to know Starmer a little as part of the pro-European left when he was shadow Brexit secretary and publicly endorsed him on February 19, saying: 'In defending the transformative economic agenda upon which he stood as a shadow cabinet member in 2019, I trust that Keir means what he has written in his ten pledges to us. It would be self-defeating for him to say one thing then act otherwise.'

Parker says: 'I got a bucketload of grief on social media for backing him.' Asked what she thinks of him now, she sighs before saying: 'I still think Keir is a decent person in as much as he wouldn't have been having parties in Downing Street during Covid or handing out PPE contracts to his mates. But is he a trustworthy politician? The evidence is pretty clear on that. Whether or not he set out to deceive, he deceived. He's no fool and he knows how he got elected. Forty per cent of people who voted for Jeremy in 2015 and 2017, voted for Keir. A lot of them now feel conned.'

Simon Fletcher, as one of the authors of the pledges, says: 'Some people have accused me of writing them so we could hold him to account for them later. That's completely untrue. I just thought it was healthy to go into an election with something to say.' He has since expressed bitter regret over his decision to join Starmer's team, saying: 'The shortfall between what was promised and what has happened since raises some very big questions for thousands on the left and soft left who voted for [him] to be leader. It sadly proved to be the wrong thing, for me at least, to have supported that leadership campaign. From my own perspective it was a mistake and ultimately a political dead end.'

There are those around Starmer who think this is no bad thing because it underlines the difference with his predecessor. 'You're either going to be criticised for the positions you defend or the positions you dump,' says one of them. 'It's a fairly binary choice and you have to do the one you feel most comfortable about.'

A reasonable assessment of the ten pledges is that, if something like this was needed to protect his policy flank in 2020, he made a mistake in allowing the pledges to be so specific when he probably should have signalled only broader principles. And Starmer, though probably inured to the left's condemnations by now, is not entirely desensitised to criticism when it's voiced by people he respects like Parker and Fletcher. Sometimes, he can become almost monosyllabic about the fate of the pledges, as if disposing of them is a rather distasteful business that is best not discussed. Asked on BBC Radio 4 in July 2022 whether they were 'dead in the water', he replied bluntly: 'Yes,' before adding: 'The financial situation has changed, the debt situation has changed.'

The combination of what he calls the 'huge damage done to the economy by this Tory government', as well as Covid and the war in Ukraine, has had a severe impact on public finances which means the most expensive items like common ownership of all the major public utilities cannot be afforded. 'A set of policies from February 2020 cannot just be cut and pasted into a manifesto for a general election, in 2024,' says Starmer, who goes on to emphasise that in any case they were by no means the 'backbone' of his leadership campaign: 'I spent most of my time telling the Labour Party we had to get serious again about winning back voters so that we could start changing lives.' Indeed, the final pledge was about providing effective opposition to the Tories and how important it was never to lose sight of what was needed for victory.

He also insists that much of the substance of the pledges is now Labour policy. This includes building a greener economy, creating the publicly owned GB Energy, investing in universal public services, bringing about the common ownership of the railways, as well as showing compassion towards genuine refugees, devolving power away from Westminster, clamping down on tax avoidance by the super-rich, introducing new workers' rights, and – eventually – abolishing the House of Lords.

But, if the pledges were protecting his left flank during the months that followed as Starmer continued to dominate the leadership battle, there was another conflict going on inside his head between his real-life concerns and those of politics. It was a time when the media was demanding he open himself up to the public more than ever before, even as his emotions were still raw from Barbara's death.

In the week of her funeral at Hoop Lane Crematorium in Golders Green, he had taken his family to the liberal synagogue in St John's Wood with Bernard that weekend to hear her name read out, as is the Jewish custom for those who have passed away. That had also been the venue for a leadership hustings on February 13, just a few days after Barbara had died. The tone was set by Margaret Hodge, the veteran Labour MP, opening proceedings by saying history had been rewritten by members of the shadow cabinet now seeking support because they had not been bold or brave enough to stand up for the Jewish community 'when we needed them most'. A series of local Jewish party members then went on to denounce the Labour Party's handling of antisemitism. Starmer began his first answer by saying: 'I'm sorry. To the wider community, I'm sorry that we let our party get into the state where you lost faith in us. I'm sorry.' Chris Ward remembers it as the only such occasion when Starmer broke with his usual practice of having a discussion about how he had done and what he could do better. 'He was very silent and upset afterwards – he just went home,' says Ward, 'as he got into the cab, Keir said, "If we win – day one – we fix this, this cannot carry on."'

The campaign rolled on, with Starmer's campaign brushing aside complaints that it had broken the letter of rules over accessing membership data or the spirit of them delaying the disclosure of donations until the contest was finished. Only once, at a hustings organised by the *Guardian* in Manchester on February 25, did the cracks really show. The journalist chairing the meeting, Anushka Asthana, picked up on an answer he had given to a radio show a few days earlier. 'Is it true that the most exciting thing you've ever done is take your kids to the football?' she asked, earning laughter from the audience.

Starmer replied: 'These questions are somehow supposed to be the measure of us.' Then he stopped for a couple of seconds before continuing, 'But – but – they're so pathetic.' There was an audible gasp from someone filling the silence. He went on to explain how his family had just lost Barbara after seventeen awful days in intensive care. 'I've been trying to be the best husband I can be to my wife and the best dad I can be to my grieving children. Then I'm asked what's the most exciting thing I've done – and I'm judged on that? I know who I am. I know what I stand for.'

He is slightly embarrassed by this answer now, which he concedes was 'tetchier than the question deserved'. Everyone has problems in their lives and there's no competition for who has the worst, so he goes to some lengths to emphasise that he wasn't seeking any special sympathy or setting himself apart from anyone else. 'I was trying to say that the ordinary, very personal, priorities of being a good husband and a father were more important to me than having some extraordinary personal story.'

But Starmer's unshakeable belief that 'I know who I am and what I stand for' is, for him at least, a better measure of his politics than any policy pledge.

Even when heading for victory in the Labour leadership contest, the circumstances of Barbara Alexander's death had pulled him back sharply to a set of values that don't come from politics and are what he always says matter most.

As we have seen, with the death of his parents and friends at other crucial moments in his career, this wasn't the first time when reality had tapped on the thin glass windows of politics.

And nor would it be the last.

Part V

Running

Back from the brink and on to
the gates of government

Rocks and hard places

Keir Starmer is in an overheated Leeds hotel ballroom telling an audience of several hundred health professionals about his mother and his sister who were both nurses, his wife who works at his local hospital and her mother who was formerly a local GP.

So far, so good. Then he says: 'So, you see, the NHS runs through my family like a brand in a rock.' He pauses because that doesn't sound right and tries again. 'A rock ... err ... of ... err ... a rock.' That doesn't sound too good either. 'Well, anyway,' he says, 'you know what I'm trying to describe!'

There is a bit of sympathetic laughter which he joins in with for a second or two as he realises, too late, that what he meant to say was 'the NHS runs through my family like a stick of rock', the sort you get at the seaside with the name of the resort running through it.

In other circumstances, this might have been a small story in a newspaper or one of those social media videos – 'Red-faced Sir Keir mangles words and leaves audience baffled' – but the purpose of telling it now is not to show he isn't always the most effortless communicator. Instead, the most remarkable aspect of the event is that there are no journalists or television camera crews there to cover the speech at all.

This doesn't seem to make any more sense than his line about the stick of rock. It's December 2022 and Starmer, riding high in the polls, is back in the city where he went to university with a

friendly audience hanging on his every word. Almost any leader of
the Labour Party before him would have regarded this as a near
perfect opportunity to deliver some passion about the NHS,
perhaps a snippet of policy about how the next government will
save it, at least a standard-issue condemnation of the Tory record.
Surely the local TV station would send someone along in case he
made some news?

The answer is that they probably would have done, if they had
been invited. The absence of media is quite deliberate and at the
insistence of the leader himself because he doesn't regard this
speech as part of political campaigning at all. Rather, he is addressing the Pancreatic Society as a way of expressing gratitude to its
president for the way he treated Starmer's brother a few months
ago.

Nick Starmer had been very seriously ill earlier that year and
taken to Leeds for major surgery where he suffered complications
and needed another emergency operation in which there was a real
risk of him dying. Although this was happening in the middle of
the local election campaign, it was serious enough for the Labour
leader to slip away to see his brother half a dozen times at the hospital, where staff let him sneak in through the back gate to avoid any
media.

'People in this room treated my brother and looked after him,'
he tells the Pancreatic Society. 'Thank you. I hope you know what
it means to me and my family.'

* * *

In the past few years, Starmer has had to become accustomed to
talking about his family background and so often has he mentioned
that 'my-dad-was-a-toolmaker', it's become something of an internet meme.

But he's been much less forthcoming about his siblings and
usually edges around the subject of his younger brother altogether.

All those years when he was being socially mobile and going where no member of his family had gone before – university, the Bar, Parliament and now maybe Downing Street – Nick had been battling very different challenges. Having been written off as 'remedial' at school, he later did some evening classes to achieve a technical qualification, before working on scrap cars and doing some scaffolding.

He had health problems and difficulties learning so didn't hold down jobs for long, but earned enough to rent a home near where he'd grown up. When Nick got engaged to his girlfriend, his elder brother was best man at a fondly remembered, if chaotic wedding. Starmer describes how he borrowed a car so that Nick wasn't 'driving his bride from the church in his beaten-up minivan, which had all his clothes in the back'. On discovering there were no plans for a reception, he raced over to the local branch of Tesco, bought every sandwich he could lay hands on and 'put some canvas thing up' in the garden of the cottage where Nick lived in case it rained when people came back.

But the marriage didn't work out and Nick ended up heading to Yorkshire, into another relationship that eventually fell apart, then into a council flat, where he was robbed by someone he had let stay. His health got worse, with breathing problems and partial deafness preventing him from doing manual work. In 2021, Starmer persuaded him to use the money he'd got from the sale of their parents' house on Tanhouse Road to buy himself a home in Yorkshire. But, having found some security at last, Nick would become sick just a year later.

Starmer, who has spoken a lot about his parents' confidence that life was 'going to get better for their kids', recognises this is a flaw in his own aspirational story of working-class-boy-made-good. 'The whole thing is so poignant,' he says, 'because Nick has had a really tough life. So that dream our mum and dad had for us hasn't come true. There's this real, deep sadness in me about that for my brother, and for them.'

He does speeches about 'breaking the class ceiling' that causes people from backgrounds like his to feel they 'don't belong' at university or 'can't do' jobs like being a barrister. But he also acknowledges not everyone will be able – or want – to bust through barriers in the way he did and that success has many faces. He takes out his phone to show a video his sister Katy has sent him of an Abba tribute gig where, on her night off, she took one of the adults with Down's syndrome for whom she works as a carer. 'She always gives them part of herself,' he says proudly. 'I couldn't do it, wouldn't know where to start. If I did a job swap with Katy, I suspect the people she works with would have a terrible day.'

This extended family, scattered a long way from Westminster, has never been far from his mind even if they're rarely spoken about. When his sister Anna got married in 1986, he was best man to her husband, Tim. When his sister Katy got divorced, Starmer stepped in and helped her buy a house. When Katy's daughter, Jess, got married to her partner, Samantha, in 2022 he was there – his first same-sex wedding – on what he says was a 'brilliant day' that made him reflect on the progress Britain had made from those days when a friend from school could be chucked out of home because he was gay.

Then, just six weeks later, he had a shocking reminder of 'how far we have to go'. He describes how Jess and Samantha were leaving a pub in the town where they live and work: 'It's a friendly place, small enough for them to know most people, it's their manor. They were hand in hand like the newlyweds they were, when three men came up to them. These cowards punched Jess many times, fracturing her cheekbone, for no reason except she's a lesbian.' He tosses his phone across the table in cold fury. It shows two photographs of her face, the first looking radiant and happy on her wedding day, the other almost unrecognisably swollen and purple after the attack.

Starmer is angry over what happened to his niece and – despite his best efforts with the police – the failure to prosecute those responsible. But he still doesn't like talking about it (and subsequently made several calls to check permission had been obtained from Katy, Jess and Samantha for it to be published here).

Much of this reluctance is about protecting them from unwanted media intrusion. When he mentioned in the House of Commons his sister's experience doing fourteen-hour shifts as a careworker during Covid, he was dismayed that the *Daily Mail* promptly arrived on her doorstep. But his unease is also about making all these complicated lives fit into a simple political narrative. At one point, he says: 'My background should be the back story, not the front story ... I can't say vote Labour because my family struggled to pay the bills when I was growing up. But you can believe that I'm going to try to fix this because I know what it's like; it's a lived experience and, through my family or the people I meet, it's a living experience.'

For instance, on all those secret visits to see Nick in Leeds, Starmer says he got a deeper understanding of the NHS from talking to hospital staff away from the cameras. At that time, Labour was making much of its plan to recruit thousands of new doctors, midwives and nurses. But Nick's surgeon, Andrew Smith, emphasised to him how much retention matters too, because losing even one member of his team could mean cancelling a series of operations. 'Staff are fed up and leaving in their droves. They feel they are doing a thankless task, that they constantly go the extra mile and are taken for granted,' he was told.

Starmer says: 'It's about who do you really have in your mind's eye when you make decisions. This is why talking to people is so important – listening to what they're actually saying – because it's these conversations which tell me what people want, what their aspirations are, what they are struggling with, the choices they have to make. I'm much happier when I'm out of Westminster just talking to people,' he says. 'You learn a lot if you take the trouble.'

Maybe that's the kind of thing a politician might say to show they are 'in touch'. But there's still a tender self-consciousness to

Starmer even about being a recognisable politician at all. For instance, when he describes how he thinks politics is too often 'done to people – not with them', he mentions visiting schools, hospitals and businesses where 'a minister had been before and just glided past, not saying thank you'. He starts worrying whether he has ever done that too. After all, this book began by describing him refusing to talk to someone on a train. 'I'm sure there are reasonable excuses for such behaviour when politicians are in a hurry, have something else on their minds or fear they will just get shouted at,' he says, blinking slowly, before looking away to stare at the floor.

In this different fashion from many politicians, Starmer's experiences outside Westminster inform what he calls 'this weird life' he has within it now. There's an old rallying cry from the feminist and civil rights movements that 'the personal is political'. But the extent to which it applies to this Labour leader is complicated because much of the time he tries to resist pressure to combine his personal with the political, even if he also concedes that keeping them separate is 'probably not the most obvious or best way to go about doing my job'. And yet, ahead of a general election that will doubtless further expand the small industry trying to find an answer to the question of 'Who is Keir Starmer?', the personal is still the key to explaining what drives him on in politics now.

It is part of the most obvious paradox about him. Watch him campaign around the country and he seems comfortable in his own skin and shows an easy enjoyment of voters' company. Then, as soon as the cameras are turned on, he too often becomes constricted. One well-known broadcaster who has interviewed him several times says: 'It's like he suddenly goes into another room.' It's a phenomenon that frustrates some of his oldest friends like Mark Adams who he first knew at school. 'I can't begin to understand the pressure he is under but there is another side to him which I wish others could see a bit more. I sometimes think he's making himself be what he thinks a politician should be and should let the brakes off a bit.'

Starmer can still reel off the names – 'Andrew, Charlotte, Ben, Lauren, Anna, Nikki and Megan' – of the medical team who treated his brother in Leeds. The stories they told seem to be more useful to him precisely because they happened in private when he was visiting, not as Labour leader, but as an ordinary citizen worried his brother would die.

The intensity of deeply painful episodes involving his own family mean they have a different quality from the usual kind of interactions he gets in politics, especially when the cameras are turned on him. He attaches a weight and significance to each of them that seems unusual, indicating it isn't just privacy he's seeking to protect, but something more like integrity. In the years since he became leader he has made successive efforts to close this gap between the personal and political. Like everything else he does, he has got better at it through practice and hard work. But the task feels all the more urgent because the closer he gets to power and the tighter security becomes around him, the further he is pulled from the reasons he went into politics in the first place.

After all, there has already been a time when many of those vital connections to the outside world were severed, not only for him but for just about everyone else too.

22

Under new leadership

The first day

Neither booted nor suited, Keir Starmer was standing in the attic room of his Kentish Town home on a conference call when he became the nineteenth leader of the Labour Party. The date was April 4, 2020 and Covid had emptied streets, suspended all sport and made politics altogether even stranger than it was already.

The last few weeks of the contest had been shrouded by a pandemic that would kill almost a quarter of a million people in the UK. But no one really doubted Starmer was heading for victory and each member of his team had been sent a bottle of champagne in advance so they could have an online celebration together. For anyone still interested, the only real question was how big his share of the vote would be.

It turned out to be 56 per cent, an only slightly smaller proportion than that gained by Jeremy Corbyn five years earlier, but exactly twice that of Rebecca Long-Bailey's 28 per cent and even further ahead of third-placed Lisa Nandy's 16 per cent.

In the brief lag before the news flashed out to the outside world, Starmer ran downstairs to the kitchen while it could still be contained within his family. His first conversation as Labour leader won't much trouble future historians. What did he tell them? 'It was probably something like me just saying, "I've won!"' What did Vic say? '"Fantastic!"' replies Starmer, adopting the customary defiance he often shows towards a line of questioning that seems unserious or might stray into his family's privacy.

In normal times, a beaming new leader would have addressed cheering crowds in a conference hall somewhere. But lockdown rules required all the candidates to pre-record their acceptance speech. Starmer had made his a few days earlier while addressing only a brown armchair in his front room. It was, he says, an odd experience to be sat in the same chair watching himself on TV delivering the speech that Saturday morning.

His message was suitably sombre and there was no trace of a smile on his face as Starmer talked about the need for the country to come together in tackling the coronavirus. He paid a dutiful tribute to his 'friend' Jeremy Corbyn, before delivering the words his predecessor had been unable to utter about the 'stain' of anti-semitism that had been left behind.

'On behalf of the Labour Party, I am sorry. And I will tear out this poison by its roots and judge success by the return of Jewish members and those who felt that they could no longer support us,' he said.

After losing four elections in a row, Labour was failing its 'historic purpose', he added. 'We've got a mountain to climb. But we will climb it … Where that requires change, we will change. Where that requires us to rethink, we will rethink.'

Opinion polls at the time gave Boris Johnson's Conservatives a twenty-point lead and very few people in either politics or the media believed Labour had much chance of victory in the next general election.

David Lammy, the Tottenham MP who was part of Starmer's leadership campaign and remains a key ally in the shadow cabinet, admits to being one of those who told him winning power would be a 'ten-year project'. The journalist Patrick Maguire probably accurately reflected the mood among MPs when he wrote that most of Starmer's supporters thought he might be the equivalent of Neil Kinnock – 'destined not to reach Downing Street, but to set his successor on the road there after cleaning the party's stables', adding that Conservatives were more likely to compare him to Ed Miliband, 'an ungainly, ideological metropolitan without the warmth or wit to bridge Hampstead and Hull. Or, put even less sympathetically, Jeremy Corbyn in a suit.' Some of those on the left who quite liked the idea of 'Corbyn in a suit' gave the new leader a wary welcome but also recognised how hard it would be for him to win. Owen Jones wrote in the *Guardian* that Starmer faced 'many challenges' but now was 'the time for critical friendship, to wish a genuinely decent and progressive politician well'.

You had to go beyond Westminster to hear a different view. Jamie Burton, a barrister at Starmer's old Doughty Street chambers and a regular in his eight-a-side games, says: 'Everyone was telling me he had no chance of victory in a general election. I said to them, "Just watch – he'll win – it's what happens to this guy." On a football pitch, just like when he was a barrister, he's always in the right place at the right time – goals out of nowhere – he only knows how to win.'

A few hours after his victory speech had been broadcast to lockdown Britain, Starmer walked into the Leader of the Opposition's offices, a suite of rooms in Norman Shaw South, the Romanesque building connected to Parliament by underground tunnels, bridges, escalators and swing doors. However, the usually fast-beating 'heart' of British democracy was almost completely deserted aside from a few security guards and about eight members of his campaign staff, who greeted him on arrival with an awkward, socially distanced round of applause.

Most of the key posts in the new leader's team had already been allocated among them. Morgan McSweeney would be chief of staff, Chris Ward would be his deputy and speechwriter, while Ben Nunn was put in charge of communications. Jenny Chapman became political secretary, liaising with MPs alongside Starmer's purple-haired parliamentary private secretary, Carolyn Harris. Another long-serving aide, Yasmeen Sebbana, was given the task of managing the office, allocating desks and working out how they would all manage to speak to each other during lockdown.

There were some complaints from left-wing staffers that they had been excluded or that jobs had been carved up too quickly. One former member of the campaign team posted a 1,500-word message on a WhatsApp group saying she'd been 'brutally' cut off and left on universal credit after failing to get a job in the new leader's team. But Simon Fletcher was given a role in planning for elections, and Starmer retained some officials from the Corbyn era, such as Helene Reardon-Bond, as deputy chief of staff, and the international officer Mark Simpson. A more recent recruit was Claire Ainsley, author of an influential book, *The New Working Class: How to Win Hearts, Minds and Votes*, as head of policy, working alongside Stuart Ingham.

Jeremy Corbyn's staff had moved out a week or so earlier, leaving behind some of the detritus of their four and a half years in charge. There was a CND flag on the wall, a duvet and some half-shredded documents on the floor. Beneath a desk was a printed sign declaring, 'I'm backing Jeremy because …' followed by the handwritten words '… he's considerate and kind'.

While Nunn earned some laughter by making a fuss about stepping in a mound of what appeared to be jelly, McSweeney gave Starmer a list of people he needed to speak to. He had brief conversations with former party leaders, who wished him well in the task of rescuing a party which so many politicians believed by then might be beyond salvation. Starmer also tried to phone his immediate predecessor but got the answer machine. He says Corbyn texted him back the next day in friendly enough fashion.

The next set of phone calls were tougher. Starmer spoke to the Chief Rabbi, Ephraim Mirvis, who a few months earlier had warned that British Jews were 'gripped by anxiety' over the possibility Labour might win the 2019 election. 'I'm not expecting you to embrace me, just give me some space to bring change,' said the new leader. 'I will judge you by your actions not words,' replied Mirvis.

Finally, Starmer called a number of party officials, including Labour's then general secretary Jennie Formby, explaining why he wanted them to resign. 'I had seen previous leaders struggle to get control over the party machine. I was determined not to repeat that mistake or have everything we tried to do dragged through some internal dispute,' he says. 'We simply did not have time for all that and we had to be ruthless.'

Although Formby, a former Unite official and a close ally of Len McCluskey, asked to be given a chance to prove her loyalty, Starmer wasn't changing his mind and a month later she was replaced by David Evans, who'd been deputy general secretary in the Blair era.

That afternoon, the new leader also began shaping his shadow cabinet. In line with his campaign promise of forging unity, he gave jobs to three of his leadership rivals, Rebecca Long-Bailey, Lisa Nandy and Emily Thornberry. He retained some Corbyn supporters but parted, apparently on amiable enough terms, with those like Ian Lavery and Jon Trickett who'd taken the hardest line. Coming in from the cold was a large group including the likes of Lammy and former leader Ed Miliband, as well as Bridget Phillipson, Anneliese Dodds, Nick Thomas-Symonds, Jonathan Reynolds and Steve Reed, who had backed him for the leadership.

A notable appointment was that of Rachel Reeves. In a sign of how little he'd mixed with Labour MPs during the previous five years, Starmer admits he had never properly got to know her before and she had initially nominated Jess Phillips for the leadership. Nonetheless, he was sufficiently impressed by this former Bank of England economist to consider putting Reeves straight into the post of shadow chancellor, before handing her the job of shadowing Michael Gove at the Cabinet Office on the still-thorny issue of Brexit.

The position that probably attracted the most attention, both then and since, was that of Angela Rayner. She had been elected the same day as deputy leader so has a separate mandate and, as someone from the left of the party, had backed Long-Bailey – who also happened to be her flatmate at the time – for the top job. Starmer, who describes Rayner simply as a 'remarkable force-of-nature', gave her the post of party chair with responsibility for co-ordinating election campaigning, as well as standing in for him at Prime Minister's Questions.

Like Reeves, she also didn't really know him at the time and admits, 'Keir wouldn't be the first on my list for a karaoke night.' When asked if they would have been friends at school, Labour's deputy leader laughs out loud, before replying: 'Probably not. I reckon he would have been too much of a good boy.'

She compares working out their new roles to the awkwardness of 'an arranged political marriage'. 'I was sort of going, "Hiya! So how do you want to do this?"' Extending the marriage metaphor, she adds: 'It took a while for us to bed it in and realise that, you know, me putting the socks on the table pisses him off, or him leaving the coffee cup out will cheese me off.'

Starmer made another phone call that Saturday afternoon: to Boris Johnson in Downing Street. He was interested to hear what the prime minister had to say about working with opposition parties on the pandemic, he says. 'But all he offered really was some matey banter about how he had a bigger mandate from his party than me.' Almost certainly to the prime minister's satisfaction, Starmer rose to the bait by nerdily pointing out there had been three Labour candidates on the ballot compared to the two for the Tories in 2019. He did notice, though, that Johnson's voice was croaking. 'He sounded so rough I felt I had to ask if he was okay.' A few days later, the prime minister was admitted to hospital with coronavirus and the front page of the *Sun* was leading with the words: 'Pray for Boris'.

In the eerie half-life of lockdowns that followed, Starmer often found himself home alone while everyone else in his family had left for the day. Vic, working in occupational health at her local hospital, landed in the thick of it as the number of cases and deaths began to soar. She faced difficult and emotionally draining work, even as she found her life was now within the goldfish bowl of politics. An occasion that upset her was when she saw 'breaking news' on the TV screen attached to the wall that one of her children had just tested positive for Covid.

But Vic also thinks she was lucky in some ways because she went off to work almost like normal and could see her friends at the hospital every day. Their children also carried on going to school because Vic was classified as an essential worker. The one member of the family frequently left behind at home was Starmer who was doing a lot of the job from a laptop in the kitchen. The team of advisers he assembled at that time also reflected how the lockdown encouraged remote working, with figures like Ainsley and Fletcher, as well as the former Treasury aide Sam White, not even based full time in London.

Ainsley had drawn up a plan for him to begin his leadership with a tour of Britain, immersing himself in the different communities and lives for two or three days at a time. She says: 'He had a real desire to go out and talk directly to people – not just the party faithful and certainly not for photo-ops – but the ones we needed to reach and had lost touch with over the years; he wanted to learn.' All of that, however, was delayed because of Covid and he was left doing 'Call Keir' phone-ins on local radio stations.

A new leader who had tried to escape the Westminster bubble, instead found himself trapped in the even smaller one of his own home.

Flashing red

The first decision Starmer took as Labour leader that affected people beyond Westminster was to offer the government broad support over Covid, letting the legislation needed for lockdowns pass unhindered through Parliament.

'Doing something else might have got good headlines, but it would have cost lives,' he says now. 'There had been a big question mark about whether people would agree to obey the rules. We had never done anything like this before as a country and some of the more libertarian Conservatives were complaining it was all very un-British. They were wrong. We all just got on with it in a very British way without too much moaning. The laws were passed and twenty-four hours later, everyone was in their house following the rules.'

Starmer's stance disappointed some in his party who were urging him to take the opportunity to split the Conservatives. But he has adopted similar positions on issues he thinks transcend party lines, such as the support he offered for Ukraine after the invasion by Russia or, more controversially, Israel after the terror attacks by Hamas. This was summed up in a strategy note written by Nunn at the time that was entitled 'A new leadership'. It said Starmer would 'act in the national interest and engage constructively with the government' while also emphasising 'competence, professionalism and a belief in Britain'.

His early appearances as leader of the opposition, in a virtually empty and socially distanced House of Commons chamber, were mostly notable for the absence of the predictably polarised politics that had characterised so much of the previous few years. Starmer's first PMQs began with him wishing the bed-bound Johnson a speedy recovery from Covid; his second saw him offering congratulations on the birth of the prime minister's latest baby.

Gradually, however, the new leader began asking more probingly forensic questions about testing, deaths in care homes, shortages of protective equipment, cronyism in the award of contracts or failures on track and trace. The BBC's Laura Kuenssberg said Starmer was 'inching rather than sprinting' towards a fight she characterised as being 'the lawyer versus the showman'. The idea that Johnson was in a competition at all was, for many, a sign of progress and his government began to wobble after his chief adviser, Dominic Cummings, appeared to break lockdown rules by taking his family on a jaunt to Barnard Castle he claimed had been to 'test his eyesight'. The *Observer*'s Andrew Rawnsley commented: 'There is indeed something very lawyerly about the Labour leader, but the public does not seem to be holding that against him. He is enjoying the best approval ratings for any opposition leader since another Labour lawyer, one called Tony Blair, was on his march towards Number 10 in the mid-1990s.'

Although Starmer generally kept a public distance during this period from Blair and other figures the left regarded as divisive including Peter Mandelson, behind closed doors there were more signs of change. Aides say Starmer had been appalled at the lack of focus and discipline in shadow cabinet meetings under his predecessor. The first under his leadership were held over Zoom, where discipline was even harder to enforce and leaks were happening in real time.

He moved swiftly to stamp out what he said were 'deeply unprofessional' bad habits. All shadow ministers were told to arrive promptly, talk clearly and to the point. Charlie Falconer, who had returned as shadow attorney general, has described how meetings under Corbyn used to be 'a shambles ... full of people intervening on topics which had fuck all to do with the topic they were talking about'. He said: 'The meetings are now being run properly.' Rachel Reeves says, 'Keir is all for having a proper discussion about things – he doesn't want people to just sit there and just agree – but, once a decision has been made, he expects people to behave professionally. He doesn't like meetings where there's not papers, where he's not being presented with evidence and options.'

Starmer was even more taken aback by the behaviour on Labour's National Executive Committee. Margaret Beckett, the former foreign secretary and longest-serving member of the party's ruling body, says: 'Keir started off trying to bring people together and be conciliatory with the left because he was serious about this unity business. He probably thought I was being a bit unreasonable when I tried to tell him that was a waste of time but, unfortunately, I turned out to be correct. They were horrible; they were insulting and very rude to him from the start. We were never like that to Jeremy whom we treated with respect. But they wanted to get their way and took the view that everybody else could go hang. They just told him to piss off.'

When she was elected chair of the NEC a few months later, ahead of a Corbyn-supporting trade unionist who had been due to take the post, thirteen of its members walked out in protest. This wasn't quite as dramatic as it might have been because one representative of Unite, having unloaded both barrels of his anger at Starmer, then spent an excruciating minute or so trying to locate the 'leave' button on his computer so he could end his participation in the Zoom meeting.

A conference call with Jewish community leaders in Starmer's first days in charge went slightly better, after he told them he'd demanded a 'report on my desk by the end of each week' of all outstanding antisemitism cases in the party, together with a timetable for their resolution. On April 12, however, a very different internal report arrived like an infection from the previous leadership: an 860-page tome, completed in the month before Starmer took over, which concluded 'hyper-factionalism' among staff opposed to Corbyn had prevented him from tackling antisemitism because 'some employees seem to have taken a view that the worse things got for Labour the happier they would be'.

The document had been leaked following a decision by the new leadership not to submit it as evidence to the Equality and Human Rights Commission's inquiry into Labour's handling of the problem. A barrister, Martin Forde, was commissioned by the party to look into the allegations and, while his investigation didn't identify where the disclosure came from, it painted a picture in which racism, sexism and bullying had been endemic among officials on both wings of the party.

Labour's lawyers subsequently began suing five former members of staff, including Seumas Milne and Karie Murphy who were key figures in Corbyn's team, for allegedly conspiring to leak the report with the intention of damaging Starmer's leadership. The allegation is steadfastly denied by those accused and, at the time of writing, is subject to a legal dispute, with costs reportedly running into seven figures.

Nor was this the only expensive legal hangover from the previous regime. In the summer of 2020, Starmer settled a libel action brought by whistleblowers in the BBC's *Panorama* documentary on antisemitism whose motives had been denigrated by Corbyn's team. The settlement, said to have been agreed against the advice of legal advisers who thought they could win the case, cost more than £600,000 and probably a further £1 million because Unite withdrew funding from Labour as a result. It was later reported that lawyers' fees were costing the party more than £2 million a year, a ten-fold increase compared to the pre-Corbyn era.

But the most visible evidence that Starmer's experiment with unity in those early months was going wrong came that summer, when Covid restrictions briefly lifted enough for him to conduct the first face-to-face campaigning since becoming leader.

He was on a train to Stevenage, masked up and with media in tow, when one of his aides showed him a message about Rebecca Long-Bailey. His shadow education secretary had retweeted, along with the words 'absolute diamond', an interview with Maxine Peake in which the actor had avowed her admiration for Corbyn and repeated an antisemitic conspiracy theory that had been proven to be totally false. It claimed that US police responsible for the racist murder of George Floyd in Minneapolis had been taught to kneel on people's necks in 'seminars with the Israeli secret services'.

Starmer told staff that Long-Bailey, as a member of the shadow cabinet, should delete the tweet immediately. But he insists he 'didn't want a fight,' saying: 'This was a day when I wanted to be getting back out to the country, talking to the people, not talking to ourselves.' Although his rival for the leadership had been seen as the 'continuity Corbyn' candidate, they'd always got on fairly well and Starmer had been impressed by the way she spoke out against antisemitism during the campaign.

By the end of the trip, however, Long-Bailey had still refused to delete the message. 'All she had to do was hit one button,' says Starmer. 'Calls were made and hours went by, but she refused to do it. I still don't know why she chose to take this course, whether she was being badly advised or egged on by others. But once it became a question about whether or not I was serious in rooting out anti-semitism, I had no choice. I sacked her.'

For her part, Long-Bailey has said she wanted to issue a 'press statement of clarification' explaining how she didn't endorse every part of the article in question and had 'asked to discuss these matters with Keir before agreeing what further action to take'. She added: 'But sadly he had already made his decision.'

Such an abrupt sacking of someone who had come second to him in the leadership race a few months earlier might, in previous years, have been seen as a big and defining moment.

It turned out to be merely a warning signal for what was to come.

'You are part of the problem'

There was little sign of any drama at Starmer's first party conference as Labour leader. Indeed, it provided proof of what many party officials have always suspected: these events would go smoothly if only there were no politicians, delegates or press in attendance.

The Covid-limited 'online conference' of 2020 still had a leader's speech of sorts on September 22, even if it was one that showed he had gone from addressing a brown armchair in his living room six months earlier to talking to a brick wall in a Doncaster arts centre. Its real significance lay in what he didn't say or, rather, who he didn't want to discuss.

He spoke from a lectern decorated with the slogan 'A New Leadership', without once referring to the old one. He mentioned the names of three Labour election winners – Clement Attlee, Harold Wilson and Tony Blair – but that of his immediate predecessor who had lost twice never crossed his lips.

Instead, he talked about things that Corbyn either would not or could not have spoken about: progress on tackling antisemitism; patriotism; family values; and becoming a competent, credible opposition. He said to voters: 'Never again will Labour take you or the things you care about for granted … Never again will Labour go into an election not being trusted on national security, with your job, with your community and with your money.' He declared: 'It's time to get serious about winning. That means we have to change and that's what we're doing.'

The next day, his first party political broadcast began with the words 'I love this country', before showing footage of him talking with army veterans and farmers. Around this time Starmer also put a Union flag in his office for TV appearances. 'That this was seen as a cause for controversy among some,' he says now, 'only served to underline the problem.'

As parliamentary business resumed, he sacked three MPs from his frontbench team after they joined Corbyn in defying the party whip by voting against measures to protect British soldiers from prosecution for crimes committed abroad. A couple of weeks later, Corbyn was among thirty-four MPs, including another seven frontbenchers, all of whom subsequently resigned, to break the whip by voting against covert human intelligence legislation – the 'spy cops bill' described in Chapter 12 – which granted legal immunity to undercover agents.

The darkest cloud hanging over these first months of his leadership, however, was the looming publication of the Equality and Human Rights Commission's investigation into Labour's handling of antisemitism complaints. Starmer had been given advance notice of its key conclusions: the party had broken the law in allowing the harassment of Jewish members and there had been interference from the leader's office in the way complaints about antisemitism were handled. It would also say that the failure of Corbyn's team to respond more effectively had been a matter of choice and the party had three months to change or face criminal prosecution.

Even so, those close to Starmer at the time insist he remained committed to the unity strategy that had been such a big theme in his leadership campaign. Despite some on the right of the party urging him to use publication of the report to launch a full-scale assault on Corbyn's record, the Labour leader told meetings with staff, legal advisers and MPs that he was still seeking to move on from – not against – his predecessor.

In a series of meetings with Angela Rayner, staff and officials, he said it was his responsibility alone to eradicate racism from the Labour Party. 'I had no intention of pinning all the blame on Jeremy Corbyn because this went deeper than any one person or leader,' he says. 'I wasn't looking for a bust-up. I wanted to look forward.'

Starmer had sat down with Chris Ward to draft a short speech for when the report was published that did not refer directly to the former leader. Instead, it spoke about this being a 'day of shame' for Labour, citing multiple 'failures of leadership' and the way the number of complaints dealt with from the backlog had doubled in the past six months, as well as the need for a more profound change in the culture of the party. But it also included this:

If you are antisemitic you should be nowhere near the Labour Party and we will make sure you are not. And if, after all the grief, all the pain, and all the evidence in this report, there are those who still think there is no problem with antisemitism in the Labour Party and that it's all exaggerated or a factional attack, then frankly, you are part of the problem too and you should be nowhere near the Labour Party either.

On the evening before the report's publication, Starmer had a phone conversation with Corbyn to talk it through. 'It was a perfectly friendly and professional call,' he says. 'It was also the last time I spoke to him.'

Rayner, sensing danger, was also on the phone, speaking to Corbyn's adviser, Seumas Milne, to warn him it would be a huge mistake to cause fresh division on the issue. Milne reassured her that no one on his side was seeking confrontation and tried to explain why Corbyn would still need to defend his record.

There have been claims that he was promised a copy of Starmer's speech but that it never arrived, although this is one of several points where accounts vary. The leader's team were by then becoming agitated over Corbyn's desire to reinsert himself into the controversy. 'We wanted to make this about how we were moving on, but Jeremy was determined to drag it back to him. I don't think they had come to terms with him no longer being leader,' says one staff member.

The EHRC report was released at 10 a.m. on October 29, with the world's media reporting how Labour, a party with a proud history of fighting all kinds of prejudice, had unlawfully discriminated against Jews. Corbyn issued a statement at 10.36, the timing of which was seen, even by some of those normally sympathetic to him, as evidence of his 'paranoia that Keir was about to put the boot in'.

The ex-leader claimed to have been obstructed by party officials in his efforts to tackle antisemitism and said he disagreed with some of the report's findings. Then he added: 'One antisemite is one too many, but the scale of the problem was also dramatically overstated for political reasons by our opponents inside and outside the party, as well as by much of the media.'

Staff at the party's headquarters in Westminster were stunned because they hadn't expected Corbyn to pre-empt their press conference, let alone put himself on a collision course with his successor by saying the whole row had been exaggerated. The

Labour leader was told what had just happened as he prepared to walk out in front of the media for his speech and press conference. There was a brief delay while he considered his options, but he decided pulling back then would have meant giving an inadequate response to the report and that was something he wasn't prepared to do.

He delivered his speech shortly after 11 a.m., then faced a barrage of questions from journalists wanting to know whether his predecessor's statement contradicted his own. To each, he replied with a prepared line about how 'there were no individual findings against Jeremy Corbyn', before saying the report had exposed a collective failure to tackle antisemitism and so 'it is incumbent on all of us to accept the findings'.

Corbyn's closest advisers were watching events unfold in an Islington community centre. 'As soon as Keir did that bit about people who say the scale of antisemitism had been exaggerated, I knew this was going to be a problem,' says one, who insists if they had known the content of Starmer's speech, they would have ensured there was no direct clash. 'Maybe it was deliberate on their part, maybe a fuck-up, maybe somewhere in between. I do know it could have been avoided.'

Shortly before noon, Starmer and Rayner regrouped in a room at Labour's headquarters with aides and party officials. The deputy leader agreed to phone Corbyn and ask him to withdraw the statement. She came back a few minutes later, shaking her head.

Remembering that day, Rayner says: 'I just felt incredibly frustrated because Jeremy has a blind spot on this and the way he handled the EHRC report was not good. All his life, he's fought racism and antisemitism and should have been on the side of people fighting discrimination. I think he saw it all as a political attack, but there wasn't any grand plan to get rid of him or anything like that. Keir had been pushing back against people who wanted to make it an issue about Jeremy; he was saying it was about the party as a whole and how we had all failed people.'

At 12.15 p.m., Corbyn gave the first of a series of interviews with broadcasters in which he doubled down on his position, once again expressing disagreement with some of the report's content and repeatedly saying the number of antisemitism cases had been 'exaggerated'. It became obvious to Starmer's team that some sort of action would have to be taken and David Evans, Labour's general secretary, went down to his office to speak with legal advisers.

Just after 1 p.m. a statement was released, saying Corbyn's membership had been suspended and that he had been stripped of the whip in Parliament. The man who had been party leader less than six months earlier could no longer even call himself a Labour MP. Although Evans had sent notice of the suspension to Corbyn by email, the former leader is said to have only found out from a photographer doorstepping him and been genuinely shocked.

Again, accounts of exactly how he came to be suspended are contested. Len McCluskey, the general secretary of Unite, claims the Labour leader told him he'd taken the decision himself because Corbyn 'put me in an impossible position'. If true, that might have been a problem because the EHRC report had criticised undue interference by the leader's office in disciplinary matters. But it always seemed unlikely Starmer would be caught out on a point of procedure or law.

Multiple sources present that day have emphasised it was Evans who had the final say. Falconer, the former lord chancellor and justice secretary, who was in the room with the party's general secretary when the suspension was agreed, says: 'There was no pre-ordained plan to push Jeremy out but, after he contradicted the findings of the report and what Keir had said, I could see no other logical way of avoiding it.' Asked directly if Evans took the decision, he replies: 'Yes, it was left to David because Keir was keen that a proper process was followed. He didn't want there to be any accusation that he was messing around in the same way Corbyn's office had done.'

Nonetheless, everyone recognised the stakes were high, not least because Corbyn still had strong support on the party's National Executive Committee. As colleagues remember McSweeney telling Starmer at the time: 'Quite frankly, we were not in a strong enough position to win a civil war.' Momentum held an online grassroots protest rally, which was addressed by John McDonnell and Diane Abbott. Back in the leader's office, Simon Fletcher was fuming he hadn't been consulted on the decision and telling colleagues it could result in a permanent schism.

Corbyn recorded a broadcast clip in which he pleaded, 'I would just say, hang on a minute, let's all just keep a bit calmer and think again about this whole issue.' The mood of the shadow cabinet that day was described as 'sombre'. The press licked its lips at the prospect of another helping of Labour Party carnage.

The following afternoon, McCluskey, accompanied by the former shadow cabinet minister Jon Trickett, arrived for negotiations in the leader's office with Starmer and Rayner. According to one of those present, the union leader said this would have to be resolved by the National Executive Committee and then handed over a piece of paper on which had been typed out exactly what he wanted it to decide. The Labour leader is said to have refused even to look at it, passing it straight back to McCluskey and saying: 'That may be how you're used to doing business, but it isn't how I do business.' He suggested that, if he was still a lawyer and Corbyn his client, his strong advice would be to mitigate the damage by issuing an apology and removing his statement on the subject from the internet.

It was eventually agreed Trickett, McSweeney and Fletcher would work on a form of words that might help solve the crisis. Although no explicit promises were made, one of those involved says: 'We got to a place where I think a deal could have been done, but it needed to be done swiftly. That was when Jeremy turned his phone off and went on holiday to the Isle of Wight.' Although McCluskey describes it slightly differently, he generally bears out this account, saying: 'Unfortunately, Jeremy wasn't prepared to move that fast. He was away; he didn't trust the other side to stick to the deal.'

A special five-member panel of the NEC, balanced equally between left and right, was convened to consider the case on November 17. The speed with which Labour's notoriously grinding machinery sprang into gear suggested to Westminster observers that 'some form of agreement had been brokered'. Corbyn finally issued a new statement on the morning the panel met. It said: 'To be clear, concerns about antisemitism are neither "exaggerated" nor "overstated". The point I wished to make was that the vast majority of Labour party members were and remain committed antiracists deeply opposed to antisemitism.'

The panel duly decided to reinstate Corbyn's membership along with a reprimand warning him about future conduct. But the delay in the new statement being issued had allowed attitudes to the former leader to harden. It was notable that his 'clarification' fell short of an apology and talked only about 'concerns' – rather than the 'scale of the problem' – not being exaggerated. He also ignored a suggestion from the panel that he take down his original statement. Indeed, at this time of writing more than three years later, it can still be found on his Facebook page.

Many people in Jewish communities responded with unbridled fury. The British Board of Deputies denounced a 'pathetic non-apology', while Margaret Hodge, who had remained a Labour MP even during the darkest days of Corbyn's leadership, threatened to resign.

The left's joy at winning an apparent victory with what some of them ill-advisedly began calling the leadership's 'climbdown' was, however, short-lived. Starmer told Nick Brown, the party's chief whip, that Corbyn would not be allowed to call himself a Labour MP.

There was a delay while Brown, who had been wily enough to hold his post in both the New Labour and Corbyn era, consulted lawyers to make sure what he was doing couldn't be challenged. Then Starmer issued a new statement. 'Jeremy Corbyn's actions in response to the EHRC report undermined and set back our work in restoring trust and confidence in the Labour party's ability to tackle antisemitism,' he said. 'In those circumstances, I have taken the decision not to restore the whip to Jeremy Corbyn.'

The Labour leader still didn't fully control the party apparatus and could not, therefore, either own or sustain the original decision to suspend Corbyn's membership. Instead, he had taken personal responsibility for keeping his predecessor out of the parliamentary Labour Party.

Brown, who would later be suspended himself because of an unrelated disciplinary investigation, says: 'My impression is that this was when Keir started to become his own man. The left went for him as hard as they could. He took a lot of abuse, made note of it, and decided – not unreasonably – to move closer to people who would support him. Jeremy's supporters thought they could push him around but they don't understand him. As the DPP, Keir had prosecuted organised crime and gangsters. He's very tough.'

Removing the whip from Corbyn was a huge risk for any politician to take, let alone one like Starmer who'd always had a reputation for caution and whose leadership was far from secure. No former leader had been treated like this since Ramsay MacDonald was thrown out of Labour's ranks way back in 1931 for the very different offence of forming a national government with the Tories.

Threats of legal action and mass resignations followed, with twenty-eight left-wing MPs signing a motion demanding Corbyn's immediate reinstatement. McCluskey accused Starmer of reneging on a deal and says: 'That was when I lost my personal relationship with Keir. I could no longer trust him.'

Yet, like in the leadership election earlier in the year, the left proved hopelessly disorganised. Different factions blamed each other for what had gone wrong and the legal action went nowhere, while threats to resign from MPs like Ian Lavery turned out to be hollow. The biggest parliamentary revolt against Starmer's leadership came six weeks later and had nothing to do with the suspension of his predecessor. It saw thirty-seven Labour MPs, including three frontbenchers, defy the whip by refusing to vote for Johnson's Brexit deal. Bizarrely, they were joined by the whipless Corbyn who, though never a pro-European, perhaps couldn't see a rebellion taking place without joining it.

Laura Parker, the former Corbyn aide and Momentum official who had backed Starmer for the leadership, says she watched the left's whole project unravel with 'this massive sense of frustration'. She thinks Corbyn mishandled the dispute over the EHRC report but points out the pandemic worked against the kind of activism and public protests the left had once been so expert at staging. 'Jeremy had brought all these different groups together and after he was gone, we just re-splintered into our subgroups,' she says. 'There was no "we" for "us" to hold Keir to account.'

Among a number of them at least was also a sense Starmer's position had some justification. The founder of Momentum, Jon Lansman, had stood down as its chair in May and then found himself being forced out of the NEC when the left decided against renominating him later that year. He strongly disagreed with Corbyn's suspension and has since spoken out against the treatment of others on the left which he warns is storing up trouble for the current leadership. However, he believes the former leader's reaction to the EHRC report wasn't just 'wrong' but 'very, very stupid' and that 'he deserved to be disciplined'. Lansman, who is Jewish and has suffered antisemitic abuse himself, says: 'Jeremy never understood the problem, he never got it, that doesn't make him racist, but we've all got to realise that prejudice is in all of us.'

Corbyn has since hinted he might stand as an independent or perhaps the leader of a new Peace and Justice Party in Islington North, which he represented as a Labour MP for forty years, at the next election. But Lansman, who lives in the constituency, suggests the former party leader would better serve the left by retiring so that he can speak freely on issues from outside Parliament without risking the position of his supporters in the party if they publicly back him. Lansman emphasises that if Corbyn runs against the official party candidate, 'I won't campaign for him – I'm Labour!'

In this extraordinary episode in the party's history, Starmer had once again relied on his judicial and legal instincts. Many of those more politically attuned would have urged him to either make it a grand gesture from the start or not attempt such a high-risk manoeuvre at all. But his stance towards the left evolved in more lawyerly and iterative fashion through his first year as leader, with each decision setting a precedent that informed the next, building a body of what lawyers would term 'jurisprudence'.

Having drifted into a position on a tide of procedure, he could then set his anchor on solid evidence and wait for the storm to blow itself out.

In the years since, the attitude of both the current and former Labour leader has hardened. At the time of writing, Corbyn says his successor has broken his pledge to build a united and democratic party. Starmer says his predecessor will not be allowed to stand as a candidate 'at the next election or any election – his days as a Labour MP are over'.

One of the few things they might agree on is that Starmer's earlier claim he'd been a 'friend' of his predecessor was the kind of thing a candidate has to say when standing in a contest to take over. Corbyn has said: 'I regarded him as a colleague. I never regarded him as a friend. I didn't spend time hanging out with him … A friend is somebody you go out for a meal with, have a chat, call their house.' Asked about this characterisation in a later TV interview, Starmer replied: 'Well, we were never friends in that sense, no, no, no.'

For all their differences, however, it's worth noting that neither Starmer nor Corbyn have resorted to the personal vitriol routinely poured over both by the other's supporters. Even now the Labour leader's decision to expel his predecessor seems 'impersonal' to the point of being almost judicial, while Corbyn has also largely attacked the decision and not the decision-taker. Although probably neither would appreciate being compared to the other, they share a slightly unworldly or old-fashioned approach to politics that is nowhere near as shrill as some of the voices who speak in their name.

Turning Labour inside out

The J-Curve

By the end of 2020, Keir Starmer's forensic approach to the government's handling of Covid began to bear fruit, with Johnson facing growing criticism for chaotic and deadly decision-making. Having started 20 per cent behind with voters, the Labour Party – now shorn of its former leader – came level, or was even inching ahead.

But the polls came down for Labour with the Christmas decorations. As Britain entered the new year, it got Covid jabs earlier than in Europe and Boris Johnson's long-time immunity to any form of criticism got a booster. 'There is undoubtedly a vaccine bounce going on,' admitted Starmer at the time, 'you can feel it.'

This went deeper, however, than a little surge of optimism in the veins of a traumatised electorate. All those graphs showing the peaks and troughs of infection waves had served to conceal underlying trends in politics. At some point, when the coronavirus was under control, life would revert to normal. And there was every reason to believe 'normal' would mean Labour slipping to election defeat in the same way it had ever since 2005.

In the previous eight months, Starmer had made a meaningful impression with voters on only two issues: the government's handling of the pandemic and the suspension of Jeremy Corbyn. The first was no longer working in Labour's favour and the second had been more a reaction to events than a political strategy. In both, his approach had been lawyerly and iterative without setting out the big vision or making the emotional connection with voters that was said to be needed if Labour was to achieve that longed-for 'cut through'.

Morgan McSweeney, who had masterminded the leadership campaign, began to argue that 'things would have to get worse before they could get better', or – as he told colleagues – 'we needed to adopt a J-curve approach'. The theory has been used to explain everything from the rise of nations to the performance of private equity, but it's also a model for turning around failing organisations. According to one academic exposition, there are five stages to a J-curve: the 'plateau' where old ways remain unchallenged; the 'cliff' over which to leap; the 'valley' that must be crossed towards change; the 'ascent' as the benefits of it become apparent; before eventually the 'mountain top' is reached.

Although not usually known for committing much to paper, McSweeney sent Starmer a nine-page internal strategy memorandum, 'Labour for the country', which warned that Labour was plateauing. It said: 'The Government is clearly benefitting at the moment from the goodwill generated by the vaccine. However, we should not take cover in this position: there is no evidence that without it we would be in a very different place from where we are now, and we must take responsibility for that.' Complaining that too many discussions were dominated by 'statues in Bristol, Meghan Markle's struggles with the Royal Family or the number of union flags in our zoom interviews', McSweeney pointed out that none of these had any real relevance for voters' primary concerns about 'jobs, livelihoods, crime and public services'.

The memo went on to add that much of the party seemed 'lost in a Twitter-driven comfort zone of its own, not pushing the boundaries and barely competitive', but seemingly more willing to listen to 'the self-identifying legions of people who inhabit social media than the voters we need to attract away from Johnson's coalition'.

The young human rights lawyer staring at his screen with 'furious intensity' at Doughty Street Chambers.

Sharing a moment with Vic.

The high-flying
QC outside the
Royal Courts
of Justice in the
Strand, 2006.

With his parents
and Vic at their
wedding in 2007.

With three of his 'best men' and oldest friends at the wedding: (*left to right*) Gordon Young, Mark Adams and Colin Peacock.

As Director of Public Prosecutions flying between international visits.

Being knighted for services to justice by Prince Charles at Buckingham Palace in 2014. Starmer rarely uses the prefix 'Sir' in politics.

As shadow Brexit secretary under Jeremy Corbyn, he almost resigned several times over antisemitism.

A sign of things to come: clashing with Boris Johnson in BBC studios before becoming leader of the opposition.

Starmer and Labour's deputy leader, Angela Rayner: they haven't always seen eye-to-eye.

'Keir's beer': the infamous picture of a working dinner in Durham miners' hall, April 30, 2021.

All smiles with the new top team: (*left to right*) David Lammy, Keir Starmer, Yvette Cooper and Rachel Reeves.

Tony Blair and Gordon Brown listen on.

With Margaret Hodge at Toynbee Hall as Labour was taken out of special measures that were imposed for the way they had handled antisemitism.

The 'Glitter-bomb' attack at Labour's party conference in October 2023. (*Left*) And then later that afternoon, with Vic, with all traces of glitter removed.

McSweeney said the damage done under Corbyn was 'such that we must change more profoundly than we have accepted until now, we must embrace the conflict that is inevitable, and we must show the public that our vision is something worth fighting for'. He was explicit that the strategy of bringing a fractious party together, for which Starmer had campaigned only a few months earlier, needed to be abandoned. 'Prizing unity above all else leads us to look inwards and away from our voters. We overvalue its importance and this narrows our thinking and shrinks our electoral appeal,' said the document.

Only a 'visible transformation' with a 'demonstrable struggle' to achieve change in the party would convince the country that Labour had listened and was 'no longer focused only on itself', wrote McSweeney. 'Keir must be seen as a break with the past decade, not a bridge to it. He must be unambiguously in the driving seat, not sharing it with Corbyn or Len McCluskey and their supporters. He must steer Labour out of the fantasy world of the far left, and the identity politics and snap judgment world of social media. He must break away from the self-regard of endless internal conversations and into the real world of people's everyday hopes and fears.'

Specific prescriptions for this coming conflict were light on detail. The paper described only 'professionalising' the shadow cabinet and transforming a 'risk averse' and 'sclerotic' party machine into one 'prepared to walk over hot coals' to win an election. But the direction of his proposed new strategy was clear and contained a deliberate paradox: internal strife was necessary if Labour was going to look outwards to Britain's voters once again.

Starmer is neither hyper-political like McSweeney, nor one of the old warriors from the right of the party who often seem to exist for this kind of factional conflict, but he found himself being pulled into the gravitational field of the battle nonetheless.

Corbyn's allies were now implacably hostile and it was by no means certain his suspension from the parliamentary Labour Party could be sustained. For several months, the chief whip Nick Brown was negotiating with trade union intermediaries over terms for the former leader's readmission. He says this was done with the full knowledge of the leader's office which, he adds, understood that a peace deal 'might still be necessary'.

Although the left-wing Richard Leonard had been eased out as Scottish Labour leader after the party won just one seat in the general election and replaced by the more moderate Anas Sarwar in February, the move had been messy. Leonard had complained of 'sabotage' while the SNP revived claims Labour's operation north of the border was always treated as a 'branch office'. In Liverpool, Starmer had backed the government's decision to send in Whitehall commissioners to take over running the city following the arrest of Labour mayor Joe Anderson in a corruption investigation, triggering not only predictable fury from the left but also expressions of alarm among allies.

There were perfectly respectable arguments against further conflict. Some warned the electorate didn't like divided parties, others that Starmer should wait until he had more control over the party, while still more pointed out that saying Labour had lost the confidence of working people was insulting millions in the 'core vote' who'd stuck by them through thick and thin. Tom Kibasi, who had been part of Starmer's leadership campaign before going off to work in the NHS, had by then joined the legions of his critics. Writing for the *Guardian* in February, he accused him of having 'provoked a completely unnecessary war with the party's left'.

By the time Starmer had signed off McSweeney's new strategy on April 17, however, the next stage of the J-curve – the cliff – was already looming into view. The party was hurtling towards the crumbling edges of a still hostile electorate. And there was little anyone could do to stop 'things getting worse'.

'A near death experience'

Labour's legal bills had so drained its finances that, initially, precisely nothing had been budgeted for the biggest exercise in democracy for eighteen months. More than five thousand English council seats and a dozen directly elected mayors were up for grabs in local elections, at the same time as campaigning was underway for the Scottish and Welsh parliaments. Although some money was later scrabbled together, there was another and even more pressing problem: Starmer had also decided to fight a by-election in a Red Wall constituency his party had held ever since its inception.

Hartlepool had fallen vacant because Mike Hill had decided to quit following a decision by the Labour leader to throw him out of the parliamentary party over sexual assault allegations. A year later, Hill was ordered by an employment tribunal to pay £434,000 in damages to a woman it found he had repeatedly assaulted and harassed after she had spurned his initial advances. Many colleagues thought Starmer was being politically naive and should have done more to avoid a contest in a constituency Labour had clung on to in 2019 only because ten thousand votes went to the Brexit Party instead of the Conservatives, who were now poised to scoop them up.

Yet he saw the swift response to the allegations against Hill, an MP who had backed him for the leadership, as a way of showing Labour was changing and he thought the by-election provided an opportunity to start winning back voters in seats like this. It was his first real chance to campaign in person since the start of the pandemic and he visited Hartlepool no fewer than three times, including on the morning after his takeaway curry in Durham that was described in Chapter 11. His campaigning style, one that had stood him in good stead when knocking on doors to get selected in Camden or having doorstep conversations out of the limelight in the last general election, also seemed to have a degree of wide-eyed innocence to it. Ben Nunn remembers them leaving their hotel in the town.

'Some lads started shouting stuff like "You're not getting our vote!" "Labour's finished here!" Keir went over to talk to them and they seemed a bit embarrassed because they hadn't expected that. He then arranged to meet one of them outside a pub the next day,' he says. 'I think this guy was astonished when I turned up,' says Starmer, picking up the story. 'We had quite a long chat. He was ex-forces, suffering from PTSD and had all kinds of problems in his life. By the end of it, I think he was saying he'd vote Labour, though whether he did or not, I'll never know.'

Such an encounter might have made for great publicity but inviting the cameras along never occurred to Starmer. Although insisting he 'always learns a lot' from such private conversations with people away from the media, he also acknowledges he 'learned the hard way that converting one voter at a time doesn't turn round a political tide'.

On May 6, the day of the election, Labour's field operation had told him there was still a chance of holding the seat. It was part of the machine that McSweeney believed had been misfiring for years, but this time its data proved even worse than usual. When the votes were counted that night, the Tories had won the by-election with a majority of almost seven thousand and a swing against Labour of 16 per cent.

Nor was there much comfort to be taken from results elsewhere. Labour was still in third place in Scotland and had lost council seats overall in England. Critics from both left and right were lining up to take a shot at him.

'Not possible to blame Jeremy Corbyn for this result,' tweeted the former shadow home secretary Diane Abbott with scarcely concealed glee. Andrew Adonis, a cerebrally centrist cabinet minister in the last Labour government, fired off a newspaper article saying, more in sorrow than anger, that Starmer had unfortunately turned out to be a 'transitional figure – a nice man and a good human rights lawyer, but without political skills or antennae at the highest level'.

For several hours that Friday, Starmer was ready to agree with this assessment. 'I felt like I had been kicked in the guts,' he says. 'The result was terrible and I had a moment where I thought we are not going to be able to do this.' When he arrived in the office that morning – after having to barge his way through a pack of photographers on his doorstep – the Labour leader told aides he was going to resign. Chris Ward recalls: 'Keir kept saying that he felt he would have to go, that the result showed the party was going backwards and he saw it as a personal rejection. Of course, I told him that was complete nonsense, and that it was far too soon for that kind of thing, but it was a rocky few hours.'

Such a reaction puzzles many people who have spent their entire careers in politics and are used to leaders whose first instinct is to cling to whatever power they have. But those are the same people who are cynical when Starmer says, as he does repeatedly, that 'I am not in this for me, this is about duty and service.' Asked about the Hartlepool result now, he talks about reading biographies of politicians who had spent their lives yearning to be leader of their party and says: 'Let me get this out of my system once and for all, I'm not fulfilling some lifelong dream here. I could happily work in the bookshop or something.' As Ward puts it: 'Keir regards his role solely as a means to an end of achieving change. If he becomes the obstacle to it, he'll get out of the way.'

This stance meant, however, that on May 7, 2021, the morning after the Hartlepool defeat, Starmer had to be persuaded not only that he could continue as Labour leader but also that he still had a viable chance of winning the next general election. Calls were made to Vic, who told him not to act in haste. Ed Fitzgerald, who had always been a source of wisdom and humour in the face of setbacks during his legal career, recalls that day as 'a rather dark one for Keir', adding: 'I think I may have told him he could always come back to Doughty Street and be a barrister again if he was finding it all too tough.' McSweeney arrived and made his case once more for 'why Hartlepool had to happen', but the theory of change he had mapped out on paper was now looking terrifying in reality. It was, said one of those in the leader's office that day, 'a near death experience'.

At around 4 p.m. that day, Starmer picked himself up off the floor and finally delivered a broadcast response to the defeat. Speaking against a backdrop of bound *Hansard* volumes in his Westminster office, he couldn't have offered a greater contrast on the evening news to Johnson. The prime minister was shown doing a victory lap around Hartlepool while above floated a thirty-foot-high – and only slightly more puffed up – inflatable version, grinning broadly with arms aloft and thumbs up.

Nonetheless, anyone who bothered listening to the Labour leader that day would have heard a very clear signal of his determination to force himself and his party through the hard yards ahead. There was none of the 'mixed bag of results' and 'making progress elsewhere' stuff that political leaders usually come up with. 'We have been talking to ourselves instead of to the country and we have lost the trust of working people, particularly in places like Hartlepool,' he said. 'I intend to do whatever is necessary to fix that.'

Into the valley

One of the more revealing interviews Starmer has done came in a podcast, *High Performance*, a slot usually reserved for sport stars like boxer Tyson Fury, who answered questions about how he copes with being repeatedly punched in the face.

Asked how he deals with the political equivalent, the Labour leader immediately referred to the Hartlepool defeat and said when 'you have lots of people saying negative stuff ... you have to somehow shut it out'. He then listed a series of mental steps – each illustrated with exaggerated physical movements of his arms. 'Take the heat. Absorb it. Put away what you can push to one side. Focus on what you're trying to achieve. Remember this isn't about you,' he said.

Just twenty-four hours after almost resigning, a steelier Starmer was back preparing for a shadow cabinet reshuffle in his office. On a whiteboard McSweeney had optimistically scrawled the words: 'Change Labour, Change Britain'. But staff were exhausted, nerves were frayed and mistakes were still being made.

There were leaks to the media about Anneliese Dodds, the shadow chancellor, and Angela Rayner, the campaign co-ordinator, being removed from their posts. The former, who was replaced by Rachel Reeves and given a new job as chair of the party overseeing policy, took her demotion well enough. Nick Brown, who says he knew he had been 'living on borrowed time', amiably stepped down as chief whip.

It was a different story with Rayner. She was downstairs in Labour headquarters on the Saturday preparing for a series of Sunday TV interviews and was told her meeting with Starmer had been put back an hour. 'I didn't know it at the time, but he was upstairs making decisions,' says the deputy leader, who has her own mandate from the party. 'My staff member comes to me and says, "I don't know quite how to tell you, but the papers are asking if we want to make a comment on you being sacked." I'm like, "What!" That was when Keir popped his head around the door and said, "Are you ready?" And I replied, "Yeah!"'

Rayner describes the conversation that followed as 'robust', which is usually a polite way of saying there was a lot of swearing. 'It was just the two of us. I made very clear what my views were at the time,' she adds.

Rumours swirled of a possible breakdown in relations or a leadership challenge. Although Starmer still got his way in removing her from the post of election co-ordinator and replacing her with Shabana Mahmood, Rayner emerged with a clutch of portfolios that included shadowing the Cabinet Office, a new post looking at the future of workers' rights, while also retaining significant influence over party matters as deputy leader. Starmer says his decision to move her 'had nothing to do with the Hartlepool result – I was beating myself up about that much more than blaming anyone else – but Ange felt I was making her carry the can'.

He concedes they had a rocky patch, 'which our relationship is probably stronger for now', adding: 'Everybody and everything had to toughen up after that week. If we kept losing, there was no point in any of us being there.'

Starmer was also making big changes among his own staff. Ben Nunn had already said he would be leaving because he wanted to start a family, while a disillusioned Simon Fletcher had made clear he would be getting out as soon as he could after the local elections. But other moves were directly related to the defeat. Jenny Chapman and Carolyn Harris, who served as the leader's lightning conductors for discontent among MPs, were swiftly scorched out of his office by the high-voltage hostility suddenly being directed towards it. One usually respectable journalist later had to pay substantial damages for an untruthful and sexist tweet that implied Chapman had been having an affair with the Labour leader.

McSweeney, whose lack of natural deference was always likely to annoy a certain kind of MP, moved to Labour headquarters as campaign director, which ultimately suited him because he was able to start clearing out and changing the party apparatus. But his departure from the leader's office was messy and unfairly reported as a demotion. It also destabilised the position of Ward, Starmer's longest-serving aide, who was to quit himself a few months later.

The break-up of this inner circle – particularly the nexus of Ward, Nunn, Chapman and McSweeney – was a difficult and emotional time for everyone. Starmer merely says: 'I had to make some really hard decisions which I thought were necessary at that time.' But it also served to underline his vulnerability.

That week, Peter Mandelson, one of the architects of New Labour and himself a former Hartlepool MP, had mused out loud that while he couldn't see 'an alternative, better leader on the horizon', Starmer's efforts so far seemed to have 'come badly unstuck'.

Those who had spoken out in support of Rayner over that reshuffle weekend ranged beyond the left and into the mainstream of the party. Andy Burnham, the Manchester mayor, publicly voiced 'solidarity' with the way this 'proud, northern, working-class woman' had been treated and hinted he hadn't given up on ambitions for the top job himself. 'If the party were ever to feel it needed me, well, I'm here and they should get in touch,' he said.

Burnham's re-election in Manchester with an increased majority had been among some slightly more encouraging results for Labour in mayoral contests. But Tracy Brabin's victory for West Yorkshire meant she would be giving up her seat of Batley and Spen in the House of Commons, necessitating another by-election – the last thing Starmer's battered leadership needed.

The constituency, formerly held by Jo Cox before her murder in 2016, had always been marginal. But its Pennines location among the disused textile mills of the Spen Valley qualified it in the eyes of London journalists as part of the Red Wall. McSweeney thought the decision to allow Brabin to abandon it another example of the party's mixed-up sense of priorities. In a phone call from a rain-lashed Hartlepool car park, he persuaded Cox's sister, Kim Leadbeater, to be the Labour candidate.

But the campaign would be complicated by the presence of George Galloway, a former left-wing Labour MP who had recently been sacked from a radio show for antisemitic remarks. He said: 'I'm standing against Keir Starmer. If Keir Starmer loses this by-election, it's curtains for Keir Starmer.' Galloway's platform was specifically aimed at the Muslim voters who made up around a fifth of the electorate in the seat, creating a toxic atmosphere the Labour leader later denounced as 'hatred, division, disinformation, lies, harassment, threats and intimidation'. Within the shadow cabinet, Starmer had faced renewed suggestions to restore the whip to Corbyn, whose criticism of the Israeli government's policies towards Palestinians had strengthened his support among sections of Muslim voters. If Labour was defeated in the contest on July 1, the rumoured leadership challenge would likely become a reality.

The newly appointed shadow chancellor, Rachel Reeves, was being talked up as a possible candidate from the right of the party, but she was never remotely interested in replacing Starmer. 'Every weekend I was campaigning in that by-election; I was desperate for us to win. On the day of the vote, I was there all day getting really sun-burnt in the heat.' She woke up at about 5 a.m. just before the result was declared and started to look through her phone, but then put it away. 'I was so worried about it, I thought I just don't want to know.'

Back in London, the leader's team had set up a 'war room' to fight back along with a '96-hour grid' of actions and announcements. In the end, all that proved unnecessary. Leadbeater prevailed, with a majority of 323 votes over the Tories. Labour had won by the skin of its teeth, its margin of victory smaller than the number of votes won at the previous election by the Green Party that had withdrawn at the last minute from this contest.

But Starmer had got himself some breathing space.

Climbing out

The last time Labour suffered a historic general election defeat, it had taken three leaders to carry the load on its long march back to power. Neil Kinnock inherited a shattered party in 1983 and fought off the hard left to change it; John Smith provided reassurance as the Conservatives' reputation for economic competence crumbled; Tony Blair offered voters that sometimes intangible but tingling sensation of hope.

Alastair Campbell had been around, either as a journalist or an adviser, for all these leaders. He hadn't always been convinced the current one measured up to any of them or, more accurately, to the scale of the challenge, but he recalls the moment when Starmer came round for a cup of tea during these dark days of 2021 'and it dawned on me he actually had a far clearer sense of strategy than even his own team were giving him credit for'.

The Labour leader was setting out how there had to be three stages to his leadership, each of which roughly corresponded to what Labour did between 1983 and 1997. First, show voters the party has changed; next, expose the Tories as unfit to govern; only then, he said, could he set out how Labour could change the country for the better.

The conversation has stuck with Campbell, although at the time there was still some way to go before even the first of these stages was reached. As Starmer later put it: 'We're trying to do Kinnock, Smith and Blair in one go and do it in five years.' But, he acknowledges, 'we were behind schedule'.

That summer he had been rebuilding his team and many of his recruits were people with experience of finding a route to power. Matthew Doyle, who'd been part of the press operation under Tony Blair, took charge of communications. Sam White, who had advised Alistair Darling when he was chancellor, was made chief of staff for the time being, while Luke Sullivan, who'd worked for the Labour whips team since the party was last in government, was given the role of liaising with MPs. Jill Cuthbertson, who had worked for Gordon Brown in Downing Street and Ed Miliband in opposition, was brought in to run the leader's office.

Deborah Mattinson had conducted opinion research for five Labour leaders before Corbyn and became head of strategy. Her appointment made ears prick up within Westminster because much of it had been reading a book she'd recently authored: *Beyond the Red Wall* described how working-class voters regarded the party as being for 'losers and scroungers' or dominated by 'naïve and idealistic middle-class students – arrogant kids … who looked down on people like them'.

She immediately began commissioning polling and focus groups to identify voters who could form a winning coalition in the seats Labour needed to capture at the next election, then built a political strategy that put them at the heart of communications and policy development. According to a strategy note Mattinson wrote for Starmer, these were 'skilled manual and administrative workers ... middle aged and older, concentrated in towns'. They were often 'economically insecure' Brexit supporters who 'care about family and country' but had lost faith in politics. She called them 'hero voters' in a deliberate effort to change the mindset of the party so that instead of being taken for granted – or 'looked down on' – they would be respected. Mattinson, who privately makes pointed references to how Starmer's own small-town working-class background has much more in common with such voters than those, inside the party and beyond, who think he 'fails to connect', said Labour needed to be relentlessly focused on issues such as the cost of living, the NHS, crime and immigration. 'We must always be using – and only be using – language that resonates with the aspirations and worries of these voters,' her memo stated. Indeed, one of the noteworthy features of Starmer's leadership has been a vocabulary of words like 'respect', 'security', 'pride' and 'country', rather than those such as 'equality', 'peace', 'freedom' and 'open' associated with his predecessor.

Around this time, Starmer had also begun to seek more counsel from Tony Blair who earlier that summer had written that the party needed 'total deconstruction and reconstruction'. The Labour leader remembers their first conversations as being less about policy than the timing and rhythm of opposition, when moves needed to be made and big decisions taken. But, as he embarked on a tour of Britain in August, there was a marked shift in the way he talked about the last time the party had been in power. He went out of his way to praise the Blair–Brown government, something neither Jeremy Corbyn nor Ed Miliband had done. And, in an interview with the *Financial Times*, Starmer hinted at a plan for fundamental reform that would, he said, 'turn the Labour Party inside out'.

The details of that, however, were only unveiled in late September as Labour prepared for its annual conference in

Brighton. Starmer announced he wanted to scrap the 'one member, one vote' system that had chosen Corbyn as leader in 2015, replacing it with the old electoral college in which trade unions had a greater say. Opposition was instant, overwhelming, and came from most of the big trade unions, grassroots activist organisations, much of the shadow cabinet, the elected mayors and the leader of Scottish Labour. Almost everyone agreed that setting forth such far-reaching proposals at short notice was a gigantic mistake.

Almost as swiftly as it had been announced, Starmer's team abandoned the idea, but then came straight back with a revised proposal that would achieve the same objective. This was to double the threshold for potential leadership candidates so they would need 20 per cent of Labour MPs to nominate them before they could go forward to a vote among party members. Such a high bar would have blocked Corbyn's candidacy. Indeed, if it had been in place when Starmer was running in 2020, his name would have been the only one on the ballot paper. On top of that, the Labour leader also proposed scrapping rules by which 'registered supporters' and those who had recently joined the party could vote in leadership elections, as well as making it significantly harder for grassroots members to deselect MPs and almost halving the number of motions debated each year at party conferences.

Some of those close to Starmer claimed the initial proposal to bring back the electoral college had been a decoy to draw opponents' fire and distract attention from the only slightly less radical package that went to the conference. Others suggest it was all a bit more chaotic than that. Either way, they had no guarantee of success. The reaction from the left was ferocious, with Momentum warning of a 'civil war', while some of the more sympathetic unions complained about being bounced and said they wanted time to consult members.

'It was touch and go on whether we had enough support for it,' says Starmer now. 'We needed nerves of steel.' The vote was scheduled for the opening Sunday of the conference on September 26 and it took a late night meeting in the Labour leader's Brighton hotel room on Saturday to secure the backing of the GMB union's general secretary Gary Smith. The next morning, he got vital support from Unison's Christina McAnea too and the proposals were approved that afternoon by 53 per cent of conference delegates. A jubilant Labour leader went off to a pub on the appropriately named Union Street to watch the second half of the north London derby in which Arsenal demolished Spurs by the more comfortable margin of 3–1.

Much of this conference drama was reported as being part of the periodic factional battles for control that Labour has gone through over the decades or, perhaps, as a way of preparing the ground for another leader in the event of this one being forced out. But it also helped move the party's points of reference away from a narrow band of activists towards winning the support of the country as a whole. From then on, MPs could stop worrying about making sure they were still a candidate in the next election and start campaigning for the support of 'hero voters', while mayoral candidates would no longer have to shower so much attention on unrepresentative party members. And, it might also be added, future leadership candidates would no longer need to parade their leftist credentials to an activist base. This is what he meant by 'turning the party inside out'.

The rule changes were far from being the only controversy at that conference. When Rayner described the Tories as 'scum', Starmer had to distance himself from her remarks. Andy McDonald resigned from the shadow cabinet over the leadership's failure to back increases in the minimum wage. On Wednesday, the day of Starmer's first proper speech as leader, organised clumps of hecklers spread out across the conference floor with the expressed intention of drowning him out.

Tension began to ease, however, soon after he began to speak. Sitting in the front row was the former MP Louise Ellman, who'd just rejoined Labour after resigning in the face of antisemitic abuse. He held his hand out to her and said, 'Welcome home.' Delegates, perhaps united only by Labour's everlasting sentimentality, rose for the first of several standing ovations. The speech proved much more personal than any he had done before, with the first real outing of the story of his working-class tool-making father. He described fights for justice in his legal career, including the murder of Jane Clough, and brought those in the hall to their feet again by pointing out her tear-streaked parents in the audience. When the hecklers tried to drown him out with chants and waved red cards at him in protest, he told them it was time to choose between 'shouting slogans or changing lives'. That got the biggest cheer of all.

Having survived a speech that could so easily have gone badly wrong, Starmer left Brighton on a high. 'I suppose this is how history is written,' he says now. 'Going in, everyone was saying how naive it was to try and do these rule changes at that conference, and then afterwards, it was always obvious to them that we would win.'

Stuck halfway?

Hostile journalists were left with little else other than to sneer at his accent, his delivery, and suggest it had all been rather dull. 'Words plopped from Sir Keir Starmer's lips like dumpling dough off a wooden spoon,' wrote a predictably rancorous sketchwriter who had taken to calling him 'the nasal knight'.

More scorn was poured over Starmer's Fabian Society essay published that week. It had been intended to answer the perennial question of what 'his vision' might be but was dismissed as long-winded and bland. 'The only thing striking about Starmer's pamphlet is how ridden with clichés, how boring, how badly written it is. It is a groaning tumbril of dead metaphors trundling along the slow road to nowhere,' declared the literary editor of the *Spectator*. John McDonnell, the former shadow chancellor whose respect for Starmer had turned sour in the past year, was equally scathing. He told a fringe meeting at the party conference the Labour leader seemed to 'lack urgency', adding: 'I have read the

11,500 words. We were told it was 14,000 words – so there is 2,500 missing. That must be where the politics was. The rest of it is banality after banality. It really is.'

On most levels, such descriptions of Starmer and what he has done are deeply unfair. In his first eighteen months, he had sacked his main rival for the leadership, thrown his predecessor out of the ranks of Labour MPs, considered resignation, had a public spat with his deputy, risked a leadership challenge, won a knife-edge vote at the party conference that most observers thought he would lose, and then faced down dozens of hecklers in the biggest speech of his life.

All of which was surely more of a white-knuckle rollercoaster ride than either boring or banal.

And yet the sense that something was missing from him as a political leader has been felt by some of Starmer's friends too. For them, his buttoned-up image has been simultaneously a puzzle and a source of frustration because they don't think of him as boring at all. The Keir Starmer they know is someone who dances at their birthday parties, lights up their weddings with best man speeches and cries on their shoulders at funerals.

This contrast was thrown into sharp relief by yet another episode of the personal pain that seems to coincide with the significant moments in his political career.

A week before that crucial party conference began, Jonny Cooper, one of his close friends from Doughty Street, died suddenly and unexpectedly on a walking holiday at the age of fifty-eight. A few days afterwards, the Labour leader boarded a train to Totnes in Devon for the funeral of an effervescent barrister who had been a driving force for LGBT rights campaigns around the world. The eulogy Starmer delivered in front of the rainbow-painted coffin is one that would make even the most poisonous pen of a sketch-writer hesitate before describing him as dull.

He talked of their struggles for justice, about jumping in freezing lakes or fast-flowing rivers, arguing endlessly and how, when they 'laughed and drank together', they always then 'laughed and drank some more'. He said: 'You all have your own stories. We must all tell them, over and over again. To remember Jonny as he was – loving, laughing, daring, vibrant, courageous – a complete one off, unique, and in our hearts. We will remember and celebrate him forever. But the loss is unbearable.'

Philippe Sands was there to see him deliver it. 'The speech he gave in the church – wow – you could just feel the depth of his passion and pain. At the wake afterwards in Dartington Hall, Keir wept with the rest of us. There is this enormous gap between Keir the human being and Keir the politician. At Jonny's funeral, I saw the real one letting himself go – in the best way – to share his grief with his friends. But, when I watched him on TV at the party conference, he had seemed to be almost a different person, holding back and distant, almost wooden compared to the generous, humorous and empathetic man I've known for twenty years.'

Andrew Sullivan, who was Starmer's Thatcherite sparring part-ner at school and has gone on to be a journalist who has known almost every major American politician over recent years, says: 'People always say, "Oh, if only more voters could see how they really are" – but the truth is that some of them like Al Gore [the former vice-president] are as insufferable in private as they are in public. With Keir it's different, over the last few years, I've seen him a few times. He'll just turn up at the pub and be a totally normal and genuinely good bloke. But his public persona is very different, I almost don't recognise him when I see him on TV.'

A view that Starmer was colourless and uncharismatic became a new orthodoxy in the media. Though most commentators gave him credit for changing Labour, they were in almost universal agreement he would be no match for Johnson's continuing allure: he had hauled the party out of the valley but was stuck halfway up and many doubted he could reach the mountain top. John Gray, the *New Statesman*'s in-house philosopher, wrote that the Labour leader was just 'a plodding lawyer' who has 'nothing of the nimbleness of mind needed', and that the party 'should replace him at once'. A big piece of research for the Tony Blair Institute concluded: 'No successful opposition has been anything like as far from the winning post in the midterm period as the Labour party is today.' A foreword by the former prime minister warned that Starmer's 'enemy is caution', adding 'more clarity and purpose' were needed if he was to succeed. Although Blair acknowledged the 'corner is turned', he said, 'the road ahead is long, and the vehicle requires an engine that can accelerate at speed'.

Feelings, factions and the 'ratchet'

At the end of 2021, the Tories comfortably held Old Bexley and Sidcup in a by-election and despite Labour's improved performance, Starmer still looked a long way off winning any kind of majority. A few days before, however, he executed another reshuffle of his shadow cabinet without the fireworks of six months earlier.

He brought back Yvette Cooper to be shadow home secretary and promoted David Lammy, another former minister from the last Labour government, to shadow foreign secretary. Charlie Falconer was sacked from the top team after being blamed – he says very unfairly – for leaking a story, while one of Starmer's closest friends in politics, Nick Thomas-Symonds, was demoted to make way for Cooper's return. 'Keir took me for a drink in Camden a couple of weeks later to soften the blow,' he says. 'We sat in a bay window of a pub which was decorated with Christmas lights and I remember how they illuminated this sort of pained expression on his face as we had a pretty frank exchange of views. But our friendship is fine – I know this is what leaders and prime ministers have to do.'

Even more complex relationships were at stake in this reshuffle too. When Starmer had been struck down by Covid that autumn, he'd asked Ed Miliband to deputise for him at PMQs and seemed sincere in his delight for him that it went well. Although a successful stand-in can often become a target for resentment, Starmer understood that this had been a cathartic moment for someone whose own leadership had ended in an eviscerating defeat six years earlier. Miliband was struck by the 'generosity' of his successor's reaction, which included not only ringing to say thank you but also sending a message to his wife, Justine, 'telling her I should stop being so modest and accept the praise'. He says: 'That is a very non-politician way of behaving – and I mean it in the very best sense.'

Little more than a month later, however, the reshuffle saw Starmer strip Miliband of half his portfolio by removing him from the post of shadow business secretary. Both went out of their way to emphasise this was to bring more focus to tackling the 'enormous challenge' of climate change. 'People underestimate the extent to which he is seized by this agenda,' says Miliband of the Labour leader. Even so, the move was perhaps inevitably interpreted as clearing the way for a charm offensive with a business community that had felt – unfairly or not – that when Miliband was leader, the party had been hostile to it.

Those promoted into the shadow cabinet included the former business minister Pat McFadden, as well as Wes Streeting and Peter Kyle. All were recognised as among the party's most effective communicators and much of the commentary was about Starmer's ruthless and cold-eyed decision-making. Robert Peston, ITV's political editor, said he had 'decisively abandoned the fatuous project of trying to form a frontbench team that could placate Labour's warring factions and had instead chosen shadow ministers for their perceived ability'.

Certainly, Starmer wasn't going out of his way to reward those allies from the 'soft left' of the party who had always supported him. McFadden, Kyle and Streeting had, like Rachel Reeves, all backed the ill-starred leadership campaign of Jess Phillips a couple of years earlier, when she had been seen as the most right-wing candidate. But Starmer, while admitting he has had to be 'quite tough' and 'unsentimental' with his reshuffles, shrugs off suggestions of being 'captured by the Blairites'. Pointing out that the petty factional battles that reduced much of the last Labour government to a soap opera happened long before he was even an MP, he says, 'I genuinely would struggle to know which side some people were on. It's a bit like asking people whether they're Protestant or Catholic, I don't care – it's about whether they can do a good job.'

Later, he says the changes to the party have not always been 'explained well enough' because 'this isn't about people getting even or whatever; it's about putting the Labour Party back in the service of working people.' Miliband himself endorses that view, saying: 'Keir is in nobody's faction. I think he is bemused by the labels – he is nobody's "ite".'

Although that's probably true about his attitude to what's been described as 'the narcissism of small differences' between Blairites and Brownites, it's less plausible about his treatment of the Corbynite faction. One of the Labour leader's allies compares him to one of the tools Starmer's own father would have used in a factory. 'Keir's like a ratchet,' he says. 'He relentlessly moves in only one direction, he never goes backwards.' And, as he tightened his grip – millimetre by millimetre – on the party, those caught in his ratchet were overwhelmingly from one side.

By January 2022, around three hundred members had been expelled by the party – often after complaints against them of anti-semitism – and many thousands of Corbynites had resigned. The following month, as Russian troops were massing on the Ukrainian border, Starmer opened up a new front by making plain he wouldn't tolerate any appeasement of the Kremlin such as had happened four years earlier over the Salisbury poisonings. Labour temporarily shut down the Twitter account of its youth wing for posting anti-NATO material and added a clutch of left-wing groups to an already lengthening list of 'proscribed organisations', support for which can lead to automatic expulsion. In an article littered with references to Cold War hawks from Labour's past like Ernest Bevin and Denis Healey, Starmer said criticism of NATO risked giving 'succour to authoritarian leaders who directly threaten democracies'.

An early test came a few days after Vladimir Putin launched his invasion, when eleven Labour MPs linked to Corbyn, including John McDonnell and Diane Abbott, signed a statement drawn up by the Stop the War Coalition expressing concern about 'sabre-rattling' towards Russia from NATO and the West. It took just forty-five minutes for them all to fall back into line after Starmer told them to withdraw their signatures or risk being thrown out of the party.

Abbott was later suspended anyway for sending a letter to a national newspaper that suggested Jewish people had never been 'subject to racism'. Even though she withdrew the remarks and apologised for any anguish caused, the Hackney North MP joined Corbyn on a lengthening list of MPs with the whip withdrawn from them. On top of that, Sam Tarry, an MP sacked from the frontbench after he defied orders by appearing on a picket line and giving an interview contradicting party policy, was deselected in Ilford South at a time when he was reportedly in a relationship with Angela Rayner.

Still more controversy bubbled up in the selections for candidates in winnable seats where those from the left have often been excluded for what they claim are spurious reasons. In Milton Keynes North, for instance, Lauren Townsend was blocked after a 'due diligence' test of her historic social media activity. Although the full reasons for why someone is not allowed to stand are never revealed, her supporters claim it was for the petty offences of 'liking' tweets such as one calling Starmer a 'prat' and another by the then SNP leader Nicola Sturgeon announcing her recovery from Covid.

According to Michael Crick, the former TV journalist who has done more than anyone to monitor the process of picking candidates, the left has been 'almost annihilated in selections', with perhaps only five left-wingers chosen out of two hundred candidates. He claims officials in Labour's headquarters have 'been very clever and effective' and that the party's regional offices often operate in a 'partisan' fashion with favoured candidates being 'tipped off' about when contests are coming up. More darkly, he alleges some have gained access to lists of local members which enable candidates to get a head start in canvassing, although it should be emphasised that senior party sources have pointed out it is possible to do this through legitimate means. Although selections have always been 'fixed and fiddled', he claims it's 'on a scale as never before' and the party's right has been far more effective under Starmer's leadership than Momentum ever was under Corbyn. 'I suspect Keir Starmer doesn't know most of what goes on, and he might be horrified if he did – or, at least, I hope he'd be horrified,' says Crick.

Some of these allegations amount to accusing party headquarters of breaking its own rules or even data protection laws and, it should be stated, there have been occasions when disappointed candidates have been asked to substantiate their accusations through a formal complaint but have failed to do so.

Often left-wing fire is directed at Luke Akehurst, who has been at the heart of selection battles both as a member of the National Executive Committee and the secretary of Labour First, an organisation that represents the most aggressively right-wing faction of the party. He's blunt about his purposes, saying: 'Why would anyone want any more MPs who are going to be disloyal?' He points out there are already about thirty members of the hard-left Campaign Group in the parliamentary party, adding it would be 'utterly irrational to allow a thousand flowers to bloom' when Starmer might have to govern with only a small majority of MPs, or even without one as a minority government after the next election.

'Keir isn't factional like me and his politics are a bit to the left of mine,' says Akehurst. 'But I think he slowly changed in the light of experience. From the start of his leadership the left behaved so badly towards him – some of the stuff on the NEC was just unhinged – that he gravitated more towards those of us who wanted to be helpful. I have no asks of him and have only ever had one proper conversation with the guy. All I want to do is stop people from the hard left alienating voters or damaging us in government.'

Although Starmer had tightened central control over selections by pushing through reforms at the National Executive Committee, he keeps away from the business end of it, with one official saying: 'Keir doesn't need to know how sausages are made.' The selections are overseen by Morgan McSweeney through a pair of lieutenants, Matt Pound and Matt Faulding – inevitably known as the 'two Matts'. The party's headquarters emphasise that due diligence tests have also weeded out several candidates from what's seen as the 'Labour right' including one or two who are personal friends of McSweeney.

It's also fair to point out that Starmer is prevented from getting involved in any disciplinary process which, under his reforms, is meant to be independent of interference from the leadership. Indeed, he is understood to have been surprised and a little perturbed when it emerged that Neal Lawson, a longstanding campaigner from the soft left for a 'progressive alliance' with the Liberal Democrats and the Greens, was under investigation for a social media post that showed him praising co-operation between parties as 'grown-up politics'. Lawson, meanwhile, vented that Labour had been 'captured by a clique who see only true believers or sworn enemies' which was behaving like 'playground bullies'.

Owen Jones, the *Guardian* columnist who in 2020 had urged Corbyn's supporters to give his successor a chance and was once on relatively friendly personal terms with Starmer, now vents his rage repeatedly on social media against what he regards as the duplicity and dishonesty of a leader who, he says, 'intends to permanently eradicate the left'.

Having helped him get elected as leader, Simon Fletcher believes Starmer has picked the right as 'his faction for now and brought in people from that side who didn't support him originally'. He points out how 'even Blair maintained a dialogue with the left that helped him through difficult situations', adding: 'That sort of relationship doesn't exist anymore. He's attached a hard face to it all, and some of the people around him seem to take pleasure in showing him as ruthless.'

Similar criticism has come from Jon Cruddas, the MP for Dagenham and Rainham and a former party policy chief under Miliband, in a 2024 book timed to mark the hundredth anniversary of the formation of the first Labour government. He accuses Starmer of abandoning policy pledges he made in the leadership election and overseeing 'a brutal centralisation of power on strictly factional lines'. But then Cruddas shows how hard it is to pin any label on Starmer by adding that he is an 'elusive leader, difficult to find' because he is also 'clearly an honest, decent man engaged in politics for principled reasons'.

Chris Ward, who was for so long one of Starmer's principal advisers, says: 'One of Keir's greatest strengths is that he's never been from or beholden to a particular faction of the Labour Party. I think that's because – unlike almost every previous Labour leader – he didn't spend his life in the Labour Party and it isn't his whole life, even now. It's why he could win a leadership contest from the soft-left, but now lead it from the centre-right. His focus is always on getting him closer to the goal of winning an election and changing the country – and he's smart enough to find different parts of the party to get him there at different times.' But Ward adds: 'The danger, of course, is that he ultimately ends up trapped by one faction or becomes isolated when the going gets tough. That's always been my biggest fear.'

The person who now has the job of interpreting this seemingly paradoxical politician to the world is Matthew Doyle, a former adviser to Blair who was persuaded to come back and become Starmer's director of communications in 2021. He remembers the moment he knew he had made the right decision. 'I was sitting in on an interview Keir was doing and he was asked "What's more important, unity or winning?" He might have come up with some equivocation about how you need to "unite to win" but, without a second's hesitation, Keir replied: "Winning."'

But then, as spin doctors like to do, Doyle immediately tempers his point by saying he's also been struck by Starmer's everyday decency. 'Keir's always polite,' says Doyle. 'He passes that "waiter test" of saying thank you – not in a formalised, over-the-top way – just straight, because he's aware of people around him. I can't say that for all the politicians I've worked for.'

Alastair Campbell, the most famous Labour 'spinner' of all, says he has slowly begun to recognise a 'winning mindset' in Starmer, a leader he describes as 'tough, resilient, serious, calm under pressure and genuinely offended by what's been done to our country'. However, Campbell also concedes, 'I don't pretend to understand him fully.'

Part of the difficulty is that this Labour leader doesn't 'narrate his motives' in the way others do. 'You rarely hear Starmer saying something overtly factional,' wrote the political commentator Helen Lewis, 'but meanwhile he's slotting a bullet in the chamber.' She suggested treating him 'like a stage magician: don't listen to the patter, watch his hands'.

Starmer himself sees no contradiction between being both decent and ruthless. 'It's not one or the other, they're just in a different place,' he says. 'I'm trying to be decent by the people that we need to help when we get into government. I'm not thinking particularly about the individuals who are going through the selection process, I'm thinking about what happens if we don't get over the line and we aren't able to serve or deliver for people.' Then he adds: 'That's why we changed the party.'

24

If not them, why him?

A lawyer's loathing

Much of the puzzlement about Starmer over the past few years comes down to the simple fact that he doesn't quite fit other politicians' idea of what a leader of the opposition should be or, in the view of some of them, appears to lack some of the core skills they might expect of someone in his job.

He is, after all, someone who spent most of his life as a barrister and, as we have seen, Starmer has often felt ill-at-ease in his latest profession. He has talked about disliking the 'song and dance' routine politicians have to perform to gain attention in Westminster; of those who think politics is 'a game', a 'pastime for people who enjoy the feeling of power' or just see it as a chance to deliver 'a sermon from on high'.

Instead of making grandiloquent speeches or throwing around condemnation and engaging in ritual abuse, he usually prefers the kind of evidence-based arguments found in a courtroom. For all his differences with the left he's never resorted to calling them names and he has also shown a nodding respect for Conservative opponents he regards as 'serious' or those he thinks have a measure of decency. In his speech to the Labour conference in 2021, Starmer was still telling his party: 'It's easy to comfort yourself that your opponents are bad people. But I don't think Boris Johnson is a bad man. I think he is a trivial man.'

A year or so later, however, the Labour leader was cheerfully admitting he 'really loathed' Johnson. 'He brings everybody down with him,' he said. 'Is there anybody who's had any relationship with Johnson – in any sense of the word – who hasn't ended up in the gutter?' In the intervening period, of course, the object of his scorn had gone from being a seemingly invincible leader looking forward to a decade in Downing Street to an ex-prime minister. The rot had begun to set in during those final months of 2021, when Johnson tried to change the law so the former cabinet minister Owen Paterson could avoid punishment for breaking Parliament's rules on lobbying friends in government. Then came the revelations of illegal parties in Downing Street that Starmer says shocked him as much as anyone else, adding: 'I had assumed holding the office of prime minister would have forced him to behave, or at least some-one around him would have called out law-breaking.'

By the time Johnson's last desperate effort to draw equivalence between his behaviour and Starmer's bottle of beer in Durham failed, Labour's electoral prospects were already showing signs of life. On May 23, 2022, the party recaptured the Red Wall constit-uency of Wakefield from the Conservatives. Two days after that victory, the vivid detail of Sue Gray's official investigation into Downing Street's lockdown parties was published. There had been a drunken fight, a karaoke machine smuggled in and abuse heaped on security guards who tried to intervene. Downing Street staff were told to be careful in case they were spotted 'waving bottles', but they still left vomit on the floor and red wine sprayed up the wall or over boxes of paper for the cleaners to sort out in the morn-ing.

Johnson had lost the trust of the public and his authority was bleeding out. But if many of his wounds appeared self-inflicted, it had often been Starmer's lawyerly scalpel that had made the first incision.

For instance, back in 2021 Starmer had asked him about reports – later confirmed by officials giving testimony to the public inquiry on Covid – that the prime minister would prefer 'the bodies pile high' than have another lockdown. When Johnson denied saying any such thing, the Labour leader replied: 'Well, somebody here is not telling the truth. The House will have heard the prime minister's answer, and I remind him that the ministerial code says: "Ministers who knowingly mislead Parliament will be expected to offer their resignation." I will leave it there for now.'

Similarly, after the *Mirror* broke the news that Johnson had attended a Christmas party in breach of the lockdown, Starmer stood at the dispatch box and said: 'I have the rules that were in place at the time of the party. They are very clear that "you must not have a work Christmas lunch or party".' At the time, Johnson wafted that away by saying all guidance was 'followed completely', before complaining the Labour leader just 'plays politics and asks frivolous questions'. This was, however, one of no fewer than ten occasions on which he provided misleading answers directly to Starmer that were cited by the House of Commons Privileges Committee report that later recommended suspending Johnson from even sitting as an MP.

The difference between these two politicians is apparent even in the way they describe each other. Johnson had thrashed around, saying Starmer was 'Sir Beer Korma', 'Captain Crasheroonie Snoozefest' or 'a great pointless human bollard'. After leaving office, however, he hinted all that name-calling had just been a bit of a game for him, as he said the Labour leader was 'far nicer and more amusing than you might otherwise imagine'. Starmer, by contrast, deploys neither puns nor baroque rhetoric to show the depth of his contempt for a former opponent he will probably carry to his grave. 'He's a liar,' says the Labour leader. 'Johnson lied so often, about anything and everything, it became priced in. He lied when he was a journalist, when he was London mayor, when he was an MP and when he was foreign secretary. Conservative MPs knew it, the media knew it, and because he had been allowed to get away with it, he carried on lying when he was prime minister.'

In the summer of 2022, however, when Johnson's lies were finally catching up with him, the question for many was why Starmer wasn't doing better than he was. Instead of giving him any credit for making Labour competitive again, there was a long queue of what were invariably described as 'senior figures' ready to say their lawyer-leader was insufficiently exciting. An unnamed member of the shadow cabinet was quoted accusing Starmer of 'boring everyone to death', while others said his ever-changing slogans – there had been a dozen by this point – showed he had no 'compelling political vision'. Angela Rayner was honest enough to go on the record, telling the BBC he needed to put 'more welly' into his job, while the *Guardian*'s Marina Hyde wrote: 'The Labour leader's got the feel of someone who'd ask for your informed consent before kissing you. You sense there'd be a waiver in the air.'

Less than a month before Johnson was forced to resign, Starmer felt the need to tell his shadow cabinet: 'What's boring is being in opposition.' One member of his team promptly confirmed to journalists that there had then ensued a lengthy discussion around the table about why he was right which was itself 'very boring'.

A view was beginning to crystallise that Starmer's law-abiding respectability was all very well as a contrast to the mayhem going on behind the front door of Downing Street, but might not be enough for him to get through it himself. And, if closing a twenty-point gap against the Tories in two years would normally be seen as a remarkable achievement, it still wasn't good enough for all those who pointed out Labour was still only at level-pegging with the Conservatives on the key indicator of economic competence.

But then, of course, along came Liz Truss. At the beginning of September, she was picked by Tory members to be Britain's new prime minister. And, over the next couple of months, the same characteristics that had so often caused Starmer to be dismissed by commentators as dreary were transformed – sometimes in the view of those same commentators – into the perfect riposte to the increasingly tragicomic politics of the Tory party.

The seven weeks Truss spent in Downing Street was the shortest of any prime minister in Britain's history and coincided with the end of a seventy-year reign on the throne that had been the country's longest. Starmer received rare praise from parliamentary sketchwriters for his tribute to Elizabeth II in the House of Commons because he captured the sense of political and national disorientation that so many MPs – Labour or Conservative – felt. He quoted lines of poetry from Philip Larkin, written for the late Queen's silver jubilee forty-five years earlier, about how she had been the 'constant good' in times 'when nothing stood but worsened, or grew strange'. Then he told MPs that Britain was once again in a period when so much seemed to be 'growing strange', saying: 'When everything is spinning, a nation requires a still point, when times are difficult, it requires comfort, and when direction is hard to find, it requires leadership. The loss of our Queen robs this country of its stillest point, its greatest comfort, at precisely the time we need those things most.'

He was still wearing this mantle of patriotic serenity when he arrived for the Labour Party conference in Liverpool at the end of September. The hall had been draped in Union flags and proceedings began, for the first time in the party's history, with a rendition of 'God Save the King'. The national anthem received warm applause from delegates, although aides accept that might have been different if Starmer had agreed to a suggestion he hold a microphone and lead the singing 'like Cliff Richard on a rainy day at Centre Court'.

In contrast to the previous year, most of the party's delegates had arrived in buoyant mood. 'You could feel something was different at that conference, you could feel it in the air,' he recalls. 'Hope turned into belief.'

Catalysing this surge of confidence had been a series of shockingly awful mistakes from Truss, who had astonished the world of politics and terrified that of finance by trying to keep promises she'd made to the Tory membership over the summer. Just a few days before Labour's conference, her chancellor Kwasi Kwarteng unveiled an autumn financial statement – swiftly dubbed the 'Kamikwasi Budget' – filled with unfunded tax cuts for the rich. Their economic experiment sent markets crashing, interest rates soaring and Labour's poll lead climbing to an all-time record of thirty-eight points.

'Is it time for Mr Boring'?

Starmer had achieved the first stage of his leadership strategy, showing the Labour Party had changed, largely on his own. But he admits that he got a leg up from the Tories themselves in reaching the second step of proving the Conservatives were unfit to govern.

Indeed, there is a school of thought that suggests the dramatic turnaround in Labour's fortunes had very little to do with its leader and everything to do with those of his opponents. Amid scandal and the resignation of Nicola Sturgeon, the SNP's grip on Scotland was being loosened, opening the prospect of Labour winning up to twenty additional seats and slashing the swing it needed in England for an overall majority. John McDonnell has dismissed Starmer as just 'a lucky general' because 'we haven't done an awful lot to gain power … it's almost like winning an election by default'.

Yet the collapse in Conservative support cannot be viewed entirely in isolation from the change being wrought inside Labour. The speed with which Starmer had transformed a party trusted neither with the nation's finances nor its security into one that appeared predictably reliable put Labour in a better position to pick up votes than at any time since the noughties. When much of the public was feeling fearful for the future, or complaining it had been betrayed by a dozen years of Conservative government and SNP hegemony in Scotland, 'no drama Starmer' had an opportunity to strike a deep bass chord with voters.

There were role models for him elsewhere in the world, where there had been a string of left-of-centre wins by candidates who had also been criticised for lacking charisma. Joe Biden had beaten Donald Trump in American presidential elections two years earlier, despite being branded 'Sleepy Joe' by his opponent. In the summer of 2022, Starmer had been to Berlin to see the German chancellor Olaf Scholz and come away saying he had no intention of emulating the 'circus' of the Tory party. The SPD leader had won with a campaign based around 'respect', even after being nicknamed the 'Scholzomat' for his dull and formulaic press conferences. The dowdily decent Anthony Albanese, who had led the Australian Labor Party to victory in May, visited London that autumn and told his British counterpart to just 'keep it simple'.

One sympathetic comedian suggested Starmer be given the title of 'God Emperor of the Centrist Dads' or 'Tedious Maximus'. Sometimes he has seemed ready to accept such a crown, saying things like: 'Good solid governance – I know, really boring stuff – is the thing that will change people's lives, not jokes.' On other occasions, however, he has objected to suggestions he's trying to bore his way to Downing Street. No one really appreciates being described as less than interesting, particularly someone who has good reason to believe his life has been more so than most. 'I don't like the boring thing,' admits Starmer. 'I might not be able to deliver a speech like Neil Kinnock or tell a joke like a stand-up comedian, but I don't think it's how I'm seen by the people who know me best.'

In a TV interview during the 2022 party conference, he was asked whether, 'given what's happening in the markets – given what's happening in politics – is it actually time for Mr Boring?' Starmer couldn't quite bring himself to deliver the answer his interviewer wanted. He went into a long reply about how 'anyone who thinks a government that loses control of the economy is somehow exciting' should ask mortgage holders and pensioners 'if that is the kind of excitement they want'. He said people would prefer a 'serious prime minister' with 'a careful, competent, confident plan'. When he finished, his interviewer looked slightly puzzled and held her arms out towards him and asked, 'So – that would be a yes?'

The Labour leader forced his head into an up and down motion before replying in the affirmative, then gave her the smile of a man who knew he had no other way out.

This conflicted relationship with the boring tag goes beyond reasons of self-image. If he recognises that being portrayed as a diligent technocrat has helped reassure voters, he also knows it's an obstacle to getting to the third stage of his strategy: giving people a positive reason to vote Labour.

Such ambivalence had been apparent in the speech he delivered to the conference the previous day. Starmer got a standing ovation for promising a 'responsible government' that would be unable 'to do good Labour things as quickly as we might like' and instead had to make 'very difficult choices'. That itself was a remarkable sign of how far the party had changed under his leadership. And, when he talked of restoring a sense of hope, he was at pains to describe it as 'not a grandiose, utopian dream' but one that was 'ordinary' and 'basic'. But then he said Labour was at its best when leading the country towards a bright new tomorrow. 'It's time to write a new chapter of Labour Party history about how we built a fairer, greener, more dynamic Britain by tackling the climate emergency head on and used it to create the jobs, the industries, the opportunities of the future.'

Any disparity in the nature and scale of his optimism didn't seem to matter much immediately. The percentage of British voters who had a favourable view of Truss nosedived into single figures and the *Daily Star* livestreamed a lettuce to see whether it would decompose faster than her premiership. It didn't.

By the end of October, Tory MPs had bypassed a party membership no longer trusted to make a rational choice and replaced Truss with Rishi Sunak. This meant Starmer, who was already trying to achieve in one electoral cycle what it had taken three Labour leaders to do in the 1980s and 1990s, was now also facing his third Conservative prime minister in as many months.

And, having established a clear advantage over the first two by being regarded as decent and competent, he found the latest one trying to contest this territory. As he entered Downing Street, Sunak promised to put 'stability and confidence at the heart of this government's agenda' with 'integrity, professionalism and accountability at every level'. Initially, at least, he seemed to have some success in this endeavour as he calmed the markets and drew some of the poison off the Brexit boil by negotiating a revised settlement for Northern Ireland.

At the same time, the rising interest rates that 'Trussonomics' had helped cause were choking off what Labour could offer, making government borrowing more expensive and rekindling the electorate's fear of any bold programme that involved spending money, such as the £28 billion the party had promised to spend each year on building a 'greener, fairer future' with historic levels of public investment in renewable energy, new gigafactories and the insulation of three-quarters of Britain's homes.

Jeremy Hunt, the chancellor, began setting traps by building in billions of pounds' worth of cuts to budgets for the years after the next election, meaning an incoming Labour government would have to raise tax or borrowing just to maintain spending on essential services.

All this meant that, just when Starmer wanted to move on to the third stage of his strategy, answering the question of 'if not them, why us?' – it was 'them', the Tories, who were still getting in the way.

The stolidity of Starmer was more than matched by Rachel Reeves, who also shares with him a relatively ungilded background and a slightly diffident public image. 'I think we're both showing that people from fairly ordinary origins can do big jobs,' she says. An editor of BBC 2's *Newsnight* once inadvertently posted on social media that she was 'boring snoring'. A decade or so ago that hurt her but, when reminded of it now, she just laughs and says: 'I think people want more sensible grown-up government and a bit less of the drama and bungee jumps, don't they?'

The tight bond Starmer has formed with Reeves is a contrast to the feuding that existed between Tony Blair and Gordon Brown the last time Labour was in government. For instance, when Reeves needed a new communications chief, she brought back Ben Nunn who had done the same job for Starmer for four years, a scenario that would have impossible to imagine under almost any previous Labour leadership. She describes how Starmer refused to rise to the bait when the *New Statesman* provocatively placed her at number one and the Labour leader number two in a list of influential people on the left. Starmer teased her with a text message saying: 'Congratulations!' She replied, 'You're stepping on my heels.' Do they ever disagree about anything? 'I think football is very boring,' says Reeves, deadpanning.

In 2022, the two of them had embarked on what became known as 'the smoked salmon offensive' – because of their preference for breakfast-time scheduling – of at least 250 meetings with chairs, chief executives and founders of firms. Much of this programme was run by Starmer's head of external relations, Vidhya Alakeson. Her efforts to prise open doors to a business community that had been closed to the party for years were helped not only by a poll lead that suggested Labour might win power, but also the craving in boardrooms for more stability than that offered by the chaos of five prime ministers, seven chancellors and nine different business secretaries since 2010.

The offer Starmer and Reeves were making was underpinned by a promise of iron-clad fiscal rules, an approach epitomised by Pat McFadden, the then shadow chief Treasury secretary whose notoriously gloomy presence proved a highly effective deterrent to any colleague tempted by profligacy. No matter how unattractive the Tories had become, Labour would have no chance unless voters trusted the party with the core functions of government: 'safeguarding national security and public finances'.

Although Starmer began 2023 by promising to set out bold ideas for the future, it was noticeable his new year speech didn't refer to the party's £28 billion a year spending plans for 'green prosperity'. Doubts within the shadow cabinet about the programme's affordability were already surfacing in public, with anonymous briefing that there would be little money left for the more mundane priorities of a cost-of-living crisis and failing public services. 'Every penny we spend on windmills will be a penny less we have to spend rebuilding crumbling schools and hospitals,' said one.

For a long time, policy announcements seemed to consist largely of ruling out proposals for expensive spending commitments that Labour had once said they would like to make. There would be no mass nationalisation of public utilities, no abolition of student tuition fees, no big offer on childcare. When Starmer talked empathetically of the cost-of-living crisis by citing the example of the family shopper who picks up an item in the supermarket, 'looks at the price tag and puts it back on the shelf', he might have been describing his own experience of finding policies an incoming government could afford.

Nor, as Reeves made plain, would there be big increases in income or wealth taxes. When she eventually announced much of the green spending would be delayed until the second half of the next Parliament, even the former Tory chancellor George Osborne, who had imposed austerity cuts on Britain, complained this was too 'sort of safe and boring'. To win an election, he said, 'you have to be a bit exciting'.

A large majority of Labour voters might have been enthused by a plan to reverse Johnson's hard Brexit deal, but Starmer's determination to win back Leave supporters in Red Wall constituencies meant he had already ruled out a return to the single market or the customs union. Instead, he said his priority was to 'make Brexit work'. Although there will be an opportunity to review the UK-EU trade deal in 2025, Starmer's priorities will merely be to find closer alignment on research, technology and security, remove strenuous border checks on foodstuffs and get mutual recognition of professional qualifications. In his new year speech in 2023, he even adopted the language of the Leave campaign as he promised to 'take back control' of legislation based on a substantial report he had commissioned from Gordon Brown on devolving power back to local communities and strengthening the role of city mayors.

None of this, however, was quickening the pulse of the electorate. In the early months of the year, Downing Street strategists took comfort from polling evidence that there seemed little positive enthusiasm for Starmer, whose popularity trailed that of his party, and suggested, if they could set up a presidential-style choice between the two leaders, they might yet pull off an unexpected comeback. They pointed out that the public's perceptions of Sunak and Starmer were remarkably similar, prompting *The Times* to predict an election would be fought between a Tory prime minister who voters saw 'as competent, smart and rich' and a Labour rival regarded as 'competent, smart and dull'.

Murmurs of discontent about a failure to set out a 'clear vision' began to rumble again, while even the mainstream centre-left voiced dismay at the prospect of replacing one technocratic prime minister with another. On Starmer's third anniversary of taking over from Corbyn, the *Guardian* ran a long editorial declaring that 'no one knows what Sir Keir or his party clearly stand for'. This so chimed with Tory attacks on him the *Daily Mail* decided to reproduce the 'withering verdict' from the 'bible of the left' on its own pages. A similar pincer movement had developed on social media, where the keyboard warriors of the left denouncing real or imagined 'betrayal' found a willing echo chamber on the right, which accused 'Slippery Starmer' of 'flip-flops'.

One Conservative strategist summed it up: 'If he says anything daring, we'll take him to pieces. But if he doesn't say anything bold, we'll take him to pieces for not saying anything bold.'

Missions and different positions

Starmer's response was to deliver what he called 'a profound statement of intent' with a plan for a 'decade of national renewal' under a Labour government driven by five missions: 'secure the highest sustained growth in the G7; build an NHS fit for the future; make Britain's streets safe; break down the barriers to opportunity at every stage; make Britain a clean energy superpower'.

They were unveiled in a big speech on February 23 at Manchester's Co-op building, with his shadow cabinet lined up in front of him and supporters packing out the balconies. Unlike previous efforts to show what he stood for, which had often seemed like forcing the proverbial square peg into the round hole honed for more obvious politicians, this one was engineered to fit the son-of-a-toolmaker. His missions were neither part of a 'vision' – a word Starmer dislikes for being too abstract and rhetorical – nor 'targets', because these don't have a clear path to delivery. And they were certainly not 'pledges' that would repeat earlier mistakes of committing him, too early, to another set of precise policies or spending programme without the flexibility to adapt to changing circumstances.

They were intended instead to be the antithesis to what he called the 'sticking plaster' politics that had seen successive governments fail to address deep-seated challenges; a deliberate contrast to the five short-term objectives set out by Sunak a few weeks earlier. 'Each of our five missions will contain this formula: a measurable goal; the building blocks of a clear strategy; and the first steps of a credible, long-term plan,' said Starmer.

Although this isn't the kind of soundbite that slips easily into a news bulletin, the missions are by no means modest in their ambition and had been designed, said Starmer, to produce a sharp intake of breath. But when he launched the first, 'to secure the highest sustained growth on the G7', no one asked how or whether such a goal could be reached. Nor did anyone ask how Labour could achieve the next sentence in his mission document about getting such growth in every region of the UK, when economic orthodoxy suggested the only way living standards could be raised in some parts of the country would be to redistribute money from richer areas like London. Sky News wanted to know why he hadn't announced any policies. The BBC had a question about whether he would back the government's cut in corporation tax that April. 'How will you change voters lives immediately?' asked ITV. The *Daily Mail* wanted to know why 'stopping the boats' wasn't one of his five priorities like it was for Rishi Sunak. And, while some commentators later suggested it might have been unwise to say the UK would outpace other economies over which it has no control, there was more criticism over the wording of this mission that not only included a reference to the textbook term 'growth' but also referred to 'the G7', an organisation of rich Western economies that was probably lost on most voters. As one of Starmer's advisers later put it: 'In any rational universe we would be in a debate about how we could achieve these missions. But all people do is criticise the way we describe them.'

The tone was set in an interview with Amol Rajan that morning on BBC Radio 4's *Today* programme. It began with a question about why his plan for a 'whole new way of governing' was different when 'we have heard that before, many times'. Starmer gave a long answer, talking about the five missions he was announcing that day, provoking Rajan to complain 'you've successfully used up time' and warn he would now be interrupting more. And, true to his word, he went on to dismiss one answer as 'literally verbiage', laugh audibly at another, then suggest this former chief prosecutor 'should be worried about crimes against the English language' when dismissing Labour's missions document with the quip, 'Hemingway it ain't'.

To be fair, the presenter's irritation may have been somewhat justified by Starmer being a bit long-winded. The purpose of singling out this interview, however, is to underline the way politicians are defined within very narrow borders, even by the supposed 'serious' end of journalism. The Labour leader was expected to serve them up with bite-sized pledges wrapped in grandiose rhetoric and sprinkled with 'vision' – which was precisely what he was trying to avoid.

The following week, Starmer used a long essay to complain that 'in a political world filled with what can seem like glib slogans, it is hard to make the case for why a particular word or phrase should be invested with real meaning'. Nonetheless, he gave it another shot, explaining how a 'mission-led' approach would be better able to create tangible change, just as the last Labour government had with its efforts to end child poverty. Positioning himself as distinct from both Johnson and Sunak, he argued he was offering neither the kind of 'populism that had debased public life' nor a technocracy 'devoid of emotion'. These missions, wrote Starmer, were 'personal to me'.

That didn't mean all of them were channelled directly from his life story. They were based on the conversations he has had with people from businesses and public services rather than being derived from some focus group report or academic think tank. 'They're alive,' he said, 'they're active.' Peter Hyman, who helped draw up the strategy, probably understands the importance of having experience outside Westminster better than most. His own career path saw him work for Blair for almost a decade, abandoning Downing Street in 2003 to take a job as a teaching assistant in a comprehensive before becoming head of a school he has set up in east London and returning to politics as Starmer's senior adviser at the end of 2022. Hyman believes sourcing the missions in the 'real world' is why, despite their difficult birth, they've survived and have slowly become recognised as a programme for government.

In the months that followed, as the Labour leader set out more detail for each mission, the 'personal' side flickered through his words. The well-worn story of growing up in a pebble-dashed semi became not just about authenticating himself as working class, but about growth being built on the 'bedrock of security' and confidence that would enable more families to invest in their own home as his parents had.

Similarly, when launching his mission to make Britain's streets safe, he described growing up in a small town and the importance of feeling safe in your community, before talking about his work as director of public prosecutions and his meeting with the parents of Jane Clough. It was, he said, 'the moment that has shaped everything I've done since, everything I think about justice' – a belief that 'incomprehensible pain can only be met with practical action'. Then he spoke about the women he'd met recently in a Birmingham refuge, where he saw 'the bruises, not just on arms and bodies, but in the souls'.

He unveiled his mission to get the NHS 'fit for the future' in a speech ending with a passage about his mother, 'a proud nurse' who'd both worked in and come to rely on the health service after becoming severely ill with Still's disease. 'Honestly – lots of people say they owe the NHS everything and I'm definitely one of them. But that's just the point. Mum's story isn't special. Behind every single door in this country, there is a family who will have their own version. This is who we are, the NHS belongs to everyone. The foundation for the comfort, security and health of working people.'

Starmer's speech on making Britain a 'green superpower' began with another part of his life: 'I know the ghosts industrial change unearths,' he said. 'As a young lawyer, I worked with mining communities to challenge the Tories' pit closure programme.' Then he talked with excitement about some of the places he'd visited in Scotland – 'the marvel of the Whitelee Windfarm outside Glasgow' – and declared the next energy revolution 'cannot be a re-run of the 1980s' with its brutal consequences for working-class communities. 'Can we change, can we grow, can we get things done, can we build things?' he asked. 'New industries, new technologies, new jobs – will they come to our shores, or will the future pass us by?'

In July 2023, he spelled out his mission to break down barriers to opportunity and smash class ceilings, once more recalling the lack of respect shown his tool-making father – a 'kind of snobbery' that had left a 'cultural bruise' and 'toxic divides'. Starmer added: 'Growing up, I saw too much unfulfilled potential; too often ambition was stifled; there were too many barriers to working-class kids getting a break.'

If there was a fluency and power to many of these speeches that hadn't been there before, none of this comes easy for a politician who lacks the effortless swagger and self-confidence of those whose families have commanded the British public's attention for several generations. If the dictum attributed to the former New York governor Mario Cuomo was 'campaign in poetry, govern in prose', Starmer is a politician with a tendency to use prose in every circumstance.

His mission on opportunity included a proposal for wider teaching of 'oracy', another unfamiliar technical term, but Starmer explained: 'It's not just a skill for learning, it's also a skill for life; not just for the workplace, also for working out who you are – for overcoming shyness or disaffection, anxiety or doubt – or even just for opening up more to our friends and family.'

Any gap in Starmer's own oracy isn't just, or even mainly, down to his background. Plenty of show-offs went to Reigate Grammar School with him and he was friends with at least some of them. It reflects a deeper objection to the practice of politics, which he thinks is too focused on such matters. According to one of his closest aides, even when persuaded to tell his own story there can be something 'begrudging' in the rendition, 'as if it has to be pulled out of him'. The Labour leader keeps telling anyone who will listen that 'this is not about me', even though that's hard to understand if you work in the 'leader's office', where – by definition – almost everything has to be about him.

An illustration of this came with a speech he was preparing for the National Farmers' Union conference in 2023. It was his third such visit and a number of drafts had been circulated because it isn't always easy to find a point of connection between the rural economy and a largely urban Labour Party led by a former barrister who represents a seat in inner-city London. In a final rehearsal, just a few minutes before the audience was due to start filing into the hall in Birmingham, he paused midway through and looked up with a quizzical expression. 'Did you know,' he asked, 'my first job was on a farm – is it worth me mentioning that?' After a short silence, while one or two advisers exchanged glances and chief speechwriter Alan Lockey buried his head in his hands, they ventured that, yes, that would be worth mentioning.

Angela Rayner, whose office is located in the same suite as those of Starmer, has her own theories about her neighbour. 'I would call him a constant professional – a real public servant – like a health and safety inspector who sees his job as not about him. He's got this real sense of purpose in what he's doing and takes it very seriously.' When it comes to feelings, Labour's deputy leader has sometimes called the party's leader an 'undersharer'.

Taking a puff on her vape, she admits to having 'overshared' at times – 'You should meet my mum, she has what you would call "no filters" at all' – then says: 'I enjoy the politics more than Keir. My first job was working in a takeaway, and the second one was working in a pub, so I find the politics of human nature easier. Keir was a lawyer and in a different occupational environment to me, his conditioning has been, you know: "don't talk about yourself".' She suggests they both have 'different needs in terms of personal development'. While she's learning the 'academic route of dotting my i's and crossing my t's', she says Starmer is now having to do 'the emotional and life stuff that I did earlier on'.

Richer, rougher and tougher

In the first half of 2023, the criticism Starmer has faced periodically since his leadership began, surfaced again with complaints his missions weren't cutting through and there was a shortage of hard policy that MPs could go out and sell on the doorstep.

Although it had always been the intention to reveal 'retail pledges' closer to the election, there was a wider unease that the absence of a big vision or transformative idea – a 'Starmerism' – meant it would be difficult to excite an electorate already alienated by politics.

In some ways, the Labour leader was a victim of his own success. The speed at which his party's electoral prospects had changed meant it had advanced to the cusp of power without establishing the supply lines for policy development usually required by parties moving into government. The last long period of opposition in the 1980s and early 1990s had been extraordinarily creative years for the centre left with a stream of ideas flowing from magazines like *Marxism Today* or think tanks such as the IPPR and Demos. This time, however, Starmer told one interviewer that Labour had 'gone from "you can't win" to "you can't lose" in the blink of an eye'.

In the course of 2023, however, his policy team ballooned in size, multiplying several times over to dozens of people, alongside the rapid expansion of a new network of think tanks and campaign groups with Labour Together now evolving into hub designed to sustain a new government in power. It's a process that's been compared by one member to 'building the plane while we take off' and much of it is being paid for by a massive injection of money into the previously cash-starved party.

The most important, and perhaps least known, of Labour's new so-called 'megadonors' is Gary Lubner. He is giving around £5 million to the party before the election, has invested millions more in what he calls the 'centre-left eco-system', and plans to continue spending similar sums over the next decade – an unprecedented level of funding for the centre-left.

The grandson of Jewish refugees who grew up in South Africa and campaigned against Apartheid before making his fortune from the global success of Belron, the owner of Autoglass in the UK, says he decided to give his money away after realising 'I had become obscenely wealthy.' His donations to the party began after he had a meeting with Rachel Reeves that was interrupted by her booking a train ticket for herself. 'I thought this is the shadow chancellor – she could be in charge of the entire economy in a few months – and here she is doing her own travel arrangements,' says Lubner.

He says what impressed him most about Starmer was not some inspirational grandiose vision or even the ruthless way he tackled antisemitism in the party, it was how he asked questions rather than gave speeches in meetings. 'He struck me as someone who wanted to understand problems, and how many politicians can you say that about?' Lubner makes plain he wants nothing in return for all his donations – neither a seat in the House of Lords nor policy influence – 'I just want to build something for the long term.'

Even so, the development of worthily thought-through policies does not guarantee media coverage. Starmer's press conferences have often been dominated by the endless culture war issues that filter through into newsdesk social media feeds. One week it would be 'deplatforming', the next climate change activists blocking roads or the 'gotcha' question that got asked again and again: 'Can a woman have a penis – yes or no?' There was deep annoyance in the leader's office after the launch of the crime mission, for instance, that the government was able to seize back control of the law and order agenda within a day. First, media attention was distracted with the shiny metal nitrous oxide canisters ministers announced they would ban. Then Suella Braverman tried to pick a pre-local election row by saying Labour councils in northern towns had failed to act against Pakistani grooming gangs because of fears of being called racist.

Back at Labour headquarters, a frustrated Morgan McSweeney recognised a clear pattern had developed before every local election campaign, in which the Conservatives would open up a trap and Labour MPs would reliably fall into it by expressing various forms of moral outrage. In 2021 it had been a report saying Britain wasn't racist and the following year an announcement the government wouldn't ban gay conversion therapy. He suspected 'grooming gangs' was set to be the 'woke dividing line' chosen by the Tories for 2023.

McSweeney decided, this time, Labour would pick a fight itself. On April 6, the party launched the first in a series of social media attack adverts: 'Do you believe adults convicted of sexually assaulting children should go to prison? Rishi Sunak doesn't.' Alongside these words was a picture of Sunak, his signature and the claim: 'Under the Tories, 4,500 adults convicted of sexually assaulting children under the age of 16 served no prison time. Labour will lock up dangerous child abusers.'

Over the next few days, condemnation rained down from almost every quarter. David Blunkett, whose sometimes populist policies as Labour home secretary had been challenged by a younger Starmer in court, wrote an article saying: 'My party is better than this brand of gutter politics.' Yvette Cooper, the shadow home secretary, was reported as letting it be known she 'had nothing to do with it', while her colleagues floundered in interviews when asked to defend the advert.

As some of the Labour leader's old friends from home and human rights law shuddered, it emerged that the factual basis of the advert's allegations was just as shaky. Sunak was obviously not responsible for judges' sentencing decisions, nor was there evidence he thought it a good idea to let dangerous paedophiles wander the streets. It all had a whiff of hypocrisy about it because Starmer, as DPP in 2012, had been a member of the sentencing council that drew up new guidelines suggesting prison wasn't the best way to deal with every sex offender.

For many observers, the advert's claim reminded them of the time Boris Johnson had falsely accused Starmer of failing to prosecute the paedophile Jimmy Savile. Even sympathetic commentators like Andrew Marr warned that Labour was losing the high moral ground, that 'ruthlessness is not the same thing as cynicism' – or the 'swaggering laddishness' of Blair's Downing Street. There was an obvious excuse available in that the Labour leader hadn't made the allegation himself and had been away in Norfolk with his family when the row began. Although aware the party was adopting new aggressive online tactics in attacking the government's record, it is understood he hadn't seen the ad before it went out.

It's instructive, therefore, that he didn't try to make this excuse and – far from washing his hands of responsibility – Starmer went out of his way to dip them in the blood. He wrote an article, splashed across the front page of the *Daily Mail*, which said: 'I stand by every word.'

Once again, the Labour leader remorselessly tried to block out the noise of criticism and keep moving on. Helena Kennedy, one of his oldest friends in the legal profession, says: 'I texted to tell him that ad was disgusting – it was terrible – but he never gets back to me on something like that.'

His decision to double down behind the advert reflected his annoyance at an outbreak of ill-disciplined briefing against his aides, and he made plain he wouldn't tolerate anyone trying to throw them under the bus. 'No matter how squeamish it might make some feel,' wrote Starmer in his article, 'I make absolutely zero apologies for being blunt about this' because 'too many people treat this as trivial, unimportant or something Labour shouldn't talk about ... When 4,500 child abusers avoid prison, people don't want more excuses from politicians – they want answers.'

By the time of his office's 'wash-up' meeting to assess the fall-out, there was a case for saying the campaign had been a success. The row created so much free publicity that the first advert was viewed more than twenty million times, sparking a belated debate about whether the Tories had undermined the criminal justice system, while Labour secured its most positive front page from the *Daily Mail* anyone could remember. When these tactics are criticised as the kind the Tories would use, it's pointed out that being compared to the most successful election-winning machine in the Western world isn't necessarily such a bad thing. 'It was important to show we can seize attention,' said one Labour strategist, 'that we now have this in our toolbox.'

To some, that sounds like the head of a weapons programme saying an atom bomb test had successfully proven nuclear capability even though it left its homeland radioactive. If Starmer's brand was built around decency and integrity, this seemed to risk cutting any high moral ground from under his feet. And yet, though many voters saw the advert, most would have only been vaguely aware of any row. What seems important inside the political bubble, where campaign strategies and tactics are endlessly debated, is really not very interesting to those living beyond. As the government embarked on yet more acts of self-harm over the summer of 2023, Labour's poll lead thickened again to around twenty points and muffled any noise of internal criticism.

The relentlessness of its leader, however, showed no sign of abating. On July 20, Labour won its biggest ever by-election victory by overturning a twenty-thousand-vote Conservative majority in Selby and Ainsty. Starmer's response was to focus on how the Tories had on the same night unexpectedly held on to Boris Johnson's former seat of Uxbridge and South Ruislip with a campaign based almost entirely on criticising the 'Ulez' clean air scheme of Labour's London mayor Sadiq Khan. 'We're doing something very wrong if policies put forward by the Labour Party end up on each and every Tory leaflet,' said Starmer.

Although the mayor largely refused to back down, the Labour leader was by then already embroiled in another row with a moderate centre left that had, perhaps naively, once thought he was one of their own. In an interview on the BBC's *Laura Kuenssberg Show*, he was asked if Labour would commit to scrapping the government's bitterly contested 'two-child benefits cap' limiting the amount in welfare payments to parents of larger families. 'We're not changing that policy,' replied Starmer, without adding even a sentence of explanation.

The baldness of his answer took many of his colleagues' breath away, not least because the then shadow work and pensions secretary, Jonathan Ashworth, had only a month earlier described the cap as 'heinous'. Announcing such a decision, without trying to offer a justification or even a nod towards those in his party who would be appalled, was almost certainly an accident. In the view of some, it was also evidence of Starmer's curiously 'unpolitical' approach to politics. Others saw the controversy as part of a deeper problem, in that he only seemed to make an impact with the media when he was reinforcing their tried-and-trusted story of taking on the left. In the same interview, Starmer had refused to rule out a multi-billion-pound hike in housing benefits but those comments had been almost entirely ignored when – under a different Labour leader – they would have made headline news.

Either way, his ratchet-like self swiftly turned the dispute into a teachable moment. Two days after the interview, he was at a conference entitled 'The Future of Britain', answering questions about some of the choices he faced. 'We keep saying collectively as a party, "We've got to take tough decisions" and, in the abstract, everyone says, "That's right, Keir". Then we get a tough decision – we've been in one of those for the last few days – and people say, "Oh, I don't like that, can we just not make that one?"'

The person who asked the questions and nodded along approvingly on the stage that day was Tony Blair. It was the first time in more than fifteen years that any of his four successors had shared a stage with a former prime minister whose Iraq War legacy had become so toxic. But the real significance of their fifteen-minute question and answer session wasn't about it being a symbolic reconciliation. Nor was it a laying-on-of-hands blessing. It showed a different Starmer, more assured as a politician than he had ever been before; someone who looked comfortable and at ease sitting opposite a three-time election winner.

Blair acknowledges the Labour leader had previously 'kept his distance from me – I understood why ... He comes from a more left position in the party than I do but he's shown that he is prepared to be pretty ruthless in getting Labour back to where it is now. Keir's taken the party back from the brink of extinction,' says Blair, with an admiring incline of his head. 'I think that's quite remarkable.'

Then he says: 'We talk a lot these days. The reason why – the difference – is that Keir's now thinking about government.'

25

Facing the future

Words, actions and a touch of sparkle

The Labour leader was perched on a red swivel chair in a BBC television studio with a nice view across the Mersey at the start of what was almost certainly his last party conference before a general election.

About halfway through his interview, he was shown a screen displaying the results of a 'wordcloud' survey of voters' responses to the question of 'What does Keir Starmer really stand for?' The most popular answer was 'Nothing'. This was closely followed by 'Don't know', 'Himself', then 'People', and the more literal 'Labour'.

'How do you feel about that?' he was asked. Starmer grinned and replied: 'I've had worse thrown at me in my life.' This was a newly self-confident leader with a twenty-point lead in the polls and the sense that mere words could not hurt him.

But two days later on October 10, at that same conference in Liverpool, something other than words was thrown at Starmer. As he began his leader's speech to a hall packed with almost three thousand people, a man climbed on to the stage, emptied a bag of sticky glitter over him and shouted something about 'a people's house', before being dragged away.

This incident lasted barely twenty seconds but, even beyond concern over how security was breached, each one of them mattered. Political consultants have long since emphasised the importance of 'non-verbal communication' because the impression formed by what voters see from a leader often counts for more than anything they read or hear. Normal folk might say this is an example of the proverb that 'actions speak louder than words'.

Anyone watching the news that night would have seen Starmer neither flinch, as so many would have done, nor start punching the protester in the manner that John Prescott so famously did a couple of decades before. Instead, the Labour leader calmly stood his ground, locked his hand unyieldingly on that of the protester and stared straight ahead.

No one was sure what would happen next, but party official Carol Linforth smartly marched up and took Starmer's glitter-covered jacket off him. The Labour leader smoothed down his hair, rolled up his sleeves and resumed his speech to roars of approval from the hall. 'If he thinks that bothers me,' he said, jabbing his thumb in the protester's direction, 'he doesn't know me.'

Yaz Ashmawi didn't know him, even though it turns out he grew up in the exact same corner of Surrey as the Labour leader and, after a few years away at boarding school and university, had returned to live in Oxted. He is now apologetic for having physically grabbed hold of Starmer but insists his protest was otherwise a 'wild success'. The glitter was apparently meant to represent the colours of the suffragettes and the ideas he wanted to promote were reforms that would make 'politics sparkle a bit more'.

In truth, however, he probably did his fellow 'Oxtedian' a favour because the images were so good some speculated it might all have been stage-managed. Linforth, who is in charge of the actual stage management at Labour conferences, might have wished that was true. After taking away the glitter-bombed jacket, she had to leave the hall for a few minutes because she felt so 'angry and upset that all the preparation we had put into Keir's speech had unravelled'. The jacket's owner later sought her out to check she was okay and sent her a bouquet of flowers. Her local florist wasn't the only one taking orders. Within a few hours, the party was selling T-shirts online with the slogan 'Sparkle with Starmer', while enterprising members of the National Executive Committee scooped up the glitter from the floor around the podium and it's since been auctioned off like the 'holy soil' tourists can buy in phials from Bethlehem.

The speech itself, however, hadn't needed to be sprinkled with anything to make it shine because this was his best so far. The missions had been shorn of some of their more technocratic language so they became about getting Britain building again, taking back our streets, switching on Great British Energy, getting the NHS back on its feet and tearing down the barriers to opportunity. The change he had brought within Labour wasn't presented as a factional conquest but a way of reconnecting, in service to the 'working people of Britain' so he could put 'country first, party second'. Starmer had his own answer – albeit one that stubbornly doesn't satisfy those demanding a simple one – to the incessant question of whether he has a clearly defined purpose to match those of past Labour election victories: 'If you think our job in 1997 was to rebuild a crumbling public realm, that in 1964 it was to modernise an economy left behind by the pace of technology, in 1945 to build a new Britain out of the trauma of collective sacrifice,' he said, 'then in 2024 it will have to be all three.'

More than anything, it showed how the missions had helped Starmer harness his 'backstory' to a 'front story' about understanding the challenges facing everyday British people. He mentioned the disrespect his father had felt, his own early doubts about whether someone like him belonged at university and how his hardworking carer sister struggles 'every week – and I mean every week – just to make ends meet'. Then he spoke about building a country 'where every contribution is equally respected, where you don't have to change who you are just to get on'.

In his most personal passage, he described his family holiday in the Lake District that summer, reminisced over how he had gone there 'every year as a child with my mum, even though she struggled so much to walk' and described how he had sat in a pub near Windermere on a sunny day eating fish and chips while 'Vic had a plant burger'. Then he contrasted that contentedly ordinary English scene with his first day back campaigning when he had met a single mother in a Worthing café who told him, 'with hurt in her eyes', how she couldn't ever think 'Oh, let's do something nice'. He said: 'That's what's this cost of living crisis does, it intrudes on the little things we love, whittles away at our joy – days out, meals out, holidays the first things people cut back.'

Afterwards, he brushed aside suggestions there hadn't been enough shiny new policy baubles in the speech, saying he had thought it more important to 'make an emotional connection' and show he understood 'what people have been going through'. He has never felt comfortable with the performative side of politics, yet he has listened to advice, practised with his usual gritty determination, and this private – often tightly bound man – was now showing he could feel the pain of others.

But the way he responded to the glitter-bomb attack had less to do with learning how to emote in public than deeper-set characteristics of a competitiveness familiar to anyone who has played football with him, as well as an almost preternatural capacity to separate himself from the heat of the moment.

When Ashmawi got on the stage, Starmer says: 'The old five-a-side skills came in handy ... I felt him trying to pull me back but I wasn't going to let myself go down on the floor.' Then he noticed some of the glitter had landed in his water and remembers thinking: 'If I drink it, how much harm is this going to do? Is that worse than letting my mouth become so dry I might mangle my words?'

Watch the tape back now and you see there are two glasses of water, one on either side of the lectern. In breaks for applause, Starmer can be seen looking down to assess which is the less polluted, going through his familiar process of weighing the evidence and taking his time over a decision of potential consequence. Even though the lights on that stage were hot, it was not until the halfway point of his speech had almost been reached that he finally took a long drink from the glass on his right. Reminded of this now, he laughs and holds his hands up in embarrassment, saying, 'Yeah, that's me telling myself I had better think this through.'

Either side of that conference, a hat-trick of stunning by-election victories for Labour, first over the SNP and then against the Conservatives, provided tangible proof that voters were liking what they saw of Labour – or, at least, as focus group reports apparently put it – that they 'can't be any worse than the current lot'.

But then Starmer was given a hefty reminder, if he had needed one, that it isn't just what people see from him that counts; words matter too.

Matters of war and peace

When Hamas attacked Israel on October 7, killing around 1,200 people and taking hundreds more back into Gaza as hostages, Starmer was widely praised for a response that closed off any possibility his party would be seen as soft on national security issues or sympathetic to Islamist terror groups, as it had under Corbyn. 'Just imagine what we'd have had a few years back with delegates waving the Palestinian flag through his speech,' said one member of the leader's office with some satisfaction afterwards. 'Today, Keir got a standing ovation for declaring Israel has a right to defend its people.'

The morning after the speech, however, the Labour leader embarked on a gruelling round of broadcast interviews including one with LBC. The presenter, Nick Ferrari, cited growing international concern over a mounting civilian death toll in Gaza and asked if Israel's response had been 'proportionate'.

'I'm very clear. Israel does have that right – must have – that right to defend herself and Hamas bears responsibility,' said Starmer.

'A siege is appropriate? Cutting off power, cutting off water, Sir Keir?' asked Ferrari.

'I think Israel does have that right. It is an ongoing situation,' he replied, before adding: 'Obviously everything should be done within international law, but I don't want to step away from the core principles that Israel has a right to defend herself and Hamas bears responsibility for these terrorist acts.'

The exchange, lasting less than a minute, soon went viral on social media. MPs' inboxes overbrimmed, while a series of clarifications, about how Starmer had been referring to the first question rather than the second, over the next few days only seemed to make the situation worse. Hundreds of Labour councillors were resigning, MPs with big Muslim communities warned their leader's words might cost them their seats, senior frontbenchers threatened to quit, and the party's hard-left faction showed signs of stirring again.

Although Starmer isn't the first exhausted politician to mess up an interview, this one had not only wobbled his reputation for sure-footedness in the face of the kind of unexpected event that he would have to face in Downing Street, it had also reinforced the sense that he can be tin-eared or even indifferent to the mood of MPs, party members and sometimes even the public.

Over the next few weeks, as he remained in lockstep with the government on the issue and refused to back calls for a ceasefire, the torrent of criticism included some from close allies such as Scottish Labour leader Anas Sarwar, who was reported to have complained Starmer's words had shown a lack of 'empathy' and 'humanity'.

Indeed, for all his desire to establish a better emotional connection with voters, he has severed a fair few of those inside Labour in the years since he became the party's leader. Some of this has been necessary, particularly given the hostility he gets from much of the left, and anyone seeking to become prime minister probably needs – if they haven't got one already – to grow a skin thicker than a suit of armour. However, the language he sometimes uses to describe this process can sound like he is trying to make himself almost impenetrable, saying, for instance, 'When you have a lot of people saying negative stuff, somehow you have to shut it out.'

For people who have spent more of their lives trying to build or sustain coalitions, however, that unrelenting – even blinkered – focus can be a risk. Angela Rayner says: 'Even though he's leader of the Labour Party, Keir is the least political person I know in politics.' Explaining why she thinks this is both a strength and a weakness, she continues: 'Sometimes, you have to understand where people are coming from, to understand their motives. And I try and help him steer away from some of the political pitfalls that can come and bite you. His natural instinct is "forget the politics – is this right or wrong?" But there's lots of grey in politics – it's not necessarily as clear cut as that.'

At the outset of the crisis, Starmer had shown little sympathy for what he regarded as posturing on a war in the Middle East over which the UK government has little influence – and a Labour opposition virtually none. This was not, he told potential rebels, an equivalent situation to that twenty years earlier, when he had himself been one of those marching against the Blair government's decision to send British troops into Iraq and when Robin Cook had resigned from the shadow cabinet. It was less of a decision about whether or not Britain should shed and spill blood, so much as one of expressing an opinion over what should happen next.

In an era of interconnected global crises – military, environmental, technological and economic – a 'polycrisis' that may dominate politics for the foreseeable future, Starmer can point out he has had more real experience of working and negotiating overseas than any opposition leader since the 1970s. His death penalty work had taken him to Africa and the Caribbean, while as DPP he had represented Britain in Washington and at international conferences, as well as running a programme to extend British systems of justice around the world. As shadow Brexit secretary, he had travelled across Europe seeking a better deal than the one the UK got.

But he has mostly operated in what Winston Churchill called Britain's 'three spheres of influence' – the Commonwealth, the US and Europe – and had little knowledge of the complexities of the Middle East.

As the destruction of Gaza ground on, Starmer's response was to immerse himself deep in detail, consult far and wide, then seek to build relations with international partners who have real traction in the region. That meant proving to Joe Biden he would be a stable partner rather than one outflanking him for the sake of votes. The Labour leader began having regular calls with Jake Sullivan, the US president's national security adviser. Later, he spoke directly to the king of Jordan and flew to Doha for talks with the Qatari emir, a visit that appeared to contradict his decision to turn down an invitation to watch England play there in the 2022 World Cup because that country outlaws homosexuality. Starmer has generally shown himself to be 'Atlanticist' in every hard test since becoming leader, with instincts that appear rooted in the Labour tradition of Ernest Bevin, the post-war foreign secretary in the Attlee government who had helped establish NATO as a Western alliance and ensure Britain was a nuclear power.

But there is a real prospect that Donald Trump may be given a second stab at the White House in 2024 and, given the views about him that have been expressed by Labour frontbenchers including Starmer himself over the years, this might seem a toxic prospect. It certainly makes the relations with the EU more crucial than ever, and the Labour leader has argued for a European-wide security pact as a bulwark against terrorism washing out of the Middle East and the influence of China, as well as Putin's Russia. Asked directly about the prospect of a Trump second term, Starmer says: 'It's up to the people of the United States who they elect as president. When it comes to working with our allies, it's so much bigger than personalities. It is about protecting our interests and ensuring the world is a more secure and prosperous place. The special relationship with the US is vital. I'll work with whoever is president.' David Lammy, the shadow foreign secretary, has talked of an approach that combines such 'realism' with progressive values and strengthening human rights around the world which are not only what Starmer has believed in all his life but also a way of extending Britain's influence and soft power.

When the Labour leader went to Kyiv to see Volodymyr Zelensky in February 2023 to reaffirm his support for Ukraine in its war with Russia, much of their conversation is understood to have consisted of the country's president asking his guest – who he had learned was a distinguished human rights lawyer – about the prospect of prosecuting the Kremlin's war crimes. And, far from offering Benjamin Netanyahu unconditional backing in his war on Gaza, Starmer has publicly backed the Israeli prime minister's political opponents, branded his rejection of a two-state solution as 'unacceptable' and warned any breaches of international law will mean 'there are going to be consequences for him when this is over'.

His argument is that, just as Labour cannot do much to fix the economy or the NHS without first winning power, internationalist humanitarian values don't have much traction unless a new government is in a position to do something about them. 'My thinking has been driven by what is actually going to make a difference and save lives on the ground,' says Starmer.

The Labour leader's speech at Chatham House on October 31, by far the biggest he had made on foreign policy, saw him refuse – 'for now' – to support the immediate ceasefire in Gaza that so many in his party and on the streets outside were demanding, because he believed such a move on its own wouldn't achieve anything. Instead, Starmer tried to look beyond the immediate conflict with talk of 'stepping stones', from humanitarian pauses towards a longer 'cessation of violence', and then a revived peace process for a two-state solution to which, he said, the world needs to pay more than 'lip service'.

Nonetheless, in a House of Commons vote a couple of weeks later, Starmer still suffered the biggest revolt of his leadership, with fifty-six MPs defying the party whip by backing a motion calling for a ceasefire and ten junior shadow ministers quitting. But no one from the shadow cabinet resigned, while many of those leaving the frontbench, such as Jess Phillips, did so on relatively friendly terms with 'more-in-sorrow-than-anger' letters. Although he says voting for a SNP resolution in Parliament designed only to split the Labour Party 'was never going to make a blind bit of difference to anyone or anything', Starmer has emphasised his 'horror' at the carnage in Gaza and that 'we all want to get to a ceasefire', adding that the rebel MPs, as well as those he persuaded to stay loyal, are 'good people' who had been 'grappling with very difficult issues'.

This change of tone reflected how, in the build-up to the vote, he had probably been spending more time listening and talking to MPs about their concerns than at any point before in his leadership. Starmer's schedule each morning also included a discussion with a core of relevant shadow ministers on foreign affairs, international development, policing and community cohesion, so that the politicians could feel shared ownership of whatever he decided. Those long discussions with backbenchers served a purpose by taking some of the heat out of their rebellion.

He had often been told by staff he needed to do more of such meetings but they aren't the kind he much enjoys. It was significant, therefore, that they were set up at the instigation of Starmer's new chief of staff, whose arrival at his side a month or so earlier was the hardest evidence yet that he was getting very serious about preparing to govern if Labour wins the next general election.

Shades of government Gray

This is Sue Gray, once such a powerful figure in the Cabinet Office that she was described by a minister as the person who really 'runs Britain', without whom 'things just don't happen'.

When she changed Starmer's diary schedule in the autumn of 2023, it wasn't merely about dealing with immediate party management difficulties on Gaza, but because she regarded it as essential to get him ready for Downing Street. She told him he needed to be engaging more regularly with backbenchers whose support would be needed to sustain a Labour government in power in the event of a small or non-existent majority, as well as developing durable systems that would enable ministers to stick together and support each other in the face of some of the crosswinds they would have to deal with in power.

'I know Whitehall and it will try to mould the new government and ministers into its way of working,' says Gray. 'What I'm trying to do now in opposition is establish our way of working so we can walk in and start delivering ... Even so, there'll still be some departments who'll struggle with that.'

She was also, of course, the official who'd taken charge of the inquiry into Downing Street's Covid parties that accelerated the end of Boris Johnson's premiership. Her arrival at the Labour Party had been delayed for several months until the autumn of 2023, while she went through the Advisory Committee in Business Appointments, but there was a strong push in government for a longer-than-usual waiting period, which felt more personal because of resentment among some senior civil servants as well as ministers over her accepting such a partisan job so soon after publication of this report. Starmer, however, had shrugged off the controversy about his new chief of staff, emphasising he'd had no contact with Gray when she was investigating the parties. He had always wanted a civil servant for the post rather than a more political appointment to help him prepare a transition plan into government. But he was particularly keen on it being her 'because I knew Sue's reputation'. He says: 'When all his nonsense blew up and some people were asking if I should still go ahead, I was willing to wait for her because of Sue's obvious integrity, rather than her lack of it.'

For her part, Gray – who has not spoken publicly about this or anything else before – makes clear she disliked being under the public gaze. Some of the profiles of her at that time had reheated old allegations that, during a career break in the 1980s when she'd briefly run a pub in County Down a short drive from the border with the Republic of Ireland, Gray had been working for British intelligence. When this is put to her directly, she bursts out laughing, then says: 'I'm definitely not a spy – and no – I never have been.'

While acknowledging that there was a certain amount of annoyance at the manner of her departure from the civil service, Gray had been dismayed by the resistance from some quarters to her investigation into Downing Street's parties. This included telling her to sack an independent adviser and efforts to tone down or remove parts of her findings, neither of which she was prepared to do. Even so, she bears no grudge towards Whitehall – far from it – because she knows the government machine will be essential if a Labour government is going to achieve anything.

'It's really important for me to say loud and clear that I love the civil service. The majority of them are absolutely people with the right values, they live by their values, and they're in public service for those values,' says Gray. 'So it was heartbreaking, really, to see the behaviour during partygate. That wouldn't have happened a few years ago. The whole culture just became very informal.' In her report, she pointed the finger of blame for this directly at the 'lack of leadership' from Boris Johnson at a time when Britain's most senior civil servant was sending WhatsApp messages to colleagues saying he had never seen a 'bunch of people less well-equipped to run a country' than those then occupying Downing Street. It is no coincidence that one of the first changes Gray has instituted to

Labour's internal processes is to limit the use of such forms of communication on serious matters. 'I don't want WhatsApp being used for policy,' she says.

As those policies are developed for an incoming government, Starmer describes with unusual relish how 'we're already deep in the detail' of reforms to Britain's notoriously sclerotic planning system so that he can meet a goal of building 1.5 million homes in five years. He has also been pressing for worked-through proposals on 'knocking out the impediments' to unblock the electricity grid so that they can achieve his mission of carbon-neutral 'clean power' by 2030. 'I don't want a discussion in the first hundred days if we win the election,' he says, 'that we could be having now.' A member of the shadow cabinet says: 'Keir's not much interested in leaning back and having a long discussion about geopolitics, even though a few of us would probably like a bit more of that. He only really comes alive when we get on to the nitty-gritty of how to get things done.'

Starmer gives an example of this himself, as he describes sitting down with Greg Jackson, the chief executive of Octopus Energy, who told him his firm could build a new offshore wind farm in eighteen months. 'Why haven't you done it then?' the Labour leader asked him. Jackson told him that getting planning permission can take five years, then a developer can face another eighteen months waiting to import materials from overseas because the stop-start nature of government support has meant there are supply chain problems. Even then there is no guarantee a new wind farm would be connected to the National Grid, which can take another five years. Starmer then got in touch with the National Grid, who told him that the rules of the electricity regulator are designed to prevent too much capacity, even though their assessment of how much there is includes projects like fossil fuel power stations that will never get built. Then, just when everyone is happy about new development taking place and the grid is waiting for the electricity, developers themselves delay projects because they don't want to be the first in an area and face having to pay all the costs of a connection. 'I'm not interested in dancing around issues, or just mouthing off about what I can do,' says Starmer. 'I'm impatient to roll up my sleeves to find answers to problems.'

One innovation specifically mentioned by Gray for Labour to look at are the citizens' assemblies introduced successfully by the Irish government with a model in which around a hundred representative voters and a handful of politicians meet to examine evidence in depth before putting a consensus proposal to the people in a referendum. She says the once socially conservative Ireland is almost 'unrecognisable' after using such innovations to thrash out answers on previously vexed issues such as abortion and gay marriage.

Starmer's team have begun work on how to use them to get agreement on constitutional questions such as further devolution to the UK nations and regions, strengthening the powers of big city mayors, or building consensus for regional development plans including housebuilding which are sometimes blocked by institutional inertia. 'This is one way we can help resolve these questions by involving communities at an early stage,' explains Gray, who adds, with a slight glint in her eye: 'Whitehall will not like this because they have no control.' Gordon Brown's Commission on the UK's Future, the recommendations of which were accepted by Starmer in 2022, proposed using citizens' assemblies to decide the shape of a new democratic chamber to replace the House of Lords.

The Labour leader himself says Camden Council in his constituency tried a similar scheme with community groups and police to tackle knife crime, but he is reluctant to present models such as citizens' assemblies as a panacea that will fix everything. 'They've worked in some areas, not in others,' he says. His focus is always on outcomes rather than single headline-grabbing measures. Often, they will look a little dull. For instance, he has contrasted unworkable but eye-catching Tory schemes to 'stop the boats' with armoured jet skis or sending illegal immigrants to Rwanda against

Labour's determinedly dour plan for what he describes as 'doing the basics better – the mundane stuff, the bureaucratic stuff' – by improving the speed with which asylum applications are processed.

This is, after all, a politician who ran a Whitehall department himself when in charge of the Crown Prosecution Service, in which one of his most effective reforms was to replace paper files with digital ones, an initiative that was never likely to generate publicity but, he says, sped up justice and improved people's lives. One of his advisers working on delivery of Labour's five missions suggests specific policies will be like 'jigsaw pieces' which on their own might seem to have little meaning but, when placed together with hundreds more, will eventually 'form a picture of recognisable change'.

Gray, who for so long was almost the archetypal Whitehall fixer, knows better than most that solutions don't usually appear in bright primary colours as much as in the nuances or ambiguities of different shades. And some of the experts being brought into policy discussions say that she's the person in the room asking, for instance, if it might be wiser to spend what funding is available for new 'Technical Excellence Colleges' on repurposing existing facilities rather than building new ones from scratch. In a discussion on crime when someone suggests locking up more offenders, she asks where all the new prisons that would be needed are going to be located.

Starmer's chief of staff has also begun attending his regular meetings with Pat McFadden, who has been promoted from the shadow Treasury team to be Labour's election co-ordinator, and its campaign director Morgan McSweeney. Gray sees part of her job as making sure that the party's desire to have an attractive offer for voters doesn't mean making promises that will be impossible to deliver in government. 'Keir's absolutely clear we've always got to be focused on what we must do to win,' says Gray, 'but if we win, we've also got to have a plan for the first day, for the first hundred days, and for the first year of the first term, if we're going to have any chance of getting a second term. He doesn't want us to forget about what we've got to do if we get to walk up that road in Downing Street.'

When Starmer launched his five missions in February 2023, Labour published a document that set out specific proposals to break up the old model of 'departments working in silos'. It said there would be data-driven 'cross-cutting mission boards' at the heart of power in the Cabinet Office so that, for example, the goal of making streets safer wouldn't just be the responsibility of the Home Office and Justice departments but also those of Health, Education and Business.

Those working on detailed proposals say these boards won't be 'one-size-fits-all' because a variety of different-shaped structures will be required to deliver each of the missions. That on health, for instance, will rely on expertise in reforming public services. By contrast, a mission board tasked with achieving 'clean power' by 2030 will be heavily stacked with representatives from the private sector. Starmer's mission on growth will require multiple structures ranging from a permanent Industrial Strategy Council involving trade unions, academic and business to the 'Infrastructure Council' with big financial institutions already convened by Reeves.

The Resolution Foundation has warned that existing plans – whether they belong to the current government or not – for reversing decline are 'not serious' and that 'world-beating' rhetoric doesn't automatically translate into a 'world-beating reality'. Others have urged Starmer to separate the Treasury's role delivering sustained growth which 'always seems to play second fiddle' from its responsibility for balancing the books.

Gray, however, seems a little wary of the kind of drastic overhaul of Whitehall that went down so badly with the civil service when Dominic Cummings tried it while he was working for Johnson. She says merely that there'll be 'a proposal for the centre' of govern-ment which will include a unit 'focused purely on mission delivery and transparency of performance'. Even more than Starmer himself, she has developed reflexes formed over decades of working on the inside which perhaps cleave towards conventional ways of doing government.

But that doesn't necessarily mean, as some party advisers have begun to grumble, she's a block on change. For instance, the chief of staff recognises that what's always been regarded as a rather 'generalist' government bureaucracy shouldn't 'have the only say in development and delivery of policy', adding: 'If we're confident in our abilities we should be embracing outside involvement working with and alongside the civil service.'

Similarly, while cautious about calls for new legislation setting out a framework under which civil servants operate, Gray believes they should be made more accountable and cites recent incidents of senior officials who appeared to have been ordered to stonewall questions from MPs. 'We should be willing to go in front of parliamentary committees and answer questions properly,' she says, 'but putting it all in statute would actually hinder the ability of the civil service to be flexible; to change and to move.'

A line that has been startlingly under-reported from Starmer's missions document talked about how he wanted to devolve 'decision-making away from Westminster to those with the experience, knowledge and expertise'. For instance, it means the skills taught in a particular area will be tailored by local politicians towards the needs of their economy rather than imposed from on top by Whitehall. This idea of no longer 'hoarding power' in the centre reflects the report Gordon Brown wrote on renewing democracy, and is maybe a distant echo of the Labour leader's left-wing youth when he advocated 'socialist self-management' as part of a 'red-green alliance'. It explains why Gray not only is keen to explore using citizens' assemblies but has already moved to repair battered relations between Starmer and the big regional mayors like Sadiq Khan in London and Andy Burnham in Manchester. 'We should learn from them about what's worked,' she says, 'as well as where things haven't worked – why would we repeat it somewhere if they've already got that experience?'

Reassuring, radical and ruthless

It is often forgotten that Tony Blair was criticised for being too cautious or defining himself mainly by what he would not do before the 1997 election when his famous five pledges included one for spending a paltry £100 million more on the NHS by 'cutting red tape'.

The former prime minister believes the attacks on Starmer for lacking a transformational vision are unfair and the five missions have given any incoming government a 'clear compass' for where it's headed. He also says that the Labour leader's experience of the government machine from running the CPS will help deliver them, adding: 'Keir has a better understanding of the process of government than I had and that will be very important.'

But then, perhaps in a little pitch for the Institute for Global Change that bears his name and has a thousand-strong staff advising governments around the world, Blair says that Starmer faces a 'policy problem' in working out how to navigate his missions through a sea of jagged rocks. 'Some of the expertise required is going to lie outside government,' says Blair. 'The world is changing very fast and finding the right people with the right capabilities on technology will be very hard.'

He believes the economic inheritance and the scale of the task facing Starmer in 2024 are far more daunting than those of 1997. Describing how 'low growth, high tax and low productivity are a big matrix of decline', he says a new government will also have to 'make sense of the European question which is incredibly difficult politically and practically' while facing 'unprecedented challenge and change' on everything from technology and climate to a deteriorating relationship between the US and China.

Acknowledging 'it will be a hard road to walk', Starmer has said higher economic growth will be his 'central mission', not least because under Rachel Reeves' ferrous 'fiscal lock' – which will give independent scrutiny of rules to ensure government debt is falling over five years and that any borrowing is only for investment – that might be the only way of generating tax revenue to pay for all the other things he wants a government to do. There are plans for some new taxes such as imposing VAT on private school fees and closing the 'non-dom' loophole used by the rich to avoid paying their fair share, while the excess profits of oil and gas companies will be targeted by another windfall levy.

Labour is said to be looking at other revenue-raising schemes to chase down evaded taxes hidden offshore or, so long as it doesn't deter investment, charge the global rich more when they buy homes here or settle their legal disputes in British courts. But, even so, Starmer has warned: 'Anyone who expects an incoming Labour government to quickly turn on the spending taps is going to be disappointed.' Sometimes he allows himself to hanker after a time when every spending decision is not always achingly painful. There are occasional hints in conversation that he would like to invest in a deeper transformation of public services so that the young people he saw ending up in the criminal justice system when he was chief prosecutor no longer 'slip through the cracks'.

Until the day when money for such things begins to flow again, he will rely on his missions to give government a 'north star' or 'single-minded purpose' in prioritising between thousands of conflicting demands. In meetings with colleagues, he repeatedly asks: 'Is this mission critical?' – or, as he once put it, 'If the answer is it helps with that mission, then the answer is yes. If the answer is it doesn't, then the answer's no.'

Those locked-tight spending taps also mean, he says, 'we will have to be more radical, not less'. Already, that has seen shadow ministers responsible for public services coming under pressure to produce detailed proposals for bigger reforms to achieve Labour's missions. In education, there would be a sweeping change to the curriculum so there would be more focus on learning the creative and problem-solving skills needed by the economy, as well as what Starmer terms an 'across the board and nothing off-limits' review of the exam system which could include amending or even abolishing

GCSEs and A-levels in their present form. In health, a new emphasis on prevention would see resources transferred from hospitals
into social or community care, as well as measures to tackle obesity
by changing eating habits. There will be more use of new technology and artificial intelligence to personalise services and reduce
bureaucracy at every level of government. As a Labour campaign
document issued to shadow ministers in January 2024 put it: 'Yes,
investment is needed, but pouring ever-increasing amounts of
money into a system that isn't working is wasteful in every sense.
The message of modernise or die is not a threat but a choice.'

All of which sounds clear and progressive until departmental
budgets are sliced under spending plans inherited from the current
Conservative government that Starmer has accused of 'salting the
earth' for an incoming Labour one. There are genuine worries in
his team about how difficult it will be for ministers to hold together
when they're scrabbling around for the last penny the Treasury can
spare. Where will the investment needed to change the NHS or
enable the UK's transition to 'net zero' come from without considerable public investment in new infrastructure and technology?

For Starmer, this is where a further level of radicalism kicks in.
In return for offering business a secure and stable environment, he
wants them investing in and helping deliver his missions. Plans for
a national wealth fund in which the government would inject £8
billion are intended to leverage in a further £24 billion of private
money. On almost every mission, there is talk about bringing not
only chief executives, but also trade union leaders, academics,
mayors, local community groups and outside experts into Whitehall
meetings as 'partners' with the government. Starmer says his
administration will neither submit to nor merely regulate markets
but seek to 'shape them' – a break with post-Thatcher orthodoxy
that has, again, been largely ignored by those who say he offers no
change.

The combination of an active state and an almost corporatist
industrial strategy, as well as a tranche of new protections for workers

in the gig economy and the creation of a publicly owned GB Energy, does not sit naturally on the political spectrum alongside tight fiscal constraint and measures to foster entrepreneurship by scrapping business rates. But Starmer's lack of a fixed factional identity or rigid ideology mean his party can claim to be both 'unashamedly pro-business and pro-worker'. Although he acknowledges most of the business chief executives 'probably aren't tribal Labour people', he tells them: 'I don't know how to run wind turbines or how to re-cable Britain. They need to do that and if they tell me what they need, we can work together to make it happen.'

He has described how Labour is planning a 'decade of national renewal' and emphasises the importance of each word. A 'decade', because fixing long-term problems will require two terms in government; 'national' because it involves the contribution of the whole country; and 'renewal' because he says that even in the most straitened of circumstances people can 'truly come together behind ideas' with a sense of a 'shared purpose for a better future'.

A lot of brows are still being furrowed and heads scratched about exactly how to create a partnership between government and so many disparate stakeholders. At the same time, there's little evidence to suggest, as yet, the public are either enthused by the ambitions of these missions or that they've cottoned on to the central role they're supposed to have in delivering them. Nor does Starmer's disavowal of the performative side of politics make it easy for him to inspire people to come together with a sense of shared national purpose.

That's why the Labour leader thinks that underpinning all five missions must be a concerted effort to restore trust in democracy. He has said: 'We need to clean up politics. No more VIP fast lanes, no more kickbacks for colleagues, no more revolving doors between government and the companies they regulate. I will restore stand-ards in public life with a total crackdown on cronyism.'

This goes beyond Labour's immediate political need to set out a contrast to the excesses of partygate, or show it has a plan for tackling the successive scandals about expenses, lobbying, waste and sexual assaults that have mired Westminster more generally over recent decades. And it's almost the opposite of the populism that thrives on such distrust. Starmer sees public cynicism as a barrier to changing the country in government. 'Trust in politics is now so low, so degraded, that nobody believes you can make a difference anymore,' he has said. Acknowledging 'there's no single "clever trick" that will easily overcome such hurdles', he says trust can only be earned back by offering 'credible solutions', showing government respects people and delivering tangible improvements. It's about what he does, not what he says.

One of Sue Gray's tasks is to finalise Labour's plan for repairing a system that has fallen into such disrepair by introducing a new Ethics Commission. This would bring together a patchwork system of standards bodies – everything from overseeing public appointments and the award of peerages to enforcing the ministerial code – into a much more powerful institution. She says it would be chaired by someone who 'isn't one of the usual suspects because it has to be independent'. At the moment, 'a complaint is quite likely to get lost somewhere in a government department' and the whole process needs to become more transparent. It is not entirely clear if the Ethics Commission would be able to initiate investigations without Downing Street, not least because such a power would become a heavy cross to bear as the media demanded it probe each and every allegation. Gray emphasises that 'Keir has very high expectations of personal integrity', but he doesn't want some sort of witchfinder-general because 'people do sometimes just mess up'. There is a difference between episodes of straightforward incompetence, she says, 'and something that needs to be called out immediately.'

There are likely to be tougher sentences against defrauding the taxpayer and a new moratorium on former ministers lobbying the government, depending on how long they served. The so-called 'Nolan principles' established under John Major – 'honesty, openness, objectivity, selflessness, integrity, accountability, leadership' – to eradicate a previous generation of sleaze are expected to form a bigger part of a ramped-up ministerial code so that they are effectively written into the contract of everyone around the cabinet table. Starmer promises he will be clear-eyed and ruthless in enforcing it. 'People will only believe we're changing politics when I fire someone on the spot. If a minister – any minister – makes a serious breach of the rules, they will be out,' he says. What if it's someone as vital to his project as Rachel Reeves? 'It doesn't matter who it is, they'll be sacked,' replies Starmer staring back, unblinking. He says that the promise he made when elected leader to 'tear antisemitism out by its roots' and enforce strict new standards within the party over the way it addressed this problem only began to be taken seriously after he sacked Rebecca Long-Bailey from the shadow cabinet in 2020 for sharing an article that contained antisemitic conspiracy theories. 'When Jeremy was suspended as an MP, they really woke up,' he adds. 'If people don't believe me when I say I want to clean up politics, I will prove them wrong. It's about showing not saying; actions not words.'

Handily, restoring standards in public life would not cost money at a time when an immediate restoration in standards of living may be more expensive and harder to achieve. Starmer, however, is adamant that rebuilding trust has nothing to do with being 'an uptight lawyer obsessed with following the rules' and that it's much more than simply being a worthy objective. For him, it's a 'means to an end and essential if people are going to believe in what we're doing'. He says: 'This isn't just a Labour issue. We've got to appeal to everyone who wants this country to succeed because we need all of them if any of this is going to work.'

As such he is looking carefully at proposals drawn up by a determinedly non-partisan commission, including a former supreme court judge, senior civil servants, politicians and crossbench peers, that is chaired by Dominic Grieve, the Conservative attorney general when Starmer was chief prosecutor. Interim recommendations are designed to 'improve ethical standards, create better relationships, lead to better decision making and law making and to underpin the core aspects of UK democracy, based on traditional British constitutional values, including the sovereignty of Parliament.'

At the start of the election year of 2024, Starmer was talking about how the past decade of polarising populism and nationalism had demanded 'your full attention, it needs you constantly focusing on this week's common enemy – and that's exhausting, isn't it?' Instead, he offered 'a politics that aspires to national unity, bringing people together, the common good, that's harder to express, less colourful, fewer clicks on social media'.

All of which will be difficult to land ahead of what promises to be a brutal election campaign. There will be those on the right who say you can't trust Starmer because they'll portray him as a 'lefty human rights lawyer'. There'll be those on the left who don't trust him because he was a tough chief prosecutor. Others from both left and right will point to his multiple shifts on policy before and since he became Labour leader as proof that he won't stick to anything for long. Still more will wish him well but look at the scale of the challenges facing him and think he's being unrealistic in believing he can achieve even a measure of success with his missions. And there's a very real danger if he fails to deliver on them, a Labour government will, far from restoring trust, undermine it still further.

Starmer himself, however, is undaunted. 'I believe that if people see the commitment to service is always there in politics, if they can see that people in power respect their concerns, then I think a lot of people across this country, after everything we've been through in the past fourteen years, will find some hope in that,' he says. 'It will feel different, frankly. The character of politics will change, and with it the national mood. A collective breathing out. A burden lifted. And then, the space for a more hopeful look forward.'

There are still reasonable grounds for doubt about whether Starmer can pull any of this off, even if the best of them are as nuanced as he is himself. A lack of political ties might leave him isolated and without allies in power, but it might also mean he can move faster than others. Although he sometimes changes his mind, that's neither so unusual in real life nor always such a sin as it's presented in politics. If he seems to lack some political skills, it's because he's not a typical politician. Indeed, without any of the fanfares or fireworks associated with more charismatic leaders, he has transformed Labour and its electoral prospects in an extraordinarily short time largely because he changed his mind about how he wanted to lead it and was not bound to a particular faction.

So much of the past few years has been about spectacle. Blair would conjure up an idea of a shining city on the hill that didn't always get beyond an artistic impression. Johnson gathered a crowd to watch him incinerate much of what value still stood. Starmer, methodically laying his building blocks one on top of another – sometimes stopping and starting again to rearrange them or finding another way for them to fit together – will never generate much excitement or attract quite the same audience, but the result could be something more solid.

As one former adviser puts it, political leaders more usually define themselves by a 'radical vision' which they are then forced to cut and trim down through compromise. Starmer begins the other way round: he exhausts conventional options before, if necessary, becoming progressively more radical.

Although it won't always make sense to those used to covering the rise and fall of big ideas, it makes perfect sense for anyone interested in achieving real change. People may still look on sceptically when he says, in spite of all the problems facing Britain, this country can still become a better place. But they had a similar expression on their faces four years earlier while Starmer was insisting he could win the next general election – and, nowadays, most of them think he will.

Touching distance

A woman walking her dog watches warily as Keir Starmer arrives outside his house in a small convoy of police vehicles that are part of the enhanced security protection he gets these days. The Labour leader climbs out of one apologising he's late and explaining he's been delayed by traffic that was at a standstill for more than an hour – 'I hate wasting time like that' – and goes inside.

His kitchen is cold because the radiators aren't working, but he makes tea and starts talking about how Whitehall will have to change if a Labour government is to achieve his missions. Then the plumber arrives – they seem to know each other – and declines an offer of tea and is shown upstairs to find the source of the problem.

When Starmer comes back down the stairs, conversation switches to the Middle East and whether Britain can do more to build long-term peace. His daughter comes home from school and hugs him, followed by his son who has just done a mock GCSE. Before long Starmer has to run into his back garden where the family cat has got into a fight. As he tries to separate them amid screeching and shouting, Vic arrives back from work and goes out offering assistance. It's not clear which cat won the fight but, by the looks of the Labour leader's hand when he comes back inside, it wasn't him.

It's a Friday evening in December 2023 and he seems to relish every last bit of everyday domestic chaos ahead of a year when, if the polls are right, Starmer will be moving from the home he's lived in for more than twenty years and into Downing Street.

He's not there yet and, even as his party embarks on a frenzy of activity to prepare for power, there are plenty of reasons why he might not win. Being leader of the opposition remains a notoriously difficult job and not many of them succeed. Eight of the ten chosen to hold this post before him never became prime minister, while the two who did started off in a much better position than that Starmer inherited in 2020. Indeed, so poor was the Labour Party's performance in the last general election, he needs a swing bigger than Tony Blair had with his 1997 landslide just to get a majority of one seat in the House of Commons. And, if such a prospect is possible because voters have become so volatile, that also means Labour's poll lead could evaporate as fast as it appeared. He knows, too, that his opponents will throw everything – not just the kitchen sink but the whole kitchen – at him in the months to come.

Yet in his relentless and sometimes inelegant fashion, Starmer has got further than almost anyone expected him to and he's now within touching distance of Number 10. That's not – just – because he has been lucky with his opponents. He's a man of no superstitions who always said he could win. The fans of his football club used to sing 'one-nil to the Arsenal' when other teams thought they were 'boring'. Would he be happy with a scrappy win? 'No, but one-nil will do,' he replies. When he meets his friends in the pub before a game, 'everyone tries to predict the score – you know, two-one, four-three and the like – I just say, "we need to get a win"'.

If he does become prime minister, Starmer will miss the pub and the football. He's already been told, for instance, that the police won't let him sit in his usual seat in the West Stand at the Emirates and the directors' box beckons. Nor is it likely that he will be allowed to grace the Kentish Town Astroturf for his regular eight-a-sides.

His eyes briefly light up when it's suggested he could do his own expensive refurbishment of the prime ministerial flat above Downing Street by building a replica of the Pineapple, the pub he likes to go to around the corner from his house. 'Maybe we could dig – didn't Churchill have a tunnel in the war?' he begins to ask. Then the shutters come down again as he realises even joking about such matters risks headlines about 'measuring the curtains' or taking victory for granted, which he really isn't.

Those bridges back to his 'real life' are beginning to wobble. Would being prime minister change him and mean he is less able to use his experiences outside politics to drive him forward within it? 'Well, all experiences change you, don't they?' says Ed Fitzgerald, his old friend and mentor from his days as a human rights lawyer. 'But I feel the core of Keir is the same ... He'll be a better PM than leader of the opposition because he'll govern in a grown-up fashion. And he's a very good judge of character. If Keir says someone's an arsehole, they usually are.'

John Murray, the Labour leader's friend from university, says: 'He just needs to be himself; if he gains the trust of the country and is elected prime minister I think we will see more of the real Keir.' Is he enjoying it? 'I don't know,' replies Murray. 'It's almost as if he has no choice. He bears the mantle of responsibility quite heavily. When I see him on TV, I can see his brain is working overtime to get the right message across – it's the most serious of serious jobs for him.'

It's even possible that the process of being in the frontline of politics has enabled Starmer to deal better with his feelings. In the same way that doing interviews on national TV eventually helped him understand a difficult relationship with his father, Starmer's sister, Katy, suggests Keir is 'opening up' more these days. She says: 'He's worked on it and has got better. He's more protective of us than ever now that Mum and Dad have gone.' Katy teasingly calls him 'the family matriarch', then says: 'Whenever I send him a message, I always say, "I love you." He didn't use to do that back, but I've noticed that he's started doing it now too.'

Back in his kitchen, Starmer is now bleeding from the scratch on his thumb that one of the cats gave him. He remembers to text his friend from school, Colin Peacock, to say there's no way he's going to have time to get down the pub now. Being unable to have a drink on a Friday evening was exactly one of the reasons why Peacock thought he was mad for wanting to be a politician in the first place and told him political careers always end in failure. He's unmoved by the prospect of what will happen if Labour win. 'It's going to take it out of him and he'll miss his old life,' says Peacock, 'but he's on the train and he can't get off it now. We'll have to figure out how to get him to make some time for himself. When it all goes wrong, I'll be there for him, of course. I'll be there going, "told you so, told you, told you".'

What does Vic think? She has told him: 'If it happens, I won't want to leave Kentish Town.' This is a corner of London where she's lived all her life and sometimes jokes that though her husband thinks it's his constituency, 'actually it's mine'. But the streak of stubborn pragmatism she shares with her husband is apparent as she tells friends who come by their house: 'We always deal with stuff that comes at us when we have to, one thing at a time. I don't think Keir will be any different. He's always been the same, he'll push through the hard stuff because it's how to get things done. And we'll do what we need to do too.'

The consequences for his family are what concern Starmer the most and keep him up at night. He's talked about his son and daughter – both of whom will be teenagers at the time of the election – and fears they'll find it hard to have their dad become prime minister. When he was his son's age, Starmer says, he was getting into all sorts of trouble. His daughter has said she won't consider moving to Downing Street and, though her parents think she's joking, you can never tell with her. 'These are really important ages, it will have an impact on their lives and I'm worried,' he says. He has described how he asks himself 'over and over again – particularly at the moment with so much online abuse directed at politicians – how I protect my family as we go into this'.

By now he has wrapped a piece of kitchen roll to soak up the blood from his wound, and is talking about a trip to Scunthorpe, describing how blast furnace workers in 'all their gear with big boots and helmets' there had told him they want to move to decarbonised steel but are being held back by delays in getting green power through the National Grid. Then he becomes enthused again, describing how business is more ready for a partnership than before, citing a conversation with former prime minister Gordon Brown who thinks firms are more likely to recognise their role in society since the financial crash, the way football clubs including Arsenal all have their own community programmes these days, as well as what his friend Colin, who he had been due to meet down the pub, has told him about working for Procter & Gamble.

All that's very 'Starmer-ish'. But is there a 'Starmerism'? The Labour leader begins replying: 'I don't—' then stops himself. 'I just want to get things done,' he says. Then Vic shouts across the chilly kitchen that if he really wants to get things done, could he start by ordering a takeaway tonight.

He'll be going on sixty-two by the time of the next election and a decade of national renewal would take two full terms of government. He is impatient to stop talking and start doing.

An ordinary-looking man in a hurry to get somewhere.

Acknowledgements

This is an unusual biography in that I've had a lot of access to a political leader at the start of an election year when the stakes are sky-high. Perhaps inevitably, the number of those who have wanted to make their mark on it has made the sometimes-solitary process of writing feel a little crowded towards the end. But any list of those who have been supportive in every way throughout this process must begin with my brilliant wife Rebecca and our amazing children, Frankie and Arthur. They've had to put up with a lot from me over the past year and I promise to try harder in the next.

Marc Stears, my collaborator on another book, has been a constant source of advice on this one too. So have those wisest of journalists: Patrick Wintour; Philip Webster; Donald Macintyre and Rachel Sylvester. My agent, Georgina Capel, has driven me forward while watching my back. At HarperCollins, I've lent hard on the fortitude and judgement of Arabella Pike, the skill and patience of Iain Hunt, the dynamic good humour of Sam Harding and Katherine Patrick. Mention should be made of my tech-savvy neighbour, Jeremy Palmer, who has let me borrow his printer.

Nor would writing such a biography as this have been possible without the professionalism and kindness of Jill Cuthbertson and Prentice Hazell in the leader of the opposition's office, the support of Deborah Mattinson, as well as the many other aides, advisers and MPs – past and present, from the Labour Party and beyond – who have given me some of their time and knowledge.

It's a book about a man with a lot of old friends from many different walks of life and all of them do him credit. John Murray and Patrick Stevens have both contributed in more ways than one. I've also been privileged to meet some of his family and I'm grateful to Katy for agreeing to be interviewed for this first time and Vic for even letting me through the door.

Most of all, I want to thank Keir Starmer himself. He does a very tough job and faces all kinds of pressure. But he has answered my questions, been generous with his time, and kept to his promise that he would not try to control what appears. Although he won't agree with every word, they've been written with the respect that a serious, grown-up leader deserves.

Notes

Chapter 1: Strangers on a train

4 'Saw @Keir_Starmer on train today': https://twitter.com/deeplydp/status/1068277364747051009?s=43&t=NZIZ9H1pdVkIXAPPY_Jv0g

6 'I knew he was dying': Keir Starmer, 'My learnings from life, loss and love', *High Performance* podcast, March 27, 2023

Chapter 2: Out of the ordinary

9 'I believe every family': Keir Starmer, speech to Labour Party conference in Liverpool, October 10, 2023

11 'If you want children': This account is taken from the eulogy written by Rod Starmer for the funeral of his wife, Jo, in April 2015

12 germinated into ambition: Lucille Iremonger, *Fiery Chariot: A Study of British Prime Ministers and the Search for Love* (Martin Secker & Warburg Ltd, 1970); Rachel Sylvester and Alice Thomson, *What I Wish I'd Known When I Was Young* (William Collins, 2022)

12 'When I was at school': Stephen Moss, 'Keir Starmer: "I wouldn't characterise myself as a bleeding heart liberal …"' *Guardian*, September 20, 2009

13 according to legend: Richard Askwith, 'Alfred Wainwright: Grumpy, reclusive and eccentric', *Independent*, July 2, 2005

13 'the hills are waiting for you': *Encounters with Wainwright*, ed. David Johnson (Wainwright Society, 2016) 184–6

14 'We knocked': From Rod Starmer's eulogy

15 'You learn to close off': Helena Kennedy, interviewed by Gaby Hinsliff for 'The reasonable case of Keir Rodney Starmer', *Tortoise* slow newscast, March 22, 2021

19 'the tool-room': Eric Hobsbawm, *Workers: Worlds of Labour* (Pantheon, 1984), 264

19 'you need not': W. H. Auden, 'Sext', *The Shield of Achilles* (Faber & Faber, 1955); Keir Starmer, speech to Labour Party conference, Brighton, September 29, 2021

20 'It is hard to accept': Michael Ashcroft, *Red Knight: The Unauthorised Biography of Sir Keir Starmer* (Biteback, 2021); Lord Ashcroft, 'King of the Middle Class Radicals', *Mail on Sunday*, June 13, 2021

20 'in my factory': 'Things we discover about Barn families', *Barn Theatre News*, Volume 18, August 3, 2014

20 'almost always worked alone': Ashcroft, *Red Knight*, 13

21 'a building site': Paul Vickers, interviewed for *Profile*, BBC Radio 4, September 26, 2009

Chapter 3: Class politics

22 'very powerful': Paul Vickers, interviewed for *Profile*

24 'We never talked politics': *Encounters with Wainwright*, ed. Johnson, 184–6

26 'a difficult man': Lauren Laverne, *Desert Island Discs*, BBC Radio 4, November 15, 2020

26 'beginning to unravel bits': Interview with Piers Morgan, *Life Stories*, ITV, June 1, 2021

26 'had carried quite heavily': Interview with Nick Robinson, *Political Thinking*, BBC Radio 4, November 26, 2021

26 'I'm not sure': Interview with James O'Brien, *Full Disclosure* podcast, February 24, 2022

26 autobiographical book: Barack Obama, *Dreams from My Father* (Times Books, 1995)

27 'My dad always felt': Sienna Rodgers, 'Starmer sets out contract with British people', *LabourList*, January 4, 2022

27 'It's a bit odd': Donald Macintyre, 'Labour leadership: Has Keir Starmer got what it takes to save the party?' *Sunday Times*, March 2020

30 talk about class: Interview with Jack Blanchard, *Politico* event, September 23, 2019

30 'the class war is over' … 'My political project': Tony Blair, speech to Labour Party conference in Bournemouth, September 28, 1999; 'Why Sir Keir Starmer wants to smash through the "class ceiling" with vision for Scotland', *Scotsman*, August 15, 2023

33 Thatcher would approve: Margaret Thatcher interview for Conservative Political Centre, January 5, 1972. https://www.margaretthatcher.org/document/102172; Charles Moore, *Margaret Thatcher, The Authorized Biography*, Vol. 1 (Allen Lane, 2013), 215–16

35 'no need to intervene': Baroness Stedman, Debate on the Education
   Bill, House of Lords, October 7, 1976. *Hansard*, Vol. 374, Col 1555

Chapter 4: The top deck

37 'always bits and bobs': Interview with Nick Ferrari, LBC Radio,
   October 24, 2022
41 he loved playing quartets: Interview with Anne-Marie Minhall,
   Classic FM, July 11, 2023
42 learning the violin: Keir Starmer, interviewed by Moira Stuart,
   Classic FM, November 24, 2023

Chapter 5: 'Reunited'

44 'Silly sod!': 'Aubs' Day', RGS Foundation, March 9, 2016, https://
   www.rgs.foundation/2016/03/09/aubs-day/
45 'the highest political office': *Reigatian Magazine* 2014, 11–12; https://
   www.rgs.foundation/2017/01/13/henry-smith-club-dinner-2017/;
   https://www.rgs.foundation/2020/04/04/breaking-news-
   congratulations-sir-kier-starmer/
45 'a blatant attempt': Andrew Pierce, 'Why is Sir Keir Starmer intent
   on denying others the private education that HE enjoyed by
   scrapping their charitable status?' *Daily Mail*, December 1, 2022
45 front-page news: Camilla Turner, 'Exclusive: "Hypocrite" Keir
   Starmer benefited from private school charity', *Daily Telegraph*,
   January 28, 2023
48 'extraordinary woman': Jonathan Cooper, 'I met Keir Starmer's
   donkeys – and they told me something about him', *Open Democracy*,
   May 22, 2020
49 'patrons': 'Opening of the New Facilities by HRH The Duke of
   Kent', Barn Theatre newsletter, February 2005, https://www.
   barntheatreoxted.co.uk/dukevisit.html
52 one newspaper alleged: Harry Cole, 'Man of the people? New
   Labour leader Sir Keir owns seven acres of land in Surrey worth up
   to £10m', *Mail on Sunday*, May 17, 2020
53 'I only once remember': Piers Morgan, *Life Stories*

Chapter 6: Feet on the ground

58 front page of the *Sun*: 'Save Our Bacon', *Sun*, May 5, 2015
58 'losing side': Ryan Sabey, 'Can you Keir kit? Labour leader Sir Keir
   Starmer ends up on the losing side during London kickabout', *Sun*,
   March 5, 2023

60 posted an edited video: 'Keir Starmer: What football means to me', Labour Party, YouTube, June 14, 2023, https://www.youtube.com/watch?v=sudfSPWfr8E

60 connections to Newcastle United: Guy Adams, 'The shocking truth: Blair did not lie about Jackie Milburn', *Independent*, May 4, 2005

61 he got confused: Daniel Boffey, 'Is it West Ham? Or is it Villa? Cameron mocked on Twitter as he forgets which team he backs', *Observer*, April 25, 2015

61 'massive fan': Oliver Jones, 'Rishi Sunak mistakes Man Utd for Leicester City in embarrassing gaffe', *Leicester Mercury*, August 20, 2022; Tom Blow, 'Fulham fans troll Rishi Sunak with chant as PM watches Southampton get relegated', *Daily Mirror*, May 14, 2023

61 'highly unconvincing': Stephen Bush, 'Football fandom doesn't come naturally to politicians', *Financial Times*, August 21, 2023

61 'Everyone stands up': 'Sir Keir Starmer on his matchday rituals, the humanity of 5-a-side and ketchup bans', *Football clichés* podcast, January 14, 2022

61 journalists have asked him: Conor Pope, 'Keir Starmer on five-a-side, Gary Neville – and whether he'd rather be PM or Arsenal win the league', *FourFourTwo*, March 23, 2023

Chapter 7: Playing hard

65 'breaking the class ceiling': Keir Starmer, speech to Labour Party conference in Liverpool, October 10, 2023

65 'illegal in the UK': 'Clinton in Harrogate', *Harrogate Advertiser*, June 15, 2001

66 'skinny indie kids': *Nag Nag Nag!*, Issue No. 1 (30th anniversary e-issue), https://sleigh-munoz.co.uk/quims/2012/01/05/nag-nag-nag-issue-no-1/

67 'David has managed': Richard Houghton and David Gedge, *All The Songs Sound the Same* (Spenwood Books, 2023)

68 'trembling residents': Jan Jacques, 'Only the innocent are behind bars on Britain's most burgled street', *News of the World*, June 8, 1997

68 'I got knocked out': Interview in 'The Real Keir Starmer, Part I', *Westminster Insider* podcast, June 23, 2023

69 'Starmer is clearly': Jonathan Jones, 'Sweet, sincere and humanising: Could Keir Starmer's oh-so-serious student picture win votes?' *Guardian*, June 2, 2021

70 no fewer than fourteen times: Interview with Piers Morgan, *Life Stories*

72 Battle of Orgreave: Tristram Hunt, 'The charge of the heavy brigade', *Guardian*, September 4, 2006

Chapter 8: Working hard

76 They have sought: Daniel Hannan, *How We Invented Freedom* (Head of Zeus, 2013), 84–7

76 Downing Street's description: Matt Dathan, 'No 10 backs threat to leave human rights convention', *The Times*, September 28, 2023

76 'on a fundamentally flawed': Alan Travis, 'Keir Starmer defends Human Rights Act against critics', *Guardian*, October 22, 2009

78 the BCL: 'Bachelor of Civil Law', University of Oxford, https://www.ox.ac.uk/admissions/graduate/courses/bachelor-civil-law

80 hit by a police baton: Nigel Cawthorne, *Keir Starmer*, Chapter 15; Ben Emmerson and Anne Shamesh, 'A case to answer? A report on the policing of the News International demonstration at Wapping', Haldane Society, September 1987; Keir Starmer, 'Trade unions in a Wapping world', *Socialist Alternatives* (July/August 1986); 'Inspiring life of Wapping warrior', *Morning Star*, November 28, 2013; see also 'Printworkers vs News International', https://www.youtube.com/watch?v=Jm9IL2Qd-2w

80 'finding the main item': Ed Balls, *Speaking Out, Lessons in Life and Politics* (Arrow, 2016), 109

80 'I am not one': Papers of the Oxford University Labour Club, Bodleian Archives, https://archives.bodleian.ox.ac.uk/repositories/2/resources/3180/collection_organization

Chapter 9: Exploring alternatives

83 One well-known: Billy Kenber, 'Keir Starmer: Radical who attacked Kinnock in Marxist journal', *The Times*, January 18, 2020; James Heale and Harry Cole, 'Posh Trot Keir is accused of hiding his hard-left past', *Mail on Sunday*, January 12, 2020; Peter Hitchens, 'Revolutionary past that gives the lie to the notion Keir Starmer is a harmless moderate', *Mail on Sunday*, June 9, 2022

83 'a Trotskyist front': Paul Mason, 'Clive Lewis and Keir Starmer are the candidates who understand how Labour must change', *New Statesman*, January 8, 2020

84 Such ideas: A. M. Gitttlitz, *I Want to Believe: Posadism, UFOs, and Apocalypse Communism* (Pluto, 2020), 66–7

85 'the community they are meant to serve': Keir Starmer, 'Wapping beyond a defeat', *Socialist Alternatives*, April/May 1987

86 'The big issue': Patrick Maguire, 'Keir Starmer: The sensible radical', *New Statesman*, March 31, 2020

87 'a goodish BCL': Geoffrey Robertson, *Rather His Own Man* (Biteback, 2019), 152

88 twenty-four formal dinners: *St Edmund Hall Magazine*, 1986–87, 8; 'General Provisions, Middle Temple', https://www.middletemple. org.uk/education-and-training/scholarships-and-prizes/bptc-and-gdl-scholarships/general-provisions

88 'someone who wears a cardigan': Robertson, *Rather His Own Man*, 152

90 'which pay much more attention': 'Would you vote for Denning?' *Socialist Lawyer*, Spring 1988, 12–13

91 'too eager to thrust': 'Reminiscences of a radical lawyer', *Socialist Lawyer*, Winter/Spring 1989, 14–15

91 'a concept of socialist law': Martin Kettle, 'Changing politics (again)', *Guardian*, July 3, 2007; Keir Starmer, 'The concept of socialist law', *Socialist Lawyer*, Spring 1991, 21

92 'that part is easy': Keir Starmer, 'Can the entrenchment of fundamental rights contribute to the realization of progressive change?' *Socialist Lawyer*, Autumn 1995, 6–7

92 'does not give electors votes of equal value': Francesca Klug, Keir Starmer and Stuart Weir, *The Three Pillars of Liberty: Political Rights and Freedoms in the United Kingdom* (Routledge, 1996), 266–77

93 'I've always been': Keir Starmer: 'My learnings from life, loss and love', *High Performance* podcast, March 27, 2023

94 Victor Mehra: 'Vice man jailed', *The Times*, August 13, 1985

95 fancy dress costumes: *Profile*, BBC Radio 4, September 26, 2009

96 'I ran upstairs': Ibid.

Chapter 10: The value of roots

100 'Wishee-Washee': https://twitter.com/ReoSurf/status/1383544081914089478?s=20

101 like the Arsenal coach ... 'a football manager': Lizzy Buchan and David Burke, 'Keir Starmer blasts Suella Braverman for being "all talk" over immigration rant', *Daily Mirror*, May 15, 2023; Keir Starmer, *Hansard*, Vol. 723, Col. 282, November 23, 2022

101 'have had the chance': Keir Starmer, *The Road Ahead*, Fabian Society, September 2021

102 'release valves': Interview with Anne-Marie Minhall, *Classic FM*, July 11, 2023

102 'Like talented footballers': 'Hello: MP Keir Starmer', *On the Hill*, November 22, 2015

104 'This is my team': Miguel Delaney, 'When the whistle goes, it doesn't matter what you do for a living', *Independent*, February 9, 2023

104 symbol for northern decline: Jason Stockwood, 'We bought Grimsby Town FC to help renew the place we love', *Guardian*, June 29, 2021

104 'same square mile': Rishi Sunak, speech to Conservative Party conference in Manchester, October 4, 2023

105 'because that's exactly': Georgia Gould, speaking at Another Future is Possible rally, Camden Roundhouse, February 16, 2020

Chapter 11: All the same?

112 bundled out: Stephen Sumner, 'Keir Starmer: Labour Party leader responds after being thrown out of Bath pub', *Bristol Post*, April 19, 2021

113 3,200 hours: Harriet Clugston, 'Keir Starmer "Beergate" investigation cost Durham police over £100,000', *National World*, September 15, 2022

113 The footage had been passed: Jim Waterson, 'Student who shot Keir Starmer Beergate video is Breitbart writer's son', *Guardian*, May 9, 2022

114 'tortuously woven web': Jane Merrick, 'Beergate', *The i*, May 6, 2022; Mick Hume, 'Posturing Sir Beer's mess is entirely of his own making', *Daily Mail*, May 8, 2022

115 handed gold stars … 'in living memory': https://twitter.com/Steven_Swinford/status/1522859702153003009?s=20; Tim Shipman, 'Boris Johnson squirms free for another run at No 10', *Sunday Times*, May 8, 2022

116 'sail through': Gaby Hinsliff, 'Keir Starmer: Who is he, really?' *Tortoise*, March 23, 2021

Chapter 12: On the outside

119 'the smug, self-satisfied': 'Reflections from Geoffrey Robertson KC, Founding Head of Doughty Street Chambers', https://www.doughtystreet.co.uk/our-history#:~:text=Doughty%20Street%20was%20founded%20in,Council%20to%20the%20Magistrates'%20Courts

120 first appearance … 'moved out of a museum': https://twitter.com/ITNArchive/status/1643203828194373638?s=20; Robertson, *Rather His Own Man*, Chapter 12

122 work for free: *Profile*, BBC Radio 4, September 26, 2009; Hinsliff, 'Keir Starmer: Who is he, really?'

122 longest in the history of libel law: Catherine Baski, 'Landmarks in law: McLibel and the longest trial in British legal history', *Guardian*, July 8, 2019

122 'If Keir hadn't offered': Ibid.

122 'We thought': Ibid; *Profile*, BBC Radio 4

122 'Even with limited resources': Ibid; Hinsliff, 'Keir Starmer: Who is he, really?'; 'Keir Starmer interviews 1996 + 2005', *McLibel: DVD Extras*, Spanner Films (Extended version, 2005)

124 'a milestone': Clare Dyer, 'Libel law review over McDonald's ruling', *Guardian*, February 13, 2005

125 'was odd': *McLibel* (Spanner Films, 1997); *McLibel: DVD Extras*

126 'a smirking Starmer': '"Patriotic" Starmer boasting he wanted to abolish the Monarchy', *Guido Fawkes*, February 3, 2021

127 'save baby killers': Harry Cole and Thomas Godfrey, 'Sir Keir Starmer worked for free as a lawyer to save baby killers and axe murderers', *Sun*, January 8, 2024

129 hundreds more escaped: Earl Pratt and Ivan Morgan, Death Penalty Project, https://deathpenaltyproject.org/story/earl-pratt-and-ivan-morgan/

129 'As we stepped': Keir Starmer, Saul Lehrfreund and Parvais Jabbar, 'Uganda's death row inmates are saved from the noose', *The Times*, August 2, 2005

130 flew to Taiwan: Owen Boycott, 'Keir Starmer visits Taiwan to lobby against death penalty', *Guardian*, September 28, 2018

Chapter 13: Seeing both sides

132 'in favour of': 'Upholding the rule of law?', Haldane Society, May 1992

133 'what was essential': Danny Penman, '"King Arthur" strikes blow for liberty', *Independent*, September 13, 1995; Clare Dyer, 'Law Lords affirm protester rights', *Guardian*, March 5, 1999; Jason Bennetto, 'Paedophile loses plea to stay anonymous on TV show', *Independent*, June 11, 2002; Ashcroft, *Red Knight*, 130–1; Martin Wainwright, 'High court upholds peace campaigner's right to deface US flag', *Guardian*, December 22, 2001

134 'I'm proud to live': Stuart Jeffries, 'The Great Defender', *Guardian*, January 25, 2007

134 more than a million: Sean Rayment, 'Million sign up for Clegg', *Daily Mail*, January 27, 1995; Nick Clark, 'Sir Keir Starmer's love of being respectable', *Socialist Worker*, July 17, 2021

136 'The 1998': Keir Starmer, 'Labour needs to look to the 2030s', Book review, *Guardian*, March 17, 2016

136 'Keir looked out': Jonathan Cooper, 'How Keir Starmer treated me as his gay colleague proves he'd make a great prime minister', *Independent*, March 7, 2020

137 'Let's get Rob': Robert Crampton, 'When Sunday comes', *The Times*, February 15, 1997

138 'from 1997 onwards': *Arsène Wenger*, directed by Gabriel Clarke and Christian Jeanpierre (Amazon Prime, 2021), 1:35

138 two books: Clive Walker, Keir Starmer, *Justice in Error* (Oxford University Press, 1993); Clive Walker, Keir Starmer, *Miscarriages of Justice* (Blackstone Press, 1999)

139 also found time: Keir Starmer, *European Human Rights Law* (Legal Action Group, 1999); Keir Starmer, Michelle Strange, Quincy Whitaker, *Criminal Justice, Police Powers and Human Rights* (Blackstone Press, 2002); Keir Starmer, Theodora Christou, Juan Pablo Raymond, Kate Beattie, *Human Rights Manual and Sourcebook for Africa* (British Institute of International & Comparative Law, 2005)

140 'He just wanted': *Westminster Insider* podcast

141 'terrorist suspects' … 'chisel-jawed' … 'very similar': Martin Bright, 'The new legal crusaders', *Observer*, August 4, 2002; Camilla Long, 'No comment from Lawyer Transparent', *Sunday Times*, April 1, 2012; Helen Pidd, 'No buts: Keir Starmer did not inspire Helen Fielding's Mark Darcy', *Guardian*, December 7, 2020

142 'Isn't that what': Sean O'Neill, 'How a British lawyer is taking the fight to Putin in the courts', *The Times*, July 5, 2023

144 'It is inhumane': Alan Travis, 'Treatment of asylum seekers "is inhumane"', *Guardian*, February 11, 2003

145 winning a series: Keir Starmer, 'Sorry, Mr Blair, but 1441 does not authorise force', *Guardian*, March 17, 2003; http://image. guardian.co.uk/sys-files/Politics/documents/2005/02/21/ GuardianFOIAAdvice.pdf; Joshua Rozenberg, 'Torture law victory for terror suspects', *Daily Telegraph*, December 9, 2005; 'Court quashes terror suspect control order', *Press Association National Newswire*, February 16, 2007

145 'This was an opportunity': Oliver Eagleton, *The Starmer Project* (Verso, 2022), 21–4

148 another pragmatic compromise: 'NI police chief denies taser link', *Irish Times*, September 25, 2007

Chapter 14: On the inside

151 'We couldn't understand' … not a natural transition: David Renton, 'Keir Starmer's past is coming under scrutiny. What can we learn from it?' *Guardian*, February 16, 2020; Keir Starmer, interviewed by Philippe Sands, Hay Festival, June 3, 2012

152 'The reality is': Basia Cummings and Gaby Hinsliff, 'The reasonable case of Keir Rodney Starmer', *Tortoise* podcast, March 22, 2021

152 'going on the offensive': Mike Sullivan, 'Crime war chief is human rights brief', *Sun*, July 26, 2008

153 Article 6: Closing submissions on behalf of Mrs Rebekah Brooks, Leveson Inquiry, July 17, 2012, 9(d)

153 no need to go further: Keir Starmer, 'Morning Hearing', Leveson Inquiry, April 4, 2012, 97

153 'one of the defining': Matt Ross, 'Interview: Keir Starmer', *Civil Service World*, November 20, 2013

154 'It's something that happens': 'Would-be suicide bombers jailed for life', BBC News, July 12, 2010

156 herself was later jailed: David Sanderson, 'Judge jails "arrogant" liar Briscoe for 16 months', *The Times*, May 2, 2014

156 'You can't always tell': Natalie Clarke, 'Seduced by King Con', *Daily Mail*, November 6, 2009

157 'chip away': Christopher Hope, 'Keir Starmer says Tory plans to scrap Human Rights Act would bring shame on Britain', *Daily Telegraph*, October 21, 2009

157 'We should tear up': Andrew Sparrow and Alan Travis, 'Tories attack director of prosecutions over human rights comments', *Guardian*, October 23, 2009

157 'What has our': 'An all too partial public servant', *Daily Mail*, October 23, 2009

158 ran an editorial … 'a good bloke': 'In praise of … Keir Starmer', *Guardian*, October 23, 2009; Stephen Moss, 'Keir Starmer: "I wouldn't characterise myself as a bleeding heart liberal"', *Guardian*, September 21, 2009

158 had already upset: 'Family of Jean Charles de Menezes end battle for justice after DPP refuses to prosecute cops over shooting', *Daily Record*, February 14, 2009

158 an open letter: 'A year on, we still wait for answers about Ian Tomlinson's death', open letter, *Guardian*, April 1, 2010

159 'head in my hands': Keir Starmer, speaking at the Legal Action Group, annual lecture 2013; 'A year on, we still wait for answers about Ian Tomlinson's death'

159 'It's been a huge cover-up': Vikram Dodd and Paul Lewis, 'Ian Tomlinson death: Police officer will not face criminal charges', *Guardian*, July 22, 2010

159 'We tried' … caution was vindicated: Hinsliff, 'Keir Starmer: Who is he, really?'; Peter Walker and Paul Lewis, 'Ian Tomlinson death: Simon Harwood cleared of manslaughter', *Guardian*, July 19, 2012

161 Defence lawyers complained: Fiona Bawden and Owen Bowcott, 'Chaos in the courts as justice system rushed to restore order',

Guardian, July 3, 2012; 'Manchester riots: Doughnut thief jailed for 16 months', BBC News, August 18, 2011

162 Such cases included: 'Benefit fraud could lead to 10-year jail terms, says DPP', BBC News, September 16, 2009

162 cases he dealt with: Jon Ungoed-Thomas, 'Gangs import children for benefit fraud', *Sunday Times*, August 3, 2009

162 'I couldn't understand it': Janis Sharp, *Saving Gary McKinnon: A Mother's Story* (Biteback, 2013), Chapter 20

163 eventually blocked: 'Gary McKinnon extradition to US blocked by Theresa May', BBC News, October 16, 2012

163 continue to find: See, for instance, Matt Kennard, 'Five questions for new Labour leader Sir Keir Starmer about his UK and US national security establishment links', *Grayzone*, June 5, 2020; David Crawford, letter, *Herald*, April 19, 2023

164 There has been talk of: Eagleton, *The Starmer Project*, 35–7; Matt Kennard, 'Revealed: After clearing MI5 of torture, Keir Starmer attended its chief's leaving party'; 'CPS has destroyed all records of Keir Starmer's four trips to Washington', *Declassified UK*, May 25 and June 29, 2023

165 'The fact the drinks': Kennard, 'Five questions for new Labour leader ...'

165 'a key role in sabotaging': Kennard, 'Five Questions for new Labour leader ...'

166 'new world order': Jonathan Kay, *Among the Truthers: A Journey Through America's Growing Conspiracist Underground* (Harper, 2011), 200–2

166 'Murdoch closed': William Turvill, '*News of the World* closure ten years on: How hacking scandal cost Murdoch's UK tabloid business £1bn', *Press Gazette*, July 8, 2021

167 'rising star': David Barrett, 'The case against the Prosecution', *Daily Telegraph*, December 12. 2015

167 'Before this trial': Fiona Hamilton, 'Brooks trial "worthwhile despite lack of evidence"', *The Times*, June 30, 2014

167 'He wasn't going to be': Hinsliff, 'Keir Starmer: Who is he, really?'

167 'Just after he was elected': Tom Newton Dunn, 'My mentor died a broken man after Keir Starmer's groundless prosecution', *Evening Standard*, May 12, 2021

168 Blair famously: John Darnton, 'Murdoch and Laborite: Britain's odd couple', *New York Times*, July 25, 1995

169 The allegation is: Eagleton, *The Starmer Project*, 29–32

170 'stem the flow': Ibid.

Chapter 15: Family values

173 made Starmer complete: Keir Starmer, 'Jonny – a eulogy', *European Human Rights Law Review*, February 1, 2022

177 On their return home: Moss, 'Keir Starmer: "I wouldn't characterise myself as a bleeding heart liberal …"'

177 condemned by everyone: William Rees-Mogg, 'Our lives are not our own to dispose of', *Mail on Sunday*, August 2, 2009; Daniel Martin, 'Tory moves to bolster law against "back door euthanasia"', *Daily Mail*, August 5, 2009

178 'Assisted Dying Bill': 'Sir Keir Starmer supports assisted dying law change', BBC News, December 21, 2023

178 found guilty of Stephen's murder: 'R v Dobson', Royal Courts of Justice, April 11–12, https://www.judiciary.uk/wp-content/uploads/JCO/Documents/Judgments/r-v-dobson-judgment-18052011.pdf; 'Stephen Lawrence: Gary Dobson and David Norris get life', BBC News, January 4, 2012

180 'We were told': Natalie Clarke, 'The mother who predicted her own murder', *MailOnline*, November 18, 2011

181 'good friends': Keir Starmer, speech to Labour Party conference, September 29, 2021

181 a second opinion: 'Crime victims offered right of review of charging decisions', BBC, June 5, 2015

181 'call on the state': Starmer, 'Labour needs to look to the 2030s …'

182 'Look, that can't': Hinsliff, 'Keir Starmer: Who is he, really?'

182 'over and over again': Ibid.

184 'watershed moment': Alison Levitt, 'In the Matter of the late Jimmy Savile', CPS, January 11, 2013; 'DPP apologises on Savile', *Counsel*, January 31, 2013

184 'As DPP, Sir Keir's job': K. Harvey Proctor, 'The real case against Starmer's term as DPP', *Conservativehome*, February 15, 2022

185 'more personal': Steven Swinford, Oliver Wright, Geraldine Scott, '"Voters feel sorry for us": Weary Tories fear by-election wipeout', *The Times*, July 8, 2023

185 'Being honest': 'Rishi Sunak distances himself from Boris Johnson's Jimmy Savile slur', ITV News, February 3, 2022

185 polling showed … sharing a video: Matt Smith, 'What do Britons make of the PM's claims about Keir Starmer regarding Jimmy Savile?' YouGov, February 26, 2022; Sienna Rogers, 'Tory MPs share doctored video of Starmer promoted by far right', *LabourList*, May 14, 2020

186 dig for dirt: Alexandra Rogers, 'Labour insiders fear Starmer's past could come back to haunt him as Tories plan to ramp up attacks', Sky News, April 29, 2023

186 Horizon scandal: Steven Swinford and Geraldine Scott, 'Why both Keir Starmer and Ed Davey face questions over Horizon', *The Times*, January 10, 2024

187 'full responsibility': Alexandra Rogers, 'Sir Keir Starmer urged to co-operate with potential public inquiry into "appalling" miscarriage of justice', Sky News, August 23, 2023

187 'can't feign outrage': Andrew Pierce, 'Boris Johnson is right. Keir Starmer's CPS did fail to prosecute Jimmy Savile. So why all the faux outrage?' *Daily Mail*, February 1, 2022

187 signed off a report: 'Child sexual exploitation and the response to localised grooming', 35, House of Commons Home Affairs Committee Second Report of Session 2013–14, June 5, 2013

188 'one of the most successful': Owen Boycott and Shiv Malik, 'Lawyers vie for prosecution role as Keir Starmer quits', *Guardian*, April 24, 2013

189 'bend to justice': Starmer, 'Jonny – a eulogy'

Chapter 16: Putting the rubbish out

197 'shallow men': Keir Starmer, speech to Labour Party conference, October 12, 2023

Chapter 17: Starting over

201 'no great personal history or affinity': Gabriel Pogrund, 'How Ed Miliband powered Labour's green agenda – but Starmer may pull the plug', *Sunday Times*, June 4, 2023

205 'Mr Everywhere': 'Mr Everywhere returns to Holborn and St Pancras', *Camden New Journal*, February 13, 2014

206 a tieless Starmer: Martin Bentham, 'Hot, ready, legal: Britain's former top prosecutor Sir Keir Starmer turns his focus to politics', *Evening Standard*, September 8, 2014

207 'One of the things': Alexandra Topping, 'Keir Starmer: "2015 will be a defining election … I can't walk away from it"', *Guardian*, December 19, 2014

210 'a battle-hardened barrister': Michael White, 'Can Keir Starmer really become Labour leader? And should he?', *Guardian*, May 18, 2015

210 Hasty denials: https://twitter.com/Keir_Starmer/status/599860284912721920?s=20

211 conflict of interest: Heather Stewart, 'Keir Starmer "decided himself not to take lucrative second job"', *Guardian*, November 11, 2021

212 'if we abandon' … 'cost and merit': 'Home Affairs and Justice', May 28, 2015, *Hansard*, Vol. 596, Col. 255; High Speed Rail (London – West Midlands) Bill, September 15, 2015, *Hansard*, Vol. 599, Col. 1006
214 'core group plus': Anushka Asthana and Heather Stewart, 'Labour MPs hostile to Corbyn named in leaked party document', *Guardian*, March 23, 2016
214 'not the Messiah' … 'It's a big mistake': 'Jeremy Corbyn "not the Messiah", says Keir Starmer', BBC News, September 29, 2015; Stephen Moss, 'If we don't capture the ambitions of a generation, it doesn't matter who is leading the party', *Guardian*, April 9, 2016
216 the exception: Natasha Lomas, 'UK surveillance bill passes House of Commons with bulk powers facing review', *TechCrunch*, June 8, 2016

Chapter 18: Brexit's shadow

219 'I sort of gulped': Interviewed by Philippe Sands, Hay Literary Festival, May 25, 2019
220 'The speed': Sarah Pine, 'Corbyn: "Article 50 has to be invoked now"', *LabourList*, June 24, 2016
221 'act or think': Eagleton, *The Starmer Project*, 72
222 'We were desperate': John McDonnell, 'Brexit Witness Archive', UK in a Changing Europe, February 19, 2021
223 'not meant about him': 'Next Steps to Leaving the European Union', October 10, 2016, *Hansard*, Vol. 615, Col. 42–4; 'Parliamentary Scrutiny of Leaving the EU', October 12, 2016, *Hansard*, Vol. 615, Col. 321
223 170 more questions … 'the will of the people': Beth Rigby, 'Labour seeks answers – 170 of them – to May's Brexit plans', Sky News, October 12, 2016; 'Comment: "Whingeing. Contemptuous. Unpatriotic"', *Daily Mail*, October 12, 2016
224 front page of the *Daily Mail*: James Slack, 'Enemies of the people', *Daily Mail*, November 3, 2016
224 'meaningful vote': 'European Union (Notification of Withdrawal) Bill', *Hansard*, Vol 621: February 7, 2017
224 'the exact same benefits': Keir Starmer, 'What next for Britain?' speech at Chatham House, March 27, 2017; 'Article 50', January 24, 2017, *Hansard*, Vol. 620, Col. 169
225 'They were never': Eagleton, *The Starmer Project*, 75
225 The calculation was: Simon Tilford, 'The limits to Labour's "constructive ambiguity" over Brexit', Centre for European Reform, July 6, 2017

225 his efforts to go beyond: Jim Pickard, 'Keir Starmer: The Brexit opponent making Labour heard on Europe', *Financial Times*, October 16, 2016

225 'Lexit': Keir Starmer, 'No "constructive ambiguity". Labour will avoid Brexit cliff edge for UK economy', *Observer*, August 27, 2017; Gabriel Pogrund and Patrick Maguire, *Left Out: The Inside Story of Labour Under Corbyn* (Bodley Head, 2020), 70; Eagleton, *The Starmer Project*, 75–7

226 A responsible government: Keir Starmer, 'What next for Britain?', speech at Bloomberg, December 14, 2016

228 fought themselves: Keir Starmer, speech to Labour Party conference in Brighton, September 25, 2017

229 Davis was sidelined … 'he didn't understand': Oliver Wright, 'David Davis sidelined as Brussels tries to undermine him', *The Times*, December 28, 2017; 'Brexit secretary David Davis resigns', BBC News, July 9, 2018

230 polling showing: Toby Helm, 'Corbyn faces clash with Labour members over second EU referendum', *Observer*, September 23, 2018

230 'I saw Seumas': Ashcroft, *Red Knight*, 230

232 'consensus': Joe Watts, 'The angry union boss, the archaic rules, the coffee breath: The inside story of the meeting that decided Labour's Brexit policy', *Independent*, September 24, 2018

233 'Isn't this a betrayal': Peter Walker, Heather Stewart and Jessica Elgot, 'McDonnell: New Brexit referendum should not include remain option', *Guardian*, September 24, 2018; https://twitter.com/Channel4News/status/1044289564746158085?s=20

235 'He wants to be leader': Eagleton, *The Starmer Project*, 94–6

236 'Listening to him': Michel Barnier, *My Secret Brexit Diary* (Polity Press, 2021), 113

Chapter 19: Towards a certain end

237 'would leave it': Theresa May, *The Abuse of Power* (Headline, 2023), 58

238 'Jeremy Corbyn wanted': Gavin Barwell, *Chief of Staff: Notes from Downing Street* (Atlantic, 2021); Gavin Barwell, 'Brexit Witness Archive', Britain in a Changing Europe, September 1 and September 25, 2020

239 likened trying to do a deal: Ashcroft, *Red Knight*, 271

240 solve the issue: Pogrund and Maguire, *Left Out*, 196

240 'I have to admit': Jonathon Read, '5,000 take part in "trust the people" march and rally outside Labour conference', *New European*,

September 21, 2019; Keir Starmer, speech to Labour Party conference in Brighton, September 23, 2019

243 'I was in Jeremy's': Aubrey Allegretti, 'Abbott denies Starmer privately defied Corbyn over antisemitism', *Guardian*, February 16, 2023

243 whether she could rejoin: JLM leadership hustings, February 13, 2020

244 'I wouldn't know': https://x.com/LordIanAustin/status/1211771593531297793?s=20

244 'thinking that Corbyn': Donald Macintyre, 'Has Keir Starmer got what it takes to save the party?' *Sunday Times*, March 15, 2020

244 'If we're not': *The Andrew Marr Show*, BBC 1, July 8, 2018

244 'We have too many': Hay Literary Festival, May 25, 2019

245 merely suspended: Rowena Mason, 'Labour expels Alastair Campbell from party', *Guardian*, May 28, 2019

245 comparing the intelligence agency: Pogrund and Maguire, *Left Out*, 75–85

246 'purely defensive action': Seumas Milne, 'It's not Russia that's pushed Ukraine to the brink of war', *Guardian*, April 30, 2014

246 'This is not': Keir Starmer, *Question Time*, BBC 1, March 15, 2018

249 later fined £14,000: Gabriel Pogrund and Harry Yorke, 'The secretive guru who plotted Keir Starmer's path to power with undeclared cash', *Sunday Times*, November 12, 2023

251 got parliamentary approval: Gordon Rayner, 'Liberal Democrats offer Boris Johnson route to an election', October 27, 2019

251 three times more airtime: Report 5, 'General Election 2019', Centre for Research in Communication and Culture, Loughborough University, https://www.lboro.ac.uk/news-events/general-election/report-5/

Chapter 20: The candidate

253 'We as a movement': Harry Taylor, 'Sir Keir Starmer says party needs to "reflect" on "devastating" election results', *Ham & High*, December 13, 2019

254 'If anybody says': Sebastian Payne, *Broken Heartlands, A Journey Through Labour's Lost England* (Macmillan, 2021), 375

256 'I have always': Keir Starmer, 'Labour can win again if we make the moral case for socialism', *Guardian*, January 15, 2020

256 'favourite to win' … 'likely to be a woman' … 'conventional wisdom' … 'stone-cold loser': Rowena Mason and Helen Pidd, 'Labour leadership race begins as senior figures back Rebecca Long-Bailey', *Guardian*, December 15, 2019; Toby Helm, 'The race is on

... and the next Labour leader is likely to be a woman', *Observer*, December 15, 2019; Oliver Wright, 'Labour leadership: It's not all plain sailing for Rebecca Long-Bailey', *The Times*, December 23, 2019; 'The Sun says', *Sun*, December 19, 2019

257 total of £455,000: The Register of Members' Financial Interests, House of Commons, June 22, 2020

258 'have ovaries': Interviewed on BBC Radio 4 *Today* programme, December 18, 2019

259 'I don't think': Zoe Williams and Heather Stewart, 'Keir Starmer sets out case for "radical Labour government"', *Guardian*, December 18, 2019

260 undisputed frontrunner: Kate Proctor, 'Poll of Labour members suggests Keir Starmer is first choice', *Guardian*, January 1, 2020

265 'I'm very focused' ... thrown its considerable weight: Elliot Chappell, 'Interview with Keir Starmer: Fatboy Slim, open selections, Trotskyism and more', *LabourList*, January 12, 2020; 'Momentum group backs Rebecca Long-Bailey', BBC News, January 16, 2020

267 The pledges included: https://keirstarmer.com/plans/10-pledges/

267 he refused to join ... 'sympathetic': Matthew Weaver, 'Labour leadership contenders split over trans group pledge card', *Guardian*, February 13, 2020; Sienna Rodgers, 'How each leadership candidate fared in the Jewish Labour Movement hustings', *LabourList*, September 13, 2020

267 'what the state': Interview with Andrew Neil, BBC 2, March 4, 2020

267 'There was an understanding': Ailbhe Rea and Agnes Chambre, 'Keir Starmer revealed his "real politics" by ditching left-wing pledges, ally says', *Politico*, June 30, 2023

267 'Low politics': Bagheot: 'Centrists need to stop worrying and learn to love politics', *Economist*, September 13, 2023

268 'If Starmer was honest': Nick Gutteridge, 'Sir Keir Starmer scraps 10 "socialist" Labour pledges', *Daily Telegraph*, July 26, 2022

268 'I don't know': Interview with Andrew Neil, BBC 2

268 'In defending': Laura Parker, 'Why I'm backing Keir Starmer for Labour leader', *LabourList*, February 19, 2020

269 'Some people': Simon Fletcher, 'I went to work for Keir Starmer because he promised to unite the party. I regret it now', *Guardian*, September 28, 2021

270 This includes: https://keirstarmer.com/plans/10-pledges/

271 'I'm sorry': JLM Labour leadership hustings, February 13, 2020

271 'These questions': *Guardian* Labour leadership hustings, February 25, 2020

Chapter 21: Rocks and hard places

279 arrived on her doorstep: Vivek Chaudhary, 'Revealed: Sir Keir Starmer's lowly-paid sister works 12-hour shifts on minimum wage for as little as £9.70 looking after the elderly at a Kent care home', *MailOnline*, September 8, 2021

Chapter 22: Under new leadership

283 'historic purpose': 'Read in full: Sir Keir Starmer's victory speech after being named new Labour leader', *Politico*, April 4, 2020

283 'ten-year project': David Lammy, remarks at Labour fundraising event in London, November 14, 2023, https://www.politico.eu/europe-poll-of-polls/united-kingdom/

283 'destined not to': Patrick Maguire, 'The man within', *The Critic*, April 2020

284 'many challenges': Owen Jones, 'Starmer can succeed, and he deserves our support', *Guardian*, April 4, 2023

285 more recent recruit: Claire Ainsley, *The New Working Class: How to Win Hearts, Minds and Votes* (Policy Press, 2018), 57

289 'inching' … 'There is indeed': Laura Kuenssberg, 'Prime Minister's Questions: The lawyer versus the showman', BBC News, May 6, 2020; Andrew Rawnsley, 'Keir Starmer's first steps are promising, but the road ahead is long and steep', *Observer*, June 21, 2020

290 'Keir is all': Jim Pickard, 'Keir Starmer: "The government has been slow in nearly all of the major decisions"', *FT Magazine*, May 7, 2020

291 'hyper-factionalism': Elliot Chappell, 'Starmer apologises to Jewish community in video meeting', *LabourList*, April 7, 2020; Tom Rayner, 'Labour antisemitism investigation will not be sent to equality commission', Sky News, April 12, 2020

291 endemic: The Forde Report, September 22, 2022

291 Labour's lawyers: Rowena Mason, 'Labour to accuse five ex-staff members of leaking antisemitism report', *Guardian*, October 11, 2020; Alexandra Rogers, 'Labour accused of trying to delay lawsuit against former employees over fears of election clash', Sky News, October 6, 2023

292 Nor was this: Michael Savage, 'Unite sounds warning over Labour antisemitism payouts', *Observer*, August 1, 2020; Greg Heffer, 'Unite cuts funding to Labour Party by £1m following warning to Sir Keir Starmer', Sky News, October 7, 2020; Jessica Elgot, 'Labour spends £2m a year on legal fees since Corbyn era, party official says', *Guardian*, September 26, 2021

292 'seminars': Alexandra Pollard, 'Maxine Peake: "People who couldn't vote Labour because of Corbyn? They voted Tory as far as I'm concerned"', *Independent*, June 25, 2020

293 'But sadly': Andrew Woodcock, 'Rebecca Long-Bailey says she was sacked before having chance to hold talks with Keir Starmer', *Independent*, June 25, 2020

294 'It's time': 'Keir Starmer: Labour must "get serious about winning"', BBC News, September 22, 2020

294 'I love this country': Sienna Rodgers, '"A new leadership" – Starmer's first Labour party political broadcast', *LabourList*, September 23, 2002

294 break the whip: Sienna Rodgers, '34 Labour MPs break whip to oppose "spycops" bill as seven frontbenchers quit', *LabourList*, October 15, 2020

298 went down: Rajeev Syal and Jessica Elgot, 'Keir Starmer had his response ready. Then came Corbyn's post', *Guardian*, October 29, 2020

298 genuinely shocked: Ibid.

298 'Yes, it was': Len McCluskey, *Always Red* (OR Books, 2021), 337–8

299 licked its lips: Syal and Elgot, 'Keir Starmer had his response …'

300 'Unfortunately, Jeremy': McCluskey, *Always Red*, 340

300 can still be found: https://www.facebook.com/330250343871/posts/my-statement-following-the-publication-of-the-ehrc-reportantisemitism-is-absolut/10158939532253872/

300 threatened to resign: Ibid.

301 'That was when': McCluskey, *Always Red*, 341

302 defy the whip: Sienna Rodgers, 'Johnson's Brexit bill passes with Labour backing – but 37 rebels defy Starmer', *LabourList*, December 30, 2020

303 'his days': https://www.facebook.com/330250343871/posts/my-statement-following-the-publication-of-the-ehrc-reportantisemitism-is-absolut/10158939532253872/; Keir Starmer, *News Agents* podcast interview with Lewis Goodall, November 17, 2023

303 'we were never friends': Keir Starmer, interviewed by BBC Breakfast, BBC 1, February 23, 2023

Chapter 23: Turning Labour inside out

305 inching ahead: https://www.politico.eu/europe-poll-of-polls/united-kingdom/

305 'There is undoubtedly': Keir Starmer, interviewed on *The Jeremy Vine Show*, BBC Radio 2, March 8, 2021

306 five stages: Jerald Jellison, *Managing the Dynamics of Change* (McGraw Hill, 2006)

308 'branch office' … alarm among allies: Neil Findlay, 'How not to save Scottish Labour', *Tribune*, January 15, 2021; Gabrielle Pickard-Whitehead, 'A crime against democracy: Outrage from Labour movement at news Starmer will back Whitehall control of Liverpool', *Left Foot Forward*, March 24, 2021

308 'provoked a': Tom Kibasi, 'Keir Starmer's leadership needs an urgent course correction', *Guardian*, February 16, 2021

309 A year later: Rajeev Syal, 'Ex-Labour MP must pay £434k damages to woman he repeatedly assaulted', *Guardian*, May 19, 2022

310 'Not possible' … 'transitional figure': https://twitter.com/hackneyabbott/status/1390553244636680193; Andrew Adonis, 'Labour needs an election winner. Keir Starmer isn't it', *The Times*, May 7, 2021

312 'I intend': 'Keir Starmer vows to do "whatever is necessary" after "bitterly disappointing" Hartlepool defeat', ITV News, May 7, 2021

312 'Take the heat': 'Keir Starmer: The reality of life as leader of the opposition', *High Performance*, March 27, 2023

314 One usually respectable: '*Sunday Times* journalist Tim Shipman pays "substantial" damages to shadow minister over tweet', *Press Gazette*, February 23, 2022

314 'come badly unstuck': Anoosh Chakelian, 'I'm afraid Keir Starmer has come badly unstuck', *New Statesman*, May 11, 2021

315 'If the party': Elliot Chappell, 'Andy Burnham defends Angela Rayner following reshuffle', *LabourList*, May 10, 2021; Dan Bloom, 'Andy Burnham breaks ranks to slam Keir Starmer', *Mirror*, May 9, 2021

315 presence of … 'hatred' … become a reality: Jim Waterson, 'Talk Radio sacks George Galloway over antisemitic views', *Guardian*, June 3, 2019; Rachel Wearmouth, 'Keir Starmer hails Batley victory of "hope over hatred" saying "Labour is coming home"', *Mirror*, July 2, 2021; Henry Zeffman and Patrick Maguire, 'Angela Rayner supporters prepare to challenge Keir Starmer for Labour leadership', *The Times*, July 1, 2021

318 'total deconstruction' … 'turn': Tony Blair, 'Without total change Labour will die', *New Statesman*, May 11, 2021; George Parker, 'Starmer urges Labour to embrace Blair's legacy as he vows to win next election', *Financial Times*, August 5, 2021

319 opposition was instant: Jessica Elgot and Heather Stewart, 'Starmer U-turns on party reform plan ahead of Labour conference', *Guardian*, September 25, 2021

319 'registered supporters': Sienna Rodgers, 'Labour NEC passes 20% MP nomination threshold for leadership contests', *LabourList*, September 25, 2021

319 'civil war': Jessica Elgot, 'Starmer risks "civil war" over Labour leadership election rules change', *Guardian*, September 21, 2021

320 went off to a pub: Jessica Elgot, 'Labour leadership rule changes pass after last-minute Unison backing', *Guardian*, September 26, 2021

320 distance himself … resigned: Lucy Fisher, 'Angela Rayner rebuked by Keir Starmer for branding Tories "scum"', *Daily Telegraph*, September 26, 2021; 'Frontbencher Andy McDonald quits in protest at Sir Keir Starmer', BBC News, September 27, 2021

321 the biggest cheer: Keir Starmer, speech to Labour Party conference in Brighton, September 29, 2021

321 'Words plopped': Quentin Letts, 'Hecklers' spit and fury sparks Starmer fan club into life', *The Times*, September 29, 2021

321 'The only thing' … 'banality': Sam Leith, 'Keir Starmer's essay is a cliché-ridden disaster', *Spectator*, September 23, 2021; Morgan Jones, 'McDonnell: Labour "lacked credibility" in 2019 but Starmer has offered "banality"', *LabourList*, September 26, 2021

323 'loss is unbearable': Keir Starmer, 'Jonny – a eulogy', *European Human Rights Law Review*, February 1, 2022

324 'corner is turned': 'From Red Walls to Red Bridges: Rebuilding Labour's voter coalition', Tony Blair Institute for Global Change, November 26, 2021

324 comfortably held: 'Old Bexley and Sidcup: Tories hold safe London seat at by-election', BBC News, December 3, 2021

325 'decisively abandoned': Robert Peston, 'Keir Starmer chooses the Labour team he actually rates', ITV News, November 29, 2021

326 By January 2022: Lee Harpin, 'New figures confirm huge increase in Labour expulsions under Starmer', *Jewish News*, January 22, 2022

327 'succour': Keir Starmer, 'Under my leadership, Labour's commitment to Nato is unshakable', *Guardian*, February 10, 2022

327 forty-five minutes: Peter Walker, 'Labour MPs drop backing for statement criticising Nato after Starmer warning', *Guardian*, February 24, 2022; https://twitter.com/younglabouruk/status/14971 49945123647498?lang=en

327 later suspended … no fewer than: Jim Pickard, 'Diane Abbott suspended from Labour party after racism letter', *Financial Times*, April 23, 2023; Morgan Jones and Tom Belger, 'Suspended, expelled, quit: Who are the MPs sitting without the Labour whip?', *LabourList*, November 26, 2023; Peter Walker, 'Nick Brown resigns from Labour over "complete farce" disciplinary process', *Guardian*,

December 12, 2023; Jessica Elgot, 'Sam Tarry deselected as MP by Ilford South Labour members', *Guardian*, October 10, 2022

327 'due diligence': Ruby Lott-Lavigna, 'Is Labour purging the left? Inside the party's embattled selection process', *Open Democracy*, April 19, 2023

329 'playground bullies': Neal Lawson, 'After 44 years, Labour moves to expel me. And my MP and activist friends are asking: who will be next?', *Guardian*, June 30, 2023

329 'intends to': Owen Jones, 'Starmer's banishment of Corbyn is one more step in eradicating the left from the Labour party', *Guardian*, February 17, 2023; George Eaton, 'John McDonnell's last stand', *New Statesman*, April 23, 2023

330 'a brutal centralisation': Jon Cruddas, *A Century of Labour* (John Wiley & Sons, 2024)

331 'treating him': Helen Lewis, 'Starmer's secret', *Bluestocking Substack*, December 2, 2022

Chapter 24: If not them, why him?

332 'song and dance': Keir Starmer, New Year speech in Bristol, January 4, 2024

332 'It's easy': Keir Starmer, speech to Labour Party conference, September 29, 2021

333 'really loathed': Keir Starmer, interviewed on Matt Forde's *The Political Party* podcast, February 20, 2023

333 avoid punishment ... illegal parties ... 'waving bottles': 'Owen Paterson: Boris Johnson backs shake-up of MP standards rules', BBC News, November 3, 2021; Pippa Crerar, 'Boris Johnson "broke Covid lockdown rules" with Downing Street parties at Xmas', *Mirror*, November 30, 2021; 'Findings of Second Permanent Secretary's investigation into alleged gatherings on Government premises during Covid restrictions', Cabinet Office, May 25, 2022

334 'the bodies' ... 'I will leave': Edward Udney-Lister, testimony to UK Covid-19 public inquiry, November 7, 2023; *Hansard*, Vol. 693, April 28, 2021

334 ten occasions: *Hansard*, Vol. 704, December 1, 2021; 'Fifth Report – Matter referred on 21 April 2022 (conduct of Rt Hon Boris Johnson): Final Report', House of Commons Privileges Committee, June 15, 2023

334 'Sir Beer Korma' ... 'far nicer': *Hansard*, Vol. 718, July 13, 2022 and July 20, 2022; Millie Cooke, 'Boris' hilarious answer on whether he'd rather be stuck in a lift with Starmer or Sturgeon', *Daily Express*, February 3, 2023

335 'boring everyone' … 'got the feel': Matt Chorley and Patrick Maguire, 'Labour leader is a slogan peddler who only paints in primary colours', *The Times*, June 13, 2022; Marina Hyde, 'Dear Keir, people say that after Johnson a bit of boring would be nice. Unfortunately, people lie', *Guardian*, June 17, 2022

335 'What's boring': Heather Stewart, 'Stop calling me boring, Keir Starmer tells shadow cabinet', *Guardian*, June 14, 2022

335 level-pegging: https://yougov.co.uk/topics/politics/trackers/which-political-party-would-be-the-best-at-handling-the-economy

336 'growing strange': *Hansard*, Vol. 719, September 9, 2022

336 'like Cliff Richard': Patrick Maguire, 'Keir Starmer offers respect but needs to give hope', *The Times*, September 28, 2023

337 'a lucky general': Anna Lamche, 'Labour in Liverpool: Don't quit the party now, urge left-wingers', *Camden New Journal*, October 12, 2023

338 'keep it simple': Heather Stewart, 'Starmer says Tory hopefuls have lost economic credibility', *Guardian*, July 16, 2022; Phillip Coorey, '"Keep it simple": Albo advises Starmer on how to beat Tories', *Financial Review*, October 7, 2022; Rachel Wearmouth, 'Keir Starmer's international inspiration', *New Statesman*, February 25, 2023

338 'Tedious Maximus': Mitch Benn, 'Psst, Tories! 27 nicknames for Starmer that are more cutting than "Sir Softie"', *New European*, April 26, 2023

338 'given what's': Keir Starmer, interviewed on *First Edition*, Talk TV, September 28, 2022

339 'not a grandiose': Keir Starmer, speech to Labour Party conference in Liverpool, September 27, 2022

339 nosedived: Camilla Turner, 'Just nine per cent have a favourable view of Liz Truss', *Daily Telegraph*, October 13, 2022

340 'stability': Rishi Sunak, The Office of the Prime Minister, October 25, 2022

342 'sort of safe': Rowena Mason and Aubrey Allegretti, 'Labour postpones £28bn green plan as it seeks to be trusted on public finances', *Guardian*, June 9, 2023

342 'make Brexit work': Emily Ashton, 'Labour's Starmer vows to "make Brexit work" as he breaks silence', *Bloomberg*, July 4, 2022

343 'as competent': Steven Swinford, 'Can Sunak's Warren Buffett gambit win over MPs and voters?' *The Times*, April 1, 2023

343 Murmurs … 'no one knows' … 'withering verdict': Henry Zeffman, 'Keir Starmer: I will be ruthless in pursuit of power', *The Times*, April 3, 2023; 'The Guardian view on Sir Keir Starmer: His party remains a mystery to voters', *Guardian*, April 4, 2023; Kumail Jaffer, 'The Guardian delivers a withering verdict on "dull" Keir Starmer', *Daily Mail*, April 5, 2023

343 'If he says': Matthew d'Ancona, 'Don't walk into the Brexit elephant trap, Mr Starmer', *Tortoise*, November 21, 2022

344 'Each of our': Keir Starmer, speech in Manchester, February 23, 2023

345 'whole new way': Amol Rajan, interview with Keir Starmer, *Today*, BBC Radio 4

346 'personal to me': Keir Starmer: 'This is what I believe', *New Statesman*, March 1, 2023

346 'bedrock of security': Ella Jessel, 'Starmer pledges huge boost in homeownership across Britain if elected', *Inside Housing*, September 27, 2023

347 'the bruises': Keir Starmer, speech in Burslem, March 23, 2023

347 'a proud nurse': Keir Starmer, speech in Braintree, May 22, 2023

347 'Can we change': Keir Starmer, speech in Leith, June 19, 2023

347 'Growing up': Keir Starmer, speech in Gillingham, July 6, 2023

348 'It's not just': Ibid.

350 'gone from': Yasmeen Serhan, 'The man who wants to fix Britain', *Time*, May 26, 2023

351 shiny metal ... failed to act: Sami Quadri, 'Nitrous oxide: Laughing gas to be banned in crackdown on anti-social behaviour', *Evening Standard*, March 26, 2023; Daniel Martin, 'Suella Braverman accuses Labour of overlooking child grooming', *Daily Telegraph*, April 2, 2023

352 'Under the Tories': https://twitter.com/UKLabour/status/1643973886311297028?s=20

352 'My party' ... 'had nothing': David Blunkett, 'My party is better than this brand of gutter politics', *Daily Mail*, April 7, 2023; Toby Helm, 'Yvette Cooper was "not told" about Labour's Sunak attack ad in advance', *Observer*, April 9, 2023

352 a member: Guy Adams, 'Not just dishonest but deeply hypocritical', *Daily Mail*, April 10, 2023

352 'ruthlessness': Andrew Marr, 'How Labour lost the moral high ground', *New Statesman*, April 12, 2023

353 'I stand by': Harriet Line, 'Tory anger as Starmer stands by "every word" of Rishi ads', *Daily Mail*, April 10, 2023

353 'I make absolutely': Keir Starmer, 'Rishi Sunak and the Tories have let criminals get away with it ...' *Daily Mail*, April 10, 2023

354 'We're doing': Donna Ferguson and Tobi Thomas, 'Starmer says Labour doing something "very wrong" after Ulez-linked Uxbridge loss', *Guardian*, July 22, 2023; 'Mayor announces massive expansion of scrappage scheme to all Londoners', Mayor of London, August 4, 2023

354 'heinous': Pippa Crerar and Patrick Butler, 'Labour would keep two-child benefit cap, says Keir Starmer', *Guardian*, July 17, 2023

355 'We keep saying': Chris Smythe and Patrick Maguire, 'Keir Starmer echoes Tony Blair and holds firm on child benefit', *The Times*, July 18, 2023

Chapter 25: Facing the future

359 'make an emotional connection': Keir Starmer, interviewed on *Breakfast*, BBC 1, October 11, 2023

360 widely praised: Robin Simcox, 'Jeremy Corbyn has a soft spot for extremists', *Foreign Policy*, October 3, 2018

361 'I think Israel': Keir Starmer, interviewed on *Nick Ferrari at Breakfast*, LBC, October 11, 2023

361 clarifications: https://twitter.com/Keir_Starmer/status/ 1716418960315330678?utm_source=substack&utm_medium=email

361 'empathy': John Bootham, 'Sarwar accuses Starmer of lacking empathy on Gaza', *Sunday Times*, November 3, 2023

362 'When you': *High Performance*, March 27, 2023

363 visit to Qatar: Ned Simmons, '"Shame on Fifa": Keir Starmer slams Qatar World Cup over LGBTQ rights', *Huffington Post*, November 23, 2022

364 strengthen human rights: David Lammy, speech to Bingham Centre, July 10, 2023

364 'there are going': Keir Starmer, interviewed by Lewis Goodall, *The News Agents*, November 19, 2023

365 'lip service': Keir Starmer, speech on the international situation in the Middle East, Chatham House, October 31, 2023

365 biggest revolt: Geraldine Scott, 'Ceasefire vote: Starmer suffers biggest revolt of leadership over Gaza ceasefire', *The Times*, November 15, 2023

365 'good people': Ibid; Henry Zeffman, 'Gaza revolt embarrassing for Keir Starmer but are there positives?' BBC News, November 16, 2023

366 'things just don't happen': Max Stafford, 'The Return of Sue Gray', Mile End Institute, March 3, 2023

367 British intelligence: Guy Adams, 'Was Sue Gray an undercover British spy when she ran a pub in the heart of IRA bandit country?' *Daily Mail*, May 6, 2023

367 'bunch of people': Peter Walker, 'Top officials called Johnson's No 10 "mad" and "poisonous", Covid inquiry hears', *Guardian*, November 7, 2023

370 'doing the basics': Keir Starmer's speech in Buckinghamshire, Labour Party, December 12, 2023

371 'Industrial Strategy Council': 'Labour's Industrial Strategy', Labour Party, September 27, 2023

371 'Infrastructure Council': Steven Swinford, 'Rachel Reeves reveals British infrastructure council for Labour', *The Times*, November 19, 2023

371 'not serious': 'Britain needs a new economic strategy', Resolution Foundation, December 4, 2023

371 'always seems to': Andy Haldane, 'Here's how to stimulate UK growth: give away power', *Financial Times*, January 12, 2024

373 'It will be a hard': Keir Starmer, speech to the Resolution Foundation, December 4, 2023

373 'fiscal lock': Rachel Reeves, 'From the OBR to new fiscal rules, we will bring back stability', *Financial Times*, September 21, 2023

374 'Anyone who expects': Keir Starmer, speech to the Resolution Foundation, December 4, 2023

375 'Plans for a national': Jim Pickard, 'Rachel Reeves to pledge new lock on Labour green fund investment', *Financial Times*, October 7, 2023

376 'We need to': Keir Starmer, New Year speech in Bristol, January 4, 2024

377 'Trust in politics': Ibid.

379 'your full attention': Ibid.

379 'I believe that': Ibid.

Illustrations

First plate section: All images courtesy of Keir Starmer
Second plate section: All images courtesy of Keir Starmer, except
  the following:

Being knighted (PA Images/Alamy Stock Photo)
As shadow Brexit secretary (Associated Press/Alamy Stock Photo)
A sign of things to come (PA Images/Alamy Stock Photo)
The Labour leader and his deputy (Associated Press/Alamy Stock
  Photo)
'Keir's beer' (Ivo Delingpole)
With Margaret Hodge (PA Images/Alamy Stock Photo)
Tony Blair and Gordon Brown listen on (Associated Press/Alamy
  Stock Photo)
All smiles with the new top team (PA Images/Alamy Stock Photo)
The 'Glitter-bomb' attack (Christopher Furlong/Getty images)

Index

Campbell, Alastair 204, 206,
    230–1, 245, 262, 316–17, 331
capital punishment 126–31
Cardiff University 174
Carlisle United FC 104
Carter, Jimmy 102, 165
Ceauşescu, Nicolae 83
Centrist Dad (punk band) 201
Chada, Raj 203, 206
Chakrabarti, Shami 159
Change UK 237, 252
Channel 4 News 233
Chapman, Jenny 196, 231–2, 246,
    247, 250, 254, 255, 267, 284,
    314
Chappell, Elliott 203
'Charter 88' 90, 91, 92
Chinn, Trevor 249, 257
Churchill, Winston 77, 382
citizens' assemblies 369
Civil Service World 153
Clarke, Ken 251
class system 30–1, 65, 278
Clegg, Private Lee 134–5, 150
Clinton, Bill 65
Clooney, Amal 120
Clough, Jane 179–80, 321, 346–7
Clough, John 179–81
Clough, Penny 179–81
Communism, Communists 83, 90,
    91, 238
Cook, Robin 362
Cooper, Andrew 35, 37, 40
Cooper, Jonny 116, 136, 167, 173,
    180, 322–3
Cooper, Yvette 78, 324, 352
Corbyn, Jeremy 317, 319; allies'
    hostility towards Starmer 307–8;
    Brexit, antisemitism and Russia,
    220–1, 224–6, 237–46, 254,
    259, 291–3, 315; leadership 87,
    115, 214, 216, 219–22, 227,
    229–31, 234–5, 236, 255,

256–7, 258, 264, 282, 290–1,
    315–16, 326; replaced as leader
    215, 247, 248–52, 253, 262,
    283, 284, 285, 286; selection
    and disciplinary process 328–9;
    suspension of 294–304, 305,
    307–8, 378
Coulson, Andy 166
Covid 111–18, 269, 270, 279, 282,
    283, 287–9, 292, 293, 305,
    324–5, 327, 333–4, 366
Cox, Jo 220, 315
Crampton, Robert 137
Crick, Michael 233, 327–8
Crown Prosecution Service (CPS)
    151–71, 179, 180–9, 202, 203,
    213, 222, 229, 370, 373
Cruddas, Jon 249, 329–30
Cruyff, Johan 34
Cummings, Anne 72
Cummings, Dominic 289–90, 371
Cuomo, Mario 348
Cuthbertson, Jill 102, 317

Daily Mail 45, 134, 135, 157, 223,
    224, 279, 343, 345, 353
Daily Mirror 334
Daily Star 339
Daily Telegraph 45, 155
Daniel brothers (Georgie, Ned,
    Mickey, Sammy) 137
Darling, Alistair 317
Davey, Ed 17, 78
Davis, David 222, 223, 228, 229,
    252
Delingpole, Ivo 113–14
Demos 350
Dignitas, Switzerland 177
Dines, John ('John Barker') 124–5
Diplock Courts 132
'DJ Fatboy Slim' (Cook, Norman;
    Cook, Quentin) 42
Dobson, Frank 202–3, 206